Civil-Military Relations in Latin America

Edited by David Pion-Berlin

Civil-
Military
Relations
in Latin
America

New Analytical
Perspectives

The University of North Carolina Press

Chapel Hill and London

Designed by Heidi Perov
Set in Fournier
by Keystone Typesetting, Inc.

The paper in this book meets the guidelines for
permanence and durability of the Committee on
Production Guidelines for Book Longevity of the
Council on Library Resources.

Library of Congress Cataloging-in-Publication Data

Civil-military relations in Latin America :
new analytical perspectives / edited by
David Pion-Berlin.
p. cm.
   Includes bibliographical references and index.
   ISBN 0-8078-2656-1 (cloth: alk. paper)
   ISBN 0-8078-4981-2 (pbk.: alk. paper)
   1. Civil-military relations—Latin America—Case studies.
   2. Democratization—Latin America—Case studies.
   I. Pion-Berlin, David.
   JL956.C58 C583 2001
   322'.5'098—dc21

                              2001035303

05   04   03   02   01   5   4   3   2   1

Contents

Tables and Figures

Foreword

As I write this Foreword, questions abound about the role and intentions of Peru's armed forces in response to President Alberto Fujimori's surprise resignation from the presidency and call for new elections in which he would not be a candidate. No one seems certain whether Peru's top military officers forced this resignation, will accept Fujimori's plan, or are prepared to take power directly.

Peru is not the only Latin American country where the political role of the armed forces is in doubt. Chile's top officers recently defied President Ricardo Lagos in staging an unauthorized welcome for former president Augusto Pinochet on the latter's return from the United Kingdom, where he had been detained for human rights violations. Colombia's top seventeen officers last year announced their resignations, together with the minister of defense, to protest President Andrés Pastrana's approach to negotiating with the guerrilla insurgency there. Ecuador's armed forces toppled the elected president last year and had to be cajoled into letting the vice president take office. In Venezuela, Hugo Chávez, a cashiered former colonel who led a bloody but unsuccessful military coup several years ago, has now won office through election and drawn on military cronies for key government positions, and the only credible alternative to Chávez in the 1999 elections was another former military leader. And in Cuba, so long ruled by Fidel Castro, experts are debating what role the Cuban armed forces will play in an eventual post-Fidel transition.

Despite the regionwide turn from authoritarian rule toward democratic governance, the thorny issue of civil-military relations has by no means been resolved. The exact form this issue takes has changed from the days of caudillo politics in the 1950s and 1960s or the bureaucratic-authoritarian regimes of the 1970s and 1980s, but the centrality of armies to Latin America's politics remains.

More than twenty-five years ago—at a time when the armed forces governed directly in almost every country of South America and in several Central American nations, as well—I focused on the political role of the region's military leaders and institutions. In my review essay in *World Politics* in 1974 and then in my edited volume *Armies and Politics in Latin America* (1975), I argued that it was important to distinguish carefully among the different political roles played by Latin American military institutions at various stages and in varying contexts and particularly to focus on the relationship between the levels of institutionalization of civilian politics and of military organizations as a key factor in determining how soldiers affected politics. I offered this hypothesis by way of illustrating the need for more comparative research and better theoretical lenses to help interpret, explain, and predict a central feature of Latin America's politics.

This field of inquiry has developed impressively over the past twenty-five years, with a great number of case studies, comparative treatments, and historical and theoretical approaches. The literature I reviewed in 1974, which seemed extensive at the time, is but a small fraction of what has been published since. Studies abound of the military as rulers, of the transitions from authoritarian regimes, of the policy consequences of military and civilian rule, and of the military's role in the initial and consolidation phases of democracy-building.

There is clearly a need to take stock of what has been learned and chart new areas of research, and that is the signal contribution of this volume. Editor David Pion-Berlin has succeeded in convening some of the ablest scholars working on the political behavior of the military in Latin America today, and with them, he has produced a comprehensive, empirically grounded, and theoretically informed symposium.

This volume succeeds in bridging political science approaches and those found in Latin American studies to give scholars greater leverage on understanding civil-military complexities. It does so by anchoring its studies around a few key analytical points that emerge from the discipline, which are informed by empirical observations from the region. By distinguishing among and illustrating three main analytic orientations in work on Latin America's military and relating these to broad schools of thought in contemporary political science as a whole, Pion-Berlin and his colleagues have shown the relevance of research on Latin America to wider political science debates, thus avoiding the all-too-familiar relegation of work on Latin America to a neglected area-studies backwater. And by tackling contemporary issues about the military's role in the processes of democratic institution-building, consolidation, and disenchantment, Pion-Berlin and his colleagues have produced a work that is both timely and policy-relevant.

ABRAHAM F. LOWENTHAL

Acknowledgments

This book has its origins, appropriately enough, in Latin America. It was in Guadalajara, Mexico, at the April 1997 meeting of the Latin American Studies Association that I first presented the idea for this volume to Elaine Maisner of the University of North Carolina Press. With her encouragement, I set upon the challenging journey of converting an eighteen-page book proposal into a comprehensive edited volume. I had considerable help along the way from numerous individuals and organizations.

Of course, this was a collective endeavor, and I owe the first debt of gratitude to my coauthors, who produced first-rate essays and who put up with my incessant reminders about page lengths and deadlines. All of their essays and my own were first presented as working drafts at a conference, "Soldiers and Democracy in Latin America," held in Riverside, California, on 19–20 February 1999. Funding for that conference was made possible through generous grants provided by the Institute for Global Conflict and Cooperation and the University of California at Riverside's Center for Ideas and Society. The center's able staff also provided valuable assistance in organizing the event.

The conference brought together not only the contributors to this volume but many other leading scholars in related fields whose thoughtful comments greatly enriched the lively discussions and debates at the symposium. In particular, I thank Carlos Vélez-Ibáñez for his welcoming remarks; James Brennan, Alison Brysk, Gretchen Casper, Edward C. Epstein, and Frederick M. Nunn for serving as panel chairs; Craig Arceneaux, Abraham F. Lowenthal, Cesar Sereseres, William C. Smith, and Daniel Zirker for serving as discussants; and Claudio Fuentes for contributing a paper. The revisions on all the essays in this symposium benefited from the oral and written comments offered by the panelists. In addition, the input of others who played no official role at the conference was much appreciated. I cannot list them all but would like to mention Jay Cope, J. Mark Ruhl, and Scott Tollefson.

The full manuscript received a careful review from the two anonymous readers for the University of North Carolina Press. Their comments were extremely thoughtful, detailed, and to the point. I thank them both. Once substantive revisions were completed, the manuscript had to then be edited for publication. In my department, I had help from William Aviles, who paid attention to numerous details on textual, table, endnote, and bibliographic formatting. At the University of North Carolina Press, the production staff was efficient, effective, and a pleasure to work with.

Civil-
Military
Relations
in Latin
America

David Pion-Berlin

Introduction

Since the birth of nation-states, civilians have grappled with the problem of how to subordinate armies to their will. Whether they presided over colonies, newly independent states, or more modern twentieth-century totalitarian, authoritarian, or democratic regimes, political leaders have always had to balance the twin goals of harnessing enough military force to defeat their enemies and ensure that that force not be turned against themselves. Many communist regimes and developed democracies seem to have somehow achieved the balance, having built professional militaries of enormous size, sophistication, and strength that still submit to civilian authority. Latin America states have not been so lucky. Leaders there face militaries that have questioned their political authority or, worse still, undermined it. For these countries, civilian control of the military often seems like an elusive goal.[1]

However elusive, civilian control is a subject that neither Latin American leaders nor scholars can easily ignore. The development, quality, and survival of democratic systems depend on governments making the armed forces their political servants and policy instruments rather than the other way around. Elected leaders cannot credibly claim to have represented popular will if they are held hostage to the will of nonelected men in uniform. Without the authority to set their own course of action, free from military constraints, threats, or vetoes, politicians and the institutions they serve may ultimately fall prey to deep public cynicism, which in turn could fuel doubts about the very legitimacy of the democratic regime. When democracies become discredited, they are most vulnerable to the designs of power-thirsty generals.

The state of civil-military affairs in today's Latin America is not so much apocalyptic as it is unsteady. Progress toward the elusive goal can be detected, but it is three steps forward and two back. The armies of the region are not in a conspiratorial mode but neither are they complacent. They do show signs of displeasure with missions, budgets, government policy, and political ineptitude, and they flex their muscles and rattle their sabers every now and then. Many have accepted civilian rule but have done so conditionally, while carving out spheres of influence for themselves within the constitutional order. Others seem more comfortable with the idea of subordination. All of this suggests that the coup or no-coup question is not the defining one for this era. Rather, there is a complex array of military behaviors and civil-military interactions, some positive and some negative, that need to be assessed in order to understand just how much further down the road politicians need to travel before they have achieved military compliance.

Thus civilian control is but one essential feature of a much larger set of ongoing relations between politicians, soldiers, and society. This volume is devoted to an exploration of different analytical perspectives that may give us some insights into civil-military interactions but with a focus on understanding what is it that leaders have (haven't) done, can (can't) do, or should (shouldn't) do to subordinate the armed forces to their will. While specific Latin American countries and their problems will be part of the narrative, the central thrust here will be on theory. Recently, a number of researchers in the field of Latin American civil-military studies have adopted and adapted innovative analytical frameworks, and their work will be showcased here.

The need for new analytical perspectives on the study of armies and politics is now more apparent than ever. It is not just that the region and world have changed in profound ways since the reemergence of democratic rule, the end of the Cold War, and the ascendancy of free market economies, thus compelling us to "recontextualize" our theoretical points of view. It is that the world of scholarship has changed as well, compelling us to keep pace with it. For all of its accumulated wisdom—and it is considerable—the Latin American civil-military field (like Latin American area studies as a whole) has suffered by standing in harmful isolation from comparative politics, political science, and even the social sciences in general. It has over the years produced some interesting, sophisticated, analytical works but has not always explicitly identified and connected these with theoretical trends and traditions in the wider discipline that surrounds it. As a consequence of having divorced itself from the discipline, it has not benefited from theoretical innovations from the outside that could have potentially valuable applications within. Instead, it has fallen back on itself, dredging up familiar ideas that have yielded diminishing returns over time.[2]

To some extent, the isolation is self-imposed. It arises from the comfort civil-military scholars have taken as members of an insular community who uncritically accept the recycling of timeworn concepts. So long as enough scholars are willing to tread the same terrain and reward others for doing so, then the publication incentives will be sufficient to sustain the enterprise within its narrow confines. To some extent, it is symptomatic of the deeper divide separating area studies in general from the mainstream discipline. Huge differences in substantive interests, methods, and modes of analysis have kept mainstream political scientists and country / regional specialists from understanding one another. Those Latin Americanists who have not found an especially receptive audience for their work in political science fall back on their own devices, reaffirming approaches more closely tied to intellectual traditions from the region. Civil-military Latin Americanists in particular do likewise.

While the results of doing so have yielded some memorable works, there are limits as to how far we can travel alone. The problem is that we have already lost touch with the larger, discipline-wide, research communities or schools of thought that we are part of or should be a part of. Those communities are important because with or without us, they are formulating the intellectual agenda, setting the terms of the debate, and devising the theoretical standards for this and future generations of comparative political scientists. The civil-military field ignores these communities at its own peril. Without explicitly identifying with theoretical traditions and trends in the wider discipline that surrounds it, it risks trailing further behind the theoretical curve. More positively, it misses an opportunity to bring its own insights to bear on broader questions and controversies in the discipline.

Despite faults of their own, comparative politics and political science *have* evolved and have done so in interesting and innovative ways. Over time, several meandering intellectual currents seem to have converged into a few thoughtful theoretical positions. Political scientists studying the rationality of choice, the behavioral impact of structures and institutions, or the normative influences of cultures and belief systems often stand at the cutting edge of their respective fields. Could civil-military specialists profit by taking notice? Could we benefit by borrowing, amending, and synthesizing analytical approaches found in political science and beyond? My colleagues and I believe so and have thus made contributions to this volume that attempt to bridge the divide separating disciplinary trends with the Latin American, civil-military field of study. In this endeavor, we have tried to be quite explicit about what theoretical premises and arguments we use.

As will be shown, each of us tries to make this connection in different though related ways. Our approaches neither converge on one dominant model or paradigm nor diverge in a display of pure eclecticism. We anchor our studies in a few distinct and important analytic traditions that compete with but also relate to one another. We do this fully conscious of the fact that each approach has its utility but also its limits and that therefore none of us can "go at it alone." A subject as complex as civil-military relations can easily befuddle the best analytical attempt and demands an assessment of theoretical alternatives. Consequently, this volume brings together a set of scholars and their alternative approaches under one editorial roof.

The rest of the Introduction will proceed as follows. First, it will make a brief tour back over four decades of writings on the Latin American armed forces. It is well beyond the limits or purpose of this chapter to survey all of it comprehensively, so instead I will highlight a few of the most influential works commenting primarily on the problems they addressed, the approaches they took, and the trends they set. Then it will explain why we need to move beyond the historical literature to consider broad theoretical trends within the wider discipline. I will review what these are, what analytical perspectives derive from them, and what advantages to civil-military inquiry they may hold in store for us. Chapter summaries will follow, and I conclude with some thoughts about future research.

Scholarly Approaches to Latin American Civil-Military Relations: A Brief Historical Review

Each generation's research interests are powerfully conditioned by the realities of the time. The turbulence of the 1960s obliged scholars to study first the forces of modernization and then the forces of unrest, turning their attention to political violence, praetorianism, and coup d'état as the decade neared its end. Once the military had seized power throughout the region, researchers set their sights on understanding the origins of authoritarian rule during the 1970s. With either the phased withdrawal or complete breakdown of these regimes by the early 1980s, attention shifted toward the causes of military extrication and the transition toward democracy. By the late 1980s and into the final decade of the twentieth century, questions of civilian control and democratic consolidation came to the fore and persist to this day.

Before the 1960s, very little had been written on the political role of the armed forces. Scholars steeped in the ideology of progress regarded overt military intervention as an uncommon, crass form of behavior not befitting societies that were developing democratically, and not worthy of comment. Thus Edwin Lieuwen could say in 1960 that "on the subject of militarism in Latin America, no important books have yet appeared."[3] Lieuwen's own book, *Arms and Politics in Latin America* (1960), followed by John Johnson's *The Military and Society in Latin America* (1964), would mark an important break with this tradition of neglect. These were the most influential works of the early 1960s, with Lieuwen arguing that the military's defense of its institutional interests could lead to harmful, predatory behavior, while Johnson insisted that the military could play a positive, developmental role precisely because of its institutional strengths and civilian weaknesses. What both authors shared was a conviction that modernization was inevitable and that the armed forces, for better or worse, would be political players in that process.

By the latter part of the decade, the seeds of doubt concerning the prospects for developing nations to progress steadily were sown with the arrival of Samuel Huntington's pathbreaking book, *Political Order in Changing Societies* (1968). Latin Americanists cannot claim Huntington as one of their own, but his thesis precipitated the demise of the modernization school, and some of his key ideas, though not embraced at the time, would later find their way into the works of influential Latin American scholars such as Guillermo O'Donnell. According to Huntington, underlying transformations in the economy create opportunities but ones that do not necessarily keep pace with the demands of socially mobile groups. Those groups turn to the political process to voice grievances but absent political institutions able to respond to their demands, instability results. Societies then descend into a near anarchic state of mass praetorianism where the military is caught up in the social and political forces swirling around it. Middle classes fearing the onslaught of organized labor "compel the military to oppose the government" and restore the status quo ante. Thus the most important cause of military coups can be found not within the organization but in the structure of society. "Military explanations do not explain military intervention," he argued.[4]

This was a curious theoretical reversal for a scholar who a decade before had published *The Soldier and the State: The Theory and Politics of Civil-Military Relations* (1957) in which he traced the origins of military conduct to the professional norms and practices in the organization itself.[5] In his first incarnation Huntington was persuaded that a military could and should dedicate itself single-mindedly to the task of professional development, thereby ensuring its political neutrality. What went on inside the profession mattered to the fate of civil-military relations. In his second incarnation with the release of *Political Order* he had become a structuralist whose views had ironically converged with those of Marxists who were formulating social class theories of military intervention.[6]

Scholars who next appeared on the scene would restore interest in institutional (meaning military professional) influences but did so by turning the *Soldier and the State* on its head. Professionalism could be the very source of harmful praetorian conduct, they argued. Borrowing from organizational theory, O'Donnell's influential article "Modernization and Military Coups: Theory, Comparisons and the Argentine Case" (1976) suggested that the military's survival hinged on its ability to reduce the threats that originate from its environment.[7] To do so, it would beat a hasty retreat from the praetorian maelstrom to tend to its corporate needs. Once having overcome its internal divisions and having crossed a threshold of institutional cohesion, professional competence, and ideological unity, it could confidently seize state power in order to transform the system and in that way attempt to ensure its survival. He concludes, "Because of their professionalism, not in spite of it, professionalized armed forces manifest a high probability of taking upon themselves the responsibility of overcoming recurring civil-military crises by way of the installation of a new political regime."[8]

For O'Donnell, the military was both an independent and a dependent variable. The organizational changes he describes could not have occurred without fundamental change in the larger socioeconomic system of which the military is a part. In identifying underlying shifts in industrialization patterns along with the growth of new, militant, and more powerful social organizations, O'Donnell established the structural bases for professional innovation.[9]

Contemporaries of O'Donnell would push the institutional and ideological dimensions to center stage, peering deep inside the military profession to its origins, education, and doctrines. Developments in the military organization, they claimed, were largely self-generated and related but less rigidly tied to changes in society. In *The Military in Politics: Changing Patterns in Brazil* (1971) and then again in his chapter, "The New Professionalism of Internal Warfare and Military Role Expansion" (1973), Alfred Stepan acknowledged that demand performance pressures combined to place "great loads" on the Brazilian system, which consumed civilian rulers and alarmed military leaders.[10] But the military's "final solution" to the systemic crisis of the early 1960s rested on an intellectual foundation constructed several years before in its Superior War College, the Escuela Superior de Guerra (ESG). The new military professionalism of internal warfare and role expansion predated and was not a reaction to the threats generated by urbanization, popular activation, and economic decline. The proof is Stepan's recall that the ESG's critique "seemed academic" to Brazilians when it emerged in the mid-1950s, so divorced was it from the realities of their country at the time.[11]

Historians would take issue with just how "new" this new professionalism was, pushing its origins back to the turn of the century.[12] But they too took seriously the capacity of the military institution to cultivate its own professional standards, doctrines, and perceptions, all of which would exert a powerful influence on its future behavior. The military had gone from being primarily the agent of social forces to the agent of its own self-generated desires. Of course, military ideas did not emerge in a vacuum. As Frederick Nunn pointed out in his book *Yesterday's Soldiers: European Military Professionalism in South America, 1890–1940* (1983), militaries in Argentina, Brazil, Chile, and Peru often emulated the thoughts and practices of European officers who had come to the region in the late nineteenth century under contract to help them professionalize. The South American armed forces aspired not only to the high standards set by Prussian and French officers but to their elitist contempt for "failed" democratic institutions and actors as well. Once the right conditions were in place a few decades later, this contempt would be unleashed in the form of military intervention against elected governments.

For some scholars, the turn toward authoritarian solutions of the late 1960s and early 1970s stood as grim testimony to the power of military traditions, thoughts, self-perceptions, and ethos to shape politics in undesired ways. It thus became apparent that just as scholars of Nazi Germany had to come to grips with Adolf Hitler's foreshadowing views in *Mein Kampf,* so too would Latin Americanists have to take seriously the words of Latin America's coup-prone generals. In bringing together and translating into English dozens of military speeches and proclamations from seven Latin American countries, Brian Loveman and Thomas Davies's *The Politics of Antipolitics: The Military in Latin America* (1978) gave a large audience of North Americans a valuable window into the military mind-set of an important era. Other political science scholars—some of whom resided outside the borders of Latin American studies but whose research was nonetheless influential—were less impressed with the military's political thinking and more persuaded by its materialism. The military's concrete corporate interests, if left unattended or threatened, would serve as the pretext for intervention, said Eric Nordlinger, Bengt Abrahamsson, and others.[13]

By the end of the 1970s an enormous body of literature on the causes of military coups had been generated. It was also clear that notwithstanding the emerging consensus about the crises that would trigger intervention, different analytical starting points for scholars had produced disagreement as to who were the prime "movers and shakers" behind coups. Marxian class analyses and institutional-professional analyses seem to be the main contenders of that era.[14]

With the military comfortably lodged in power during the decade of the 1970s, the next logical step in scholarship would have been to analyze the morphology of those dictatorships. But then a curious thing happened, as Karen Remmer relates it: "Scholars moved from the study of democratic breakdowns to the study of democratic transitions without pausing to analyze the authoritarian phase that came in between."[15] Few comparative studies ever provided so much as a glimpse of the inner structure or workings of these regimes, focusing instead on societal factors that caused their installation.[16]

Whatever military policies and practices emerged were then traced back to conditions existing before the takeover. This was a mistake because "the forces that shape authoritarian rule are not fixed at the time of regime emergence."[17] What was needed in the civil-military field was a decisive shift from society to the state, but that would have to wait until the end of the 1980s with the release of Genaro Arriagada's *Pinochet: The Politics of Power* (1988) and Remmer's own book *Military Rule in Latin America* (1989).[18]

In her book, Remmer examines how authoritarian regimes are organized and how that organization directly affects the strength, professionalism, and cohesion of the armed forces, which in turn affects the life span of the regime itself. In establishing the relationship between institutional arrangements, decision-making processes, and regime durability, she successfully brought the state back into the study of the armed forces. It is not that other researchers had abandoned interest in the military as a relatively autonomous, institutional actor. It is that they had not grafted those interests to an analysis of regime dynamics once the armed forces had seized state power.

The military's lengthy immersion in power became the springboard from which analyses of extrication were launched. One can note several trajectories. The first was to concentrate on the harm done to military professionalism. The military came to realize that its managerial skills were not enough to cope in the sphere of governance, which demanded that it make tough decisions about contentious issues. Politics divides, and so it divided the officer corps, which was forced to choose sides in policy disputes that eroded professional unity and discipline. In the end, María Susana Ricci and J. Samuel Fitch conclude, "military government is a contradiction in terms; the armed forces cannot govern without subverting their own essence."[19] Already weakened and wishing to avert any more damage, they exit hastily from office. Some military governments, however, recognized and then eliminated the divisions early on, enabling themselves gradually to extricate from power with minimal damage to the institution. This second trajectory is most closely associated with Stepan's *Rethinking Military Politics: Brazil and the Southern Cone* (1988), which contends that regime moderates, fearing the breakdown of the hierarchical command because of renegades in the repressive intelligence community, launch an "aperture" intended to expose their misdeeds and thereby undermine them.

The third trajectory, taking off from Remmer's book, notes how the organization of power in the dictatorship conditioned how well the armed forces managed divisive issues such as economic crises. In those regimes that were better able to concentrate decision-making authority at the top in a few hands and shield the rank and file from policy debates, the military hung together.

Hence they could either delay their withdrawal, liberalize the regime, or pursue a full-scale transition on terms favorable to them. In those regimes not so institutionally blessed, economic policy crises would split the military wide open, causing it to lose any ability to set the timing or terms of its own extrication.[20]

Developments in the authoritarian regime would have, it seems, conditioned the next phase, namely the transition toward a democratic future. But the impact of different dictatorships on the transitions that followed depended on what analytical point of view scholars embraced. Authoritarian legacies mattered less to those who focused on elite decision making. For them, the transition was a period of great fluidity, uncertainty, and opportunity that provided political actors with a menu of expanding options. What decisions were made had less to do with the past and more to do with the future. Hard-line and soft-line officers and moderate and radical civilians alike would strategically jockey for position, exchange offers, issue threats, make bluffs, and finally negotiate, all with the objective of working out arrangements for the transfer of power to democrats. O'Donnell and Philippe Schmitter's *Transitions from Authoritarian Rule: Tentative Conclusions about Uncertain Democracies* (1986) best typifies this voluntaristic approach to civil-military affairs in a transitional setting, while Adam Przeworski's *Democracy and the Market: Political and Economic Reforms in Eastern Europe and Latin America* (1991) formalized this approach through the use of game theory.[21]

Authoritarian legacies mattered more to those who adopted a path-dependent analysis to transition. They looked behind the strategic choices to prior conditions that shaped the "opportunity set" from which decisions could be made. Choice was contingent on but not uniquely determined by socio-economic regime allies, the performance of the ancien régime, and the strength, unity, and resolve of the outgoing military elite. In varying contexts, strategic interactions would commence, resulting in formalized agreements (pacts, constitutions, and the like) which in turn would set the constraints for future interactions. These approaches are best exemplified by Terry Karl's article "Dilemmas of Democratization" (1990) and Felipe Agüero's *Soldiers, Civilians and Democracy: Post-Franco Spain in Comparative Perspective* (1995).

Today's Political Agenda

The completed transition in Latin America has naturally shifted the center of scholarly focus again, this time to the patterns of civilian-military relations developing under democratic auspices. Researchers have been appraising the degree to which respective civilian and military spheres of influence have narrowed, widened, or changed at all since the inauguration of democratic rule. If elected leaders have greater authority by virtue of their positions in democratic regimes, does that extend fully to their command of the armed forces? If the military is more compliant today than it was a decade or two before, how deeply rooted is that compliance? Is it unconditional and professionally grounded or contingent on the civilians' politics or performance? If civilian control is conditional or partial in nature, can democratic regimes sustain themselves nonetheless? These questions indicate that in a sense we (the field of civil-military behavior) have come full circle since the publication of Samuel Huntington's *Soldier and the State*. Then as today, the issue was (is) what would it take for politicians to achieve supremacy over their armed forces in a democratic system?

Achieving civilian control—let alone democratic civilian control—is a tall order for any Latin American nation to fill.[22] Indeed, scholars are justifiably skeptical about the prospects and would probably not have even broached the subject were it not for the persistence of democratic rule in Latin America. The passage of time uninterrupted by military praetorianism has given elected officials and their defense policy makers a new lease on life, justifying the natural rise of civilian control to the top of our intellectual agenda. In decades past, democracies were teetering on the edge of collapse, frantically trying to appease power-hungry officers to avert disaster. By and large, that is not the case today.

At the dawn of a new century, civil-military relations in Latin America are more stable than they were a decade or two ago. In most countries of the region, the military has been diminished in size, resources, influence, and stature. It cannot wield the threat of coup d'état as convincingly as it had in the past, nor is it clear that it would want to. Two safe generalizations can be made about the Latin American military: it is less oriented toward regime overthrow and more preoccupied with retaining some influence within the regime; and it is less interested in confronting civilians about national policy and more concerned with protecting its institutional well-being.

At the same time there remain significant differences in the state of civil-military relations from subregion to subregion and country to country. In the nations of the Southern Cone and Brazil, the armed forces have generally had cordial relations with civilian leaders. Most have been more occupied with issues of professionalism, external defense, and regional security. The one exception would be Paraguay, where the inward-looking military maneuvers for position and influence.

By contrast with the Southern Cone, the Andean region is a more troubled place. In the face of weak, ineffectual civilian institutions, the military has become politically embroiled by arbitrating legislative-executive disputes, clashing with armed insurgents, and propping up some leaders while undermining others. Yet Bolivia stands out as an example of an Andean country whose civil-military relations have become more stable since the era of perpetual coups. Finally, Central America has made significant headway since the civil wars of the 1980s. Militaries are smaller, more compliant, and less interventionist than they once were. Honduras and Nicaragua have probably made the greatest strides toward civilian control, followed by El Salvador and then Guatemala.

Debilitated democracies, coup plots, and near misses in countries such as Paraguay, Peru, Venezuela, and Ecuador post warnings that all is not well and that there are stresses and strains in these political systems that are spilling over into the civil-military realm in disturbing ways. While the survival (not the consolidation) of democratic states since the early 1980s has been unprecedented and satisfying to note, political stability cannot be simply defined as the absence of military intervention. Avoidance of coups is not the same as civilian control. Even where the armed forces do refrain from provocative actions designed to upset the legal framework, they may not fully accept their subordinate status. Spheres of influence that lie at the civil-military border could remain contested even within the constitutional order.

Thus government leaders still face significant challenges even in an environment that is more secure than in decades past. Let us review some of these. First, they must curb military influence while preserving or enhancing military professionalism. It is one of today's ironies that the militaries that are the most subordinate to civilian authority are least able to secure funding for their own modernization. In a country like Argentina, politicians squeezed between pressures from the International Monetary Fund (IMF) to reduce the budget deficit and societal pressures to ease the pain of structural adjustments have had enough power and motivation to divert budget shares away from defense toward other needs, leaving the military professionally undernourished. Conversely, those militaries that are less subordinate have the clout to insist that civilians give them the revenue guarantees they want. Chile's armed forces are arguably the most professionally well equipped on the continent but less respectful of civilian control. Governments must strike the middle ground, searching for ways to modernize the armed forces in a cost-effective manner while retaining their political authority and attending to societal needs.

The second challenge for civilians is to respond to the forces of globalization and market-oriented reform. They will have to devise strategies to deal not only with the social groups victimized by these economic changes but with the armed forces' responses to these groups. If Venezuela and Ecuador are indications, then the military has already become the pivotal actor between coalitions in favor of and against economic reforms of this kind. Witness the military's role in first suppressing IMF-induced riots in Caracas in 1989 only to take up the banner of resistance against neoliberal reforms with the birth of the rebellious military movement led by Hugo Chávez. Witness too the events of January 2000, when swarms of indigenous protesters, angered over Ecuadorian president Jamil Mahuad's latest austerity plan to secure external financing, stormed the congressional building in Quito to demand the president's ouster and his replacement by a civil-military junta. Military units joined in solidarity with the protest movement, but the military chief of staff, fearing international consequences, disbanded the junta and ushered Ecuador's vice president to the top executive post.[23] Governments must somehow calibrate their neoliberal economic policies to minimize such explosive opposition while ensuring that officers with populist sympathies do not add fuel to the fire.

The third challenge is to better design and manage the missions assigned to the armed forces. When soldiers enmesh themselves in internal security operations against drug producers or guerrillas and do so without sufficient civilian input and oversight, political problems arise. Soldiers can seize control of an operation as a vehicle to expand their own authority, demanding a say in policy making, encroaching on political jurisdictions, or interfering in civilian life. All of that raises disturbing questions about the government's own authority. Colombian soldiers sent out on search and destroy missions against narco guerrillas seem to be untethered and have already been accused of countless human rights transgressions.[24]

Civilians share some of the blame because they turn their backs on the conduct of these operations for lack of expertise and trust in their own judgments. This leads to the fourth and final challenge. Civilian governments must empower themselves with defense knowledge so that they can earn the confidence of their commanding officers. The Chilean military's insistence on near total control over its frontier and sea missions is also a reflection of political leaders' hesitancy to assert their own views on these matters.[25]

In brief, democratically elected regimes continue to survive, albeit some more precariously than others. But within these democratic systems elected leaders have yet to demonstrate enough interest or competence in military affairs. Questions concerning the military's resources, its professional development, and its roles and missions beyond defense still linger. The longer these questions remain unresolved, the more tensions will arise in the civil-military relation and the more doubts will be cast about the politicians' capacity to lead. As the equation shifts from one of regime survival to governmental performance and civil-military interaction in democratic systems, so too must our analytical orientations.

Choosing Analytical Perspectives

Consequently, the main challenge confronted in this volume is to decide what theoretical directions should be pursued in grappling with the issues of civil-military interaction and civilian control in democratic states. Changing contexts provide partial clues. For example, many military institutions in Latin America have assessed that the professional and political costs of reintervention are higher than in the past, given their anticipation of widespread and unprecedented condemnation from the international community, the regional neighborhood, and their own public. Political and economic forces in favor of democratic sustenance are much stronger than they were in the past. Such changes alter the preferences and perceptions of military elites, who now seem more interested in carving out a niche of influence within the democratic order than overturning it. The forces that may have propelled them into office before would not necessarily do so today. Whatever analytical perspectives are chosen must factor in the military's self-imposed limits and revised calculations about the risks and benefits of authoritarian rule.

This is why the Latin American civil-military literature of the past could not simply be imported into the present to serve as a guide. While many of the heretofore mentioned analyses were persuasive, they were also subject- and time-bound and could not possibly have anticipated some of the dramatic changes that have unfolded. But changing conditions force us to reconsider specific research questions, causal relations, and hypotheses embedded within theory more than the premises underlying them. A general theory of regime change should remain viable whether we are witnessing the rise or the fall of a democratic order. Likewise, a theory of civilian control should (if it is a good one) tap into fundamental forces that shape civil-military relations, forces that are so important and basic that they persist across different eras and contexts.

On the one hand, the fact that many underlying premises remain valid does invite us to build on *some* core theoretical elements found in the historical literature. All the contributors to this volume have benefited from the works previously mentioned. On the other hand, it does not invite a wholesale return to the past in order to move into the future. Even if the accumulation of good civil-military scholarship had pushed the frontiers of research forward, it is not clear in what direction. J. Samuel Fitch lamented back in the late 1970s that the field had already become disturbingly eclectic, bordering on the anarchic. Everyone had his or her own pet projects, but no one seemed committed to the collective endeavor of theory building. While there were some discernible theoretical trends at the time, many scholars were not self-consciously identifying with these, he argued. A decade later, Fitch would renew similar concerns, suggesting that although explanations of military behavior had become "increasingly sophisticated and complex," he still concluded that "given the slow pace of scholarly research and the enormous number of unanswered questions about military politics and military rule, more research needs to be directed to *theoretical issues* with direct policy consequences" (emphasis added).[26] To this day, there remains a need for research direction, with an explicit convergence of civil-military scholarship around a few key theoretical positions.

Some have said that a state of near anarchy has reigned in comparative politics and political science as well. But disciplines evolve, and over the course of several decades, a scattering of intellectual trends seems to have finally crystallized into a few schools of thought. An important recent volume suggests that the current field of comparative politics is more coherent than imagined.[27] Today's research revolves around three paradigmatic points: rationalist, culturalist, and structuralist. They help to order the substantive, methodological, and philosophical orientations of a wide range of scholarship in the field and arguably in political science and the social sciences as well. Rather than specific theories, these are ideal types within which theorizing occurs. Structuralism, for example, can include analyses of society, the state, and the global order and can include everything from social class, to governing institutions, to international systems. What unites them is attention to the impersonal forces that drive individual behavior. There is a similar unity and coherence to rationalist and culturalist paradigms.

This volume is conceived on the notion that Latin American civil-military specialists might find some advantage in situating their critiques more explicitly within these disciplinary paradigms while at the same time preserving their Latin American orientations. We do so with a premise in mind: that the objects of our inquiries, while certainly different, are comparable to and in fact integrally connected to objects beyond themselves. We who study politicians and soldiers in Latin America may be wrestling with questions shared by those in the mainstream discipline who study civil-military relations in other regions. Similarly, our pursuits may link with those who study other actors, including executives, legislators, parties, interest groups, and regimes. If so, then answers to our questions may be found with the help of analytical perspectives applied more generally.

For example, security specialists in the structural school have advanced theories to account for changes in the civil-military relation based partly on the international political context. Michael Desch argues that changing security environments affect the chances that civilians can render the armed forces subordinate. Those chances are greatest when external threats are high and internal threats low and least when external threats are low and internal threats high. But the effects of threat environments are sometimes ambiguous, and in these situations, argues Desch, doctrines guide the military either to diverge from or to converge with civilian leaders.[28] In light of Latin Americanists' long, abiding interest in doctrines of national defense and security, it would make sense to take a closer look at how or whether the tremendous changes in the regional and international environments of recent years are affecting contemporary military thinking.

Whereas structuralists often look at large, remote influences on behavior, rationalists perform close-up examinations of civil-military conduct. Peter Feaver's analysis of conflict between U.S. government and military officials relies on game theory. By demonstrating the logic of a series of interactions between civilian principals and military agents, he exposes the process by which outside forces make their presence known inside the relationship. Even as we acknowledge the huge differences between civil-military affairs in the United States and Latin America, we can at the same time find creative applications of game theory to model the conflict-ridden interactions between politicians and soldiers in this region.[29]

Beyond the civil-military field, there should be benefits to drawing on general theories of political action. Whatever may be said about civilians who interface with soldiers and the special burdens they bear, they are also politicians and political appointees. They worry about how to get elected; get reelected; survive in office; satisfy party leaders, voters, and constituents; run agencies; balance budgets; make laws; and formulate and execute policy. And they operate in familiar institutionalized contexts, be these executive, judicial, or legislative. Accordingly, notwithstanding important country differences, rules of behavior that apply to politicians everywhere should apply to them, meaning that theories of general political behavior should have relevance to them as well.

Armies are professional organizations like so many others. True, only they monopolize the means of coercion. Only they practice coups. But they share with countless other organizations features such as hierarchy, roles, rules, rank, and rewards and problems such as coordination, compliance, and delegation. They, like other organizations, have institutional legacies, memories, embedded norms of behavior, and methods of socialization. Like other agencies of state, they must compete for federal funds, and like the interest groups they sometimes mimic, they resort to pressure tactics to get what they want. These parallels invite us to draw on broader theories of organizations, institutions, the state, or interest groups found in the mainstream discipline.

There are several advantages to adapting for our own use more general analytical approaches once applied to subjects far removed from civil-military affairs. They enable us to ask intriguing questions that may not have occurred to us before. Those new questions drive the search for new evidence. Facts that may not have seemed relevant before take on significance within the framework of a different analytical model. Those facts also take on new meanings because our interpretation of them is shaped by our prior theoretical approaches. When all is said and done, perhaps the most important reason for considering alternative approaches is that they may provide us some powerful explanatory tools for solving puzzles that arise from theoretically informed observations in our field or heuristic devices for suggesting fruitful avenues for theory building. There is much we still do not know about what it is politicians and soldiers either want to do, can do, or are likely to do, given the contexts in which they operate, the previous interactions between them, the preferences they hold, the strategies they adopt, and the beliefs they espouse. It is worth exploring some new analytical directions to see if we could get some added leverage on addressing these problems.

The costs to not moving in this direction are considerable as well. The first is that we will continue to suffer from a double isolation as Latin America area studies specialists and then again as civil-military specialists. That isolation has occurred because, as Peter Smith noted, we (as Latin Americanists) have not "sufficiently engaged the theoretical and methodological discourse of the mainstream disciplines."[30] We have too often been divorced from the major intellectual traditions, currents, and debates in political science and in the field of comparative politics. This is truer still for civil-military experts. We live a sheltered existence, turning inward upon ourselves to revisit the same themes and concepts with diminished returns for our endeavor and without regard for innovative developments elsewhere. As a result, we have not persuasively communicated to other researchers our findings or that those findings may have implications for other areas of inquiry.

The second cost is that as a result of this divorce, we in area studies have invited assaults from some quarters in the discipline for not living up to the standards of political science research. Accusing us of having "defected from the social sciences into the camp of the humanists," critics take us to task for accumulating country studies that are too descriptive, atheoretical, noncomparative, and ill suited either to sustain or to refute a theoretical body of

TABLE 1.1 *Paradigms and Perspectives*

PARADIGM	ANALYTICAL PERSPECTIVE
Rationalist	Analyses of strategic action (includes coalition building, game and bargaining theory)
Structuralist	Analyses of institutions (includes organizations, rules, and regimes, at domestic, regional, and international levels)
Culturalist	Analyses of the subject (includes individually held or shared ideas, beliefs, attitudes, interpretations)

knowledge.[31] We have, they say, been unable to answer the question, What has the study of your area contributed to the broader discipline? Divorce is a two-way street, and certainly some of the generalizations about area studies have been unfair. It is a gross distortion to set up false dichotomies between humanists (meaning all area studies specialists) and scientists (those from the mainstream discipline) or between those committed to in-depth study of cases against those designing "sophisticated research."[32] In the field of Latin American studies, one can find a growing number of well-researched, theoretically informed, social scientific studies on a range of topics. Nonetheless, there is also a kernel of truth to the critics' observation that we have been too inattentive to intellectual developments outside the confines of our field.

The critics have gotten it about half right, which means we in the field of Latin American civil-military relations have to meet them halfway. One way of doing so is precisely by taking greater interest in applying some of the respected theoretical approaches found in the larger discipline to *la cuestión militar*. What are these?

The heretofore mentioned tripartite division in comparative politics between rationalist, structuralist, and culturalist approaches is a useful starting point. But as one of the authors, Mark Lichbach, says, the ideal types must be "judged on pragmatic grounds. They are useful or not for this or that problem from this or that conceptual point of view."[33] Civil-military specialists must then find the specific applications within these schools of thought that are pertinent to the analysis of issues that concern them. The contributors to this volume have done just that. A few of us can arguably be typecast as advocates for a specific analytical point of view. The rest cannot and have instead chosen to incorporate ideas from more than one theoretical tradition. The analytical perspectives represented in this volume can be identified and usefully grouped within the three schools of thought shown in Table 1.1. What lies ahead are succinct summaries of these analytical perspectives. Under consideration will be their units of analysis, their premises, their conclusions, and differences among them.

Strategic Action Approaches

Theories of strategic action argue that political behavior is driven by self-interest. Motivating all behavior is a set of desires, beliefs, and preferences grounded in material or careerist pursuits. Since only people desire, believe, and choose, either they are the units of analysis, or groups and organizations are treated as if they were individuals. Action is intentional; there are reasons for what we do, having to do with fulfilling our objectives, some of which are valued more highly than others. We rank order our objectives, assign probabilities to achieving each, and then plot how we will fulfill them.

Action is strategic, meaning that the road taken is thought to be the best one to arrive at a predetermined set of prioritized ends. Not all roads can be traversed, and it is the context that defines what options (or opportunity structures) are available. Most (not all) strategic action theorists therefore admit that the available courses of action depend on what structured environment the actor finds himself in. If we know his interests, his contextualized options, and we assume his rationality, we can reasonably predict what course of action he and any other actor in his position would choose. Consequently, disciples of strategic action theory believe that political actors are interchangeable.[34]

Of course, individuals do not act in isolation. The chances that they could achieve their ends have something to do with conditions and constraints imposed not just by a context but by a rival actor. Here, models of strategic action such as coalition building, game theory, and bargaining theory will have great relevance. These models are extensions of rational action theories because they make the same assumptions about individuals but factor in the behavior of others. Bargaining, for example, often commences when neither party to a dispute has the power to impose its preferences on the other unilaterally, yet both share the common interest of deriving a settlement. Occurring under conditions of uncertainty and incomplete information, bargaining is a form of conflict resolution that depends on communication in the form of bids and counterbids between the two sides.

Institutional Approaches

While strategic action theorists focus on the individual and his or her interests, calculations, and actions, institutional theorists put their stock in the enduring

influence of organizational rules, patterns, and traditions on personal behavior.[35] Strategic action theorists believe that any organization can be reduced
to its component parts: its members, whose interactions, taken in the aggre-
gate, constitute the life force of the institution itself. Most institutionalists, in
contrast, believe the whole is greater than the sum of its parts. Institutions not
only are forces in their own right but are fully capable of compelling rational
individuals to behave in ways they might not have chosen on grounds of pure
self-interest.

Institutions can be generally defined as "formal or informal procedures,
routines, norms and conventions embedded in the organizational structure of
the polity."[36] The central issue today is not whether these structures have an
impact on individual behavior—a point that most rationalists concede—but
how. Do they influence strategic calculations, or do they alter values and
identities? Do individuals adhere to embedded rules because they stand to
gain, because they must, or because they want to?[37]

Some institutionalists situated close to the border with strategic action
theorists maintain that institutions matter primarily because they constitute
strategic environments within which individuals plot a course of action. Rational actors can still pursue their self-interests, so long as they discover the
most optimal strategy within the limits set by the institution. Others hone in on
the long-term constraints and antagonisms imposed by the organized environment on the individual's advantageous pursuits. Actors may have to settle for
suboptimal solutions[38] because they confront entrenched rules of the game
they cannot overturn—rules that constitute the embedded interests of the
framers of the original accords who first set up the institutions. Thus while
institutions are susceptible to change, change is either difficult or path dependent.[39] As a result, frustrated actors make adjustments not only in strategies—a
move consistent with rational choice arguments—but oftentimes in preferences as well. A third variation on this thinking contends that institutions
themselves can be the source of preference and preference change. For example, individuals "discover" career-oriented values derived from the structure
of incentives established by the professional organization. Professors covet
unstructured time, lawyers covet clients, and so on.[40]

Subjective Approaches

Featured prominently in the work of such contemporary theorists as Clifford
Geertz and James C. Scott, subjective approaches to the study of politics have
had an important, lasting impact on disciplines of political science, sociology,
and anthropology.[41] There are variations on the theme ranging from analyses

of individual leaders to those of large groups. These perspectives are united by their general concerns about ideas and more specifically about beliefs, attitudes, and interpretations that guide political behavior.

Ideas offer perspectives—angles of vision—for their proponents that bring certain objects into sharp focus and blur others. Whereas proponents of strategic action would argue that ideas originate from, reflect, and serve an individual's interests, subjectivists would claim that ideas help interpret interests or even generate their own. Groups of people could be as easily united through outlook as they are through material relations. Subjectivists will therefore make content analyses of ideologies, doctrines, and other sources of shared vision to discover how these provide groups with persuasive frames of reference.

They will also explore the ways in which individuals absorb and then act on those ideas. Rather than dispassionately observe behavior from afar, these analysts crawl under the skin of the political agent, to comprehend *his* angle of vision, to know the significance that events have for *him*. In short, subjectivists agree with Max Weber, who said that events have qualities and importance that are "conditioned by the orientation of our cognitive interest."[42]

Orientations, says Harry Eckstein, are learned via socialization, and socializing experiences are often similar from one individual to the next by virtue of membership in the same collectivity.[43] When these experiences nurture common, guiding assumptions about political life at a national level, we speak of political culture.[44] A similar process could occur in subnational collectivities, be these social classes, religious groups, or armies. Once the beliefs of individuals in those groups converge, we may find a consistency to their interpretations and actions derived not from interests or institutions but from ideas.

The Expected Payoff

What could be gained by adopting these analytical frames of reference? What can we learn about civil-military relations that we might not otherwise? What are the limits that each approach comes up against, and how might the alternatives overcome these?

Strategic action approaches may give us a deeper understanding of what underlying interests, goals, and strengths, respectively, motivate and enable politicians and soldiers to behave the way they do. The challenge of politicians is always twofold. They must consider those strategies that will most likely engender military subordination. But they must simultaneously weigh the impact their moves will have on their political goals, those being to survive in office, to get reelected, to serve constituents, and to help their party. In some contexts, these goals may be compatible. In other contexts, they are not, forcing the political leader to trade off between satisfying the military's wants and voters' wants. A decision in favor of an additional defense expenditure must be weighed against the loss of revenue for constituents or some prized national program. A decision to bring a military officer into the cabinet makes one less ministerial post available to a political ally or coalition partner, and so forth.

Meanwhile, the armed forces have their agenda. Their core objective is to preserve if not enlarge their coercive capabilities, projecting them outward against foreign foes and, if need be, inward against domestic foes. To do so, they are further motivated to maintain standards of material well-being and organizational control, including budgets, living conditions, equipment, discipline, cohesion, and esprit de corps in the ranks.

Strategic choice theory would tell us that each side's rational pursuit of its own interests could result in a collective irrationality.[45] For instance, politicians have an incentive to divert scarce fiscal resources away from defense toward sectors that will have a more beneficial electoral impact for them. In doing so they deprive the military of resources needed to elevate its professionalism. A military so deprived cannot contain its impulse to act unprofessionally—like an unruly interest group—pressuring the government for more resources and knowing that if it does not, others will. The result may be a clash between soldiers and civilians that not only upsets the quest for more stable civil-military relations but may have a destabilizing effect on the democracy itself.

But conflict is not inevitable. The decision to accommodate or contest is influenced not just by interests but by the availability or scarcity of resources to either side. Politicians' resources vary, and they come in the form of good performance, defense knowledge, electoral mandates, popular legitimacy, and votes of confidence from the region and beyond. The military's resources are multiple, too, and are organizational (a monopoly on the means of coercion; unity in the ranks), societal (status), and historical (earned reputations) in nature. The strengths of one side set limits for the other. Politicians armed with great assets can choose from a more diverse portfolio of options, unless they are up against a formidable military. If so, accommodation or negotiation may be wiser than contestation. Likewise, it is well known that the armed forces do cautiously consider politicians' voter appeal and the government's legitimacy before contemplating threatening action. Strategic options for either actor depend, then, on the civil-military balance of power established at a particular historical juncture.

Of course, things are not perfectly symmetrical. The military and only the military could, in theory, advance its goals by playing its ultimate card, coercion. That most don't most of the time is one of the fascinating stories in civil-military history. Strategic choice arguments would suggest that in today's context, armies of Latin America do not resort to their ace in the hole because they have other means (persuasion, bargaining, intimidation, bluffs, threats) at their disposal that will produce the same results while forgoing the higher costs now attributed to intervention.

Typically, therefore, civil-military relations in the contemporary Latin American era invoke a mixture of conflictual and cooperative impulses. Both sides may compete over the same set of scarce goods (power, policy, budgets), yet each has an incentive to avoid grave outcomes. Certainly civilians want to avoid coups at all costs. But coup mongering is a risky venture for the armed forces: a coup attempt could fail because of internal dissent; or it could succeed but trigger disaster soon thereafter in the form of domestic uprisings, international repudiation, or economic blockades. As a result, they interact in ways that can be modeled as either positive sum games or bargaining scenarios. Neither side has so much power that it can impose its preferences on the other; each must contemplate the moves of the other before deciding what to do; the equilibrium outcome to a civil-military conflict depends on their combined moves and can accrue (however unevenly) benefits for both sides.

Strategic action theory's application to civil-military affairs has its limits. For politicians to make sound strategic judgments, they need information about military intentions—information often not available from an organization that is exceedingly guarded about its priorities. Accordingly, it is easy for political leaders to miscalculate, making suboptimal choices that trigger unwanted military reactions. Also, there is a problem regarding the unitary actor principle. Even if we had information on military views, exactly whose views do we take to be representative of the institution? And is there an archetypal view? The armed forces are not only a huge organization with many members but a divided one. It may be a stretch to presume that it behaves as if it were one. Institutional theory, in contrast, does not make that simplifying assumption.

At a fundamental level, institutional analyses should help us understand how armies resolve their collective action problems. How can huge, unwieldy collectivities such as these ever achieve any unified goals with so many disparate members who bring with them differing values and interests? Any complex organization confronts the central challenge of coordinating the activities and interactions of large numbers of people without the aid of a market.[46] While instruments of coordination vary, organizations like the armed forces put a premium on hierarchy and socialization. Hierarchies centralize authority and delegate tasks along a ladder of influence. Labor is divided, information is channeled, goals are shaped, obedience is rewarded, and dissent is punished—all for the purposes of getting members to cohere around institutionally mandated objectives. In this respect, soldiers would comply because they are situated at lower rungs of the ladder, their tasks and options are structurally limited, they look forward to material compensations (via promotion), and they are fearful of reprisals. But soldiers are also dutiful. Through a means of institutionally controlled indoctrination, they have been socialized to accept the goals of the organization and their place in it. Although the content of military doctrine leads us into the arena of ideas, the process by which that doctrine is designed and disseminated is organizationally determined.

Consequently, those in positions of authority expect those below to execute their orders faithfully, and most of the time they do. But even in the stoic environment of the armed forces, soldiers do not always comply, and institutional analyses can help explain why. Sometimes the institution invites its own dissent by enforcing rules of conduct that, however rational in their organizational intent, trigger dissatisfaction from those below. For example, a decision to induce interservice or joint action will improve military responses but will also eliminate service redundancies, which in turn could result in terminated assignments, triggering objections from below.

Dissatisfaction has a mixture of causes: subordinates may resent the orders handed down to them, they may be disgruntled with the reward system, or they may have lost respect for those who do the ordering. In response to dissent, superiors must be prudent with how much punishment they mete out because they are also dependent on subordinates who, despite their lack of official authority, have their own sources of power either in the form of knowledge or control over troops. That power could be used strategically to pry concessions out of superiors or to undermine them. The military hierarchy must strike the delicate balance between command of and respect for those below them. It is principal-agent dilemmas such as these that are brought into sharp relief by organizational theories of political behavior.[47]

Institutional approaches also have application on the civilian side of the ledger. They teach us that armies of the region do not automatically translate their preferences into policy whenever and wherever they wish. Their will is mediated by governing agencies via procedural and structural mechanisms that can either open or restrict the military's channels of influence. Thus even in systems where the armed forces maintain considerable stores of power, institutional arrangements on the civilian side should be observed to know where the military influence makes a decisive impact and where it does not.[48] Finally, institutional analyses can be applied at the regional or international level. Conceived broadly as bundles of rules and networks of agencies that shape interactions between states, institutions—be they trade, border, or security agreements—can also have an impact on domestic civil-military affairs. They do so by shifting the military incentives toward or away from support of civilian-led foreign policy initiatives, while altering incentives of societal actors either to conspire with the military or to join to constrain its reach.

Institutional analyses effectively reveal the rules that govern behavior but not all the underlying forces that drive it. The passions stirred by interests and the principles forged by beliefs that lie behind military or civilian action often go undetected by institutionalists. Moreover, while it can usefully posit the "rules of the game" in civil-military spheres, it cannot tell us how each of the "players" interprets those rules. Thus institutionalists would not pick up on the differences in perceptions that could be at the root of conflict between politicians and soldiers. For leverage on these dimensions, we must turn to subjective analyses.

For subjectivists, military views matter. Whether these views are held by the entire institution or by a few, their content must be unveiled so that we can understand how soldiers down through the ranks "size up" events around them. Subjective analyses can give us explanatory leverage regarding continuity and change in the armed forces and in its relations with politicians and society. If military interpretations are based on deeply held beliefs, they may persist despite changes in the environment that should otherwise challenge their premises. Knowing this could help explain why some militaries cling to an idealized past rather than adjust their mentality to a changing world. An examination of age-old military notions, myths, and symbols may give us insights into why soldiers believe they remain the custodians of national interest while civilians more commonly reject such claims.

Not all soldiers in a given military institution believe the same things. The typical Latin American military is a divided one, with officers clustered into factions that reside within or across services, functions, and ranks and embrace their own ideas. Because the military is not immune to external influence, those ideas can creep in from society to different levels and corners of the organization without official detection or endorsement. Should they also give rise to impassioned subgroup loyalties, they can constitute the driving force behind change in the form of internal revolts against leaders or conflict between units. At the very least, they could help explain why differences in ideology and role perceptions persist in the same institution and thus why the military does not always act in unison.

Subjectivists also concern themselves with the society. Scholars concur that civilian support or opposition has often tipped the balance in favor of or against military intervention. Whether or not citizens embrace military solutions for political problems ultimately hinges on their attitudes regarding the military's proper role in the political system. In sum, to the extent that individual or groups of soldiers and citizens come to believe in a premise—whether that premise is correct or not or self-serving or not—their behavior is more likely to be influenced by it. That is why subjective perspectives have an important place in civil-military scholarship alongside strategic and institutional analyses.

At the same time, subjective analyses face difficulties. How do we really know whether military beliefs drive behavior? After all, we identify beliefs by listening to the military voice. But words may be rhetorical disguises for the underlying pursuit of political or economic gain. Proclamations or interviews after the fact may be post hoc rationalizations for behavior motivated by self-interest, not conviction. If what the military ultimately does seems consistent with the strategic pursuit of a predetermined set of core interests, then might not reason and rationality be the guiding forces behind military action? And despite the diversity of views within the ranks, we must remain impressed with the ability of most military organizations to mute internal differences, silence dissent, and compel allegiance when the chips are down. Institutional features probably have much to do with achieving these outcomes.

The Contents of This Volume

Each of the contributors to this volume draws on one or more of the analytical traditions described above and relates these to specific civil-military questions in Latin America. The chapters are ordered according to levels of analysis. The first three deal at the level of the individual, with Wendy Hunter's chapter focusing on the actor's rationality, while J. Samuel Fitch's and Ernesto López's chapters concentrate more on the actor's beliefs. The next two chapters, by Deborah L. Norden and David Pion-Berlin, move to the organizational and institutional planes, respectively. The next three chapters, by Harold A. Trinkunas, Felipe Agüero, and David R. Mares, blend concerns with the broad and the narrow. Trinkunas and Agüero look at the impact of regime changes, power relations, and institutions on future strategic choices, while Mares examines regional level influences on domestic actors. Finally, Brian Loveman presents the broad sweep of historical influences on contemporary occurrences.

In Chapter 2, Wendy Hunter assesses the usefulness of a strategic action approach to analyzing civil-military relations with application to Brazil. While acknowledging the utility of cultural and structural analyses in the literature on Latin American civil-military affairs, Hunter finds that rational choice theory has the distinct advantage of being able to reveal the powerful impulses and calculations that respectively motivate and steer specific political behaviors. The politician is motivated principally to compete for and survive in office, which under certain conditions prompts him to contest the military for influence. Meanwhile, the military has its own interests to defend, but in today's political environment, where heavyhanded tactics could damage its reputation, it is more prudent in its responses. In turn, this situation renders the politician "less fearful of upsetting the military." Hence the strategies one side chooses influence the choice of strategies adopted by the other. But rational choice theory has its limits. It cannot adequately explain why, if it is in their self-interests to contest the armed forces, politicians do not do it more often and why some militaries manage to retain so much power. Hunter argues that cultural and structural approaches may fill in some of the explanatory gaps.

J. Samuel Fitch reveals the limitations to behavioral approaches to civil-military affairs by way of an analysis of military subjectivity in Chapter 3. We cannot simply observe what the military does because it may exercise its roles behind the scenes or not at all, yet enjoy tremendous influence. Moreover, when the military does act, its behavior is susceptible to different interpretations. Which interpretation would we choose? For Fitch, testing competing explanations for conduct demands evidence on military beliefs. Military officers are "boundedly rational actors" who pursue their self-interests in a given context *as they understand it*. To uncover the military's self-understandings, the author conducted extensive in-depth interviews with Argentine and Ecuadorian officers and found that there are "competing conceptions of the role of the armed forces in a democratic regime" and variations in the extent to which "democratic norms of civil-military relations are accepted or contested, internalized or rejected." Through an analysis of military journal writings, the author is also able to discern variations in military doctrinal views on national security.

In Chapter 4, Ernesto López draws on the subjective approach in arguing that Huntington's concept of civilian control will have to be revised if it is to be made applicable to the Latin American context. In a region where the military exhibits tendencies toward intervention, autonomy, and professionalism without social responsibility, subordination to civilian authority is not a given, as Huntington had implied; it is something to be constructed. But if civilian control is to be constructed so that it is sustainable, it must be rooted in military convictions, not material interests. Specifically, it must be predicated on the military's firm belief in the legality of the democratic order and of the right to command of those who exercise authority. Thus López characterizes the civil-military relation as one of domination (borrowing from Max Weber) which rests on legitimate consent and not imposition. It is only when the military consents to the government's rule over it that subordination can become a reality. Responsibility for that change in mentality lies not just with soldiers but with politicians, who have to demonstrate they can lead. Brief case studies of Argentina and Chile illustrate some key points.

Deborah L. Norden deploys organizational theory to analyze military bureaucracies and the conspiratorial movements they may give rise to in Chapter 5. Normally, the military is a rational organization featuring hierarchy, strict rules of behavior, and division of labor designed to ensure top-down control in pursuit of unified goals. Yet competing sources of authority and contacts with the external environment render it vulnerable to capture by small pro-coup groups from within. To counter this vulnerability, methods are chosen that succeed in creating obstacles to coups but ironically "contribute to the motivation to attempt one." Norden assesses how in Venezuela, democratic governments enacted bureaucratic reforms to weaken the political power of the army, impede coordination between the military's service branches, speed the ascension and retirement of officers, and develop party networks in the armed forces. While the intent of these reforms was to prohibit organized unrest in the ranks, they stimulated it by obstructing the military from carrying out some of its professional functions, thus giving rise to grievances among officers that would spill over into military rebellion in the form of Hugo Chávez's Movimiento Bolivariano Revolucionario (MBR). But the rebellion could not topple the government in part because of those very same bureaucratic reforms. Having failed at coup d'état, the MBR adapted organizationally to follow a political movement path to power.

In Chapter 6, David Pion-Berlin explores the paradox that the Argentine military remains subordinate despite a ministry ill suited to enforce that subordination. Using an institutional approach, he argues that there has been a compensation for ministerial frailty in the form of other civilianized centers of power in the executive and legislative branches of government. Autonomy, namely the insularity and independence with which policy makers can work, and institutionalized expertise in the form of governmental schools, institutes, and research centers are the two principal sources of institutional strength. Combined, these features have allowed civilians to strip the military of resources, roles, and rationales that in the past constituted vital sources of strength. Policy makers without *formal* authority over the armed forces could nonetheless exert considerable influence over them because they made policies that directly and adversely affected their interests and could do so because of the strengths of the institutions they inhabited.

Harold A. Trinkunas employs elements of institutional and strategic action theory as components of a path-dependent model to explain civilian control efforts in Argentina and Venezuela in Chapter 7. To render the military subordinate to their will, civilians must enjoy first the leverage to "compel the armed forces to accept reduced jurisdictional boundaries" and then the capacity to solidify those boundaries through monitoring and supervising military conduct. Leverage is a function of strategy and opportunity. Not all options are available, and the choice depends on how much "room for maneuver" politicians enjoy as a result of the type of transition to democracy. Still, opportunities may be squandered or new ones created, depending on the strategic acumen of political leaders. Because the armed forces will employ countermeasures to stem the loss of their influence, civilians must generate the regime capacity necessary to maintain authority on a more permanent basis. They do so by transforming their actions into institutionalized oversight, enforcement, and expertise. "Depending on what combination of opportunity, strategy, and institutions are available," writes Trinkunas, "an emerging democracy can follow a path toward one of four potential outcomes: regime collapse, regime persistence, weak institutional control, and strong institutional control."

In Chapter 8, Felipe Agüero combines elements of historical-institutionalism and strategic action to understand the shaping of civil-military relations in postauthoritarian regimes. He is concerned with how conditions before and during the transition to democracy determine the power resources soldiers and politicians will have at their disposal as they bargain with one another over issues vital to them. What either side ultimately achieves depends on the resources they brandish during their interactions. Yet the unexpected does occur because in a dynamic process such as this one, actors may fail to exploit the opportunities that arise or, conversely, succeed in overcoming the limits that are imposed. Bargains are important because the outcomes to these encounters not only "differentially empower the military and civilian officials for the ensuing process" but institutionalize arrangements well into the future, making it difficult to undo what has been done. These ideas are applied to empirical capsules on two southern European and five South American countries.

David R. Mares resorts to a rational-institutional approach to examine the relationship between regional economic integration and democratic civilian control in Chapter 9. Free trade zones are institutions because they are made up of a complex of rules, norms, and agencies that govern the economic interactions between member states. Mares hypothesizes that if integration were to affect civil-military relations it would do so by shifting the power and interests of key domestic actors. Where the rationale for integration is protectionist, the prestige of the military and its nationalistic allies at home is heightened, making democratic civilian control less likely. Where integration is inspired by openness to international capital, the military is weakened, ceteris paribus. But outcomes also depend on whether the gains derived from any economic union are enjoyed by many or few. The maldistribution of benefits can generate social disruption among the losers, prompting winners to court the military for their own protection. As a result, the military's influence will rise and civilian control will become less likely. Case studies of integration between El Salvador and Honduras and between Argentina and Chile reveal that while the economic rationales are supportive of greater democratic control, sources of tension and threat perception remain that attenuate the influence.

In the final chapter, Brian Loveman examines the historical transmission of institutional and subjective influences on contemporary civil-military affairs. Loveman finds that over the course of centuries, there has been an accumulation of overlapping and reinforcing laws, practices, concepts, and norms that have established a "permanent regime of protected democracy" that persists to this day. These regimes are constitutional but are rigged to allow undue military influence over courts, policies, politicians, and common citizens. Today, civil-military relations in these regimes stand as "living legacies" of a premodern past. What survives are practices and beliefs, sustained through the years via the replication and reinforcement of laws, regulations, rituals, and myths that have become so embedded that they constitute a "political culture" of militarism. There is, for example, a continuity of discourse that stretches from the 1800s to virtually any twenty-first-century military website on the continent to speeches of politicians themselves regarding the military's right to be the ultimate custodian of national interest. That right is based on the notion (whether accurate or not) that there is an institutional continuity between the armies that helped build the nations of the region and today's armed forces.

The Future

None of us has the last word on the study of civil-military relations. Undoubtedly, our chapters will raise as many questions as they answer, given the fast-paced changes in and around the civil-military world, the complexities of the subject, and the limitations of our approaches. That is all for the good, since it is those questions that will inevitably lead to new research. But what directions might or should that research take?

In 1976, in an influential review essay, Abraham Lowenthal exhorted his fellow scholars to take on the challenge of theoretical integration. He said, "The most exciting task is to *synthesize and integrate within an inclusive theoretical formulation* the by now abundant literature on the political roles armies play in Latin America and in other regions" (emphasis added).[49] Is this advice still helpful? Perhaps it is, if we consider that the three main analytical perspectives represented here, however useful they may be, are still incomplete. The weaknesses of one seem to point to the strengths of another. This raises the idea that there may be beneficial synergies in bringing them together. Differences in philosophical premises, units of analysis, and methods of inquiry would certainly complicate the effort, but it still may be worth a try. Without detailing what such a synthesis would look like, let me conclude by briefly relating the merits of considering one. To sharpen the discussion, I will consider only the question of civilian control, leaving aside the full array of civil-military issues and interactions.

Civilian control is a relation of power, and power is about influence. In a Dahlian sense, that means that civilians must get the armed forces to do what historically they have been reluctant to do, namely not only to restrain their interventionist impulses but more positively to accept their subordinate status. What would be the bases and the means on which such a result would be achieved?

The armed forces could derive a material preference for it. They would come to see that self-restraint was self-serving. Civilians would reward compliance through provision of goods coveted by the armed services. Alternatively, they could put up with it as a matter of necessity, owing to rules of behavior with which they were forced to comply. The method would be to build a state-centered, organizational infrastructure to channel influence, contain harmful pressures, and monitor and supervise activities. Or they could accept it on principle, believing that compliance was a virtue. The means used would be persuasion at the hands of respected civilian and military authorities.

Subordination therefore would be rooted in either interests, institutions, or ideas, meaning that each basis of compliance would connote a different analytical starting point. If any one of these bases were both necessary and sufficient for civilian control, there would be no need for a discussion of analytical unity. Politicians could put all their eggs in the basket of interest satisfaction, institution building, or indoctrination. Likewise, scholars could put all their eggs in the basket of one theoretical approach, be it strategic, institutional, or subjective in nature.

Latin American realities suggest that a singular approach in practice or in theory is unlikely to succeed. Political and military leaders will most likely have to resort to multipronged strategies to grapple with an issue as hugely complicated and sensitive as this one. None of the aforementioned paths to subordination will be suffice, but each will be an essential ingredient in a more inclusive approach.

For example, fulfilling military corporate wants may be in principle an attractive device to foster compliance, but in an age of economic scarcity, how practical is it? Politicians face enormous international pressures to rein in defense spending on financial grounds and domestic pressures to redistribute the fiscal pie to other well organized interests on political grounds. If reasonable cuts are made in defense but soldiers become angered nonetheless, what is to be done? Without rewards, rules must be established so that whatever complaints officers are likely to have are routed through legal channels. The expression of dissatisfaction within the organizational confines of the democratic system places beneficial constraints on the military's behavior.

Fine and well, but institutions matter only when powerful protagonists agree to work within them. Armies of the region have been known to sidestep official channels when it was self-serving. What is to restrain them from doing so again? The probability of repudiation or punishment would be one solution, but that depends on an uncertain civilian ability to inflict such costs. Hence we must consider value reorientation as a means of self-restraint. Institutional circumvention is less likely when the military has internalized the norms of subordination. When the notion that a soldier executes but does not challenge policy or those who made it becomes an article of faith, then civilian leaders can more comfortably trim defense budgets and demand rule-based compliance without fearing harmful reprisals.

The interrelated dimensions of this problem invite an interrelated analytical response; a synthesis of some nature is in order. Advocates of different theoretical points of view should put their heads together and find ways of combining the virtues of each perspective into a more comprehensive but parsimonious model. Such a model would involve theorizing about interests, institutions, *and* ideas, and their combined impact on civilian control. It would consider the rational preferences, the relations of power, and the resonating principles that drive, guide, constrain, and change the actions of politicians and soldiers alike.

The potential benefits to future research of this analytical synthesis are several. It would avoid an adhesion to a single paradigm and yet overcome the atheoretical tendencies also noticeable in the field. The focus on strategic action, subjectivity, and institutionalism cuts a third research path that will allow us to congeal around a few key analytical approaches that have problem-solving potentials.

For many decades, Latin Americanists seemed to be consumed by one dominant paradigm after the next. First came modernization theory, then dependency, and then bureaucratic-authoritarianism. While each was compelling in its own way in its own time, all of these grand theories were guilty of sweeping, unfounded generalizations, excessive aggregation, and idealized abstraction that made hypothesis confirmation *or* refutation difficult.[50] Civil-military literature did not particularly benefit when it came under the domination of a single paradigm. But neither did it profit from exercises in barefoot empiricism. Studies that avoided the theoretical and focused primarily on descriptive case study narratives provided us with an abundance of facts on countries in the region but left us without comparable constructs, concepts, and testable hypotheses.

Together the three approaches are useful because they should give direction and focus to our inquiries yet allow for a broader view of the same subject. For example, strategic action theory will force us to think in terms of motivating interests and goal-oriented choices each time we investigate a civil-military problem. Add an institutional component and we are compelled to think in terms of how those interests and goals are either enabled, disabled, or refracted by embedded rules, procedures, and power relations within organized contexts. Throw subjective analyses into the mix and we must come to grips with how politicians and soldiers interpret their interests and the rules they come up against. The integration of the three perspectives thus permits us simultaneously to explore different dimensions of the same civil-military relationship.[51]

This avoids the temptation to isolate on one set of arguments believing it to be the most compelling without laying it side by side with others that may prove equally or more persuasive on their own terms. By first comparing analytical approaches, we get a better sense of the strengths and limitations of each. By then combining them, we may be able to get beyond the partial critique of the civil-military subject each theory produces to find a more comprehensive, realistic, if not powerful explanation for a complex phenomenon.

There are also policy implications to such a synthesis that researchers might contemplate. If political leaders in this region are ever to achieve lasting supremacy over their militaries, they will have to deal with interests, institutions, and ideas. Soldiers who are called on to practice political self-restraint cannot be asked to forsake self-interest. Politicians must see to it that enough resources are spent on military upgrades so that officers perceive that their professional careers are advancing. But the willingness of the military to obey is related to the capacity and desire of civilians to command. Thus politicians must fortify the defense-related institutions along and outside of the chain of command that are responsible for channeling influence, delegating tasks, and supervising activities. Civilians placed in charge of these institutions should demonstrate enough competence in defense affairs to elicit the respect of their military subordinates. And if military ideas about democracy and civilian control are to change, there has to be a greater intellectual exchange with civilians. Politicians and soldiers alike must try to tear down the walls separating the military academy from the civilian university.

Scholars and students then have good reasons to give serious consideration to each of the analytical perspectives discussed in this book, as well as to their possible integration. We invite them and others to read the chapters in this volume and then contemplate the intellectual challenges that lie ahead.

NOTES

I thank Craig Arceneaux, J. Samuel Fitch, Wendy Hunter, Mark Lichbach, and Deborah Norden for their comments on earlier drafts of this chapter.

1. Definitions of civilian control abound, but most converge on a few interrelated themes relating to power, functions, organizations, rules, and values. There must be a distribution of power that allows the constitutional authorities to make policy with the expectation that the military will carry it out. There is a functional division of labor with civilians setting the general course and the military filling in the technical details. Defense institutions must be in place to channel, regulate, and routinize the flow of influence and information from the political to the military sphere and back again. And the armed forces must not only act professionally and nondeliberatively but also come to believe in the civilians' right to rule over them.

2. On the one hand, it is a compliment to scholars whose classic texts we refer to time and time again. On the other hand, the recycling of concepts found in those texts displays the absence of competing landmark works and the failure of the field to move decisively forward. Among the most familiar and cited works are the following: Samuel Huntington's *The Soldier and the State* (1957) and his *Political Order in Changing Societies* (1968), S. E. Finer's *Man on Horseback* (1962), Guillermo O'Donnell's *Modernization and Bureaucratic-Authoritarianism* (1973), and Alfred Stepan's *The Military in Politics* (1971) and his *Rethinking Military Politics* (1988). Some of these works will be addressed below.

3. McAlister, "Recent Research and Writings on the Role of the Military in Latin America," 5.

4. Huntington, *Political Order in Changing Societies*, 213, 194.

5. An observation also made by Dominguez, "Samuel Huntington's *Political Order* and the Latin American State."

6. Ibid., 2–4. For example, Huntington's work shared great similarities with Nun's "The Middle Class Military Coup," written in 1967 and reprinted in Lowenthal and Fitch, *Armies and Politics in Latin America*.

7. O'Donnell, "Modernization and Military Coups."

8. Ibid., 120.

9. The structural bases for regime change were best elaborated in his classic book *Modernization and Bureaucratic-Authoritarianism.*

10. Stepan, "New Professionalism."

11. Ibid., 56.

12. The principal sponsors of this view were Nunn, *Yesterday's Soldiers,* and McCann, "Origins of the New Professionalism."

13. Nordlinger, *Soldiers in Politics*; Abrahamsson, *Military Professionalization and Political Power.*

14. Fitch, "Armies and Politics in Latin America." "Institutionalists" of the time confined their studies to the evolution and characteristics of military professionalism and did not consider more general questions of institutional design and rules of behavior, which have since characterized the "new institutionalists."

15. Remmer, *Military Rule in Latin America,* 24.

16. The exception would be the radical Peruvian military regime of 1968–80 to which numerous detailed studies were devoted. For references, see Lowenthal and Fitch, *Armies and Politics in Latin America,* 43, n. 30.

17. Remmer, *Military Rule in Latin America,* 31.

18. Since then, other works have emerged. For example, see Munck, *Authoritarianism and Democratization.*

19. Ricci and Fitch, "Ending Military Regimes in Argentina," 68.

20. Haggard and Kaufman, *Political Economy of Democratic Transitions.*

21. These works, like the vast majority of those on democratization, did not bring civil-military relations to center stage. They are included here because they have influenced scholars in the civil-military field.

22. Civilian control can occur in nondemocratic regimes as well. Democratic civilian control refers to a condition in democracies where there is both presidential-executive authority and legislative supervision over the military.

23. On Venezuela, see Agüero, "Debilitating Democracy," 139; on Ecuador, see "Ecuadorian Crisis over Presidency Ends Peacefully," *New York Times,* 10 February 2000, 1, 6.

24. Vargas Meza, *Drogas, Máscaras y Juegos.*

25. Hunter, *State and Soldier in Latin America,* 32–33.

26. See Fitch, "More on the Military in Politics," 206, and "Armies and Politics in Latin America," 40.

27. Lichbach and Zuckerman, *Comparative Politics.*

28. Michael C. Desch, *Civilian Control of the Military: The Changing Security Environment* (Baltimore: Johns Hopkins University Press, 1999).

29. Feaver, "Crisis as Shirking." Wendy Hunter, a contributor to this volume, has applied a game theoretic model to explain why civilian governments in Argentina and Chile yield to the military on human rights issues while holding firm on other issues. See "Negotiating Civil-Military Relations." Notwithstanding this piece, it is a rarity to find game theoretic approaches to any topic in Latin American studies, let alone civil-military affairs.

30. Smith, "Changing Agenda," 22.

31. Johnson, "Preconception," 170. Latin Americanists have taken their own colleagues to task for similar reasons. See Remmer, "New Wine or Old Bottlenecks?," 492.

32. Bates, "Area Studies and the Discipline."

33. Lichbach, "Social Theory and Comparative Politics," 266.

34. A useful overview of this theory can be found in Monroe, *Economic Approach to Politics*. Major rational choice works are too numerous to mention, so here are three: Arrow, *Social Choice and Individual Values*; Olson, *Logic of Collective Action*; and Elster, *Ulysses and the Sirens*.

35. Key contributions to this school of thought are March and Olsen, "New Institutionalism"; March and Olsen, *Rediscovering Institutions*; and Steinmo, Thelen, and Longstreth, *Structuring Politics*.

36. Hall and Taylor, "Political Science and the Three New Institutionalisms," 938.

37. Ibid. Answers to these questions separate rational, historical, and sociological variants of institutional thought.

38. Simon, "Behavioral Model of Rational Choice."

39. Krasner, "Sovereignty."

40. March and Olsen, "New Institutionalism."

41. See Geertz, *Interpretation of Cultures*, and Scott, *Weapons of the Weak*. Also see Monroe, *Heart of Altruism*. And finally refer to these classics by Weber: *Methodology of the Social Sciences* and *The Protestant Ethic and the Spirit of Capitalism*.

42. Weber, *Methodology of the Social Sciences*, 64.

43. Eckstein, "Culturalist Theory of Political Change."

44. Inglehart, *Modernization and Postmodernization*.

45. Levi, "A Model, a Method, and a Map," 20, 22.

46. March and Simon, *Organizations*, 2.

47. Kiewiet and McCubbins, *Logic of Delegation*.

48. For this theoretical perspective, see Pion-Berlin, *Through Corridors of Power*, 19–41.

49. Lowenthal, "Armies and Politics in Latin America," 18.

50. Geddes, "Paradigms and Sand Castles."

51. Even so, such a synthesis is not all-inclusive. It leaves out certain structural perspectives that consider large economic and political systems at national and international levels. The calculations, beliefs, and power resources of key civilian and military players are admittedly influenced, however indirectly, by changes in the global economy, balance of power, and security environment, none of which cannot be easily reduced to lower levels of analysis.

Wendy Hunter

2

Reason, Culture, or Structure?
Assessing Civil-Military Dynamics in Brazil

The wave of authoritarian regimes that swept Latin America in the 1960s and 1970s, followed by democratization in the 1980s and 1990s, gave students of civil-military relations in Latin America much food for thought. While explaining the causes of military interventionism was relevant in the first instance, accounting for why the military stepped down from power became the burden of subsequent analyses. The remote prospect of military coups in the current period, coupled with the more subtle forms of military influence that continue to exist, prompts present-day scholars to try to understand the forces that keep the military at bay yet at the same time allow officers to retain some degree of political influence.

Despite the many excellent and informative studies conducted on given cases of military rule and retreat in Latin America during the last four decades, little work has been done to compare and appraise the strengths and weaknesses of the different theoretical frameworks that scholars have used to approach the subject of civil-military relations in the region. The aspiration to build knowledge depends on appraising existing beliefs, explanations, theories, and approaches. This has yet to occur in an explicit way among scholars of civil-military relations.

In this chapter I hope to contribute to filling that gap. I concentrate on assessing an approach to civil-military relations that is based on the premise that politicians and leading officers are rational actors who interact with one another in strategic ways. First, I present a broad overview of civil-military relations in Brazil since 1985 and explain that preexisting theories had little ability to account for the noticeable decline in military influence after 1988. Second, I present the fundamental features of three major analytical frameworks into which many prominent studies of Latin American militaries fall: rational choice, cultural, and structural. Third, I provide an elaboration of the rationalist explanation for civil-military dynamics, as well as examples of structural and cultural accounts. Fourth, I assess the merits and drawbacks of the rationalist line of analysis in relation to competing analytical models as applied to civil-military relations.

Overview of Civil-Military Relations in Brazil since 1985

In 1985, the Brazilian military stepped down from the seat of government after twenty-one years in power. Since military leaders had negotiated the terms of the transition from a position of strength, they managed to preserve for the military a wide array of institutional prerogatives. These included six cabinet positions and a marked presence in the National Security Council and National Information Agency, two organizations that were central to controlling the Brazilian population and putting the military's stamp on economic, social, and political policies under the dictatorship. Other prerogatives included a continuing role in the management of strategic industries such as informatics and telecommunications; a predominant voice over nuclear issues and the development and occupation of the Amazon; the retention of some influence over the militarized state police; and protection from legislative oversight in areas such as military intelligence. Hence it seemed in the early days of Brazil's new democracy that the officer corps would enjoy a high degree of insulation from civilian politics. Many scholars predicted that the political positions and economic resources that gave the military significant clout would remain virtually untouched over time and, therefore, that the organization would continue to have a strong say over broad social, political, and economic decisions, in addition to defense and security policies.[1] Were their expectations borne out?

The Brazilian armed forces today are far less influential and privileged than they were in the initial period of civilian rule. They have experienced a notable diminution in the number of positions, civilian decisions, and resources they control. The number of high-level government positions they occupy has fallen dramatically. Whereas active-duty officers headed six ministries in 1985 (the three traditional service ministries, the heads of the intelligence service, National Security Council, and armed forces general staff), this number dropped to zero in 1999. President Fernando Collor (1990–92) eliminated the intelligence service as a ministry and appointed a civilian at the helm of a revamped organization. He also took away the ministerial status of the National Security Council, formed a new agency, and put a civilian in charge. President Fernando Henrique Cardoso's (1994–2002) decision in 1998 to create a unified civilian-led ministry of defense replaces the traditional service ministers and the head of the armed forces general staff.[2] This measure breaks with Brazil's long-standing status as one of the few remaining countries in the world without a unified defense ministry. Because these institutional changes take the military out of the cabinet entirely, senior officers will be less likely to influence high-level decisions—especially those not strictly related to security and defense—on an ongoing and regular basis.

But even before the military experienced such a visible loss of official institutional power, its actual ability to prevail over civilian decision making had been slipping since roughly 1988. For example, under President José Sarney (1985–90) Congress defied the military and expanded the right of workers to strike in 1988 and 1989. This action came after a series of efforts by senior officers to convince legislators to preserve the restrictions on worker mobilization and bargaining put in place under the military regime. These restrictions were countered by lobbying efforts on the part of workers and their representatives to give labor a stronger position in the new democracy. The military suffered another defeat when President Collor signed an agreement with Argentina allowing for inspections by the International Atomic Energy Agency, which broke the organization's previously unchallenged control over nuclear issues. Against discreet but visceral military resistance, President Cardoso subjected the officer corps to a symbolic assault in his decision to offer financial compensation to the families of those who died at the hands of the dictatorship, including the families of guerrilla leaders Carlos Lamarca and Carlos Marighella. Finally, the military's ability to keep budgets and troop size at levels satisfactory to its members has fallen short of previous predictions that the organization would readily be able to translate its political clout into economic influence. For example, whereas the Brazilian armed forces numbered 496,000 in 1985 (equivalent to 3.6 soldiers per 1,000 people), by 1995, their numbers had been reduced to 285,000 (equivalent to 1.8 soldiers per 1,000 people).[3]

But perhaps the most telling indicator of the lower profile of today's military is the scant amount of public attention it receives. The military ministers frequently made the front page of Brazil's major dailies during the Sarney administration, when they were often featured issuing proclamations about pressing debates. Several times during these years, military troops were pictured breaking up strikes, occupying ports and refineries, and quelling land invasions. Similarly, meetings between the civilian executive and senior military leadership used to set off rumors about the specter of saber-rattling and behind-the-scenes military influence. Today, they go largely unnoticed. Indeed, the scope of military influence has contracted over time.

This does not suggest, however, that the officer corps retains no political role. Especially compared to their counterparts in advanced Western democracies, Brazil's armed forces continue to exercise influence over policies that go well beyond defense and security, strictly defined. For example, through the Strategic Affairs Secretariat, they retain considerable say in issues related to the Amazon, even those not directly related to border defense (for example, land policy, indigenous rights, drug interdiction). Moreover, soldiers are sometimes still deployed for purposes that are more police than military in nature (for example, quelling land invasions organized by the landless movement, Movimento Sem Terra, under the first Cardoso presidency). Brazil's armed forces are subject to little legislative oversight, whether the issue concerns the actual use of allotted military funds or the conduct of military intelligence. In any event, it is certainly true that many officers are not prepared to abandon a political role altogether and continue to see their institution's contribution in broad nation-building terms. This applies more to the army than to the navy or air force.

Military autonomy over corporate issues (salaries and retirement benefits, promotions, the socialization of officers and recruits, and the like) as well as defense issues (for example, the specific kinds of weapons purchased and training pursued, defense organization) also remains ample. Politicians have exerted little effort—much less effort in any case than they have made in more civilian issue areas—to make inroads into these matters. In fact, the tacit arrangement that appears to have emerged is that civilians are willing to grant officers considerable autonomy in their own sphere of influence in exchange for noninterference in civilian decision making.

Hence, while an argument about the reduction of military power and privilege in Brazil needs to be qualified by recognition of remaining enclaves of autonomy and military evasions of civilian control, an important trend toward the diminution of influence exists nevertheless and requires explanation. That military power has eroded in Brazil is especially noteworthy and worthy of examination given the marked strength of the institution at the onset of civilian rule. The relative popularity of the military governments from 1964 to 1985—as a result of the economic successes many Brazilians associated with them, the relatively low incidence of human rights violations that occurred, and savvy public relations—allowed Generals Ernesto Geisel (1974–79) and João Figueiredo (1979–85) to preserve important institutional prerogatives for the armed forces. Moreover, the conservative cast of the Congress,[4] coupled with the fact that the first two postauthoritarian presidents—José Sarney and Fernando Collor—had held political office under the military regime, seemed to bode especially well for the military. Hence the erosion of military influence that has occurred in Brazil is unexpected, and stands out as demanding explanation. It also has implications for other cases, raising doubts about the military's capacity to remain a preponderant political actor in other countries, especially where the military entered the new democracy from a less privileged position.

Rationality, Culture, and Structure: Frameworks for Understanding Civil-Military Relations

Rationality, culture, and structure form the basis of three major ideal type research schools.[5] Much of the political science literature written about the military in politics in Latin America can be classified within these analytical frameworks, although authors often did not self-consciously or explicitly design their studies to achieve such theoretical ends.

The rational choice approach (including strategic game theory) is based on the following core assumptions. (1) The individual (or some analogue of the individual) is the fundamental unit of analysis. (2) Individuals are thought to be rational in the sense that—given their goals and alternative strategies from which to choose—they will select the alternatives that maximize their chances of achieving their goals. (3) The goals of individuals are basic, fairly consistent, and capable of being roughly ordered. It is generally assumed that most individuals prefer more material goods to less and more autonomy to less. Similarly, it is assumed that they prefer their careers to advance rather than regress or end and the organizations they are members of to survive rather than undergo demise. (4) Individuals have a certain capacity to assess situations accurately, to identify other actors and their goals, and hence, to decide what their strategies will be.[6]

To the extent that rational choice approaches regard most individuals as purposive, intentional, interest-driven, and capable of gathering relevant information most of the time, they underscore the role of agency and deliberation. The implication of the rational choice framework is that actors are pragmatic, as opposed to highly ideological or principled.

Theoretical clarity and parsimony are among the major strengths of explanations based on rationalist principles. Although there are certainly phenomena that are unexplainable in rational choice terms, when rational choice can explain, it usually does so well. Because of its theoretical clarity, rational choice generally lends itself to stricter empirical tests than most other analytical approaches.[7]

Proponents of rational choice models defend the use of deductive reasoning for reasons that go beyond parsimony. If their models lead to predictions that turn out to be false, the starting assumptions have to be modified or additional ones need to be added. In this way, rational choice has heuristic value and can contribute to the accumulation of knowledge: even when it does not predict reality, rational choice lays bare the lack of fit between theory and reality. In this instance, practitioners of rational choice should return to the theory and adjust it rather than resorting to ad hoc explanations.[8]

The most convincing rational choice analyses are those that specify a priori the interests and goals of actors rather than inferring them from behavior. Ideally, these theorists should formulate predictions that are empirically falsifiable, instead of first looking at the empirical evidence and then designing a model that fits. In any case, rational choice arguments become less persuasive when actors' goals are only loosely specified or allowed to be idiosyncratic, or when anomalies are described as "rational" in trying to amend predictions post hoc. These inadequacies, common to rational choice analyses, accept wide-ranging behavior as theory confirming.

In this connection, critics such as Donald Green and Ian Shapiro contend that given the failure of most rational choice analysts to specify clearly what it means to act rationally, it is not obvious what behaviors would be unaccounted for by rational choice. These authors argue that many scholars of this genre engage in post hoc theorizing: they design assumptions so that the model's predictions fit the data. Seldom, in their view, do authors clearly state what observed data would compel them to reject the specific hypotheses they advance.[9] This objection is sound but does not seem to condemn rational choice in a fundamental way. Rather, it puts the burden on analysts to proceed with an awareness of this potential criticism. What "rationality" implies and conduct that would falsify what a rationalist perspective would predict needs to be stated clearly.

Because the rational choice approach assumes that the conduct of individuals is an optimal response to a given environment and to the behavior of others, a successful explanation must first describe that context, which usually includes prevailing institutions. "Rational choice institutionalism" focuses on the strategic choices of actors in the context of extant political institutions. Such explanations must also make a compelling argument for why interchangeable individuals would adopt the same course of action in the same situation. The implication is that if these variables alone explain outcomes, more explanation or added complication is unnecessary.

In this connection, Green and Shapiro charge rational choice analyses of erring on the side of explanatory minimalism and bias. The problem involves comparing the performance of rational choice models against competing theories. How should explanations be sorted out and assessed if the predictions of the rational choice perspective overlap with those derived from other analytical models? What is the true cause, in other words, if two or more models predict the same outcome?

> Alternative theoretical accounts, it should be noted, occupy a small pedestal in the rational choice pantheon. The drive for sufficient accounts of political phenomena often impels rational choice theorists to focus instead on what the theory *does* seem to explain. As Russell (1979:11) notes, this style of analysis is often accompanied by a striking disregard for alternative explanations, leaving open the question of whether the data conform equally well to the predictions of competing theoretical accounts. . . . Ironically, the insistence on pressing one form of explanation to the exclusion of others has the effect of diminishing the persuasiveness of rational choice accounts.[10]

This criticism, while insightful and sound to some extent, does not fatally condemn rationalist lines of analysis but instead demands that their practitioners recognize that an emphasis on the formulation of *sufficient* explanations leaves them open to this "pathology." In other words, facile assumptions should not be made about rational choice being the superior or only explanation if viable contenders exist.

In contrast to rational choice models, culturalists begin by examining not individuals but communities, groups, and nations and the values, ideas, and orientations that people in these entities have in common. A culturalist would not assume that individuals from different cultural backgrounds would respond uniformly to a given situation. The incentives and disincentives that any set of circumstances presents could well be interpreted differently depending on the community, group, or nation at hand. Paraphrasing one author, the touchstone of cultural theory is that actors do not respond directly to "situations" but respond to them through mediating "orientations."[11] These orientational frames of reference take the place of (or at least complement) decision costs and calculations based on "objective" criteria such as material or professional gain.

A culturalist approach sees great limits to generalizing across countries since political predispositions and outlooks are thought to vary so greatly from context to context. Because culturalists assign primacy to ideas and values as filters of material or institutional structures, they are interested in gaining interpretive understandings of meaning. They are interested in the role of history in creating and reproducing culture and in socialization practices in perpetuating cultural norms. In short, "interpretivist accounts illuminate the power of ideas, the influence of history, the significance of intellectuals, and the persuasive power of political rhetoric and dramaturgy."[12] Culturalists tend to explain the continuity in political outcomes even when material and structural conditions (that is, objective factors) change.[13]

Whereas rationalists focus on individual calculations and actions and culturalists on norms, structuralists focus on underlying material or institutional conditions as key determinants of political outcomes. Structuralists regard structures—whether economic or political in nature—as having independent and causal status. Choice and culture are thought to be derivative of structures. Extreme versions of structuralism minimize the significance of actors and their freedom to choose. More relaxed or complex versions examine how the rationality and nonrationality contained in structures are manifested in actions and orientations.

Lichbach provides an excellent summary comparison of the three approaches. Paraphrasing him, choice, culture, and context are the specific domains of study of the three schools.[14] Whereas rationalists study how actors employ reason to satisfy their interests, culturalists study norms that constitute individual and group identities, and structuralists explore relations among actors in an institutional context.[15] Rationalists generalize, culturalists particularize, and structuralists typologize.[16] Because the three schools are treated here as ideal types, sharp boundaries are drawn among them, bringing out the distinctive assumptions they have about human nature and expectations of behavior. In practice, many studies invoke ideas and methods from more than one research tradition. For heuristic purposes, however, this chapter proceeds by way of forcefully confronting the unique features of each.

Analytical Models as Applied to Civil-Military Relations

Rational Choice and Strategic Interaction

In my study of the military in Brazil,[17] rationality plays a large role in influencing how much political involvement the military pursue and how much the politicians allow. My fundamental premise regarding politicians is that they are first and foremost interested in their own political survival. They may take an intrinsic interest in certain programs and policies, but staying in office is a requisite to pursuing these interests. Even if politicians do not run for immediate reelection, maintaining popularity is important for the sake of their future political careers and those of their political cronies and allies, which often include family members.

Under conditions of relative political stability, electoral competition creates incentives for politicians to contest the military when military actions conflict with their opportunity to expand their appeal to voters. When might this occur? First, electoral competition can be expected to motivate politicians to search for economic assets to distribute as pork barrel as well as for more programmatic purposes, thereby improving their chances of reelection. This pursuit of state resources may well pit them against soldiers. Second, elected leaders often try to improve their standing with the mass citizenry by supporting policies that appeal to popular yearnings for change and participation, whether they be socioeconomic (for example, land reform) or political (for example, labor rights) in nature. An expansion of popular participation, especially if accompanied by populist politics and social mobilization, might well run counter to the frequent military goal of maintaining the status quo.

Third and more generally, politicians concerned about effective governance tend to seek maximum control over events and processes that occur within their jurisdiction, territorial or functional. Large bureaucratic organizations like the military can compromise this autonomy and latitude. Thus politically inclined, resource-hungry officers typically interfere in both the making of policy and the distribution of patronage, thereby creating costs for politicians. At the same time, in contrast to alliances with other established groups and institutions, close relations with the armed forces rarely enhance a politician's electoral fortunes. This is especially true in contemporary Latin America, where the military have little currency to trade in the electoral area.

Presidents and legislators alike are subject to pressures to reduce military influence, but because of the slightly different nature of their incentives, capacities, and support bases, the dynamic unfolds somewhat differently in each case. A military inclined toward excessive interference is especially problematic for presidents, who need to govern effectively, build political organizations with strong personal loyalty to themselves, and survive in power if they hope to maintain long-term influence. The future political careers of presidents, more than those of legislators, depend on enacting programmatic goals with broad cross-regional support. And in a highly clientelistic system like Brazil, presidents also rely on the distribution of large-scale patronage to win support for their programs in the Congress and the bureaucracy and among governors and mayors. A politically active military can jeopardize all of these goals.

If electoral competition creates incentives for politicians to diminish military influence, popular support through electoral victory enhances their capacity to do so. A military would incur considerable reputational damage in forcefully opposing a government with strong public backing. This could well, in turn, result in a loss of material privileges. The greater the mandate a government enjoys, the less likely military elites will be to work aggressively to offset civilian attempts to diminish their political standing.

But when deep economic and political crises put the survival of governments in doubt, presidents can be counted on to court the military—even at the cost of their own political autonomy. Similarly, efforts to reduce military clout become detrimental if they go too far in antagonizing the military and thus put the electoral regime at risk. In the event of a coup, the civilian president is usually the main target of overthrow. In this context, the rational survival strategy for a president is to concede power to the armed forces rather than to retract it. Allowing the officer corps greater political influence and budgetary concessions are typical ways in which beleaguered presidents try to secure their governments.

Legislators also have a strong interest in not antagonizing the military. But because a military takeover would not place them as directly in the line of fire, they are generally slower than presidents to respond to saber-rattling in the context of crisis. Until there is unequivocal cause for concern, the rational strategy for legislators is to keep promoting policies that enhance their popularity with large numbers of people in the electorate, even at the risk of antagonizing the military. I do not posit that all politicians behave according to these predictions all of the time but rather that enough do in a sufficient number of instances to erode military influence progressively.

Turning to the military side of the ledger, how can a rational choice approach be used to explain the behavior of soldiers? Several issues need to be confronted in applying such an approach to the military. The first has to do with what the relevant unit of analysis is: is it the (sum of) individuals within the officer corps, the senior officer corps, or important service, rank, and factional elements? A second and related issue concerns the incentives that officers follow: are officers' decisions motivated first and foremost by their own career goals or considerations about the organization? How valid is it to think in terms of the self-interest motivations of officers who are steeped in traditions and mythologies of self-sacrifice and corporate pride?

There are some limitations in treating the military as if it were a unitary actor. Factional politics sometimes help shape civil-military outcomes. For example, as Deborah Norden's work on the Argentine military rebellions of the 1980s illustrates well, rank and past experience played a large role in how officers responded to civilian efforts to break the political and economic power of the Argentine armed forces.[18] Junior officers had an ax to grind and were particularly unrestrained in voicing their grievances, in part because of where they sat in the organization. The junior ranks were vital in the unfolding of conflict throughout the presidency of Raúl Alfonsín.

Notwithstanding some exceptions, however, it is reasonable to assume that the choices of the senior leadership basically govern the institution's practices and policies. The military, much more so than most other organizations, has strict rules and norms of obedience. That there is a formal hierarchy that tries to ensure some level of internal cohesion and generally succeeds in doing so lends justification to the unitary actor assumption. As a rule, the more professional a military, the more likely the hierarchy speaks on behalf of the institution as a whole. Thus, the "choices" as discussed here are conceived primarily as choices of the hierarchy.

But do senior officers act in accordance with the broader interests of the organization, or do they have career advancement and other self-interests in mind? While the substantive policy positions associated with the two motivations undoubtedly differ at times, more often they converge since senior officers are more likely to be promoted if they adhere to the organizational goals being espoused by the top brass.

What substantive organizational goals do militaries typically have? Core corporate concerns include the following: a monopoly over paramilitary organizations, autonomy of the rank and seniority system from political interference, obedience to hierarchy (especially between officers and enlisted men), relative unity among the officer corps, and budgetary resources sufficient to maintain essential training, education, and equipment.[19] Generally, Latin American militaries also have ideas and preferences about what the political, economic, and social order should look like. Ideally, most senior officers in the region desire some degree of influence over these broader concerns. At times, strong objections to the extant or emerging economic and political situations, coupled with visions of change, have inspired their forceful intervention in politics. But for the most part, absent extreme crisis, concerns about organizational survival and viability are primary. Usually, corporate concerns are present (either alone or in combination with broader concerns) when the military has been willing to incur the risks of coercive action against elected governments.

In the current (post–Cold War) period, most Latin American militaries are mainly interested in defending the status quo rather than pushing for greater influence. In the vast majority of cases, no fundamental challenges to military integrity—such as the operation of subversive groups or parallel armed institutions—have arisen. In the interest of corporate autonomy and the protection of individual officers, the officer corps' first priority has been to avoid prosecution of human rights abuses committed under the previous regimes. The armed forces have sought also to defend their salaries and budgetary appropriations and to preserve decision-making autonomy over explicitly military matters like force structure and weapons acquisition. Some militaries have even tried to retain influence (and associated institutional prerogatives) over broad political, social, and economic matters. This aspiration is generally not as pronounced or as uniformly present as desires to ensure basic organizational maintenance and advancement.

What courses of action can Latin American militaries take to defend their interests? The political strategies that the armed forces employ at any given time correspond to the prevailing political climate. In the current era of democracy and post–Cold War politics, the armed forces face considerable restrictions on their bargaining power and behavior more generally. The costs of employing coercive tactics have risen. Most officers are very aware that large sectors of society, as well as the international community, would now condemn heavyhanded solutions—a military coup, in the extreme. The cumulative weight of these costs exercises a taming effect on the military, making an overthrow (and even highly visible forms of saber-rattling) unlikely. The low credibility of military force renders elected politicians less fearful than previously about upsetting the military. Thus, while officers can be expected to lobby to stem the erosion of their political influence and material privileges, unless core corporate interests are involved, the military leadership generally proceeds with care. This is because the armed forces can in fact overplay their cards. Excessive threats can wear down the reserve of goodwill that the armed forces need to retain long-term credibility. The major exception to military restraint has been over human rights. Long permitted to commit such misdeeds with impunity, the region's armed forces reject fundamentally the notion that civilians can bring officers to trial. Over this issue, the stakes are considered high enough to justify the use of force.

In earlier times, the armed forces were more willing than they presently are to stand up for and advance their corporate and political interests if elected governments threatened them. In Brazil, for instance, developments of the early 1960s challenged the military's core corporate principles as well as its preferred political and economic order. In officers' eyes, efforts by labor organizers to unionize enlisted men and President João Goulart's pardon of mutinous sailors put military preservation in question. The specter of the officer corps' demise loomed especially large in light of the executions that had taken place in Cuba five years earlier. Also, the mobilization of popular sectors raised concerns among officers as well as civilians about maintaining their privileged socioeconomic position. In the context of the Cold War, important sectors of domestic society as well as the international community supported military interventionism to defend the status quo. The costs, then, of using force were lower and militaries overthrew democratically elected governments throughout the region.

In summary, under the fairly stable political and economic conditions that currently exist in most of Latin America, self-interested politicians can be expected to check military influence when it interferes with their own goals and the military can be expected to be somewhat restrained in its reactions. This is not to say that ideology is irrelevant or that all politicians will follow the stated course of action all the time. Neither does it imply that all officers will be equally balanced and temperate in their response. But at the very least, the rational actor framework presented here suggests that conflict will develop between electoral politicians and militaries and that the survival interests of politicians are sufficiently compelling—and the pragmatism and foresight of leading officers sufficient—to contain the military's reach.

Culture

Cultural accounts toward Latin America typically refer to orientations such as elitism, authoritarianism, corporatism, and patrimonialism. These principles had a strong foundation in traditional Spanish Catholicism. The tendency of Latin American societies to be hierarchically structured by rank and vertically structured into major corporate groups (for example, the military, the church, the bureaucracy) is understood to stem from Iberian patterns.[20] The persistence of strong domestically involved militaries—with missions such as civic action tasks that contribute to nation-building—is also seen in this light.

While culturalists recognize that the nineteenth century gave rise to a new framework of ideas and values—liberal, republican, sometimes egalitarian, secular, and rationalist—they do not regard these as having replaced earlier orientations but rather as having coexisted (somewhat uneasily) alongside them. Questioning the degree to which these latter values have actually taken root, culturalists study their variable impact across the countries of Latin America.[21]

Brian Loveman exemplifies a culturalist/historical understanding of civil-military relations.[22] Tradition itself has causal status, in his view. Going back to independence, Loveman traces the historical connections of the military to the nation-state and its role in the founding and development of Latin American republics. The role it played in these early developments led it, in his view, to arrogate itself as progenitor and permanent custodian of these countries. For Loveman, returning to the distant past is essential to understand what he sees as important and underlying strains of continuity into the present. What, more substantially, connects the present to the past? He writes: "As in the past, when Latin American armed forces participate in politics, they will do so in the name of *la Patria*, convinced that when 'the politicians' fail to protect their nations' sovereignty and transcendental interests, it is the duty of the Armed Forces to carry out their historic and constitutional missions. Despite the 'democratiza-tion fad,' they remain, in their doctrine, in military lore, and in the minds of many of their fellow citizens, the 'ultimate reservoir of sovereignty' who guarantee 'the historical continuity of the nation.' "[23] Hence, while the specific threats and enemies facing *la Patria* may change over time, as well as the specific form of the response, the mission of the armed forces is immutable. This pattern of maintaining change is captured well by the adage, "The more things change, the more they stay the same."[24]

Structure

Structural explanations for the military's political involvement take various forms. Some structural explanations are based on economic and sociological variables. Others focus on political institutions. Three prominent and quite different examples of a structuralist approach are Guillermo O'Donnell's work on bureaucratic-authoritarianism,[25] the democratization literature that under-scores the importance of *modes of transition* for explaining subsequent grada-tions in military power and autonomy,[26] and David Pion-Berlin's book on postauthoritarian Argentina.[27]

O'Donnell's concept of "bureaucratic-authoritarianism" refers to the re-gimes that existed in Argentina (1966–73 and 1976–83), Brazil (1964–85), Chile (1973–90), and Uruguay (1973–85). Bureaucratic-authoritarian govern-ments were characterized by a technocratic, bureaucratic, nonpersonalistic approach to policy making. One of the most salient features distinguishing these systems from previous nondemocratic regimes was the institutionalized presence of the military.

In O'Donnell's view, notwithstanding certain variations across countries, bureaucratic-authoritarianism emerged in reaction to three broad develop-ments: (1) economic problems that came about when the initial phase of industrialization was completed and countries aspired to "deepen industrial-ization" (that is, pursue the expansion of production beyond consumer goods to include the intermediate and capital goods used in the production process); (2) increased popular sector activation, in the wake of urbanization and mod-ernization; and (3) the increased importance of technocratic roles. Intent on curbing popular mobilization and promoting major changes in economic pol-icy, civilian technocrats joined with military officers, conspired in the making of coups, installed themselves in power, and co-governed.

The argument is structural in orientation insofar as broad developments in society, the economy, and the polity are seen as coming together at a certain historical point and (somewhat inevitably) leading countries toward more or less the same regime outcome. Factors like choice, leadership, and agency are given little play. "Culture" has little or no relevance.

The *modes of transition* argument also contains elements of a structuralist explanation. Karl is an articulate proponent of this perspective. She explains the variety of postauthoritarian outcomes that have emerged in Latin America:

> What is called for is a path-dependent approach which clarifies how broad structural changes shape particular regime transitions in ways that may be especially conducive to (or especially obstructive of) democratization. This needs to be combined with an analysis of how such structural changes become embodied in political institutions and rules which subsequently mold the preferences and capacities of individuals during and after regime changes. In this way, it should be possible to demonstrate how the range of options available to decision makers at a given point in time is a function of structures put in place in an earlier period.[28]

Many scholars in addition to Karl have applied this basic framework comparatively. Felipe Agüero uses it to explain the attainment of greater civilian supremacy in the new southern European democracies relative to the new democracies of South America.[29] Taking Brazil as an example, Alfred Stepan,[30] Frances Hagopian,[31] and Jorge Zaverucha[32] posited that Brazilian democracy would suffer from a serious handicap. They claimed that the negotiated nature of the transition to civilian rule would provide the military, along with civilian elites who enjoyed strong standing under the authoritarian regime, with long-lasting political clout. More specifically, they contended that institutional privileges the armed forces retained in the transition process would give them a strong and indefinite foundation of political leverage. The military would be able to exercise undue influence in nonmilitary spheres as well as resist civilian direction over defense issues. The considerable political interference of the army in the first three years of the civilian regime seemed to provide empirical verification for this theoretical expectation.

A third example of structuralism—with a clear institutionalist bent—is David Pion-Berlin's *Through Corridors of Power: Institutions and Civil-Military Relations in Argentina*. This study sets out to explain the loss of military power in different issue areas since 1983. Its guiding premise is that political power does not translate automatically into policy but rather is mediated through governing institutions. Specifically, the higher the concentration of authority and decision-making autonomy enjoyed by civilian executives, the more able they will be to reduce military influence. Conversely, the greater the dispersion of authority across different civilian actors, the more the armed forces can preserve their privileges by playing civilians off against one another. Invoking the institutional variables of authority and autonomy, Pion-Berlin explains the considerable success of postauthoritarian civilian governments in reducing defense spending; their only moderate success in human rights policy; and their virtual ineffectiveness in defense reform (integrating the services, eliminating unnecessary support structures, and so on). It stands to reason that regardless of what the impetus for policy change consists of (for example, self-interest or principle), extant institutions will indeed influence the success of any given civilian challenge.

Assessment

The Merits of a Rational Choice Understanding of Civil-Military Relations

More specifically, my defense of a rationalist perspective vis-à-vis civil-military dynamics in the region revolves around the following issues. (1) Rational choice provides a sense of the impulse that drives politicians in their conduct toward the armed forces. (2) It can account for the undeniable loss of military power and influence that has taken place in wide-ranging cases in recent years. (3) Similarly, it provides insight into the pragmatic accommodation and adaptation that the officer corps in many countries have made to the new order. (4) It can explain variations in military influence among different issue areas. (5) It sheds light on the slightly different strategies and postures that presidents versus legislators assume toward the military. Each of these points is elaborated below.

A model that uses rational choice principles lends itself much more readily than cultural or structural approaches to explaining the immediate impetus or impulse driving politicians' behavior, especially conduct that overtly challenges the armed forces. Because they focus on general underlying orientations, cultural models do not provide this sense of agency. Neither do structural models, which also focus on broader background conditions that facilitate or impede human action. Both these schools, hence, leave an important gap, one that rational choice is equipped to fill. The focus on the actual decisions of political actors—and the calculations that go into these decisions—is a crucial dimension of the explanatory power of rational choice. By explaining the mechanism of or trigger for action, rational choice analysis makes an important contribution to explanation beyond that which culturalism or structuralism can provide.

The principles of rational choice can explain instances of marked loss of military power and autonomy better than many competing alternatives, especially culturalist alternatives. Although there is disagreement about how much change has occurred, even those most sensitive to signs of continuing military power have to admit that civilians have succeeded in reducing some military prerogatives—political and economic—over time. Reductions of the number of military officers in the cabinet, the occupation of other government positions by civilians that used to be held by officers, declining budgets, smaller force levels, and the like are irrefutable signs of change that those who stress cultural/historical patterns are ill-equipped to deal with. A cultural approach can accommodate change in the event of a major trauma to a society such as war or economic devastation, but with the possible exception of Argentina under the Proceso de Reorganización Nacional (1976–83) this does not describe the recent history of most Latin American countries. Structural models are more compatible with change—specifically, in this instance, the loss of military influence—than most cultural models. David Pion-Berlin's study of the military in postauthoritarian Argentina is a case in point. Structures themselves can change (more easily than culture, at least) or simply be designed in a way that facilitates policy innovation. But in any event, a rational choice approach can still provide a more proximate cause for the decline of military power than a structural orientation.

In relation to declining influence, the leadership of most professional-leaning militaries of Latin America has reacted in fairly levelheaded, balanced ways. An awareness that a strategy of defection from the current democratic order would not be in the ultimate interest of the organization (and the careers of individual officers) has prevailed. The prevalence of reason over emotion has contributed in significant ways to the stability of postauthoritarian Latin America. Notwithstanding three admittedly disruptive military rebellions in Argentina[33] and two episodes of visible saber-rattling over human rights issues under President Patricio Aylwin in Chile,[34] officers have kept their troops in the barracks. Only in Peru, where a serious guerrilla threat remained, was there a (temporary) reversion to authoritarian government after President Alberto Fujimori's *autogolpe* in April 1992. And even here, the initiative lay with Peru's civilian president, not the military leadership.[35] Although this brief period of autocratic rule increased the political role of the military, it is telling that in the wake of that period, President Fujimori tried to reassert control over the military institution.

Beyond exercising a certain judicious restraint when challenged, senior officers have made rational adaptation to the new rules of the game in other ways. In Brazil, for instance, the officer corps recognize that since the Congress now controls the lion's share of resources and legislates over policy, they (just like any other organization) need to deploy their own lobbyists in the congressional forum. These lobbyists work in a fashion typical of other political lobbyists to persuade legislators of their cause. A stronger and perhaps more controversial example of adaptation would be what has happened in Venezuela. Following the defeat of Hugo Chávez's coup attempts in earlier years, the former officer decided to join the electoral system rather than continue to try to beat it.

In comparison to cultural explanations, which effectively homogenize political outcomes because of the undifferentiated role of norms and values, a rational choice model has more ability to explain specific outcomes across distinct issue areas. This ability stems from the association of different issues with different incentives and goals. For example, in Brazil, politicians have displayed a much higher propensity to try to curb military influence and privilege when matters affecting electoral popularity (for example, public resources, labor rights) have been at stake. By contrast, in spheres where politicians have seen little to gain with constituents by challenging the military (for example, issues such as defense organization and military education), they have generally allowed military leaders to dictate. Structural explanations can also be issue-specific in nature. What are seen as the structural barriers to or facilitators of change often differ depending on the policy in question.

Unlike culturalist accounts, applications of rational choice can often distinguish between the behavior of presidents and that of legislators. They do so by going back to the basic incentives, goals, and strategies that apply to the two categories of politicians. While democracy provides some common inducements for both to push back military influence, the strength of the incentives and the capacity of politicians to act on them vary. This variation explains distinctions in how, why, and when executives (versus legislators) choose to challenge the military. Some structural explanations, such as advanced in Pion-Berlin's 1997 book,[36] although not others (for example, modes of transition arguments) also differentiate between presidential and legislative roles vis-à-vis the armed forces.

Two qualifications of rational choice as an appropriate explanatory framework for civil-military relations should also be noted. First, if rational choice is correct, we might expect to see even more instances of civilian challenge to the military than in fact have taken place. This acknowledgment makes a certain recognition of culture necessary. Second, a rational choice analysis may account for the decline of military power over time across cases, but the starting point of the downward trend (that is, where military power was at the onset of democratic rule) does in fact influence the end point. This fact warrants a certain concession to structure. I elaborate on each of these points below.

Although many Latin American governments can claim some degree of accomplishment in reining in military autonomy, as J. Samuel Fitch correctly points out, "Given the relatively low short-term risk of a military coup, most governments appear to have erred on the side of excessive caution in dealing with the armed forces."[37] Certainly, nearly nowhere has there been a profound and secure institutionalization of civilian supremacy. As Consuelo Cruz and Rut Diamint contend, "Domestic political actors repeat the old mistake of accommodating—with varying degrees of comfort—the military's self-insulation. Elected officials, in the main, favor streamlining military establishments; but after making resource allocations, they leave the armed forces to their own devices. Politicians tend to avoid the military question. . . . Like medieval lords, the armed forces are becoming, all at once, guardians of their own limited autonomy."[38]

If the incentives that rational choice postulates are that compelling, why are military autonomy and power as conspicuous as they are? Specifically, if politicians can benefit from contracting the organization's influence, why have they not gone further in their efforts? There are several possible answers to these questions. The first is compatible with a rational choice perspective: politicians have not done more to rein in the military because most politicians are instrumental rather than principled and would not benefit in a clear and immediate sense from challenging the officer corps over a host of issues in which the military continues to enjoy autonomy (for example, defense organization, officer training, strategic planning). An example of where politicians employ rational calculations but fall short of full civilian control involves the way budgets are typically handled. Legislatures in many countries have made reductions in military personnel and cuts in defense budgets to rationalize public finances. But beyond cutting the defense budget to divert resources elsewhere, they have manifested little interest in the application of allotted military funds.[39] Also, there is an objective cost to contesting the military, not the least of which is that it takes time and attention away from other, more pressing and electorally significant issues, often of an economic nature.

Admittedly, the heavy hand of culture or history also figures into the equation. How precisely does the tradition of military autonomy affect contemporary Latin American politics? To be on firm ground, cultural explanations need to specify the ways in which historical practices influence present-day patterns. For example, because civilians have never played a significant role in matters ranging from the formulation of defense policy to the oversight of military intelligence, few legislators or presidents know anything about the sphere of defense. This lack of knowledge, in turn, renders them less effective in trying to shape or guide military policy. Civilians can certainly be educated in this respect—in fact, some countries have tried to build a core of civilian defense experts—but the results have not been quick in materializing. In any event, it remains clear that in a region where officers have long meddled in politics and placed themselves above reproach, establishing institutions that would truly and unconditionally subordinate the military to civilian authority requires formidable legislative initiative. In such a context, the "default option" remains one of accommodation.

At the same time, it needs to be stressed that culture is not an insurmountable barrier to change. As my research on Brazil shows, politicians have proved willing to challenge the military when they can clearly benefit from doing so, that is, over specific policies that interfere with their own opportunities for advancement. And as Pion-Berlin's more structural approach also shows, when institutional arrangements are propitious, politicians can not only contest the military but also effectively shape relevant policies and wrest control from them.

The second qualification of my rational choice approach is as follows. Although initial institutional constraints that derive from modes of transition (or other structural factors, for that matter) do not create enduring limits on the expansion of democracy, as the weakening of the Brazilian military since 1988 suggests, for at least some period of time, they do influence the relative strength of militaries in the region. This is revealed by a comparison of the Argentine, Brazilian, Chilean, and Peruvian militaries in their respective post-authoritarian periods. Clearly, an overall downward trend of military influence exists across countries, a fact congruent with my rational choice analysis. At the same time, however, the absolute level of military influence that prevails at present in each of these countries corresponds to the strength of the military there immediately after authoritarian rule. For example, the Argentine military was comparatively the weakest of the four at the onset of civilian rule in 1983. It remains so today. Conversely, the Chilean military was the strongest relative to its three counterparts. It persists in that status to the present time. While it is possible that factors other than structural/institutional ones are at work, a certain "path dependency" appears to exist here. That the strength of the Chilean military is incongruent with the historic strength of democracy and civilian rule in that country—before the drastic reshaping of authority relations under General Augusto Pinochet, who institutionalized military power in a series of legal provisions not easily overturned—enhances the credence of this view. In sum, the comparative assessment here does not constitute a refutation of rational choice thinking but merely shows that such an analysis may need to be placed in the context of a broader structure.

Conclusion

This chapter has attempted in an explicit and deliberate fashion to confront and draw out the merits of the rationalist approach and to assess the potential contributions of other schools of thought, namely, those that are cultural and structural in nature. In doing so, it concurs with the assessment in the volume's Introduction that Latin Americanists could profit from explicitly incorporating ideas from these schools of thought. In particular, it affirms that theories of strategic action have the capacity to, as Pion-Berlin says, "give us a deeper understanding of what underlying interests, goals, and strengths respectively motivate and enable politicians and soldiers to behave the way they do." While stressing the analytical value provided by rational choice analysis, I have proceeded following Hagopian's advice that scholars "recognize that their scholarship is better because of the challenges raised by those comparativists whose work is framed by alternative paradigms."[40] Indeed, analytical insight is to be gained by subjecting one's analysis to the scrutiny and challenges of rival ideas.

The core differences among these approaches with respect to their basic assumptions about human nature (especially the rational choice and cultural perspectives) belie an easy coexistence or complementarity. But the above comparison of these analytical frameworks as applied to civil-military affairs suggests that "both acts and contexts matter."[41] Through its stress on agency, rational choice provides a vital addition to structural and cultural perspectives. Decisions, after all, do not originate from cultures and structures in unmediated fashion. Political actors, operating within historical and institutional constraints—make them. Without attention to actual decision making, explanation remains incomplete. Prediction suffers as well.

Yet standing alone, rational choice premises remain too thin and uncontextualized. Structure and culture provide the context in which reason is employed and hence must be taken into account. Whether or not a decision is rational usually depends on circumstances against which the decision is made. This is the major premise followed by "rational choice institutionalists" or even rational choice analysts who focus on the strategic manipulation of cultural symbols. Along these lines, Lichbach distinguishes between "thin" and "thick" rationalists. "Thin rationalists are pure intentionalists who see reasons as causes of action. They have a reductionist view of conditions and culture. . . . One can extend the boundaries of the rationalist approach by deepening the micro, and hence studying culture, and exploring the macro, and hence examining institutions."[42] This is advice that scholars of civil-military relations in Latin America would do well to heed.

NOTES

1. See, for example, Stepan, *Rethinking Military Politics*.
2. Fleischer, "Cardoso Second Term Cabinet."
3. From U.S. Arms Control and Disarmament Agency, *World Military Expenditures*, 62.
4. See Power, "The Political Right."
5. This discussion is based on Lichbach, "Social Theory."
6. This discussion of rational choice draws from Geddes, "Uses and Limitations of Rational Choice."
7. Tsebelis, *Nested Games*, 40.
8. Ibid., 42–43.
9. Green and Shapiro, *Pathologies of Rational Choice Theory*, 34.
10. Ibid., 37.
11. Eckstein, "Culturalist Theory," 790.
12. Bates, de Figueiredo, and Weingast, "Politics of Interpretation," 635.
13. Eckstein, "Culturalist Theory," discusses a limited number of instances in which change can be integrated within a cultural explanation.
14. Lichbach, "Social Theory," 263.
15. Ibid., 249.
16. Ibid., 256.
17. Hunter, *Eroding Military Influence in Brazil*.
18. Norden, *Military Rebellion in Argentina*.
19. Needler, "Military Motivations in the Seizure of Power."
20. Wiarda, "Toward a Framework for the Study of Political Change."
21. Wiarda and Kline, "Context of Latin American Politics."
22. See Loveman, "Latin American Civil-Military Relations." See also Loveman, *For la Patria*.
23. Loveman, "Latin American Civil-Military Relations," 29.
24. Eckstein, "Culturalist Theory," regards this "pattern-maintaining change" as one of the ways in which a cultural approach can accommodate change.
25. O'Donnell, *Modernization and Bureaucratic-Authoritarianism*.
26. Karl, "Dilemmas of Democratization"; Stepan, *Rethinking Military Politics*.
27. Pion-Berlin, *Through Corridors of Power*, 24.
28. Karl, "Dilemmas of Democratization," 7.
29. Agüero, *Soldiers, Civilians, and Democracy*.
30. Stepan, *Rethinking Military Politics*.

31. Hagopian, " 'Democracy by Undemocratic Means'?"

32. Zaverucha, "Degree of Military Political Autonomy." See also Zaverucha, *Rumor de Sabres*.

33. See Norden, *Military Rebellion in Argentina*.

34. See Hunter, "Negotiating Civil-Military Relations."

35. McClintock, "Breakdown of Constitutional Democracy in Peru."

36. Pion-Berlin, *Through Corridors of Power*.

37. Fitch, *Armed Forces and Democracy*, 164.

38. Cruz and Diamint, "New Military Autonomy," 116–17.

39. Ibid., 120.

40. Hagopian, Review, 665.

41. Lichbach, "Social Theory," 261.

42. Ibid., 259.

J. Samuel Fitch

3

Military Attitudes toward Democracy in Latin America
How Do We Know If Anything Has Changed?

It has now been more than twenty years since the latest round of democratic transitions in Latin America began in Peru and Ecuador. Most observers were initially skeptical that the return to elections and civilian governments would lead to lasting changes in the political power of the armed forces.[1] The checkered history of earlier democratic cycles suggested that democratic transition would probably not lead to democratic civil-military relations. Most of the structural conditions contributing to military intervention in the 1960s and 1970s remained. Moreover, handing over the presidency to a civilian did not in fact mean the military was returning to the barracks. In Brazil, Chile, and Guatemala, military leaders made it clear that they intended to play an active role in the successor regimes.

In fact, these new democracies have proven more durable than expected, despite being born amid the worst economic crisis since the 1930s. Nearly all of them have now survived multiple elections and transfers of power. Despite successful coups in Haiti, Panama, and Ecuador and military uprisings in Argentina and Venezuela, military rule has not returned to Latin America.

There is, however, little agreement about the nature of the military's role in posttransition regimes in Latin America. Are these in fact democratic regimes or simply the continuation of military domination behind a civilian facade? Is the military's power a major or minor factor in these regimes? Is the military's influence rising or falling? Are the changes (if any) in civil-military relations temporary or permanent?

Some of the disparity in scholarly responses to these questions undoubtedly stems from the differences among Latin American democracies. Even within the Southern Cone, the Andean region, and Central America, there are marked differences in civil-military relations and also significant changes over time.[2] Generalizing from disparate cases or time periods probably accounts for some of the conflicting views of the relative power of civilian and military leaders in contemporary Latin America. Still, scholarly assessments are strikingly divergent even in cases that have received extensive attention over the last fifteen years.

In what is generally considered the most favorable case in the region for significant changes in civil-military relations, J. Patrice McSherry argues that the Argentine military's political power is still considerable and "important sectors of the military [remain] only conditionally committed to democracy." Although she acknowledges some advances relative to other Latin American countries, such as a civilian minister of defense, McSherry describes Argentina as a "mixed case" where the armed forces are still a "factor of power, with guardian capabilities and propensities."[3]

In contrast, David Pion-Berlin argues that civilian governments have been successful in making deep cuts in the Argentine military budget and in reducing the military's role in internal security, despite Alfonsín's forced retreat on the human rights trials. Where McSherry portrays an unremitting military struggle to retain or regain traditional military prerogatives, Pion-Berlin notes "a growing military willingness to live under democratic administrations" and to work within the normal rules of a constitutional democracy.[4]

In the Brazilian case, Wendy Hunter argues that democratic control has not been achieved but that the trend has been toward a reduction of the military's ability to control key areas of national policy. From its initial position as the dominant tutelary actor in a weak democratic system, the military has become a relatively minor player in the new regime, although it retains a very high degree of institutional autonomy.[5] In contrast, Jorge Zaverucha argues that military prerogatives are virtually untouched after nearly fifteen years of ostensibly civilian rule. In his view, the military remains a powerful, if not dominant, political actor.[6]

Similar disagreements exist with regard to less widely studied cases. Enrique Obando credits Fujimori with achieving a high degree of civilian control over the armed forces through co-optation of senior officers and new laws enhancing Fujimori's authority as commander in chief. In contrast, Dirk Krujit describes Peru after Fujimori's *autogolpe* as "civil-military co-government."[7]

Notwithstanding the special difficulties of studying the Latin American armed forces, such disparate evaluations are troubling in a field that aspires to be treated as serious social science. The lack of even minimal consensus on seemingly basic questions undermines our authority as scholars to speak on policy issues that are crucial for democratic consolidation. This chapter is an attempt to clarify the origins of these discrepancies and to suggest how to move toward a more systematic understanding of the political role of the military in contemporary Latin American democracies.

It begins with the question of standards and different approaches—behavioral and attitudinal—to measuring progress to more democratic civil-military relations. I argue that changes in military attitudes are a necessary, though not sufficient, condition for institutionalizing democratic regimes. Then I consider the advantages and disadvantages of two sources of data on military attitudes, personal interviews and military journals. Finally, I argue that evaluating evidence from either source requires greater attention to theory and more explicit hypotheses connecting empirical evidence to conclusions about the nature of civil-military relations in the new democracies. Taking military ideas, culture, and ideology seriously requires greater rigor and more systematic attention to how we study military attitudes.[8] The chapter offers a set of guidelines for how we might move in that direction.

Defining Standards

While "civilian control" as practiced in the United States and Western Europe is generally taken as the standard against which civil-military relations in new democracies should be evaluated, there is no agreement on what in fact that standard is and how it should be measured. In his influential early work on posttransition regimes in Brazil and the Southern Cone, Alfred Stepan focused on the persistence of military prerogatives—privileges and powers assumed rightfully to belong to the armed forces—such as the presence of active duty officers as voting members of the cabinet or military control over domestic intelligence agencies.[9]

Taken together, these prerogatives defined a Brazilian regime that was clearly closer to "military tutelage" than civilian control. McSherry and Zaverucha both follow Stepan in focusing their analysis on military prerogatives.[10]

While that approach may serve well for establishing the direction of change—that is, increasing or decreasing powers exercised by the military—it does not really define what would constitute a democratic system of civil-military relations except by negation: a high level of military prerogatives is necessarily incompatible with democracy. But the converse of that proposition is not necessarily true; democratic civil-military relations cannot simply be defined as the absence of military prerogatives. Even in the United States, promotions of military officers below the four-star rank are normally subject to only limited civilian review. Despite congressional oversight and occasional investigations of "wasteful military spending," military budgets are generally accorded a degree of civilian deference not ordinarily extended to civilian agencies. While the political power of the military may be limited in Western European democracies, the armed forces exercise varying degrees of political influence in democratic regimes.

Military prerogatives are almost invariably matters of degree. Legal provisions guaranteeing certain budgetary resources to the military, independent of the appropriations process, seem clearly undemocratic, but how much oversight of military spending do civilian authorities have to exercise to qualify as democratic? The large number of possible military prerogatives further complicates evaluation. Stepan lists eleven prerogatives enjoyed by the Brazilian military in the mid-1980s; a recent paper by Zaverucha lists seventeen military prerogatives under President Cardoso.[11] In addition, the prerogatives approach implicitly treats all military prerogatives as more or less equally important.[12]

The absence of a civilian minister of defense may be troubling, but it is surely less threatening to democracy than military threats to overthrow the government or the presence of active duty officers as voting members of the National Security Council. The large and variable number of potentially relevant prerogatives, of varying degrees of centrality, multiplies the potential sources of disagreement in characterizing particular cases. On conceptual grounds, then, it makes more sense to define democratic civil-military relations affirmatively, by what they are rather than by what they are not.

If democratization of civil-military relations is a long-term process, how would we know when we have reached the threshold for democratic consolidation? What are the essential attributes of civil-military relations in a democracy? As I argue in greater detail elsewhere,[13] the first requirement is that the armed forces must be politically subordinate. The traditional role of many Latin American militaries as the "guardian of the national interests" and ultimate political arbiter in times of crisis is fundamentally incompatible with even weak notions of political democracy as a system of government characterized by majority rule, minority rights, and the rule of law. However noble or dedicated they may be to the *Patria*, military officers are not accountable to the citizenry in elections nor do they possess any institutional mechanism for determining the will of the people or for securing popular consent for any particular military interpretation of the "national interest." Likewise, military claims to tutelary powers as the "guardians of national security" effectively subordinate elected civilian authorities to nonelected and unaccountable military authorities. In established democracies, the armed forces often have significant political influence, but that influence is typically circumscribed to areas in which military officers have specialized professional expertise. Even within the military's professional sphere, civilian governments can decide to disregard military advice without fear of military disloyalty to democratic norms.

Second, the armed forces must be subordinate to the rule of law. While it is common in established democracies for military personnel to be subject to special military laws and regulations—and to trial in military courts for violation of those regulations—military personnel are held accountable for violations of military and criminal law. In a democracy, the armed forces cannot be above the law; military personnel cannot operate outside the law. Nor can national security laws be used to strip civilians of their rights by subjecting them to the jurisdiction of military courts. Torture, disappearances, and execution without due process of law are grievous violations of national and international law, regardless of whether the president is a military officer or a civilian, regardless of whether he or she is popularly elected.

Finally, the armed forces in a democratic regime must be subordinate to the policies established by duly constituted civilian authorities. State agencies are normally granted some degree of autonomy in implementing government policies within their particular sphere of expertise. Still, in a democracy, autonomous self-governing armed forces would be as illogical as an autonomous self-governing Ministry of Foreign Relations. In democratic regimes, the military does not set its own budget, choose its missions, define the threats to national security, or formulate its own defense policies. With due allowance for the differences between parliamentary and presidential regimes, the armed forces advise civilian authorities on matters of national security and carry out the policies of the government.

Taken together, these constitute a clear but stringent set of standards for democratic civil-military relations. None of the current Latin American democracies could claim to meet all of them. Though Argentina and Uruguay come close, both militaries refused to submit themselves to the rule of law when faced with charges arising out of human rights violations during the previous regime. In established democracies, all three elements of democratic control are in fact usually taken for granted. There is, therefore, no a priori reason to consider these standards utopian or unrealistic.

Assessing Changes in Military Behavior

Given this set of standards for democratic civil-military relations, one could assess changes over time or differences between countries in actual behavior, attitudes, and/or legal norms.[14] Particularly for American political scientists, the behavioral approach has a strong intuitive appeal. In this view, what counts in the end is not what military officers say but what they do. The bottom line is whether the armed forces comply with democratic norms or violate them. On its face, the argument is compelling. The standards, as stated above, are a matter of behavior.

Nothing so clearly demonstrated the decay in Venezuelan civil-military relations as two attempted coups in 1992. Notwithstanding the claims of Argentina's *carapintadas* that they were not trying to overthrow the government, the Semana Santa revolt in 1987 forced the Alfonsín government to end the human rights trials of junior officers in clear violation of the norm of political subordination and the rule of law.[15] Still, the behavioral test is almost never as simple as it sounds.

First, the behavioral test works only if military loyalty to democratic norms is in fact being challenged. As Stepan pointed out over a decade ago, perhaps the least democratic outcome is where the military has many political prerogatives and those institutional privileges are simply accepted by the civilian leadership.[16] In such a case, the military need not resort to a coup or even threats against the government because its interests are amply served in a system of civilian deference to the armed forces. Still, in situations of high military power in nominally civilian regimes, there should be observable signs of violations of democratic rules such as unpunished human rights violations and autonomous military participation in high-level policy processes. Regimes characterized by "conditional subordination"[17] present greater difficulties because the military normally does not speak publicly on policy matters and maintains its formal subordination to the president as commander in chief except in times of crisis. Even in crisis situations, under current international conditions, military leaders may prefer to exercise their "arbiter" role quietly behind the scenes rather than appear publicly as the "guardians of democracy."

Thus assessments of military behavior are also assessments of the context of that behavior. If the power of an argument is demonstrated by the range of critiques that it has withstood, by analogy the strength of democratic control might be judged by military adherence to democratic norms when military interests have been seriously threatened. Following this line of reasoning, David Pion-Berlin distinguishes between "strong tests" of civilian control and "weak tests." A strong test requires civilian policies that adversely affect military interests on significant issues.[18] Military compliance with civilian policies that favor military interests or challenge them only on peripheral matters is at best a weak demonstration of civilian control.

Still, the application of "strong tests" has to be done fairly. For some critics, it seems as if the only acceptable proof of civilian control would be to put every single officer accused of human rights violations on trial in civilian courts. Often the military is doubly damned if it contests civilian policies inimical to its interests. Military criticism of those policies or attempts to change them is taken as evidence of the lack of military subordination to civilian authority. In the extreme case, this leads to a standard of democratic behavior that can never be attained. The only fully convincing proof of civilian control would be to abolish the military and see if its members went home without complaint. This suggests the following guidelines for strong but fair tests of civilian control:

1. Behavioral assessments of military compliance with democratic rules should reflect the significance of the military interests adversely affected by that compliance.
2. Military officers in new democracies should not be held to higher standards of democratic behavior than those enforced in established democracies.
3. Military contestation of civilian policies that threaten their interests should not be taken as a violation of democratic norms as long as the resultant conflicts are handled within normal democratic channels.

The Argentine government's decision to put military officers on trial for human rights violations during the "dirty war" was thus a strong test of civilian control. When the trials expanded to include hundreds of junior officers indicted and hundreds more called to testify, the intensity of the "test" clearly exceeded that experienced by the military of any established democracy. When the *carapintadas* resorted to force in defiance of civilian authority, the limits of military acceptance of democratic norms were clearly exposed.

The Argentine example also points to a second source of complexity in the behavioral approach. In principle, the virtue of the behavioral test is that it is straightforward. Faced with difficult circumstances, the military either behaves in accordance with democratic rules or it doesn't. In reality, even the rules above admit degrees of transgression, for example, holding only soldiers and lower-ranking officers responsible for human rights violations or inappropriate military lobbying on issues of special concern to the armed forces. Civilian leaders may simply not be interested in exercising policy control on issues like military reform or defense policy that have no real civilian constituency. If the violations of democratic norms are relatively minor, the regime may remain democratic, even if civil-military relations are not always so.

If, however, the armed forces commit human rights violations that intimidate certain sectors of the society from freely exercising their rights as citizens, then that regime is at least as undemocratic as one that holds fraudulent elections. If the armed forces operate as an autonomous "state within the state," that regime is at least as undemocratic as one in which a colonial ruler allows free elections only for certain offices. To the extent that the military state within the state can effectively veto policy decisions by the elected government, it is little different from a colonial system of limited self-rule in which the native government is subject to the veto of the colonial governor. Depending on the scope of that veto power, the civilian government may be nothing more than a figurehead, a puppet dancing to the strings of the military. The power relations between the armed forces and civilian authorities are thus a matter of degree. Even if we agree on the clear examples of what is democratic behavior and what is not, many cases will lie between those extremes. Hence analysts will have to make difficult judgments about the degree to which democratic norms have been met or the degree to which those norms have been transgressed.

In many instances, assessing military behavior is far less straightforward than proponents of the behavioral approach would have us believe. A given behavior may have quite different meanings, depending on the context. Consider the example of military resistance to civilian attempts to restrict or eliminate the military's role in internal security. Military lobbying in Congress to regain or expand its internal security mission could be interpreted in very different ways:

- as evidence of military refusal to accept civilian policies restricting its activities, that is, lack of subordination, or as evidence of military willingness to work within the democratic system to change policies that it considers to be unwise
- as evidence of the persistence of "national security doctrines" hostile to democracy or as evidence that civilian and military leaders disagree about the magnitude of the internal threat, the ability of other security forces to contain that threat, or both
- as evidence that the military is unwilling to give up its traditional prerogatives or as evidence that the military resents the increasing budget of other security agencies when its own resources and personnel are being cut

Likewise, if we observe that posttransition military budgets are declining as a percentage of GDP, that behavioral outcome could be read as evidence that

- the military's power is declining relative to other claimants on government resources
- military spending is returning to normal levels after a high level of expenditure under the military regime

- military spending is declining as a result of diminished threats because of the end of the Cold War, regional integration, or peace treaties to end internal wars
- the private sector of the economy is growing faster than the public sector
- the military is hiding more of its resources in nonmilitary or off-budget accounts as a result of increased scrutiny by international financial institutions

A strong claim for the first explanation logically requires evidence ruling out alternative explanations. In the case of military expenditures, these competing explanations can—and should be—tested empirically.[19] Testing competing explanations for military resistance to reducing its internal security role requires evidence on military attitudes and motives for that resistance. Characterizing military behavior is thus inevitably a matter of judgment and interpretation. Unfortunately, that means there will inevitably be disagreements about those interpretations, particularly when analysts have different implicit theories about military behavior.

Assessing Changes in Military Attitudes

In principle, attitudinal measures could help clarify what these behaviors mean to the officers involved. Measuring military attitudes and assessing their significance also requires complex interpretations, but these are in principle no more difficult than those involved in evaluating whether military behavior meets democratic norms. In both cases, I argue that we need more explicit procedures for making such judgments.

Military attitudes are central to assessing to what extent democratic norms of civil-military relations are accepted or contested, internalized or rejected. Behavior alone—including "passage of time" tests—cannot tell us whether democratic norms have become institutionalized in military belief systems or whether the absence of overt violations of those norms is a result of (1) military adherence to democratic norms; (2) military perceptions that actions violating those norms are unnecessary; or (3) military judgments that such actions are desirable but politically unfeasible given opposition from other actors, foreign or domestic. Depending on the answers to such questions, we would obviously make very different assessments of the current state of civil-military relations and different projections for the future.

In-depth personal interviews provide the most direct means to measure military attitudes, but these are perhaps the most difficult to obtain. Military officers are not readily accessible to outsiders, including academics. Lists of the names of all officers in a given rank are normally not available outside the institution, and hence random sampling is usually impossible.[20]

In practice, interviews are normally secured through personal contacts, especially introductions and references from other officers. Thus interview samples are vulnerable to bias according to the ideological makeup of the personal networks to which one has access. Institutional rules limiting public statements by military officers or requiring permission of one's superior to participate in outside research offer multiple excuses for declining the interview for those who do not want to talk, although such rules rarely prevent officers from talking if they want to do so and if they trust the interviewer. There is, therefore, a very real danger of selection bias from oversampling of certain segments of the officer corps and undersampling other less accessible groups. Particularly when the samples are relatively small, the issue of the representativeness of interview samples needs to be addressed explicitly. Information on the nature of the sample, how it was constructed, and possible sources of bias should accompany any interview data. Although interviews with military officers, like other elites, normally follow an open-ended questionnaire format, the wording of questions can make a significant difference in the responses one elicits, hence it would be helpful to include interview schedules in publications based on military interviews.

In my own work, I have found retired officers to be useful sources of information on military attitudes. Regardless of their de jure status, retired officers are under fewer effective institutional restrictions about speaking on politically sensitive questions. During periods of turmoil, the turnover in senior officers is often substantial, so there are frequently significant numbers of officers who have retired in the last one to five years. In that time frame, it is unlikely that officers are going to change their belief systems and unlikely that they would react differently to current events than their soon-to-be-retired colleagues. Retired officers are also critical sources for reconstructing why the military reacted the way it did in past crises.[21] Still, there is a strong, perhaps exponential, decay factor in the ability of retired officers accurately to represent the attitudes of their active-duty contemporaries, especially if there are significant generational differences among junior and senior officers.

Differences in how one analyzes interview data can also lead to different substantive conclusions. It is well known in the survey literature that respondents tend to give answers they think the interviewer wants to hear or to give the socially approved answer.[22] Particularly when responses are not confidential, self-censorship may bias military responses. Based on historical experience, professions of military commitment to democracy warrant a certain degree of skepticism. If not practiced carefully, however, skepticism may simply become a warrant for disregarding evidence contrary to one's existing hypotheses about military attitudes.[23] Inevitably, investigators will have to make complex judgments about how to interpret the data from military interviews.

For example, in response to an open-ended question about what the military's role should be in the posttransition regime, in 1991 a majority of the Ecuadorian officers I interviewed argued that the military should carry out the missions assigned to it in the Constitution (see Table 3.1). Others said the military should be subordinated to the constitutional authorities or stay out of politics. Only 20 percent argued that the military should play a "guardian" role in politics. At first glance, then, more than three-fourths of these officers gave "democratic" responses, nearly as many as a 1992 sample of Argentine officers.[24]

Closer inspection of the Ecuadorian responses to other questions, however, suggested that officers held widely different interpretations of the military's constitutional duties; some argued that the military's constitutional mandate included a politically autonomous guardian role. Based on their responses to a series of questions, the respondents were classified according to four competing conceptions of the role of the armed forces in a democratic regime. According to this classification, barely half the Ecuadorian respondents accepted the subordination of the armed forces to civilian authority; half argued that the military should play a guardian or arbiter role "if necessary."

Based on the whole set of interview responses, respondents were further classified according to the degree of ambiguity of their role beliefs and the degree of coherence or contradiction between their professed role beliefs and other attitudes. Of those espousing role beliefs consistent with democratic norms, only a few Ecuadorian officers had responses fully coherent with that position; roughly a third evidenced major contradictions; nearly half had significant ambiguities in their positions.[25] (Ecuadorian advocates of a guardian or tutelary role also often gave ambiguous or contradictory responses.) In contrast, Argentine officers were more consistent and unambiguous in accepting their political and professional subordination to civilian authority, although there were still proponents of alternative role beliefs, especially among retired officers associated with the *carapintada* movement.[26] While it may be tempting either to accept Ecuadorian officers' professions of loyalty to the Constitution at face value or to seize on the ambiguities and contradictions as evidence of only superficial commitment to democratic norms, careful examination of the interview data as a whole provides strong evidence that Ecuadorian officers' role beliefs were in fact conflicting and often ambiguous and contradictory.

TABLE 3.1 *Role Beliefs of Ecuadorian and Argentine Officers*

ECUADOR 1991

Open-Ended Question: Political Role of the Armed Forces?

	Agree
Subordination to constitutional authorities	18%
Constitutionally assigned missions	56%
Arbiter / guardian of national interests	15%
Guardian of national security	3%
	(N = 39)

Role Beliefs Classified on Multiple Questions

	Role Belief Proponents	Among Proponents of Each Role Belief	
		Major Ambiguities	Major Contradictions
Democratic professionalism	38%	43%	36%
Classic professionalism	16%	50%	33%
Arbiter / guardian	35%	42%	31%
Tutelary guardian	11%	75%	50%
	(N = 39)	(N = 38)	(N = 37)

ARGENTINA 1992

Open-Ended Question: Political Role of the Armed Forces?

	Agree
Subordination to constitutional authorities	55%
No intervention in politics	8%
Constitutionally assigned missions	22%
Participant in national project	10%
Arbiter / guardian of national interests	3%
Guardian of national security	2%
	(N = 67)

Role Beliefs Classified on Multiple Questions

	Role Belief Proponents	Among Proponents of Each Role Belief	
		Major Ambiguities	Major Contradictions
Democratic professionalism	36%	0%	4%
Classic professionalism	48%	25%	16%
Participant in national project	6%	75%	0%
Arbiter / guardian	6%	50%	75%
Tutelary / guardian	5%	33%	33%
	(N = 67)	(N = 67)	(N = 67)

This analysis suggests several guidelines for assessing military attitudes toward democracy based on interviews with military officers:

1. Information on sampling procedures, characteristics of the interviewees, confidentiality conditions, and possible sources of selection bias should be presented, so readers can make independent judgments of the representativeness or unrepresentativeness of the sample.
2. Particularly where there are officially approved positions on the attitudes in question, interview responses should be checked for consistency and credibility.
3. Interview responses should be judged in the context of the whole set of interview data. Data on ambiguity and coherence of the responses are critical descriptors of military belief systems.
4. With rare exceptions, military officers do not all think alike. Hence claims about military attitudes should include evidence on minority or dissenting attitudes as well as majority views. Ideally, such descriptions should include the distribution of those attitudes across the ideological and institutional subgroups that collectively constitute the "armed forces."

Finally, it is striking that arguments about progress (or the lack thereof) in constructing more democratic civil-military relations almost always focus on military attitudes (and behavior) rather than civilian attitudes. In Latin America, the most ardent advocates of a politically autonomous military have often been civilians. These have usually been elites, but civilian reformers and radicals have also frequently advocated an activist role for officers sympathetic to their cause. In Ecuador, a 1991 survey of two major cities found strong public support for an active military role in politics (see Table 3.2). In the Southern Cone, in contrast, survey data suggest that striking changes have occurred in civilian public opinion toward the military as a political actor.[27] While there is impressionistic evidence of significant changes in the attitudes of civilian elites as well, the civilian side of the civil-military equation deserves much more careful investigation than it has received to date.

Military Journals and Military Attitudes

Given the practical difficulties of getting access to active-duty officers to obtain data on military attitudes directly, military journals offer a potentially attractive alternative source of data on military thinking about democracy and civil-military relations. Although military publications are sometimes irregular,

TABLE 3.2 *Civilian Attitudes toward the Military's Role in Politics: Ecuador, 1991*

STATEMENT A. "If national interests are threatened in times of crisis, the armed forces should intervene to change the government."

Strongly Agree	Agree	Disagree	Strongly Disagree
20%	56%	16%	9%

STATEMENT B. "If national security is endangered, the armed forces should assume power."

Strongly Agree	Agree	Disagree	Strongly Disagree
19%	58%	14%	9%

STATEMENT C. "The armed forces should avoid coups d'état but should pressure the government when they see that the country is doing badly."

Strongly Agree	Agree	Disagree	Strongly Disagree
21%	64%	10%	5%

most Latin American militaries publish multiple journals. In the larger countries, the army, navy, and air force publish separate journals that might be used to investigate the similarities and differences in military thinking across the different services. The most attractive feature of military journals as a source of data about military attitudes is that they have been published for decades, in some countries back to the turn of the century. No other source offers such potential for analyzing changes in military thinking in historical perspective, including earlier waves of democratization and periods of military reform. But that potential has not been systematically evaluated. Given clear evidence from interview sources of significant differences in the attitudes of Ecuadorian and Argentine officers toward their role in posttransition politics, the empirical question is to what extent these differences are reflected in military writing.

As an initial test, I examined articles published in Argentina's *Revista de la Escuela Superior de Guerra* (RESG) and Ecuador's *Revista de las Fuerzas Armadas* (RFFAA), the first published by the army, the second by the Estado Mayor Conjunto. Although both journals feature occasional articles by foreign authors and invited civilians, most are written by military authors for their fellow officers. There is some distribution of military journals outside of the military, but it is rare to find anyone outside of the military (or the exceptional scholar)[28] who reads them. The time periods covered in this analysis are somewhat different for each journal, 1973–92 for Argentina and 1979–91 for Ecuador. The former covers the return of Juan Perón and the ill-fated government of his widow, the military regime, and the first nine years of the democratic regime. The latter begins with the democratic transition and covers the first three civilian administrations.

A simple content analysis of the titles of signed articles in each journal reveals that neither pays very much attention to democracy or civil-military relations, at least not directly. Out of nearly six hundred articles published in the RESG over nineteen years, only two focused primarily on democracy and two others on issues of civil-military relations such as military intervention in politics. The Ecuadorian journal, RFFAA, was published somewhat more sporadically, but out of over four hundred articles in a twelve-year span, only one dealt extensively with democracy and one more with civil-military relations. Most references to democracy or civil-military relations occur in articles about other subjects, for example, revolutionary war, international relations, and national security. Even so, the frequency of any statements about democracy is low.

Hence there are serious questions about whether the opinions expressed in these few articles are in fact representative of "military thinking" about democracy or the political role of the military. We would obviously be skeptical about generalizing about military attitudes from one or two interviews. The same skepticism seems warranted in generalizing from small numbers of statements in military journals.[29] In fact, if we were to take these statements, direct and indirect, as evidence about military attitudes toward democracy, affirmations of the need for democracy are perhaps more frequent in the Ecuadorian journal than in its Argentine counterpart. Based on the interview evidence above, judging military attitudes solely from the statements in these journals would have led to the wrong conclusion.[30]

If military journals do not tell us much about military attitudes toward their political role, what do they tell us? I would argue that military journals can tell us quite a bit about military doctrine.[31] The debate over "national security doctrine" in Latin America is too complex to deal with adequately here,[32] but certain questions of doctrine do receive more or less regular attention. The basic concepts of national security planning are explained (usually without reference to the type of government doing the planning); threats to national security are described and analyzed; and finally, strategies for dealing with those threats are recommended. The military's concern with the internal security threat presented by guerrilla warfare is evident in both journals, though it is probably true that in a typical year there were more articles about military history than about internal security. Both journals feature frequent articles on international relations, external conflicts, and conventional warfare, which contradicts the conventional image of Latin American militaries as single-mindedly devoted to stamping out internal security threats.

There are also discernible differences in what these military authors say about the nature of the internal threat and how to combat it. In general, Ecuadorian writings stress the socioeconomic origins of the discontents revolutionary groups try to exploit to advance the Marxist cause. "Outbreaks of insurgency occur when the right conditions exist. . . . Hunger and misery are the worst enemies of social peace."[33] The interaction between security and development is clear and obvious. Progressive development is indispensable for security because it provides the resources necessary for increasing the common good by making available abundant satisfactions. In this way it diminishes the possibility of generating resentments and frustrations capable of being translated into violent actions against the established order.[34]

> On the domestic side, there are various causes that give rise to the formation and presence of groups outside the law. In many cases, youth decide to take up arms in response to the intellectual frustrations of experiences of popular injustice; in other cases, there is a clear maladaptation to one's surroundings because of grave socioeconomic disequilibria, given a society of privileges and the privileged. . . . What should be done to establish the social and economic peace demanded by the population of the world, especially those that debate between hunger and poverty . . . ? Perhaps a democratic-pluralist form of government, real, pure, with the full exercise of liberty, the law, and social justice; a government which respects institutions and individuals; a government that fights with social measures the subversion that has in many cases not been defeated by arms.[35]

In contrast, Argentine military writings stressed the ideological threat of "subversion," which seeks to undermine the core values of "Western Christian civilization."

> There is a spiritual and cultural wealth in Latin America, because of the fact that its inhabitants are Catholics and because of its Greco-Roman heritage. The strategic implications of this unity of beliefs are enormous and decisive, because . . . the terrain on which the real battle is fought is the mind and soul of man, and the alternative is to be destroyed morally by the materialism of the consumer society or the materialism of Marxism-Leninism and its allies, direct and indirect, or rather to be elevated to the Highest by the grace of the Church of Christ.[36]

> To achieve the goals [of the subversion], many weapons are employed, not all of which physically attack the enemy; to the contrary, most are oriented to achieve that which is more important than the physical death

of a combatant, which is to produce [his] moral and spiritual death. . . .
This arsenal . . . runs from drugs, blackmail, sex, political and ideological
indoctrination, deforming secular and religious education, psychological
action in all its forms of compulsion, such as selective terrorism, kidnap-
pings, assassinations, etc.[37]

Marxist-Leninism . . . attempts to destroy the morality of the West [and] its
cultural cohesion, in order to overcome its resistance and seize power. . . .
Marxist ideology absolves, promotes, sustains, and exalts any incident
which helps weaken western values.[38]

In this dirty fight, produced by this new type of ideologue and complacent
officials who have made negligence their way of life, there are no ambiguous or uncertain positions based on the fear of being mistaken. As long as
one acts in good faith, and with the precision appropriate to the circumstances, every excess, every error, no matter how lamentable, should be
excusable.[39]

Even here, however, the differences are not simple. Some Argentine authors
acknowledge socioeconomic problems that make the poor susceptible to alien-
ation or Marxist propaganda.[40] Conversely, some Ecuadorian military writings
warn of the dangers of ideological "subversion."[41] So here again we need to
characterize military attitudes, quantitatively or qualitatively, in ways that
capture differences in military doctrines about internal security without reducing them to a stereotypical "Ecuadorian view" versus the "Argentine view."

Finally, military journals are good sources for data on military myths and
self-images. Military life features many ceremonial occasions—the graduation
of new cadets, anniversaries of historic battles, and days dedicated to each
of the military forces. These are often reported in military journals, with
congratulatory editorials and reprints of speeches delivered on these ritual
occasions.

The army that was born with the *Patria* is conscious of that fact. From
there comes the unbreakable will to serve her, to reaffirm the inescapable
duty to give the best of its efforts for the fulfillment of its mission at all levels of the national life. . . . Its commitment is to the *Patria*, as the worthy
successor to that heroic army that gave even the supreme sacrifice, leaving
in every latitude and height [of the battlefield] inspiring examples of valor
and sacrifice.[42]

The critical question is, however, what relationship these myths have to attitudes about democratic civil-military relations. It is certainly possible that
officers who consider the armed forces to be "the guardians of the sacred altar

of the *Patria*" are more likely to believe that the military should have an arbiter or tutelary role in contemporary Latin American democracies.

But it is also possible that this ceremonial rhetoric has relatively little to do with whether military officers are (or are not) willing to accept the fundamental norms of democratic civil-military relations. In either case, these institutional myths are one or more causal links removed from military attitudes about their political role in a democracy, in a relationship that is almost certainly not a perfect correlation. Thus it would be useful to compare institutional self-images in military journals in Latin American countries that lack democratic control of the military with a country like Spain where the same myths have historically been common, despite the general consensus that Spain has now consolidated and institutionalized a system of civil-military relations consistent with democratic norms.[43]

Based on this preliminary analysis, I would suggest the following as guidelines for using military journals as evidence of military attitudes toward civil-military relations:

1. Questions of sampling and representativeness apply to military journals, as well as military interviews or surveys. Researchers therefore have an obligation to provide readers with sufficient information to judge the representativeness of any sample of military writing.
2. Descriptions of military writings should include appropriate measures of the variability of the military attitudes in question, including evidence of dissenting or minority viewpoints.
3. The utility of indirect indicators of military attitudes toward democratic norms of civil-military relations is inversely proportional to the number of causal linkages between the attitudes being measured and democratic attitudes and behavior.

Theory and Evidence

Finally, it is also apparent that even if given the same evidence, for example, the change in the number of active-duty officers holding cabinet status in Brazil, different scholars will come to different conclusions about what the evidence proves or does not prove. Notwithstanding Popperian arguments about the importance of falsification in scientific research, in reality our data are not independent of the theories that guide our interpretation of the evidence. Thus a significant portion of the variance in scholarly descriptions of contemporary civil-military relations is perhaps less a result of the method-ological issues addressed above than it is a consequence of the different theo-retical assumptions and approaches that scholars bring to the study of the Latin American military.

To take an extreme example, some authors seem to hold the (usually im-plicit) theory that military officers in Latin America are evil people who terrorize and torture civilians who disagree with them. Given a military jour-nal article advocating military subordination to civilian authorities and respect for human rights, advocates of this view of the military are likely to dismiss the evidence as simply public relations for external consumption or as a statement unrepresentative of military opinion, citing multiple instances of military im-punity for human rights violations.

Others view the military as an ideological actor, permeated with right-wing authoritarian conceptions of the internal threats to national security.[44] In this view, military acceptance of democracy would be likely only if democracy posed no threat to military efforts to stamp out "subversive" ideologies chal-lenging the status quo. To the extent that the military's ideological agenda is seen as institutionalized in the state apparatus—intelligence agencies, military schools, the Chaplain's Corps—and ties to like-minded civilian elites,[45] it is even less likely that the military could change the way it thinks about democracy or civil-military relations. The culturalist view of military attitudes as deeply rooted in the Hispanic legacy must likewise be skeptical of newly found military commitments to democracy or to U.S. conceptions of military professionalism.

In contrast, a rational actor approach, particularly one that sees the military as concerned primarily with institutional interests, offers much more theoreti-cal latitude for the possibility (though certainly not the inevitability) of civil-military relations that accommodate the armed forces without violating demo-cratic norms.[46] My own work assumes that military officers are boundedly rational actors, pursuing individual and institutional self-interests within the national and international context as they understand it. Those understand-ings are, however, mediated by the differing ideological lenses of individual officers, institutional and other identifications, and learning from experience. Military "interests" are therefore subject to redefinition. Individual and collec-tive behavior in the military is also subject to formal and informal institutional norms. Behavior, particularly compliance with or violation of democratic norms, is assumed to be a conscious decision, influenced by imperfect projec-tions of the consequences of that behavior but also by belief systems specifying what the armed forces should do in different situations.

In this view, military behavior—like human behavior in general—is imperfectly correlated with military attitudes.[47] Under certain circumstances, military officers may behave in ways that contradict their beliefs. Changes in behavior may lead to changes in attitudes rather than vice versa. Nevertheless, like voters with strong party identifications, military officers are likely to act in ways consistent with their belief systems and identifications. In practice, attitudes and behavior exist not in isolation but in interactions with other actors. Hence military officers cannot simply believe whatever they want or whatever suits their interests. Argentine officers, for example, are painfully aware that the last military regime was a political, economic, and military failure. That "fact" cannot be ignored in discussions of the role of the Argentine armed forces in politics. To assume otherwise is to assume that military officers are incapable of learning or changing their behavior in response to changes in the world around them.

Conflicting theoretical visions of the Latin American military are in turn typically part of a broader set of theoretical assumptions about Latin American democracies that shape the way one looks at civil-military relations in those regimes. Marxist conceptions of Latin American politics assign the military a role as the guardian of a certain class structure, though they would not necessarily rule out civilian control of the military in societies where dependent capitalism has achieved hegemony. Liberal pluralist conceptions of the "new democracies" in "developing societies" are obviously much more open to the possibility that military and civilian elites could learn to play by democratic rules of the game, given the right historical and institutional circumstances.

Regardless of what we might wish the situation to be, the reality is that our theoretical priors influence the way we interpret the evidence about military attitudes toward democratic civil-military relations. Thus I would suggest two final guidelines for the serious researcher:

1. Insofar as possible, theoretical assumptions about the nature of the Latin American militaries and the larger political systems of which they are a part should be made explicit. Empirical findings should be examined from the perspective of alternative theoretical assumptions.
2. Theoretical predictions about the evidence one expects to find should be made in advance of the data gathering rather than post hoc. These theoretical predictions should specify what evidence would be disconfirming, or at least challenging, to the theory on which those expectations are based. Any researcher should be able to specify what evidence would lead him or her to change his or her mind.

Ecuador and Argentina Reconsidered

By the standards proposed here, Argentina has made substantial progress toward a democratic system of civil-military relations.[48] During the Alfonsín government (1983–89), Argentine leaders deliberately sought to eliminate the military's traditional prerogatives and impose democratic control. In short order, the powers of the civilian minister of defense were strengthened; the service commanders were replaced by a chief of staff for each force; and military industries were transferred from the individual services to the ministry. Military salaries and budgets declined sharply. Particularly in comparison to the past, the policies of the Alfonsín government constituted a sharp reduction in the political power and autonomy of the armed forces.

The toughest test of the military's subordination to democratic norms came in the trials of military officers for human rights violations during the military regime. After military courts refused to act, the nine members of the three juntas were tried in civilian courts; five were convicted and sentenced to prison. Despite belated efforts by the government to limit the scope of the trials, human rights groups and sympathetic judges mobilized to file charges against hundreds of other officers. Junior officers revolted in 1987, demanding an immediate end to the trials. Shortly thereafter, the government sent to Congress the Law of Due Obedience, which exonerated most of the accused. Clearly the Argentine military's commitment to the rule of law did not extend to letting officers be judged in civilian courts for what they considered to be "acts of war." In this and two subsequent uprisings, rebel leaders made it clear that they were not attempting to overthrow the government. Nevertheless, the revolts did force civilian authorities to accept an outcome that neither the courts, the Congress, nor public opinion really wanted.

Alfonsín's successor, Carlos Menem, came to power in the midst of a deep economic crisis. Facing skyrocketing inflation, the government sought to defuse conflicts with the military in order to focus on economic stabilization. More officers were exonerated, and the imprisoned members of the juntas were eventually pardoned. Although Menem praised the armed forces, military budgets continued to decline. When retired *carapintada* leader Colonel Mohamed Alí Seineldín publicly criticized Menem's policies, he was arrested. His supporters revolted several months later. This time military officers carried out the president's orders to suppress the revolt. As the issues shifted from institutional and individual self-defense against the trials to the more narrowly ideological agenda of Seineldín and his followers, the *carapintadas* lost support within the army and dissident officers were purged. With the human rights issue more or less resolved, the political subordination of the armed forces to the democratic regime now appears solidly established. Subordination to the rule of law is generally accepted, though the extent of the military's commitment to that principle has not really been tested since the 1980s trials.

Evaluating the subordination of the armed forces to the policy direction of civilian authorities is more difficult because of civilian disinterest and lack of expertise in defense policy. The Alfonsín government pursued a largely reactive policy, trying to contain military opposition to the trials and budget cuts while sustaining the reduced level of political prerogatives. Having reached a political accommodation with the armed forces on the human rights issue, President Menem was content to leave it to the military forces to determine how they would adapt to continuing budget cuts. Menem also pushed for the participation of Argentine forces in international peacekeeping operations. That mission provides important benefits to the armed forces—societal legitimacy, professional experience and training, and extra pay and resources—so the peacekeeping mission has been accepted despite nationalist criticism.

Arguably the best test of the policy subordination of the military to civilian control is the controversial question of the military's role in internal security. Seeking to prevent a recurrence of the human rights abuses of the previous regime, a broad alliance of center and leftist groups supported the legal exclusion of the armed forces from internal security matters. Military leaders lobbied intensely to keep their traditional role, given their belief that the communist threat was still present. Giving up the military's responsibility for internal security also meant giving up claims for the resources to perform that mission, at a time when military budgets were shrinking and civilian governments were working hard to resolve border disputes with Argentina's neighbors.

Ultimately the 1988 National Defense Law defined the military's mission as external security; internal security was assigned to the police and paramilitary security forces. Military intelligence agencies were limited to external security questions, and military planning for internal conflicts was banned. Still, the military was not expressly banned from participating in internal security operations. First Alfonsín, then Menem, issued decrees authorizing the use of military forces to maintain public order under certain circumstances. In 1992, a new Internal Security Law reaffirmed that internal security was the mission of the security forces rather than the military and assigned responsibility for planning and coordination to the Ministry of the Interior. But it also provided for the president to use regular military forces, if the security forces were overwhelmed, by declaring a state of siege.

In the end, the armed forces have been substantially, but not entirely, removed from internal security operations. Military opposition to limiting its internal security role has been consistent and continuous, but that opposition appears to have been waged within the normal channels and methods of democratic politics rather than through military revolts or threats of military disloyalty to the regime. In Argentina, neither Alfonsín nor Menem nor the congressional majority has been willing to rely entirely on nonmilitary forces for internal security. Arguably, civilian reluctance to give up the option of using military force in domestic disturbances or insurgency has been the critical barrier to categorical exclusion of the military from internal security, not the military opposition to such exclusion. The 1992 interviews cited above, and others since then, indicate a decline in military perceptions of internal security threats and a growing willingness to live with their role as the instrument of last resort in internal security. In my view, persistent military opposition to more restrictive policies is less troubling than reports of failure to comply with the new limits, particularly the restriction on domestic intelligence activities.[49]

Other instances of policy subordination despite substantial military opposition include the elimination of the Condor missile program under pressure from the United States and Menem's sudden decision to eliminate mandatory conscription in favor of an all-volunteer military. Except, then, for the human rights question in the 1980s—a very large exception—Argentine civil-military relations have generally been consistent with democratic norms as practiced in established democracies. The interview data described above show substantial, though not universal, military acceptance of the norms of political and policy subordination to civilian authority. This does not mean civil-military relations in Argentina are necessarily harmonious or that undemocratic attitudes are nonexistent. Still, the new system of civil-military relations has been increasingly institutionalized in new laws, in military attitudes, and in the organizational mechanisms for the exercise of democratic control of the armed forces. The remaining defects in that system stem largely from the lack of civilian will or motivation to use those mechanisms as they are normally used in established democracies.

In contrast, Ecuador has made little progress toward democratic civil-military relations during the last two decades. The overthrow of President Mahuad in January 2000 marks the first successful military coup in Latin America since the Haitian army overthrew President Jean-Bertrand Aristide in 1991. The abortive attempt by nationalist officers to install a civil-military "Junta de Salvación Nacional" is dramatic evidence that a sector of the army has largely given up on the current democratic regime.

In contrast to the dramatic failure of the Argentine military in the Malvinas/ Falklands war, Ecuadorian military governments under Rodríguez Lara (1972–75) and the Triumvirate (1976–79) were mildly progressive, nationalist, and largely devoid of human rights abuses. The military regime presided over an unprecedented economic boom, fueled by oil exports and lavish government spending on infrastructure projects. After a gradual negotiated transition, the armed forces turned over power to what they hoped would be a new generation of democratic leaders. Despite grumbling from conservative officers, the first civilian government survived the death of the president and the beginnings of the debt crisis. The second, headed by conservative León Febres Cordero, was rocked by repeated confrontations with Congress and the courts, punctuated by two minor military revolts. A short-lived guerrilla movement aggravated military relations with Democratic Left president Rodrigo Borja, who nevertheless amnestied captured rebels over strong military objections. For the most part, civilian presidents avoided confrontations with the armed forces and accepted the substantially increased institutional autonomy, which the military regime had written in law and military regulations.

With all of the major parties in disrepute, an independent swept the 1992 election. Austerity policies and a growing recession quickly eroded support for the Durán Ballén government. After the vice president was caught trying to buy votes in Congress, military pressure finally broke the political deadlock over the naming of a new vice president. The 1996 elections brought to power the populist leader Abdalá Bucarám, who presided over a series of scandals and a deepening economic crisis. He was deposed a year later by a popular mobilization that spurred Congress to declare the presidency vacant by virtue of the president's "mental incompetence." The crisis over who would succeed Bucarám—the vice president or the president of Congress—had to be resolved in a marathon session in the office of the commander of the Joint Staff.

After a two-year interim, Ecuadorians elected Popular Democrat Jamil Mahuad, who promptly ran into a major banking crisis that led to a spiraling devaluation and near-default on the foreign debt. Economic discontents turned to outrage when it was revealed that Mahuad had accepted multimillion-dollar campaign contributions from bankers at the center of the financial crisis. When Indian and labor groups seized the Congress and Supreme Court buildings, a group of junior officers moved to take power. Under intense pressure from the United States and opposition by more senior colonels in critical troop commands, the revolt collapsed, but having fled the presidential palace, President Mahuad never returned. The vice president, a political independent from Guayaquil, took the oath of office as president in the Ministry of Defense. Although the leaders of the initial revolt were purged from active duty, it seems clear that a sector of the armed forces is no longer willing to subordinate itself to civilian authority. Even the "constitutionalist" officers who backed vice presidential succession seem resigned to an active political role as the de facto "guardians of democracy," given the incompetence of civilian political leaders.

A full analysis of the causes behind these trends is beyond the scope of this chapter, but two factors stand out. First, the hyper-fragmentation of the Ecuadorian party system leads inexorably to weak presidents in more or less continual confrontations with an opposition-controlled Congress. Second, the nature of the previous military regime in combination with the poor performance of civilian institutions since 1979 have produced a severe loss of military and civilian confidence in the current regime. Not surprisingly, a substantial majority of the civilian public favored the January coup.[50]

Military attitudes reflect the contradictory influences of an international environment hostile to military governments and an unstable domestic context inhospitable to democratic civil-military relations. The broad military consensus on living in a constitutional democracy masks growing division about the meaning of democracy in the Ecuadorian context and substantial uncertainty about the proper role of the military in a democratic regime. Most officers acknowledge the conventional norms of democratic civil-military relations, while explicitly and implicitly questioning whether such norms can be applied in Ecuador.

Policy subordination to civilian authority has been mixed. Lack of civilian expertise in defense and military matters is clearly a major problem. But there is also a strong tradition, encouraged by the armed forces, of civilian deference to military expertise on matters related to national security. Perhaps the most striking manifestation of the high degree of civilian acceptance of the military's institutional autonomy was the absence of any provision in the 1979 Constitution for a permanent defense or armed forces committee in Congress.

During the 1980s, there were few real tests of the military's formal subordination to presidential control. Rodrigo Borja's amnesty for the "Alfaro Vive ¡Carajo!" guerrillas was opposed by conservative officers to no avail. Military opposition to Durán Ballén's attempts to privatize military industries was waged both within channels and publicly through the Association of Retired Generals and Admirals. Faced with other pressing problems, the government dropped the privatization proposal. As real salaries began to decline in the 1990s, military criticism increased, but budgetary and salary complaints were pursued within channels, with the minister of defense, generally a retired officer chosen by the president, acting as the intermediary between the military and the executive. Nevertheless, under the leadership of nationalist general Paco Moncayo, senior army officers often spoke publicly on policies they considered matters of national security.

Probably the most serious challenge to policy subordination came with the decision of Presidents Bucarám and Mahuad to seek a negotiated settlement of the disputed border with Peru, which had caused a brief war in 1941 and periodic military confrontations ever since. Partly because of Ecuador's superior military performance in the 1995 clash, officers and civilians hoped that Ecuador could negotiate from a position of strength. Though it contained some concessions, the final agreement was disappointing to many officers. Still, military opinion was divided, given the strengthening of the Peruvian military position in the late 1990s and new threats along the Colombian border. More research is needed to clarify the terms of debate in the armed forces and the reasons behind their acceptance or rejection of the alternatives under discussion. My impression is that the lack of politically viable alternatives, especially alternatives acceptable to the United States and other guarantors of the 1941 Rio Protocol, weighed far more heavily than military agreement with government arguments for the treaty or any commitment to the principle of civilian supremacy.

In Argentina, the outcome thus far has been significant progress toward a working system of democratic civil-military relations. Significant defects remain in that system, and reversions to older practices remain possible, though improbable under current circumstances. In Ecuador, the military remains the ultimate arbiter of political crises and a strong policy voice on security issues broadly defined. Although the military has a good human rights record and has bowed to civilian authority on some difficult issues, the domestic political context is inimical to both the principles and the practice of democratic civil-military relations.

Conclusion

As noted in the Introduction to this volume, ideas matter. Ideas provide the cognitive frame of reference within which boundedly rational actors—including military officers—interpret the options available to them and calculate the advantages and disadvantages of alternative courses of action. Belief systems contain implicit and explicit conceptions of proper values, correct behavior, and beliefs about "the way the world works." Military beliefs thus structure military behavior.

These beliefs do not exist in a vacuum. They reflect perceptions of the national and international context and learning from experience. Military beliefs are also shaped, in ways we still do not adequately understand, by institutional interests and socialization and by premilitary socialization and inter-actions with the larger society. Understanding whether or not civil-military relations in Latin America have in fact changed thus requires careful analysis of the extent to which military belief systems have changed. Institutionalized democratic control implies significant changes in military beliefs. Taking military ideas seriously, in turn, requires more systematic attention to problems of sampling, measurement, and interpretation. Still, in the study of military attitudes, as in the study of civil-military relations, theoretical progress also requires clear and explicit attention to our theoretical priors and the standards by which we assess the evidence.

NOTES

This essay is an outgrowth of the panel "Civil-Military Relations in Latin American Democracies: How Do We Know If Anything Has Changed," Latin American Studies Association annual meeting, Chicago, 25 September 1998. I am indebted to the participants in that panel—Wendy Hunter, Brian Loveman, David Pion-Berlin, and Jorge Zaverucha—for stimulating my own thinking on this subject. I also benefited from comments by Craig Arceneaux on an earlier version of this chapter presented to the "Soldiers and Democracy" conference at the University of California, Riverside, 19–20 February 1999.

1. See, for example, Fitch, "The Armed Forces and the Politics of Democratic Consolidation."
2. See Fitch, *Armed Forces and Democracy*, 36–60.
3. McSherry, *Incomplete Transition*, 266, 289.
4. Pion-Berlin, *Through Corridors of Power*, 9.
5. Hunter, *Eroding Military Influence*, 139–46.
6. Zaverucha, "Sarney, Collor, Itamar," 2–3, 33–34. See also Zaverucha, "A Constituição Brasileira de 1988." Compare Rizzo de Oliveira, "A adaptaçao del militares a democracia no Brasil."
7. Obando, "Power of Peru's Armed Forces," 112–15; Krujit, "Peru," 284.
8. On the general issue of more rigorous grounding for the notion that "ideas matter," see Berman, "Ideas, Norms, and Culture."
9. Stepan, *Rethinking Military Politics*, 93–114.
10. McSherry, *Incomplete Transition*, 25, 272–89; Zaverucha, "Sarney, Collor, Itamar," 2.
11. Stepan, *Rethinking Military Politics*, 94–97; Zaverucha, "Sarney, Collor, Itamar," 3–33.
12. Hunter, "Assessing Military Power and Privilege," 3.
13. Fitch, *Armed Forces and Democracy*, 36–38, 176–77.
14. On judging democracy on the basis of legal norms, see Loveman, " 'Protected Democracies' and Military Guardianship" and *Constitution of Tyranny*.
15. Norden, *Military Rebellion in Argentina*, 99–124; Pion-Berlin and Arceneaux, "Tipping the Civil-Military Balance."
16. Stepan, *Rethinking Military Politics*, 68–102.

17. Fitch, *Armed Forces and Democracy*, 40.

18. Pion-Berlin, "Strong Tests of Civilian and Military Power," 7–13. Pion-Berlin also argues that the historical context—the prior history of military intervention, the nature of the prior military regime, the type of transition, and the historical strength of civilian institutions—should be taken into account (ibid., 4–7). But this confounds the measure of the outcome—democratic control under difficult circumstances—with (independent) variables normally used to explain differences in the outcome in question.

19. Despite UN and IMF efforts to standardize the accounting and reporting of military expenditures, conventional data sources frequently report depressingly different spending figures. Careful attention to what is and is not included in publicly reported budgets is rare, despite wide variations in the accounting treatment of military pensions, police and paramilitary budgets, payments and interest on loans for foreign arms purchases, and income generated by military enterprises or auxiliaries. See Scheetz, "Evolution of Public Sector Expenditures," 188–89.

20. An approximation to the universe of officers can sometimes be constructed from the annual promotion lists in the official register, but finding those officers is often difficult. In Argentina, the problem was compounded because active-duty and retired officers unlisted their telephone numbers (and home addresses) during the 1970s.

21. Key participants are often anxious to talk about their role in important events. Indeed, one systematic source of bias in military interviews is the tendency to see oneself as playing a more pivotal role than was actually the case.

22. Williams, "Interviewer Role Performance," 224–31; Zaller, *Nature and Origins of Mass Opinion*, 6–75; Weisberg, Krosnick, and Bowen, *Introduction to Survey Research*, 86–87.

23. In the methodological worst case, evidence about military attitudes is admitted when it supports one's argument and dismissed as window dressing or propaganda when it does not.

24. Both samples were nonrandom; both had substantially more army officers than representatives of the other services; both were constituted mostly by colonels and generals. The Ecuadorian sample consisted overwhelmingly of officers retired since the 1979 transition; the Argentine sample included roughly half retired and half active-duty officers, including junior officers down to the rank of captain. Interviewees were promised that their responses would not be individually attributed to them. The interviews typically lasted one to two hours, following a more or less standard set of questions. For further details, see Fitch, *Armed Forces and Democracy*, 64–65.

25. An example is Peña, "Military and Democracy in Ecuador."

26. For a similar conclusion, also based on interview data, see Fontana, "Percepciones militares acerca del rol."

27. See the Instituto de Estudios de Opinión Pública in Quito. Compare Catterberg, *Argentina Confronts Politics*, 56.

28. Frederick Nunn is the outstanding exception. For a persuasive demonstration of the utility of military journals in understanding the historical development of the Latin American militaries, see *Yesterday's Soldiers*.

29. See Lustick, "History, Historiography, and Political Science," 606–14, on the problem of selection bias in the use of historical materials. Compare Nunn, "South American Military."

30. See, for example, Moncayo, "Poder militar, partidos políticos," 12–13, and "Introducción al conocimiento," 58–61; Monteverde, "La Democracia," 103–5; Hernández Cajiao, "Disciplina," 29–32; and "Editorial: Afirmación de la conciencia institucional." The contradictions in Ecuadorian military thinking are nevertheless evident in the editorial defense of the previous military regime and the ambiguous role accorded to the military as the defender of the Constitution in the Monteverde article. Hernández argues that "the norm of 'non-deliberation' constitutionally imposed on the armed forces guarantees their position as the Arbiter, Judge, and Guarantor of the nation's order, security, and development" ("Disciplina," 32). A less encouraging view is offered by a retired Argentine officer a year after the democratic transition: "Democracy should not be understood only as a particular form of government, but also as a *style of life*, where the rule of law marks the harmonious operation of the Republic and the guarantees and rights of its inhabitants" (Magallanes, "Estrategia psicosocial y opinión pública," 55).

31. See Stepan, *State and Society*, 130–44, for a carefully executed study of changes in Peruvian military doctrine based on an analysis of military journal articles.

32. See chapter 4 of Fitch, *Armed Forces and Democracy*, for a detailed analysis of posttransition continuities and changes in national security doctrines in Ecuador and Argentina.

33. Carrillo, "La guerrilla y los derechos humanos," 45.

34. Donoso, "A propósito de desarrollo, seguridad, y presupuestos," 7.

35. "Guerrilla y delincuencia."

36. Piccinali, "Perspectiva estratégica," 71–72.

37. Quintana, "Técnicas psicológicas," 8.

38. Camps, "La subversión," 44–45.

39. Vilas, "Reflexiones sobre la guerra subversiva," 12; Carillo, "La guerrilla y los derechos humanos."

40. See, for example, Picciuolo, "La caballería del futuro," 78–79.

41. See, for example, Pauker, "Movimiento revolucionario," 110–11; Hinostroza, "Subversión comunista"; Pazmiño, "Las fuerzas armadas"; and Almeida, "La guerra revolucionaria."

42. "Editorial," 7. See also Alvarez, "El militar, educador, y técnico."

43. Agüero, *Soldiers, Civilians, and Democracy*.

44. López, "National Security Ideology."

45. McSherry, "Military Power, Impunity."

46. See Hunter, "Reason, Culture, or Structure?," in this volume.

47. This view of the relationship between attitudes and behavior draws heavily on the work of Lasswell, McGuire, and Abelson. See in particular Lasswell, *Power and Society*, 103–41; McGuire, "Attitudes and Attitude Change," 241–50; and Abelson, "Beliefs Are Like Possessions." On the relationship of military role beliefs and coup decisions, see Fitch, *Military Coup d'Etat*, 129–45.

48. This section draws on Fitch, *Armed Forces and Democracy*, 72–91, 136–44, 150–53. In addition to the works of Pion-Berlin, McSherry, and Norden, see López, *Ni la ceniza ni la gloria*.

49. McSherry, *Incomplete Transition*, 274, 2.

50. Data provided by Santiago Nieto, director of Informe Confidential.

Ernesto López, translated by Ian Barnett

4

Latin America
Objective and Subjective Control Revisited

Intentions

The redefinition of the relationship between civilians and the military in order to achieve some degree of subordination of the armed forces to the political powers that be has always been one of the central themes in the transition to and consolidation of democracy in Latin America.[1] The examples of such centrality are many and various: some of the best-known cases involve the four military uprisings in Argentina between March 1987 and December 1990 and the detention of General Augusto Pinochet in London and its immediate aftermath of political disruption in Chile.

Looking at the question from the civil-military point of view, transitions to democracy from authoritarian or dictatorial regimes will entail setting up processes capable of causing the military to abandon its ascendancy and autonomy both in the state and in politics, while at the same time encouraging conditions suitable for the installation of a democratic regime and the re-emergence of civilian political control over the armed forces.

The process of consolidation ensues after the replacement of an authoritarian or dictatorial (military) government with a democratic one (which in the same terms means "civilian"). One should not, however, lose sight of the fact that the term "consolidation" carries with it the implicit acknowledgment that democracy does not automatically follow from this replacement; rather, it has to be built up over time.

Neither should it be forgotten that the political relationship between civilians and military in this period of consolidation will entail as many steps backward as forward. It is a complex process in which subordination is a goal but in which the military's tendency to act autonomously is also recurrent. Quite apart from the ups and downs in any process of consolidation, when the question is examined in the medium to long term, subordination of military institutions to constitutional powers must occur to some degree for a democratic regime to be effective. Hence it emerges that the problems involved in military subordination constitute one of the most delicate and significant aspects in the evolution of stable democracies. As a result, drawing up a conceptual framework that adequately accounts for whether or not the military becomes subordinate is, far from a mere academic exercise, a crucial tool in producing workable analyses of the region's democratic processes.

As is well known, the investigation of the real world is always tackled by way of concepts. This is as inevitable as painters expressing themselves on canvas with brushes. Nevertheless, an understanding of both the natural and social worlds does not immediately present itself to either the intelligence or the senses. This complexity (vis-à-vis our human limitations) renders inescapable the need to conceptualize;[2] to trim, select, weigh, define, and characterize certain events, processes, and relationships in the real world, which for whatever reason are advanced as being more relevant or significant than others.

The central task of this chapter is to examine the well-known concept of civil-military relations and, intimately associated with it, the concept of subjective and objective civilian control on the understanding that they constitute particularly useful springboards for the study of the problems stated above. It is well known that the first person to use these concepts was Samuel Huntington in his renowned book *The Soldier and the State*.[3] The central notions of this exceptional work (in particular those which deal with subjective and objective civil control) later on served to bolster numerous works. Here, Huntington's text is reviewed with a critical eye in order to extract from it the considerable amount it has to offer.

The complementary task is to discuss Huntington's notion of power, one of the book's founding principles, alongside Max Weber's now-classic concept of domination in an attempt to throw into relief some of the rigidity the Huntingtonian model presents for the examination of the various cases in Latin America. Finally, a reconceptualization of the categories of subjective and objective control is proposed as the outcome both of this review and of the critical analysis of the experiences of the different countries in the region in the recent past. The problems involved in how civilian control is articulated with the necessary construction of legal-institutional regimes and democratic, political systems in today's Latin America are set out, and finally, the cases of Argentina and Chile are summarily examined with the aim of putting the proposed reconceptualization into practice.

The Huntingtonian Approach

As mentioned above, a very revealing conceptual frame of reference and one that is widely used in the study of the relationships among the armed forces, the state, and society was devised by Samuel Huntington around the concept of civil-military relations in his book *The Soldier and the State*. This seminal text has inspired numerous theories about civil-military relations in Latin America and the need for their restatement regarding the subordination of the military to democratic authority. As a rule, however, nobody has followed this work to the letter. As a result, it has been worn thin with successive reworking and reformulation and revised over and over again owing to its limitations in the face of Latin American realities.[4]

According to Huntington, civil-military relations are those established "between the military and the civilian environment that runs a nation" (6). This first point establishes a fairly precise field of influence for the concept: the various relational configurations that can be established between the civilians who govern a nation and its military. This concept would not be applicable to situations in which the military rules directly, though it certainly would apply to nondemocratic political regimes in which there is a civilian political administration and civilians are in charge or to communist regimes not formed as military dictatorships.[5]

The same field of influence is established in Chapter 4 of Huntington's work, in which the issues of subjective and objective civilian control are laid out. There would be no point in talking about civilian control without taking as a given that it is civilians who govern a nation. That distinguished military leaders can launch themselves into the world of politics to occupy some of the highest governmental positions is something that does not escape Huntington's discerning mind. This occurred in Weimar Germany and in the United States under General Dwight D. Eisenhower. But in these cases it was a question of men at arms becoming politicians and not climbing to the heights of power with the backing of the armed forces.

An observation of unquestionable significance by this author, and one that cannot be omitted however straightforward it may seem, is the following: the web of relationships tying civilian political leaders and the military together works as a "system of interdependent elements."[6] This means that its components tend to function in an articulated way and that, given modifications in one part, modifications in another will occur, from which it is clear that civilian-military interaction is a relational concept.

Civilian Control

The civil-military relations question is coupled with two major sets of issues in Huntington's approach. The first has to do with the degree to which civil-military relations produce national security for states. The second forks in two directions: (1) the way in which a nation's civilian leaders relate to its military and how this resolves itself and (2) the way in which this relation may have a bearing on the distribution of political power among the various actors in the political system.

If in the first set of issues, the cadre of superior officers becomes politically active, this may result in a loss of military professionalism, thus diminishing the armed forces' capacity to provide a nation with security. This, according to Huntington, is what may have happened in Germany in World War I.[7] The second set of issues forms a central knot of concepts in his approach. Huntington posits that "the essential premise for any system of civilian control is the minimization of military power" (122). To put it in a schematic and simplified way, the observation aims at solving the problem of *who* should command and more particularly of *how* they should achieve command. His general drift here is plain: it is the dimension of power that must be examined, and in Huntington's opinion, there are two routes this work should take: the subjective and the objective.

Subjective civilian control attempts to stem military power, both materially (the size of the armed forces, the resources available to them, and so on) and in the officer corps' capacity to wield its influence in the political and societal spheres. To achieve this, civilian groupings try to persuade the military to identify with their particular interests, to adhere to their points of view, or both. Thus this type of control makes "the military more civilian by turning them into the mirror of the state" (121), which in turn brings about a decline in military professionalism. On this matter Huntington says that "the essence of subjective civilian control is the denial of an independent professional sphere" (121).

Objective civilian control, in contrast, is oriented toward "the recognition of autonomous military professionalism" by trying to establish an "independent military sphere" (121). It is presumed here that a highly professional corps of officers will have the ability to subordinate themselves to the decisions and orientation of a legitimate state authority, whatever its political colors may be. Hence this type of control aims at making the military "politically sterile and neutral" (122) and at persuading it to function as an "instrument of the state" (121) instead of its mirror.

A reduction in military power brought about subjectively generates a relative increase in civilian power, but according to Huntington, it also gives rise to a new problem. In his words, "An increase in civilian power always implies an increase in power of some particular civilian group" (117). Accordingly, subjective civilian control tends to have a distorting effect on the political system insofar as it accrues power to the group (or groups) linked with the armed forces to the detriment of those not so linked. Moreover, subjective civilian control, inasmuch as it politicizes the military and therefore deprofessionalizes it, tends to lessen the armed forces' capacity to furnish the nation-state with security.

Objective civilian control, however, is perfectly capable of correcting both of these disorders. By rendering the military politically neutral, it avoids distorting the political system. And insofar as it proposes autonomous military professionalization and does not require significant reductions in the size of the armed forces, it is capable of resolving problems of national security more effectively. Accordingly, Huntington states that "objective civilian control not only reduces the power of the military to the lowest possible level as compared to civilian groupings; it also maximizes the chances of achieving military security" (123).

Professionalism, Ideology, and Power

In his historical examination of civilian control situations, Huntington proposes a typology that combines three dimensions: the level of professionalism reached by men at arms, the ideology prevailing in society or the state, and the relative power of the military. Before examining this typology, it is advisable briefly to review its component parts.

As he sees it, professionalism has three dimensions: capacity, corporateness, and social responsibility. The first of these refers to the acquisition of specialized knowledge, forms of training and drilling that distinguish some professional activities from others. The second refers both to the development of an esprit de corps and to the regulatory power over professional practices (through colleges, associations, or similar bodies) these activities normally possess. The third dimension is linked to the responsibility required by society in the exercise of a profession. A doctor, for example, is normally authorized to prescribe medicines without any external controls, and society delegates the responsibility to him or her.

For Huntington, military activity (in particular that of officers) is a professional one. In terms of capacity, it enjoys a competency peculiar to it, summarized by Harold Laswell's phrase, "the management of violence" (25). Regarding corporateness, it is a highly bureaucratized public activity, organized hierarchically and according to a strict normative code. Similarly, the functional requirements of security "lend to the officers corps the form of an autonomous social unit" (31) reinforced with special powers such as wearing uniforms or carrying arms. Last, on the subject of responsibility, Huntington states that "an officer's capacity imposes on him a special social responsibility. The illicit use of his capacity to his own ends would bring down the edifice of society" (29). Thus he adds that "his capacity can only be used to ends approved by society through its political agent, the State. . . . His responsibility toward the State is the responsibility of an expert adviser. . . . He can only explain to his client his needs in this area, give advice about how to meet them, and then, after his client has made up his mind, assist him in carrying them out" (30). From this arises the obligation to be subordinate to the political powers that be, an essential component of the Huntingtonian model of military professionalism.

Regarding the ideological dimension, he devises four ideal types that correspond to the doctrines that are "most significant in western culture" (129): liberalism, Marxism, fascism, and conservatism. This is not the place to go into them in detail, but it is appropriate to remember that, in his opinion, only conservatism is logically compatible with military values. The remaining three are, for different reasons, destined to clash with the axiological world of the military and its representations.

As regards power, Huntington manages with simple concepts. He defines it as "the capacity to control other people's behavior," and he posits that it breaks down into two dimensions: "the degree of power or, in other words, the point to which somebody's particular behavior is controlled by another, and the scope or field of power, in other words the types of behavior which are influenced by another individual or group" (124). Similarly, he believes that power exists in two forms: formal authority and informal influence.

On the basis of these definitions, he undertakes a historical analysis of civil-military relations: "The general relationships between power, professionalism and ideology make five types of differing civil-military relations possible. . . . Three of these five types allow for a high degree of professionalism and objective civilian control; the other two presuppose a low level of professionalism and subjective civilian control" (137). In a nutshell, these are as follows:

1. Antimilitary ideology, high military political power, and low military professionalism. In this category he situates the cases of the Near East, Asia, and Latin America, as well as that of Germany during World War I (because the military's excessive political participation eventually damages its professionalism) and the United States during World War II.
2. Antimilitary ideology, low military political power, and low military

professionalism. In this category he places Germany in World War II[8] and, generically speaking, modern totalitarian states.

3. Antimilitary ideology, low military political power, and high military professionalism. This would apply to the United States from the rise of military professionalism until World War II.

4. Promilitary ideology, high military political power, and high military professionalism. As Huntington sees it, the best example of this model of civil-military relations is that of Prussia and Germany in the days of Bismarck and Moltke (1860–90).

5. Promilitary ideology, low military political power, and high military professionalism. The case of Great Britain in the twentieth century is the key paradigm here.

This is as far as Huntington's conceptualization goes. His use of the concept of power is conspicuous throughout. The Latin American experience in the last fifty years, however, throws doubts on his application.

The Discrepancy between the Huntingtonian Approach and the Latin American Historical Experience

There are three levels on which the Latin American historical experience distances itself considerably from the Huntingtonian model. The first of these is the validity of the principle of subordination. Almost all the historical cases examined by Huntington (barring his general mention of Latin America, the Near East, and Asia in the first of the above types) show a clear tendency toward the military's subordination to the civilian powers. From this evidence is deduced the statement with which he begins his book: the relationship is between the military and the civilian forces that govern a nation. This is self-evident, but although his prose is subdued on this point, it is also categorical: government *is* by civilians. Men at arms, as citizens and *not* as soldiers, may from time to time occupy governmental positions. This conviction turns Huntington's proposition into a *given*: it is a fact that civilians govern nations. What eludes his analysis (probably because it did not come within the bounds of the visible, historical events that served as a basis for his conceptualization) is the notion that the military may govern nations.

Latin America clearly presents other historical forms. Almost without exception, what has distinguished the region during the course of the twentieth century has been *military interventionism* and not subordination to civilian will. Rather than subordination being a fact, the recurrent tendency in the region has been for the military to launch itself again and again onto the political stage. This excessive intervention in politics inevitably damages or shatters the prevailing legal equilibrium. Its best-known avatar is the coup d'état, but it is not the only one. The military has also played a variety of excessive roles such as "the power behind the throne"; a *moderating role* in Stepan's well-known conceptualization, according to which the military came to the defense of Brazil's political system between 1945 and 1964 whenever it considered itself overwhelmed by the clashes occurring in the political system;[9] or, as a guarantor, a tutelary role, as happened in Argentina between 1955 and 1966 and perhaps is still the case in today's Chile.

Things being as they are, no analysis of civilian control can base itself on the axiom that civilian control occurs in a natural or normal way in Latin American political systems. Therefore, this axiom cannot be elevated to the rank of premise on a general conceptual plane.

The second level on which one must inevitably underscore the differences between Huntington's approach and the course of Latin American history is that of the military sector's relative power and the nature of its potentially autonomous actions. No matter how much power the armed forces may gather unto themselves in Huntington's schema, they are always subordinate to some civilian grouping. They are a *mirror*, as he rightly points out. He does acknowledge in his finely tuned inquiries into real historical situations that the military may become powerful and autonomous (as was the case in Japan from the onset of military professionalization to the end of World War II) despite being subordinated to a pattern of subjective civilian control.

In Latin America things have happened differently. The armed forces have had and still have a strong tendency toward total or unconditional autonomy. There are plentiful examples of this in Argentina, Brazil, Chile, and Peru as well as in the majority of Central American countries. To account for this situation, Latin American analysts have preferred to use the concept of *autonomization*.[10] In my own work, I have used it to refer to the high degree of independence from society and public figures that military institutions have enjoyed as regards their performance and decisions, their capacity for defining on their own terms missions, goals, doctrines, and modes of relation with the world of politics. This capacity sooner or later makes them politically powerful actors when compared to their civilian counterparts.[11]

Given the high degree of total or unconditional military autonomy evident throughout Latin American history, no analysis can presuppose that Huntington's subjective route, which aimed at turning military institutions into a mirror and thus politicizing them, leads by definition to civilian control. Neither is it feasible to suppose that the objective route, which encourages professional autonomy but not at the expense of military power, will by definition redound to civilian control.

The third level on which one must underscore these differences is that of professionalism. For all the foregoing reasons, one aspect of professionalism in the Latin American context leaves much to be desired: the level of social responsibility. It is obvious that military interventionism in politics violates this principle. The following question arises: If professionalism depends on three conditions, what happens if one of these is not met satisfactorily? Is the result the same if one, two, or three of these variables are unfulfilled? Apart from the problem of logical consistency that this question contains, Latin American realities underscore the fact that the application of a typological schema constructed on the basis of Huntington's three proposed dimensions (the relative power of the military, the predominant ideology in society, and the level of military professionalism) lacks any meaning. Abundant historical experience demonstrates that in this region, the military tends not to fit this model of subordination. It thus can be deduced that this schema would be inappropriate for any historical examination of civilian control in the region since one basic assumption underlying it—the tendency toward military subordination—is not fulfilled.

Power, Domination, and Civil-Military Relations

As has been shown, Huntington's formulation rules out total or unconditional military autonomization, as it does military governance. It follows that this schema implicitly entertains the idea that the military *agrees* to being subordinated: positing subordination as a *fact* presupposes acceptance of a prior consensus between the actors involved for this to come about. As a result, his analysis of the interaction between relative power, professionalism, and ideology takes place within a basic consensual framework: the military *does not* govern nations itself.

For Huntington, there is a consensual substratum (military subordination as a given) on the basis of which a power play unfolds. Latin American problems demand an inversion of Huntington's model in which power constitutes the substratum on which consensus must be built. Consequently, power-shaping events (glaring examples are the 1982 Malvinas defeat in Argentina, the No's victory in the 1988 Chilean plebiscite, and the serene supremacy of an armed forces that chose liberalization and oversaw the transition in Brazil without any mishaps) decisively conditioned transitions to democracy and served (as they still do) as the groundwork on which the search for consensual civilian control unfolded. Since the historical starting points are different, they demand an adjustment in one's conceptual starting points.

In Latin America, as has been laid out in the previous section, there has not been any basic historical consensus over military subordination to the public powers that be. This absence is perhaps the most important determining factor in military interventionism, unconditional autonomy, and deficient professionalism. All things being equal, consensus building will clearly be a sine qua non for the development of the kind of civil-military relations that will make civilian control possible. One could in exceptional circumstances resort to power or, in other words, work to reduce the military's influence to a minimum, thus ruling out any chance that it might be able to launch itself into the political arena. Or the armed forces could even withdraw themselves directly, as has happened in Costa Rica and more recently in Panama. But for historical reasons I will not go into now, this is not a viable alternative for the vast majority of countries in the region.

Weber Revisited

The most appropriate general frame of reference for handling issues on consensus and political action remains, in my opinion, the one outlined by the well-known German sociologist Max Weber in *Economy and Society*. Weber distinguished between power ("the likelihood of imposing one's own will in a social relationship against all resistance") and domination ("the likelihood of finding obedience to an order with a definite content").[12] It is clear here that the former is bound up with imposition and the latter with consent. Consequently, both are linked to completely different realms of social action.

As Weber sees it, "the concept of power is sociologically amorphous"[13] because it refers to a set of issues with hardly any relief or nuance and considerably less rich in detail than the concept of domination. Insofar as domination involves "a minimum of will to obedience or, to put it another way, an interest in obeying," this is much more substantial. It is this interest in obeying that constitutes one of the keys to the concept of domination. Weber warns that obedience can be the result of various factors: economic interests, habit, and so on; but he also notes that a degree of conformity is constantly present in relationships involving domination. In his words, "From experience, no form of domination is willing to have purely material motives as the probable basis of its persistence. . . . Rather, it tries to foment belief in its legitimacy."[14] In other words, a minimum of conviction ("belief") must again be present.

It is advisable to note that Weber's interest in distinguishing between these two dimensions (power and domination) is an exclusively analytical one. It is simply a heuristic resource (as are most Weberian conceptualizations as a rule) that tells us nothing about the nature of any particular historical process. In other words, in a given reality, practices and institutions that blend or combine different forms from both dimensions may coexist.

On what grounds must the construction of a consensus about conditions of high interventionism, total autonomy, and professionalism deficient in social responsibility take place? Answering this question requires an examination of another of Huntington's initial propositions. He argues lucidly that civil-military relations form a system of interdependent elements. What happens in any one of the system's components reverberates in another. Shifts and transformations in any one part will bring about alterations in other parts.

Civil-military relations in Latin America have on the whole been characterized by the combination of *excesses* and *defects* in this interrelated system. Subordination has been hit doubly hard: from one side by interventionism, autonomy, and insufficient professionalism; from the other by the limitations and the repeated capitulation of the political classes (an example of this was Fujimori's *autogolpe*). On one side, the excessive behavior of the military has tended to prevail, while on the other, there has been the inconsistent, permissive, and even obliging conduct on the part of the politicians.

Subordination requires the obedience of the military but also responsibility from the politicians in command. The most clearly recognizable facet of the Latin American experience is military disobedience, as expressed in the various manifestations of the coup d'état and the search for privilege or autonomy even in fairly democratic contexts, a clear case being Chile. A lack of civilian responsibility, however, has been just as frequent an occurrence as military "nonobedience." When a civilian's duty to assume command is not fulfilled, "de facto nonsubordination" occurs; the absence of a mandate undermines the leader's authority and the commitment of those who should obey it. Politicians are perceptibly lagging behind in assuming a position of leadership toward the armed forces. It is almost as if they suddenly realize they have a command obligation just when the situation becomes critical but not beyond it. Thus several attempts by the military to assert its autonomy and privilege were suppressed during Raúl Alfonsín's government (1983–89) and in the early part of Carlos Menem's administration (1989–99). Military "excesses" were subdued, and in their place developed a healthy tendency among military chiefs to consent to subordination. But political leadership was still lacking. Thus, to build a consensus, changes must occur in the military's awareness, self-perception, values, education, and doctrine *and* in the politicians' willingness to draw up and enact a mandate.

Bearing in mind the issues outlined so far and using the Weberian notion of domination, I propose the following conceptualization, which brings together both the critical comments made about Huntington's schema in light of Latin American historical experience and the broad theoretical outline expounded above.

Subjective civilian control must be understood as an attempt to draw up, attain, and sustain military subordination to public authority on the basis of the uniformed classes' particularistic adherence to some civilian public group or sector. This adherence could, among other things, be founded on the coincidence or similarity of opinions; personal loyalty; material, institutional, or individual expediency; and accords.

Objective civilian control must be understood as an attempt to draw up, attain, and sustain military subordination to public authority based on rational/legal legitimization.[15] In this case the obedience of the military is the fruit of its attachment to the letter of the law. The uniformed classes owe allegiance to public authority because an abstract and impersonal normative order respected by all its citizens applies. This order, among other things, is what ordains that the armed forces be subordinated to the state's political management.

I use the word *attempt* deliberately in both definitions because I realize, as I have established above for Latin America, that obedience (or subordination) is a result and not a postulate, a goal that must be reached and not a premise.

The Legal-Institutional Regime, Political System, and Civil-Military Relations

If one admits that the quest for a form of military subordination that would overcome the disagreements of the past depends on consensus building, one may wonder under what general conditions such construction should take place and which of the proposed alternatives (subjective or objective control) would be the best to adopt.

In Latin America (particularly in those countries undergoing democratization subsequent to the dark days of military dictatorship), the construction of the kind of civil-military relations that would ensure a model of military subordination should run parallel to the construction of a democratic political regime and a democratic political system; in other words, the building of a legal-institutional regime (also a republican order)[16] and the practices, organizations, and identities that develop are strengthened and operate inside the legal-institutional framework, which I will refer to as a *political system*.

A legal-institutional regime is normally based on a constitution and a set of constitutionally congruent laws that give representative democracy a juridical, ethical, and normative grounding. Within this set of laws, those that govern political life (representation, the electoral regime, and so on) are especially significant in terms of the question being examined here. Political systems are social constructs; they result from social practices and the play of institutions that include but go beyond the conduct of politicians and soldiers. While political systems usually operate within the juridical bounds laid down by the legal-institutional regime, circumstances within the system could give rise to regime changes.

Thus civil-military relations are but one facet of this multidimensional system, which includes specific types of political parties, relationships between governors and the governed, and patterns of demand articulation. The opportunities for civilian control will vary with the terms set by a legal-institutional regime and the evolution of the political system and its actors. It may be that the legal-institutional regime contains safeguards that protect the military's autonomy and thus neutralize civilian control efforts. Or it may be that in the attempt to build up control, the political leadership of a country fails to use regime resources at its disposal. The first is the case in present-day Chile, the second, in Argentina, both of which I will come back to later.

Let us turn to the second issue brought up at the beginning of this section: whether a system of objective rather than subjective civilian control (as redefined in Weberian terms above) provides a more solid foundation for the construction of civilian control. It would appear that the objective form is preferable for two reasons. First, military subordination based on obedience that stems from conviction is qualitatively superior to one deriving exclusively from "purely material motives," as Weber put it. The German sociologist believed that domination could not be sustained on material grounds but rather needed a more secure base, namely its own legitimization. In his view, conviction (a belief in legitimacy) is better grounds for obedience than self-interest (although for Weber this was a question of degree and not of mutually exclusive options).[17]

Because the system of objective civilian control rests in part on military convictions regarding the legitimacy of those who rule legally, it is a more secure and longer-lasting means of building consensus about subordination. The system of subjective civilian control, in contrast, runs the risk of becoming circumstantial and episodic: "Purely material and goal-oriented rational reasons imply here as everywhere, a relatively fragile relationship," as Weber saw it.[18] There are no assurances that enhanced corporate interests or administrative benefits can be bartered for compliance; commitments in this area are inevitably uncertain. In Argentina, for example, a military Restructuring Law (Ley de Reestructuración) stipulating a gradual, almost 30 percent increase in the military budget over five years was passed in 1998. Since then, as the result of a recession and a decline in tax-collecting capacity on the part of the state, military budgets have actually declined in absolute terms.

Other particularistic reasons for advocating support of subjective civilian control, such as personal loyalty, do not offer many guarantees either. It is enough to witness how the once-strong link between former Argentine president Carlos Menem and the *carapintada* colonel Mohamed Alí Seineldín quickly dissolved in the midst of the December 1990 military uprising.[19] Taken too far, subjective methods of control based on fidelity between politicians and soldiers have brought political systems dangerously close to the brink of military interventionism. One is reminded of the vastly popular phrase, "to dream of one's very own general (or colonel at least)," an allusion to the politician's misplaced desire for a military confidant. In relying on and confiding in "his general," he ends up solidifying the military's power more than his own.

But the system of objective civilian control is also more suitable for another reason. It is the system that best connects with the construction of a rational / legal democratic (republican) order. Such an order, predicated on consensus, requires that the primary foundation of its legitimacy rest on a belief in the legality of the established regulations and the right to command of those who are called on to exercise legal authority. All of this is based precisely on those arrangements laid down by Weber for every legitimate, rational domination.[20] Constitutional laws and other laws make up a universe of impersonal, abstract rules that in principle apply to all citizens. These rules enshrine the founding principles and procedures of representative democracy: sovereign power, the division of powers, the periodicity of terms of office, periodical elections, and so on.

In this context those who govern do so according to these impersonal, abstract rules, and the governed obey "the law." As citizens themselves, members of the armed forces must be subordinate to the public powers that be. It is the civilian leaders who are responsible for the political management of defense and therefore of the armed forces. Given that this order holds sway and they must comply with the law as any citizen or institution in a republic must, the armed forces owe subordination to the constitutional authorities, whatever the political color of those in power. If one observes the definition of objective civilian control propounded above, the resemblance between what has just been raised and the problems alluded to in this definition becomes clear. What follows is its greater aptness for building up subordination.

All in all, if civilian control is something to be constructed in Latin America, it will be because (1) it takes the form of regulations and practices performed by politicians and the military tailored to the exercising of this control and (2) the construction of legal-institutional regimes and political systems that contribute to establishing a democracy without limitations or deformations is completed. When these two conditions have been satisfied, perhaps subordination will become a given, as in Huntington's schema.

Argentina and Chile

To put the categories and conceptual insights just formulated into action, the cases of Chile and Argentina will now be briefly examined. These cases will not provide exhaustive explanations but will instead illustrate how the definitions and concepts heretofore presented might work in practice.

Like no other country in Latin America, Chile sets forth the dilemma of a political class (strictly speaking, a coalition in the government) seeking to strengthen its predominance and control over military institutions from inside a deficiently democratic legal-institutional regime. It is common knowledge that both transition and consolidation in Chile have developed within the framework of a regime that placed restrictions on republican principles and allowed the armed forces to play a tutelary role.[21] General Pinochet's 1980 Constitution is still in force, even though it has been amended. The so-called *leyes de amarre* (literally, "mooring laws"),[22] aimed at maintaining the military's autonomy and its capacity for political control, still hold sway. Modification of the Constitution and its "mooring laws" requires special majorities in Parliament—an extremely difficult task for the government coalition given the present electoral regime, which has allowed the political right to hold a percentage of seats disproportional to its actual strength. So the safeguards imposed by the military in the legal-institutional regime limit opportunities for the construction of civilian control regardless of how resolute the Chilean leadership is in asserting this control.

As a result, a situation is taking shape in Chile rarely seen on the Latin American stage: on one side of the fence, a military maintaining its autonomy and sheltered by a restrictive legal-institutional regime while at the same time bolstered by a minority of the electorate; and on the other side, a constrained government coalition that is equally persistent in its desire to achieve civilian control. In the final analysis, it might be said that attempts at gaining civilian control collide with the regulations of a deficiently developed republican order and with the political will of an electoral minority. Under these conditions it is inadequate to speak of civilian control in any one of its variants (subjective or objective) because what is in dispute is the mere possibility of that civilian control.

Developments in the national and international political system could surmount this situation, however. A hemispheric context that is auspicious for the development of democracy coupled with the maturity of the Chilean political class could give rise to a reform of the legal-institutional regime that would make possible some form of effective civilian control. Obviously, time and history will always have the last word.

On the contrary, a nonrestrictive legal-institutional regime was reestablished in Argentina because of the military's scant capacity to influence the transition after its defeat in the Malvinas. The military had no safeguards, nor could it effectively resort to stonewalling tactics. From the point of view of the legal-institutional regime, nothing stood in the way of the advance toward civilian control.

This ideal situation was disturbed between April 1987 and December 1990, however, when four military uprisings led by middle-ranking officers (the *carapintadas*) occurred. It was not just these acts of insubordination that were so disquieting but the actions chosen by the political leadership responsible for defense. Raúl Alfonsín's government was inclined toward subjective civilian control,[23] as evinced by the appointment of chiefs of staff (Generals Ríos Ereñú and Dante Caridi among others) based on ideological affinities rather than professional merits. These measures proved counterproductive, and the policies in general exhibited delays and discontinuities that suggested a failure to command the armed forces. Thus, while Argentina has registered greater legal-institutional advances than Chile, its politicians have underutilized the resources and opportunities available to them.

The course of time and political action have gradually removed obstacles (especially those concerning the military's responsibility for crimes committed during the so-called dirty war) to the establishment of even minimally adequate civilian-military relations. President Menem, who succeeded Alfonsín, could begin to occupy himself with the military's professional needs. Thus, contrary to Alfonsín, he privileged professional merits over political or ideological positions in the selection of his military chiefs. In part this occurred because the Menem government demonstrated a somewhat stronger preference for objective civilian control.

Conclusion

Since the book's appearance in 1957, Samuel Huntington's *The Soldier and the State* and, in particular, his conceptions of civilian-military relations and civilian control have become unavoidable reference points for studies of the relationship between the armed forces, the state, and society. But Latin America's peculiar historical traits call for not only an attentive rereading of Huntington's text but a reworking of his concepts as well. Military subordination to the civilian political powers that be is not deeply ingrained in this region. Quite the contrary, it is repeatedly absent and must be constructed and cultivated.

As the foundations for military subordination are constructed so too must they be for the legal-institutional regimes and the democratic political systems of which civil-military relations are a part. The restoration of republican orders and political systems in line with them is unavoidable because the current processes of democratization began as the conclusion of military dictatorships. Both constructions must be based on actions of a consensual nature. It is difficult to imagine sustaining a republican regime on an authoritarian basis. In the same way, it is also difficult to think that civilian control might for any length of time rely on imposition and not on consent.

All these circumstances demand an inversion of Huntington's point of view. Steeped in the historical experiences of the United States and Western Europe, his treatise considered subordination as a given and thus quickly turned its attention toward other issues: making civilian control consistent with national security and stopping civilian control from causing distortions in the political system. With subordination as a fact, Huntington worked these problems from the viewpoint of power, as we have seen. The necessary inversion advocated here privileges the concept of consensus. Thus this chapter has attempted to redefine subjective and objective civilian control from the vantage point of consent and not imposition or, in Weber's terms, domination and not power. Similarly, it has shown that the "consensual" definition of civilian control allows us to grapple with a relatively unidentified but frequently occurring facet of civilian-military relations in Latin America: the political class's failure to assume command. If subordination is not a given, neither is the leadership's ability to wrestle with the military question.

The briefly outlined cases of Chile and Argentina demonstrate the problems of simultaneously constructing a legal-institutional regime, political system, and civilian control. Without legal-institutional regimes and political systems that give shape to unfettered democracies and without a political class willing to assert its lawful authority over the military, it will be difficult to pursue the option of objective civilian control. For this reason, either we will be navigating through murky institutional waters or we will be resorting to subjective civilian control with all the uncertainties that have accompanied it.

There is a clear affinity between this chapter's central assertions and a key point made in the volume's Introduction regarding subjective analyses. If we are to understand the potential for longer-term continuity in relations between soldiers and politicians, we must cut below the political surface to explore the depths to which the military does or does not *believe* in civilian control. Only a military compliance rooted in conviction offers the basis for more lasting forms of subordination. Soldiers must come to believe in the efficacy of the legal-institutional order of which they are a part. They must also be persuaded that those executive political figures bestowed with legal authority to command the armed forces are prepared to wield that authority. It is on the basis of such firmly held beliefs (and not material interests) that the consensus necessary to sustain a stable civil-military relation can emerge.

Finally, I wish to point out that I do not believe (as so many others from Protagoras to Isaiah Berlin do) that the explanation of historical matters has a final theoretical resolution. I would consequently like what has been expressed here to be taken as one starting point among other possible ones, as a front door that gives access to "the incalculable and enigmatic reality" (as Jorge Luis Borges once wrote) in order to study its singularity, its uniqueness, its one-and-onliness.

NOTES

Translator's note: Quotations from English-language authors have been translated into English from Spanish versions. This may in places give rise to discrepancies between the English of original texts and that of the versions to be found in this translation. Spanish titles are in the original language.

1. The concepts of *transition* and *consolidation* are used here following Guillermo O'Donnell's definitions. From his point of view, transition is to be taken as the "interval which stretches between one political regime and another." More specifically, O'Donnell goes on to add that "transitions are demarcated on the one hand by the initial steps toward the dissolution of the authoritarian regime and, on the other, by the establishment of some form of democracy, a return to some kind of authoritarian regime or the emergence of a revolutionary alternative." After the emplacement of a new regime (especially when this is a democracy), the use of the term *consolidation* is essential. See O'Donnell, Schmitter, and Whitehead, *Transiciones desde un gobierno autoritario*, 19.

2. In *El mundo como voluntad y representación*, the German philosopher Arthur Schopenhauer has left us some memorable ideas and arguments about the inevitability of representing the world through concepts. (See especially the opening pages.)

3. This chapter refers to the first Spanish version of Huntington's book, *El soldado y el estado*, published in Buenos Aires in 1964 by the Argentinean Officers' Library of the Argentinean Military Circle (Biblioteca del Oficial del Círculo Militar Argentino). The page numbers for quotations from this book are given in parentheses in the text.

4. References to Huntington's conceptualization can be found in one form or another in many works, too numerous to list here. His conceptualization figures in almost all the latest works published in the United States, including Fitch, *Armed Forces and Democracy*; Hunter, *Eroding Military Influence*; McSherry, *Incomplete Transition*; Norden, *Military Rebellion in Argentina*; and Pion-Berlin, *Through Corridors of Power*.

5. In collaboration with Zbigniew Brzezinski, Huntington applied the concept of the civilian-military relationship to the comparative study of the former Soviet Union and the United States. See their excellent *Poder Político U.S.A.-U.R.S.S.*

6. Huntington, *El soldado y el estado*, 10.

7. See ibid., 138. The excess of political participation on the part of members of the military, who were very prestigious in Wilhelmine Germany, might have led to overmilitarization in the political management of the war and to an overestimation of Germany's military capacity. This situation may in the end have proved fatal because the German military's setting of unattainable goals hastened its defeat in war.

8. In the case of Germany, the clash between fascist ideology and military ethics acts as the trigger for a low level of professionalization. This clash manifested itself tangibly in the splits between Hitler and the high command of the armed forces. The latter tended to oppose the former's will to expansionism. Hitler, moreover, glorified war and believed himself to be in possession of a fundamental truth. In reply to his high command's skepticism and cautiousness and to impose his own designs, Hitler manipulated command positions and used perks and corruption to "soften up" the higher-ranking officers while infiltrating the middle and lower ranks.

9. See Stepan, *Brasil*, 67–71.

10. See, among others, Fitch, *Armed Forces and Democracy*; López, *Ni la ceniza ni la gloria*; Pion-Berlin, "Military Autonomy"; and Varas, *La autonomía militar en América Latina*.

11. See, for example, López, "Argentina 1991," 158–59.

12. Weber, *Economía y sociedad*, 43.

13. Ibid., 43.

14. Ibid., 170.

15. On the concepts of *legitimacy* and *rationality/legality*, see ibid., 170–80.

16. In political debate at the end of the eighteenth century and during a good deal of the nineteenth, the concept of republic was used as a synonym for representative democracy. Such was the case with Madison, who differentiated it from pure or direct democracy (see Hamilton, Madison, and Jay, *El Federalista*, 39). A republican order, in my opinion, presupposes representative democracy, implies the existence of a state, is based on the law, and is deployed as a legal code functioning as a pyramidal structure after Hans Kelse's well-known image.

17. Weber, *Economía y sociedad*, 171.

18. Ibid., 170.
19. See Saín, *Los levantamientos carapintadas*, 170–76.
20. Weber, *Economía y sociedad*, 172.
21. See, among others, Arriagada, *Por la razón o por la fuerza*, 267–73, and Valenzuela, "La Constitución de 1980," 26–30.
22. See Valenzuela, "La Constitución de 1980," 26–28.
23. See López, "Argentina 1991," 166–72.

Deborah L. Norden

5

The Organizational Dynamics of Militaries and Military Movements
Paths to Power in Venezuela

On 4 February 1992, Lieutenant Colonel Hugo Chávez Frias helped lead a dramatic and popular coup attempt in Venezuela. The coup failed. Seven years later, on 4 February 1999, an inaugural parade celebrated the installation of a newly elected president, retired Lieutenant Colonel Hugo Chávez Frias. Chávez failed to gain power militarily, despite his apparent popularity, yet he succeeded dramatically at the polls, when success required many more supporters. Why?

To answer this question, this chapter will explore the roles of two forms of organization in military movements: (1) the organization that serves as the context for a military movement, the military bureaucracy, and (2) the movement organization, as it develops from a conspiratorial to a more popular movement. The nature of these different organizations and their relations to the surrounding society can help explain the evolution of Chávez's movement, the (Movimiento Bolivariano Revolucionario), and the contrasting outcomes of Chávez's quests for power. In the Venezuelan case, the two organizations—military bureaucracy and military movement—differed considerably in form, organization, and function. The military movement was born from the armed forces and initially sought to gain power by conquering its "host" organization. Failing this, the MBR sought to gain power through a different method, recruiting the support of the society. I argue that Chávez's contrasting insurrectional and political fortunes were at least in part a consequence of organizational factors. With respect to the military bureaucracy, the established organization provided a propitious atmosphere for the birth of the new movement but offered a less welcoming home for its continued advance. This situation helped propel the new movement into the political arena. To succeed in this new arena, however, the movement would need to adapt to the requirements of a broader public. Chávez's movement proved capable of doing so largely because of the combination of two factors: (1) the fortunate popular resonance of the movement's stated goals and (2) the movement's ability to retain a consistent project while adopting a flexible discourse.

The chapter begins with an analysis of these two forms of organizations, military bureaucracies and military movement organizations, looking at the nature of these organizations and how they may alternately provide or prevent paths to power. The term "movement organization" may appear contradictory, as social movements are generally presumed to lack an organizational structure. Military movements, however, integrate both the more fluid, amorphous characteristics of a social movement and organizational components, especially at the center. The nature of this core organization evolves as leaders attempt to define and redefine the movement's goals and, concomitantly, to attract the appropriate support to, and within, the movement. Thus, in this chapter I use organization theory, as well as some of the social movement literature, to provide insight into the origins and transformation of military movements. I then turn to the Venezuelan case, looking at the organization of Venezuela's military bureaucracy and the origins, evolution, and transformation of Chávez's military movement.

Variations in Organizations

Under most circumstances, it would appear that carrying out a coup d'état would be much simpler than winning an election at the polls. Certainly the number of active supporters required is considerably more for the legal than the illegal approach. Successful coups require primarily passive or cautious neutrality, both by members of the military and members of society; they do not require an explicit demonstration of support by the majority (or plurality) of voters. But neither winning over an existing organization nor successfully creating a new one is a question of mere popularity. Organizations vary, and the methods that work to progress within them—or to defeat them—vary as well. An established military bureaucracy and a new military movement are vastly different organizational forms.

According to W. Richard Scott, all organizations share certain similarities, having to do with their nature as goal-oriented social structures: "All must define (and redefine) their objectives; all must induce participants to contribute services; all must control and coordinate these contributions; resources must be garnered from the environment and products or services dispensed; participants must be selected, trained, and replaced; and some sort of working accommodation with the neighbors must be achieved."[1] In addition, there are vast differences among organizations. The military, as a large, permanent bureaucracy of the state, has some guarantee of personnel and resources, highly developed rules to regulate internal behavior and ensure control, and more functionally defined goals (goals involve fulfilling a function or providing a regular service). Given the high probability that the organization will continue, less adaptation to the environment is required. The infrequency with which militaries are called on to exercise their primary function—defending the country—reinforces this tendency toward bureaucratic insulation and sluggishness. In contrast, an incipient voluntary organization—like a military movement—must be very sensitive to its environment and will likely have relatively undeveloped rules and structures, no reliable means for recruiting personnel and resources, and, using Mayer Zald and Michael Berger's term, more "*purposive goals.*"[2]

These differences imply that the concerns and structures of the two organizational forms are likely to differ. An established bureaucracy is more likely to function as a "rational" organization, "oriented to the pursuit of relatively specific goals and exhibiting relatively highly formalized social structures."[3] For the sake of efficiency, as well as the security of those at the top, hierarchy becomes a central attribute of the organization and internal control a key focus. In this model, those at the top make any key decisions about organizational goals and their implementation, while those further down enjoy little discretion and are charged primarily with executing orders. The nature of the model prevents a high level of flexibility with respect to either structure or goals. At the same time, though, when carrying out its expected tasks and functions, a "rational" organization is designed to respond quickly to the commands of its senior officials. This feature is both its strength and its weakness, as will be discussed.

New movements may originate around the pursuit of particular goals, but as organizations, they cannot concentrate solely on the attainment of those goals. Leaders must also ensure the movement's survival. Thus leaders concentrate on organizing, recruiting participants, and directing the group's activities in such a way that the originating goals *could* eventually be pursued. These organizations thus function more as "natural" systems. According to this perspective, "the structural features and programs of the organization . . . [change] over time in response to changing conditions."[4] With survival primary and by no means guaranteed, organizations adapt to their environments, changing their structures and modifying their discourse over time. In sum, while a bureaucracy seeks to sustain itself and its position, a military movement seeks to achieve a position.

Organizational Dynamics of Military Bureaucracies

The professional military approaches Weber's ideal-type of a "rational" bureaucracy at least as much as any other modern organization. Yet militaries stand alone in one particular way: only they execute coups. Control, therefore, becomes a central element in the design of militaries and civil-military relations, so much so that organizational "rationality"—structuring an organization to maximize efficiency in goal achievement—may, in some instances, be set aside. This section will explore the parallels between Weber's model of the rational modern bureaucracy and military institutions. It will assess the extent to which militaries are "rational" organizations and the ways in which the complexity, missions, and external contacts of militaries may still generate problems with control. In particular, I will look at the means through which the military structure can be used to subvert control of the organization and some of the methods that have been adopted to prevent this outcome. I propose that a high level of rationality is both an advantage and a disadvantage for civilian control of the military. A highly rational military structure does not *encourage* military insurrection, but it does *facilitate* it. In contrast, a less rational organization may encourage dissenting movements, but it may also block their success.

Weber's model of the rational bureaucracy is calculated to maximize efficiency in goal achievement. The bureaucracy is portrayed as a finely tuned machine, in which each part performs carefully delimited tasks in order to fulfill the organization's central functions. According to Weber, the requirements for a modern bureaucracy include (1) "the principle of official *jurisdictional areas*, which are generally ordered by rules, that is, by laws or administrative regulations"; (2) hierarchy, with superior offices overseeing subordinate offices; (3) office management "based upon written documents," with support of a staff; (4) specialized training of officials; and (5) office management based on "*general rules*, which are more or less stable, more or less exhaustive, and which can be learned."[5] In other words, Weber's "rational" modern bureaucracy is presumed to be highly hierarchical, based on a system of formal, established rules and specialization of training and tasks. Advancement is also expected to occur along predictable lines, with officials progressing in rank based on seniority and merit.[6]

The Military Organization and Weberian Bureaucracy

Modern militaries tend to be structured as rational organizations, emphasizing hierarchy, formal rules, and division of labor. At least in theory, most modern militaries also have careful procedures for ensuring seniority and merit-based promotions. Such a structure should allow strict top-down control, emanating from a political strata that is organizationally superordinate to the military leadership, and should result in an organization capable of efficiently pursuing the military's national defense and security goals.

Of Weber's bureaucratic elements, hierarchy stands out most clearly as a characteristic of modern militaries. As Jacques Van Doorn writes, "Hierarchy is the backbone of all military performance of all rights and duties, and of the entire process of all personnel allocation."[7] Organizational diagrams tend to depict near classic pyramids, with senior officers occupying the pinnacle and enlisted personnel at the base of the triangle. Military personnel not only are assigned offices according to rank but also wear their ranks on their uniforms and attach their ranks to their names. Obedience stands out as one of the first requirements in a military institution—a necessity for an organization designed to fight wars. Personnel are thus assigned to a limited domain, responsible to those directly above them in the chain of command.

The structure of modern militaries also includes Weber's model of specialized areas of competence. Far from a collection of interchangeable individuals, modern militaries are divided into a variety of specializations, beginning with the traditional division of army, navy, and air force. Specialists in nonmilitary areas—that is, such professionals as engineers, medical doctors, and lawyers—may also be incorporated into the armed forces, but because of their lack of expertise in the management of force, they remain relatively peripheral to the central power structure. Thus, while expertise does tend to create some degree of autonomy and discretion, these professionals do not pose any real problem for internal control. As will be discussed, other forms of specialization can be less innocuous for cohesion and control.

Modern militaries also follow elaborate written rules and administrative procedures. These may begin with benchmark guidelines set forth in a national constitution. From there, a body of laws and regulations tends to detail everything from military missions to training, personnel policies, uniforms, pensions, security procedures, and forms for documents. In other words, the vast majority of behavior in a modern military is likely to be based on a formal set of rules—probably too vast for any individual to know in its entirety but theoretically obtainable.

Finally, the modern military incorporates, at least in principle, personnel policies based on seniority and merit. Officers are generally admitted through a competitive system of examinations, following which they are given extensive training, usually by the organization itself (depending on the military's capacity, some officers may be sent to military schools abroad). With respect to professional advancement, most militaries use elaborate procedures for evaluating personnel and determining who may be promoted. A certain number of years may be required in a rank, with additional educational requirements for some steps.

This ideal-typical rational military would presumably minimize the possibilities for a coup because such practices as fair personnel policies and decision-making patterns that confine politics to the top strata would limit the motivation for insurgency. Coup prevention in a "rational military" thus coincides with Samuel Huntington's classic model of "objective" civilian control. Objective control relies on differentiating military and civilian responsibilities, accomplishing "its end by militarizing the military, making them a tool of the state."[8] Thus the military would carry out solely military functions, exercising considerable autonomy in the execution of its duties. This separation of political and military duties, according to Huntington, would make the armed forces less prone to political interference. The problem with the objective control model is that while it may encourage the military to focus on military questions, it does not necessarily provide the oversight that would allow for more meaningful control.[9] Differentiating functions can also mean granting the military considerable autonomy on defense matters and limiting political leadership in this area. Furthermore, with a fully rational model, the political leadership and military organization may be poorly equipped to combat an insurgent movement *were* it to arise.

Limits to Rationality and Control in Modern Militaries

Most militaries nonetheless do deviate somewhat from Weber's tightly knit model of the rational bureaucracy. Challenges emanate particularly from two areas: competing sources of authority and contacts with the external environment. Both of these areas potentially disturb cohesion and control within the military, which make political leaders inclined to pursue other—sometimes counterrational—means of ensuring control.

To begin with, large, complex organizations tend to suffer from competing sources of authority. According to Herbert Simon, " 'Authority' may be defined as the power to make decisions which guide the actions of another. It is a relationship between two individuals, one 'superior,' and the other 'subordinate.' "[10] The intrinsic diversification and specialization that occur in complex organizations, however, mean that subordinate personnel will inevitably possess information and knowledge not shared by their superiors. Those with positions of power therefore may not always be able to exercise their official authority. As Simon explains, "An individual who does not have a recognized status, or who is not recognized by his associates as expert with respect to a certain kind of knowledge will have a more difficult time convincing his listeners that a recommendation is sound than one who possesses the credentials of 'expertness.' "[11] This imbalance between official authority and expertise has been referred to as the "principal-agent" problem.[12]

In militaries, competing authority may come from a variety of sources. While specialized expertise in such areas as medicine and law are unlikely to interfere with the formal hierarchy, other kinds of military expertise may. In particular, those in more heroic, war-fighting roles—such as special forces— enjoy an area of autonomy and authority that may challenge more senior officers. According to Morris Janowitz, "The history of the modern military establishment can be described as a struggle between heroic leaders, who embody traditionalism and glory, and military 'managers,' who are concerned with the scientific and rational conduct of war."[13] Not only do heroic, war-fighting roles carry prestige within the armed forces, but the accompanying autonomy and discretion tend to make personnel in these capacities more difficult to monitor and control. Military personnel at lower ranks may also possess expertise distinct from their superiors through improvements in training. When such changes occur, junior officers enjoy educational benefits their superiors may not have had, leaving the latter at a disadvantage. *Position* may also offer a source of competing authority. The very structure of the military organization means that mid-level officers control a critical source of power within the institution, which can leave those at the top vulnerable. With the highest ranks fulfilling essentially managerial ranks, it is those in the middle—the field grade officers—who have direct control of troops and weapons. Militarily, generals must rely on the compliance of these subordinates to be able to take any action. Such compliance is by no means always guaranteed.[14] Military rebellions and even many coup attempts tend to come from the middle ranks.

Finally, other aspects of the modern military that hinder control involve the difficulty of "containing" the institution or preventing official contacts between lower-ranking personnel and the external environment. Because the military is an administrative "tool" of political elites,[15] it would be presumed that most meaningful contacts between the outside world and the institution would take place at the top. Although the armed forces may approximate "total" and closed systems more than most, however, they still are in many respects "open" systems. First, like any institution, militaries must procure equipment and personnel, which requires external contacts by those at lower ranks. Second, domestic missions such as "civic action" duties place lower-ranking personnel in regular contact with civilians, often exposing the former to different values and priorities than those of their superiors. And third, despite rules designed to limit politicization within the armed forces, officers below the top levels may have their own political connections, which may help them compete for appointments and resources.

Military Coups and the State

Coups, however, require more than connections and exposure to alternative concerns (although these may help to motivate insurgency). A successful coup requires achieving dominance over the armed forces so as to take control of the government. According to Edward Luttwack, "The apparatus of the state is . . . to some extent a 'machine' which will normally behave in a fairly predictable and automatic manner. . . . A coup operates by taking advantage of this machine-like behavior: during the coup because it uses parts of the state apparatus to seize the controlling levers; afterwards because the value of the 'levers' depends on the fact that the state is a machine."[16] This machinelike character of the state stems from the very "rationality" of its components: the specialization of tasks, the division into functional areas, the existence of standard operating procedures, and, above all, the hierarchical and relatively rigid nature of the bureaucratic structure.

As long as the majority of the population does not participate in politics or remains neutral in the face of a coup, coup conspirators should need relatively few active participants to be successful. With respect to public supporters, Luttwack claims that "as the coup will not usually represent a threat to most of the elite, the choice is between the great dangers of opposition and the safety of inaction. All that is required in order to support the coup is, simply, to do nothing—and this is what will usually be done."[17]

Within the military itself, coup planners need to be able either to incorporate or to "neutralize" those units whose position and equipment would allow them to reach and counter the coup forces before they could take control.[18] Effectively taking over a sufficient portion of the armed forces, however, without informing and involving too many individuals means relying on the structure of the organization: linkages between different sectors or branches of the armed forces and clear lines of control within each branch. In other words, as described by Luttwack, the modern military coup requires an essentially "rational" organization of the armed forces. The very hierarchy and organizational specialization that allow battlefield efficiency can also provide an opening for coup conspirators.

The mechanics of coup planning and execution have not gone unnoticed by those who have sought to initiate or strengthen democratic regimes. In new democratic regimes, concerns about the threat of military intervention or obstruction have often led to measures to prevent such occurrences. Some of these methods *use* the "rationality" of the organization, while others are more likely to *subvert* the rationality of the organization. The methods used to ensure control of the military in Venezuela have tended to diminish organizational rationality, handicapping the organization's ability to achieve its primary stated goal, national defense.

One method used to achieve control that does subvert bureaucratic rationality is what Harold Trinkunas describes as "Divide and Conquer" strategies. These strategies appear to be those most likely to interfere with a Luttwack-style coup attempt, in that they tend to use the structure of the armed forces to create obstacles to intervention: "Divide and Conquer strategies generate regime leverage by exploiting internal cleavages and encouraging competition within and among state security forces, raising the costs of military intervention. Civilians either create new counter-balancing security forces, such as gendarmeries or national police forces, or they induce existing military units to balance against each other, creating deterrence within the armed forces."[19] Such strategies tend to encourage organizational inefficiencies. For example, competition between forces may prevent them from working together. Notably, in Argentina, the inadvertent competition that arose between military branches during the military regime—a consequence of carefully dividing up ministerial and geographic domains—proved devastating during the Falklands/Malvinas war.[20] Creating alternative security forces, such as a national police or National Guard, has mixed implications. On the one hand, this may be a source of inefficiency if it means the duplication of functions. If this force is under the control of the Defense Ministry, it may also increase the likelihood of military forces being used to suppress popular mobilization. On the other hand, if such a force is organizationally separate, perhaps under the auspices of a different ministry, it could actually deter the use of the conventional forces in suppressing civil unrest and could also conceivably protect the conventional forces from the politicizing influences of many other domestic roles.

If the divide and conquer strategy seeks to use the military's structure to enhance control, other strategies attempt to bypass the structure so as to create allegiances, if not subordination. Huntington's second form of control, "subjective civilian control," depends on "civilianizing the military, making them the mirror of the state" by strengthening the power of ruling civilian groups over the military.[21] Along these lines, powerful political groups may pursue political ties especially to senior members of the armed forces to ensure their loyalty in times of crisis. These political networks contradict organizational rationality both by introducing a damaging bias into the system of promotions and appointments, impeding a meritocracy, and by "opening" the institution to unofficial outside influences that could inspire political, rather than functional, organizational adaptations.

In sum, the stability of the modern military, with its reliable resources and predetermined goals, allows for the development of a highly rational organization. Such an organization may be very efficient; however, it may also be vulnerable to capture by a relatively small coalition. Many of the strategies designed to counter this vulnerability thus also hinder institutional rationality, altering the organizational structure or co-opting personnel. These strategies may succeed in creating obstacles to carrying out a successful coup, but they may also contribute to the motivation to attempt one. Thus, regardless of careful strategies to prevent coups d'état, military bureaucracies may still find themselves hosts to challenging military movements.

Organizational Dynamics of Military Movements

In contrast to military bureaucracies, which are essentially conservative in nature, military movements stand for change—at the very least, a change in military or political power holders. The nature of the movement organization thus differs considerably from that of the bureaucratic organization described above. Unlike bureaucracies, ongoing military movements or movements with military origins must also undergo radical changes if they are to survive. Created initially using the structure of the military bureaucracy, movements evolve from closed, relatively controlled voluntary organizations during the conspiratorial phase, to more open and inclusive movements as the original leadership attempts to gain wider appeal.

Military movements function as a particular a form of social movement that originates inside an institution and may or may not move beyond the boundaries of that institution. Social movements differ from bureaucratic organizations with respect to both their structure and the incentives they offer for participation. As Zald and Roberta Ash Garner write, "First, they have goals aimed at changing the society and its members; they wish to restructure society or individuals, not to provide it or them with a regular service. . . . Second . . . , MOS [movement organizations] are characterized by an incentive structure in which purposive incentives predominate."[22] Movement organizations, unlike bureaucracies, cannot offer many selective benefits such as salaries and pensions. Instead, social movements are, by nature, voluntary associations, recruiting supporters or members primarily by appealing to a shared interest in change.

Structure of Authority

Perhaps the greatest difference between a social movement organization and a bureaucracy is thus the *structure of authority*. Most voluntary associations cannot rely on command or hierarchy to the extent a bureaucracy might. Any bureaucracy can apply such threats as termination (and the corresponding loss of salary and benefits) to encourage compliance with the leadership's wishes. In a military organization, the power of enforcement is even stronger—military personnel often face strong legal penalties for such infringements as disobedience and desertion. Under these conditions, a decision to leave the organization could be quite costly. Not surprisingly, most would opt to comply with orders rather than to leave.[23] In contrast, voluntary associations have little capacity to coerce compliance from their participants or supporters, although in a conspiratorial movement, risk may convince participants to *offer* their obedience. These organizations are thus likely to be "flatter" in nature,[24] with a less developed hierarchy and relatively more influence by lower-level participants. Decision making would need to at least appear more inclusive because the leadership needs to attract and maintain participation. Such a movement may get much of its direction from a charismatic leader at the helm, but the layers between the leader and his or her following are likely to be relatively less refined.

Relation to Environment

The voluntary nature of a social movement also influences its relation to the environment. Voluntary associations—especially social movements—face a more precarious existence than bureaucracies. All their resources, including personnel, depend on their ability to find support in the surrounding environment, whether that environment is intra- or extrainstitutional. According to Sidney Tarrow, "When they succeed, even resource-poor actors can mount and sustain collective action against powerful opponents."[25] Organizations that do not find external support may perish. Movement organizations thus require a certain amount of flexibility and adaptability. Structures may need to change, and even goals—or their portrayal—may require modification.

Changing Goals and Organization: The Military Movement

The nature of the challenges facing a military movement and the changes the movement is likely to make over time can to some extent be predicted. Military movements begin as the natural offspring of the bureaucracy from which they emerge. The composition of the leadership will often have recognizable ties to particular organizational sectors or generational cohorts within the armed forces. The movement develops its own organization, however, based on the intrinsically conspiratorial nature of its project and the essentially military nature of its methods. Given the risk and the necessity for eventually acting with military efficiency and speed, coup conspirators will likely grant their leadership some authority to issue commands, more so than in most volunteer organizations. These movements nonetheless do retain their voluntary character, drawing participation through the loyalty and shared goals of their membership rather than through material inducements. As movements become more public, they are likely to evolve from the conspiratorial structure, becoming relatively more open—and more similar to typical volunteer organizations—because of the need to find support from a wider audience.

Bureaucratic Contributions to Military Movements

Born within a bureaucracy, military movements benefit considerably from the institutional context, with organizational resources that may not be available to more independent social movements. As Tarrow notes, "Institutions are particularly economical 'host' settings in which movements can germinate."[26] The social networks and organizational linkages that social movements seek to use can easily be located in a military bureaucracy. Military officers have a variety of ties, both structural and experiential, that can be used to help build a conspiratorial movement. For example, officers who go through military school together tend to share a very close bond; potential insurgents engaged in a conspiratorial project can more securely approach their cohorts than others in the military. Membership in the different military arms and specializations also contributes to the available network for a military movement. Perhaps most important, however, is simply the regular contact among military personnel through their work, their clubs, and their living arrangements. A military constitutes a vast system of social networks within a single shared organization. If the initiators have the motivation and a popular mission, they will probably be able to mobilize allies through these many intraorganizational networks.

Coup Conspiracies as Military Movements

The movement's initial form is likely to be conspiratorial, given its intent to challenge authority. At this stage, the movement more nearly resembles an "exclusive" organization, despite its voluntary nature. According to Zald and Garner, "exclusive" organizations tend "to require the recruit to subject himself to organization discipline and orders, and to draw from those having the heaviest initial commitments."[27] Such a high level of commitment is necessary for a coup conspiracy, given the dangers that conspirators face. Therefore at this stage, few are brought into the movement, and they tend to be recruited through the safest connections possible. Those who do participate tend to have a very strong commitment to the movement's goals. Few would be likely to risk their careers, and possibly even their lives, if they did not believe something of value was at stake.

From Military Movement to Political Movement

Once a coup attempt or a military rebellion has taken place (emergence), the nature of the movement organization will almost necessarily change. If the movement succeeds in taking power, its survival ceases to be an immediate concern, although institutionalization will still be required for organizational longevity. If, at the other extreme, the movement is defeated and its emergence from underground reveals its lack of potential support, then the movement organization is likely to wither and disappear.

The middle alternatives present the more interesting challenge. If a coup fails or a rebellion either fails or succeeds partially (attains concessions but not control of the military apparatus), and the movement's emergence reveals the presence of some support inside or outside of the armed forces or both, then the movement may have the means and motivation to reorganize for longer-term survival. The movement then faces a variety of requirements: it must define its purpose beyond the ouster of military or political elites; it must recruit broader support; and it must begin to create the organizational structures necessary to endure and incorporate new recruits.[28]

The problem with carrying out these tasks simultaneously is the inevitable but potentially conflictive relationship between goal definition and recruitment. Defining goals is both crucial for the movement's expansion and dangerous to the process. The movement is still voluntary and thus must continue to find members largely on the basis of common purpose and beliefs and, at best, the promise of *possible* access to power some time in the future. This means that objectives need to be clarified sufficiently to attract followers. But doing so may also alienate supporters who may previously have shared only antagonism toward the incumbents, and it may even create enemies. During Argentina's military rebellions of the late 1980s, the more the movement defined itself, the more internal foes it produced, eventually leading to its defeat in 1990.[29] Goals that are too narrowly defined may be clearer and enhance the movement organization's cohesion, but they also may restrict the movement's wider appeal.

Another difficult requisite for the movement's continued development is organizational expansion—creating new units, defining "offices," assigning responsibilities, and the like—all necessary for stability and the effective incorporation of more personnel. To facilitate recruitment, the movement—as an inclusive organization—will probably also change its entrance requirements from those that were selective and limited during its conspiratorial days to ones that require minimum levels of initial commitment such as a "pledge of general support without specific duties, a short indoctrination period, or none at all."[30] With material compensation still limited and authority still contingent on the consent of the participants, the leadership may find it even more difficult to retain its grip over the growing movement. The structure may become even "flatter" as the core leadership reaches out to potential allies to whom it would be inappropriate to issue orders.

This period of transformation, in which the military movement adapts to its emergence into a broader arena, brings no more guarantee of success than did its initial insurgency. Combining goal definition and expansion may well lead to some division or diversification within the movement as groups displeased by the changing (or unchanging) objectives, leadership, and composition separate from the original organization. This diversification may easily weaken the core, offsetting efforts to expand. Or goals may become so diffuse in the process of adapting to new allies that the initial agenda may be entirely lost, and the original goals become impossible to fulfill. Here, timing is likely to play a critical role in the movement's survival. If the movement's goals and priorities were relatively well defined *before* expansion, either during an interim period between emergence and expansion or, as in Venezuela, during a long period of germination before expansion, and those goals are sufficiently marketable, then the movement may still be able to sustain its essence.

Venezuela's Military Movement: The MBR

In the Venezuelan case, the original nature of the military movement contributed to both its military failure and its political success. The military organization from which the MBR emanated provided both the social networks necessary for constructing the movement and some of its motivations. But the structure of the military bureaucracy—designed at least in part to prevent coups d'état—created obstacles that these middle-rank, unpracticed coup leaders were unable to overcome. In contrast, as a political movement, both the origins and strategies of the MBR worked to the leadership's advantage. The emergence of the MBR at the head of an unsuccessful coup attempt against an unpopular leader and regime validated Chávez's subsequent political position as the one true representative of change.[31] Organizationally, the MBR's early years, spent underground before the 1992 coup attempt, allowed it to consolidate its central ideas and goals *before* reaching out to the broader public. This foundation kept the movement from disintegrating once it began to expand. At the same time, the combination of Chávez's charisma, the leadership's willingness to reach out to compatible allies, and the movement's flexibility with respect to structure and the details of its projects meant that the movement *could* succeed in attracting widespread support.

Origins of the MBR

The Movimiento Bolivariano Revolucionario began to take shape long before the February 1992 coup attempt launched the charismatic Hugo Chávez into the limelight. During approximately a decade of planning, the leaders had plenty of time to formulate ideas and projects, as well as to solidify the group's commitment to the insurrectionary cause. The leaders pulled together a network of reliable conspirators using the organizational structure of the military bureaucracy. Initially, the incipient movement appears to have functioned as a very "flat," discussion-oriented volunteer organization, with minimal authority to command granted to (or demanded by) the leadership. As it drew closer to taking action, the risk involved compelled a somewhat tighter, more hierarchical organizational structure—although authority remained contingent on the consent of members—and group members appear to have assumed organizational roles based on their military ranks.

According to Lieutenant Colonel Francisco Arias Cárdenas, Chávez's primary partner in the coup attempt, the two officers began meeting informally with a group of friends as early as the late 1970s, discussing concerns about the military and politics but "without a concrete plan." After around 1982, Chávez and Arias Cárdenas began to plan to work together "to change the direction of the state." The two were then separated for several years, when Arias Cárdenas was first at the University of the Andes and then in Colombia, while Chávez went to another part of the country. According to Arias Cárdenas, around 1986, while he was still at the university, "we already began to establish more formal working groups, to come together and approach a discussion between professors, with groups from small and medium businesses, to make proposals about the working of the state and the reorientation of the country."[32]

Many of the ties between movement members, at this time as well as in February 1992, could be traced to networks provided by the military organization. At first, the members of the coup coalition were almost entirely army men. An effort had been made to involve a sector of the air force as well, but the links to that service were so weak that the unavailability of a single key ally prevented air force participation. In the army, the paratroopers—led by Chávez—would be particularly important. Generational ties were also central: the five lieutenant colonels who headed the 1992 efforts had all been through military school around the same time; Arias Cárdenas graduated in 1973, and the remainder graduated one year later.[33] Teaching military courses, the 1973 and 1974 graduates were able to reach more junior officers, thereby expanding their numbers.

By the 1986 San Cristobal meeting, the group was more cohesive and larger, with some fifty or sixty active officers, although the leadership still occupied relatively low ranks in the armed forces. Arias Cárdenas reports that "at the time, I was a major, Hugo was a captain, and other *compañeros* who were there were lieutenants." This situation precluded taking early action, but the participants continued building their ideas and biding their time. At meetings, "we brought papers which we discussed, we discussed lines of action, and we made decisions about the composition of the organization and the leadership within our *planteamiento.*"[34]

In February 1989, riots broke out in Caracas in reaction to the neoliberal reforms of President Carlos Andrés Pérez. Unable to regain control easily, the president placed the matter in the hands of Minister of Defense Italo de Valle Alliegro. The minister of defense called in the military, National Guard, and traditional forces; the riots were successfully suppressed, but at considerable cost of blood and governmental legitimacy.

For the MBR nucleus, the 1989 riots and their aftermath added fodder and impetus to the movement. Already, corruption in the administration (Pérez was impeached in 1993) and in the military had become a central concern of the movement. In particular, members took offense at the politicized nature of promotions and appointments, a practice related to the democratic regime's strategy for civilian control.[35] The riots exacerbated the group's dismay at the military's increasing assumption of "policing" roles, from controlling protests or "civil disturbances" to combating narcotics trafficking.[36] The MBR was also disturbed about the nature of the event. From its leaders' perspective, government corruption was to blame for the Venezuelans' poverty; they therefore identified more with those they fought than with those they obeyed in the confrontation. According to Arias Cárdenas, at the time of the riots, "there was a deep desperation in the group because we weren't ready; that is, we had proposed that this situation would explode, that it was moving toward a situation of civil violence, but we had not prepared sufficiently to respond."[37]

Nevertheless, the riots did encourage the MBR to accelerate its plans, beginning by reorganizing the movement. During the early years of its development, the MBR functioned primarily through collegial "working groups," kept relatively small because of the need for secrecy. Following the 1989 riots, the group began planning more actively for a coup d'état. At this point, the loose, cooperative organization of the working groups became inappropriate. To function in a coup-oriented military operation, the MBR required more hierarchy, specialization, and discipline. Thus the leaders began tightening the structure, creating a more "exclusive" and orderly organization that would be more appropriate for a coup. At the head of this new MBR, a "triumvirate" was formed, including Chávez, Arias Cárdenas, and an air force officer who, in the end, was blocked from participating. By February 1992, the leaders determined that the moment to act had arrived.

4 February 1992: Dissecting a Failed Coup d'État

After more than thirty years of relatively stable democracy, the coup attempt of 4 February 1992 took Venezuela by surprise. Yet it was not unwelcome: public opinion polls following the event would reveal that, though Venezuelans did not seem interested in a military regime, a "moderating" coup to replace the incumbent regime was a popular option.[38] Between Carlos Andrés Pérez and Hugo Chávez Frias, the latter looked somewhat more appealing. Over the next few years, the balance of public opinion would shift even further in this direction.

Nonetheless, the coup attempt was clearly defeated. It failed for many reasons, having to do with both errors on the part of the coup conspirators and successes on the part of those who designed the system of military control. The coup conspirators failed to take over the media—identified by Luttwack as a key tactical necessity—and recruited perhaps too carefully, bypassing potential allies because of their caution. Felipe Agüero argues that the coup failed "as a result of the rebels' inability to marshal the participation of the high command, which pointed to the fact that the rebels' attempt encountered an elite that, despite appearances of divisions, was fundamentally unified."[39] This, too, undoubtedly played a role, although coup attempts by mid-level officers are a real possibility. Yet the coup's failure also reflected the success of the daunting system of organizational obstacles created by Venezuela's democratizers.

In their efforts both to reduce certain tensions in the armed forces and to prevent the resurgence of military activism, the Venezuelan democratizers incorporated some important structural changes in the armed forces. Several of these reforms could be considered counter to bureaucratic rationality, in that they impeded organizational efficiency and effectiveness. Yet politically, the reforms made sense at the time they were implemented.

For example, reforms weakening the linkages between and equalizing the

political weight of the different armed forces branches eased interforce jeal-
ousy at the time but also prevented improved interforce cooperation. The
reform was carried out essentially by moving the coordinating office, the
Estado Mayor Conjunto (Joint Chiefs of Staff), to an advisory role, peripheral
to the line of command in the armed forces. Each of the armed forces thus
would relate directly to the executive through the minister of defense (an
active-duty officer). The move was ostensibly designed to pacify the other
forces by taking away the army's dominance, but it also served the democratizers' goals of politically weakening the potentially most threatening branch
of the armed forces and making multiforce coup coalitions much more difficult
to achieve.[40] At the same time, though, the reform hindered the potential of the
forces to cooperate for legitimate military purposes, a clear requirement for a
"rational" organization.

A later structural reform had to do with the National Guard. The National
Guard (Fuerzas Armadas de Cooperación) was formed in 1937 as a national
police under the control of the minister of the interior.[41] In 1946, the National
Guard was unified with the military forces as a result of the merger of internal
security issues with national defense in the government's conceptualization of
national security.[42] Subsequently, in 1958, the Guard was formally converted
into a fourth branch of the armed forces, under the authority of the minister of
defense.[43] As a fourth service, the National Guard also became the second
ground force and thus served as a potential counterbalance to the army—even
the uniforms look very similar. During the February 1992 coup attempt, the
National Guard faithfully executed this role, standing out as the key military
loyalists. Again, though, the overlapping functions of the two ground forces
meant some sacrifice of overall organizational efficiency.

Democratizers also instituted personnel policies aimed at easing internal
pressures—this time from junior officers rather than the navy and air force—
with similarly problematic consequences for organizational rationality. To
begin with, a 1959 decree established a limit of thirty years of service for
officers.[44] The policy, originally designed to appease frustrated junior service-
men[45] with the arguable added benefit of speeding organizational renovation,
also served to inhibit the solidification of coup coalitions. This policy allowed
officers to move through the ranks more rapidly and leave before they could
cultivate an independent following. A related personnel practice has been to
limit to one year the period during which officers occupy the top positions in
the armed forces. Both of these practices have inhibited the consolidation of
military leadership, with positive and negative consequences: they have weakened possibilities for a successful coup coalition but have also diminished the

effectiveness of the leadership (along with its ability to rally support *against* an insurgency) and may have contributed to even greater anxiety about quick professional progress within the ranks.

Informal practices joined with the above formal structures and policies to block the potential for successful coups, in this instance by boosting support for the governing elite. In particular, political leaders developed party-related networks throughout the "apolitical, non-deliberating, and obedient" military.[46] Acción Democrática (AD), Venezuela's largest political party since 1958, has been known to have the strongest network in the military. Such ties have reputedly helped officers succeed in promotions and achieve desirable assignments. The requirement that promotions to the rank of colonel or general be approved by Congress has contributed to the suspicion by junior officers that their superiors had risen politically rather than meritoriously. But such networks probably also contributed to the apparent loyalty of senior officers observed by Agüero.[47]

The irony of these control measures is that while they may make it difficult for a coup attempt to succeed, they actually help *create* the motivations for such attempts. Measures that increase the pressure to progress rapidly through the forces, as well as those that contribute to politicization of the higher ranks, exacerbate discontent within the armed forces. In this respect, these practices may contribute to insurgencies, even though they may block their successful execution. The structural mechanisms for coup prevention also impede rationality in the organization, in that the same obstacles to interservice communication and the development of leadership that discourage coups also would impede the military from effectively carrying out its defense missions, if called upon to do so.

Finally, these methods of coup prevention are not equivalent to true control. While the structure of the military may have impeded the emergence of a successful coup coalition, it has not given political leaders the ability effectively to "control" the armed forces through democratic means. Because the minister of defense was a military man and few opportunities were available for civilian oversight, the military has traditionally enjoyed a very high level of autonomy, with relatively little direction or intervention by political elites.[48]

How did these countercoup measures affect the events in February 1992? To begin with, the efforts to control the armed forces through politicization of the top elites, as well as through the counterbalance of the National Guard, certainly contributed to rebel dissatisfaction. The military elites were perceived as merely a reflection of the corrupt political elites. By preventing the development of strong leadership by senior officers, policies such as the rapid rotation in top positions and the short term of service also contributed to the birth of the military movement.

Once the movement commenced, however, these preventive measures essentially worked. The lack of linkages between the separate service branches made it much more difficult for the rebels to use organizational networks to locate allies in the other forces. Similarly, the National Guard performed the counterbalancing role, emerging as the dependable loyalists in the conflict. Finally, as the senior military officers had developed allegiances to political elites, the rebels could not count on their participation. To compensate for the lack of senior officers, who could conceivably command the obedience of a larger sector of the organization, the field officers would have had to gain the participation of many more of their peers. Because they were unable to do so, the MBR failed in its first attempt to attain power. Most certainly, though, this was not to be its last effort.

From MBR to MVR: Political Transformation of a Military Movement

Following the February 1992 coup attempt, the MBR began to change, seeking a more successful route to power. Plans for a second coup, which continued for a while from the MBR's prison headquarters, were mostly replaced by a more political project after a group of senior officers led a failed coup attempt in November 1992. To succeed as a political project, however, the movement would have to modify both its form of organization and its relation to its environment. The MBR thus began seeking new allies, expanding to adapt to more political projects and paths to power. Nevertheless, because of the prolonged germination of the MBR, the central agenda items—sweeping away the existing political structures and the incumbent elite and improving conditions for the poor—remained intact throughout.

The November coup attempt probably helped encourage the MBR to abandon the coup path by alienating much of the public previously receptive to a military option. At the time, Chávez and Arias Cárdenas could do little more than place their followers at the command of Rear Admirals Hernán Gruber Odreman and Luis Cabrera Aguirre and air force general Francisco Visconti Osorio, abandoning their own plans for a follow-up *golpe* from the prison. It was not, in the end, a coup attempt with which the MBR would want to be associated. As the plot began to unfold, the leadership found itself entirely without the support of ground forces; the ill-fated venture thus ended as a disastrous and unnecessarily violent air force coup, which concluded with many of the participating pilots flying directly to Peru. Fortunately for Chávez, the public nevertheless seemed willing to distinguish his movement from the distinctly unpopular November attempt.

The period of imprisonment contributed more productively to the MBR's maturation in that the leaders had the opportunity to continue developing their ideas and begin expanding their organization. New contacts were forged, particularly with members of the political left who paid visits to the coup leaders in their prison cells. But the movement also began to show signs of stress. After charming the Venezuelan public in February 1992, the charismatic Chávez began to emerge as the central figure in the movement, leaving aside the more serious and bookish Arias Cárdenas. Chávez, too, seemed inclined to assume sole leadership of the movement, accepting the title of "supreme leader" and rejecting the collegial leadership of the conspiratorial phase.[49] Naturally, this generated some tension with Arias Cárdenas and foreshadowed the parting of ways that would occur following the officers' release from prison and once again before the May 2000 elections.

In some ways, this shift would appear to be a natural offshoot of the transformation from a conspiracy to a political movement. At this juncture, the two leaders continued specifying their goals, but differently. Both had shared the aim of displacing President Carlos Andrés Pérez and ending the two-party dominant *partidocracia*. After Pérez was removed from office in 1993 and a nonparty candidate—Rafael Caldera—was elected to office, Arias Cárdenas considered their mission to have been essentially completed. He accepted a position in the Caldera administration as head of PAMI (Program for Mother-Infant Nutrition) and later ran a successful campaign for the governorship of Zulia as a candidate of a nontraditional party.[50]

In contrast, Chávez refused to be co-opted into the system, aspiring instead to create an independent political movement. He shifted his focus toward the idea of a Constituent Assembly as an institutional means of overthrowing the regime. With diverse allies, including Rear Admiral Hernán Gruber, leader of the failed November coup attempt, and various representatives of the political left, Chávez began organizing support for the Constituent Assembly, with the Frente Amplio Pro-Asamblea Constituyente as a base.[51] Chávez then traveled around the country to organize bases. In 1994, a march was planned, with the hope that "thousands of people from all the country would go to Caracas by foot, by car, by burro, by tractor, however, and surround the National Congress with the greatest demonstration that has been seen in the country, and tell the National Congress, we don't want you."[52] The dramatic march never materialized, but the campaign did succeed in coalescing public resentment toward the governing elites into a specific program, one clearly identified with

Chávez. By early mid-1998, public opinion polls revealed that a strong major-ity of those surveyed believed that the political system required significant reform, many looking to a constitutional assembly to do the job.[53]

Through the campaign for the Constituent Assembly, Chávez and the MBR were able to build the national foundations that they would need for a political campaign. Throughout the country, the MBR created a strong organizational network, with bases oriented toward the Constituent Assembly. New allies were brought in around this shared program, at least temporarily leaving aside the other facets of the MBR's agenda. Finally, in early 1998, Chávez officially became a candidate for the 1998 presidential election, claiming that the Con-stituent Assembly "is the only thing that justifies my presidential candidacy."[54]

The MBR now created the MVR (Movimiento Quinta República), the official political organ (technically, a political party, although Chávez and his allies still avoided that term) for the campaign. The name of the party was chosen less as a reference to the "Fifth Republic" than as a means of keeping the same initials, since "B" and "V" are pronounced identically in Spanish. While retaining the popular cry for a Constituent Assembly, the new organization needed to broaden its agenda somewhat to win the presidency. Chávez formed alliances with some smaller political parties, most notably the MAS (Movi-miento al Socialismo), and formed a new umbrella organization to join the MVR with MAS and other independent supporters of the Chávez presidency. The need to appeal to a much wider audience and to satisfy a diverse coalition led Chávez to adopt a rather vague discourse, often characterized by inconsisten-cies. He continued to discuss social justice, as he had since 1992, but also met with businessmen and indicated his support for free trade. Chávez traveled to Cuba and lauded the Cuban system but also made an effort to reach out to the United States, despite the latter's continued refusal to grant him a visa. The shifting discourse confused many but ultimately succeeded. The former coup leader won the December 1998 elections by a landslide, garnering 56 percent of the vote, in contrast to the 40 percent won by his closest competitor.[55] On 2 February, Chávez was inaugurated as president of Venezuela.

Why was the MBR able to launch Chávez to the presidency? Much had to do with the movement's ability to retain some internal cohesion while projecting extreme flexibility. Externally, the movement appeared eminently adaptable and eager to please. Drawn to the dynamism of Chávez, many saw in him and his campaign precisely what they wanted to see: the promise of change and change in whichever direction they desired.[56] Throughout Venezuela, voters disaffected with the traditional parties embraced the possibility of a true op-position. Nevertheless, internally, the movement retained the essence of the original 4 February platform, and though new members continued to flood into the movement, Chávez's closest allies still came from either the initial insurgency or from loyalists during the prison period.

Conclusion: Consistency and Change in the MBR

Moving from its origins in the Venezuelan military bureaucracy to serve as a vehicle that elected a Venezuelan president, the Movimiento Bolivariano Revolucionario would appear to have undergone vast changes. From the beginning, the MBR sought to alter the Venezuelan political system. Initially, the movement attempted to do so by taking control of its host organization and launching reforms from there. Yet the structure of the Venezuelan military made it especially difficult to capture, even for a coup coalition with a charismatic leader and a popular agenda. The MBR thus gradually shifted toward a different path, in the process also modifying its organization and discourse.

As this chapter demonstrates, the use of organization theory, along with social movement theory, can help to explain both why this movement emerged from within the military and why it successfully transformed itself into a political movement. Thus the first part of the story draws from an essentially institutional approach. As David Pion-Berlin suggests in the Introduction to this volume, institutional analyses reveal how the rules and structures of organizations influence the choices of their members. He argues that even a profoundly regimented and hierarchical organization like the armed forces can invite dissent from within and that institutional theory can help explain why. It does so by revealing the contradictions embodied in rules designed ostensibly to enforce compliance. Hence, in Venezuela, a largely rational military structure facilitated, and in some ways even encouraged, military insurrection. In an effort to curb military insubordination through bureaucratic reforms, the Venezuelan authorities impeded the military's professional functions, thus giving rise to grievances from within the ranks, which then led to open rebellion.

The remainder of the MBR story, however, has taken place *outside* the formal structure of the armed forces. From the moment the members of the MBR began meeting in their early discussion groups, they had started to form a separate entity. This group began developing its own organizational characteristics as it sought to mobilize first a military movement and subsequently a political movement. Thus, to tell this latter part of the story, this chapter has focused on the strategic choices of the movement's leaders in combination with the dynamics of organizations and movements.

Has the MBR become an entirely new entity in the process, relinquishing all of its original aims in the quest to attain power? I would argue that it has not. First, the MBR remains a movement in that it has not converted completely to a political party. Second, once Chávez had been elected, it became clear that many of the original players would remain active in the movement or even return to it and that the essence of his original project—radical transformation of the Venezuelan political system—would continue to shape his agenda as president.

The organization did follow Venezuela's electoral rules, declaring itself a party in order to compete; however, in many respects, it remains more of a movement. In an analysis of Peronism in Argentina, James McGuire discusses the contrasts between political parties and political movements. According to McGuire, "First, parties tend to view opposition as permanent and legitimate, whereas movements seek a form of national unity in which political opposition withers away. Second, parties tend to see fair elections as the only appropriate road to power, whereas movements tend to try to achieve or retain power by the most expedient means at hand. Third, parties tend to portray their leaders as less important than their philosophies and policy goals, whereas movements tend to exalt leadership and to give their leaders great programmatic and procedural flexibility."[57] On each count, the MBR resembles a movement rather than a party. The MBR made it plain that its principal opposition, the two parties that had dominated Venezuelan politics—AD and Copei—would not be considered legitimate. Instead, the MBR would accept only the complete elimination of the political system that had supported those parties. Given the history of the movement, it was also clear that for the MBR (or MVR), elections were only one of several acceptable routes to power—albeit the route least likely to incur international censure during the "democratic" post–Cold War period.

Finally, the movement increasingly focused attention on Chávez's leadership instead of the movement's policy goals, another characteristic of movements as opposed to parties. Such an approach proved a convenient way of allowing a shifting and ambiguous discourse during the election campaign, while still attracting followers. Supporters of the MBR appeared to be drawn to the most consistent element in Chávez's discourse: the promise of change. As a charismatic leader (in Weber's terms), Chávez gained his authority from his status as an agent of change. Unfortunately, Chávez found it difficult to achieve sufficiently rapid economic change to satisfy the electorate, particularly after Venezuela's disastrous floods in 1999. It was only at this point that his charismatic mantle began to disintegrate, and his allies began to desert him.

Yet change had been the goal of the MBR since its inception. Long before an adoring public transformed Chávez into "the" leader of the movement, the

MBR had planned for the total reconstruction of the political system into a model more commensurate with its vision of democracy. This model required the political elimination of the entrenched elites—especially those from the dominant two parties—a new constitution, and a greater focus on "economic" democracy (at a minimum, attention to the basic needs for the poor). In this sense, the movement retained a certain continuity from the beginning, deterring either its disintegration or its transformation into a purely personalistic vehicle.

After the election, Chávez's words and actions revealed consistency with respect to both the promise of change and the composition of his closest associates. Allies from the insurgent and prison periods were quickly placed in a wide range of public positions. Many of these newly appointed public servants were retired military officers; Rear Admiral Hernán Gruber, leader of the second coup attempt, was one of those placed in a top position. Chávez also initially made a point of lauding his former partner, governor of Zulia Arias Cárdenas (who had thrown his support to Chávez during a critical point in the elections), indicating that he would be the president's key intermediary with the governors.[58]

Yet it was Chávez's statements at his inauguration that most clearly showed that his intentions remained unchanged. President Hugo Chávez Frias was inaugurated on 3 February 1999, one day before the seventh anniversary of the coup attempt. Taking his oath of office, Chávez dramatically demonstrated that power had not yet moderated him, declaring before an astounded audience: "I swear before God, I swear before the Fatherland, I swear before my people and before this defunct Constitution to carry out the democratic transformations necessary for the Republic to have a new Constitution suitable for new times."[59] Chávez then immediately moved to order a referendum that would begin the process of convoking the Constitutional Assembly and presumably would complete the task of abolishing the post-1958 Venezuelan political system. The 1992 coup was now complete.

NOTES

I thank Wendy Hunter, David Mares, David Pion-Berlin, Mina Silberberg, Bill Smith, and Scott Tollefson and an anonymous reviewer for their helpful comments on earlier drafts of this chapter.

1. Scott, *Organizations*, 10.
2. Zald and Berger, "Social Movements in Organizations," 215.
3. Scott, *Organizations*, 23.
4. Ibid., 67.

5. Weber, *Economy and Society*, 956–58.

6. Ibid., 963.

7. Van Doorn, "Officer Corps," 264.

8. Huntington, *Soldier and the State*, 83.

9. Norden, "Democracy and Military Control in Venezuela."

10. Simon, *Administrative Behavior*, 125.

11. Ibid., 128.

12. See Feaver, "Crisis Shirking," for an application of principal-agent theory to civil-military relations.

13. Janowitz, *Professional Soldier*, 21.

14. During the 1987–90 military rebellions in Argentina, at least two of which achieved considerable ground for the rebels, the generals' orders to repress the insurgents were largely disobeyed. See Norden, *Military Rebellion in Argentina*.

15. Clausewitz, *On War*.

16. Luttwack, *Coup d'Etat*, 21.

17. Ibid., 36.

18. Ibid., 70.

19. Trinkunas, "Crafting Civilian Control," 12.

20. Norden, *Military Rebellion in Argentina*.

21. Huntington, *Soldier and the State*, 83.

22. Zald and Garner, "Social Movement Organizations," 123.

23. According to Zald and Berger ("Social Movements in Organizations," 193), the costs of leaving the institution mean that junior officers may have much more motivation to fight for change internally—possibly through conspiracies to take control.

24. Scott, *Organizations*, 12.

25. Tarrow, "Collective Action and Social Movements," 17.

26. Ibid., 21–22.

27. Zald and Garner, "Social Movement Organizations," 125.

28. According to Ken Jowitt, any successful movement must pass through three stages: transformation, consolidation, and inclusion. See Jowitt, "Moscow 'Center.'"

29. Norden, *Military Rebellion in Argentina*.

30. Zald and Garner, "Social Movement Organizations," 125.

31. The extent to which Chávez formed public opposition against the democratic regime, versus merely reflecting it or anticipating it, still remains to be determined.

32. Interview with Francisco Arias Cárdenas, 12 July 1994, Caracas.

33. Machillanda, *Cinismo político*, 106.

34. Interview with Arias Cárdenas, 12 July 1994, Caracas.

35. Interview with Hugo Chávez Frias, 14 July 1994, Caracas. See also Agüero, "Debilitating Democracy," 150, and Burggraff and Millett, "More than Failed Coups," 57.

36. Interviews with Arias Cárdenas, 12 July 1994, and Chávez Frias, 14 July 1994.

37. Interview with Arias Cárdenas, 12 July 1994.

38. Philip, "Venezuelan Democracy and the Coup Attempt of February 1992," 459.

39. Agüero, "Debilitating Democracy," 138.

40. See Burggraff, *Venezuelan Armed Forces*, 174; Gil Yepes, "Political Articulation of the Military," 166–67; and Agüero, "Fuerzas armadas," 197.

41. Müller Rojas, *Relaciones peligrosas*, 39.

42. Ibid., 41.

43. Ibid., 42.

44. Ibid., 147. The 1983 reform to the Organic Law of the Armed Forces expanded the limit of service to thirty-three years. The law also set age limits for staying in each rank, which meant that officers could stay in the military only as long as they were promoted (Congreso, Nacional República de Venezuela, *Ley Orgánica de las fuerzas armadas nacionales*).

45. Müller Rojas, *Relaciones peligrosas*, 148.

46. Congreso, Nacional República de Venezuela, *Constitución de la República de Venezuela*, 1961.

47. Agüero, "Debilitating Democracy."

48. See Norden, "Democracy and Military Control."

49. Interview with Arias Cárdenas, 13 July 1994, Caracas.

50. During the February 1992 coup attempt, Arias Cárdenas briefly assumed the position of de facto governor of Zulia.

51. Interview with Rear Admiral Hernán Gruber, 27 June 1994, Caracas.

52. Interview with Freddy Bernál, 14 July 1994, Caracas.

53. *El Universal Digital*, 18 June 1998.

54. Ibid., 1 February 1998.

55. "A Message from the People," *Economist*, 12 December 1998.

56. As a charismatic leader, Chávez also benefited from the popularity of "strongmen" in Latin America (as David Mares has reminded me), but this is not sufficient to explain his electoral support. Other "strongmen," such as former Lieutenant Colonel Aldo Rico in Argentina, have had much less success transforming military movements into political movements, at least in part because of difficulties with organizational modification.

57. McGuire, "Political Parties and Democracy in Argentina," 203.

58. Within a year after Chávez took office, however, his alliances with his former comrades began to falter. Arias Cárdenas became his principal opposition in a new national election in 2000, after the 1999 Constitution was enacted. Arguing that Chávez had failed to implement their collective goals, several of the former coup leaders shifted their support to Arias Cárdenas.

59. "Despedida a una Constitución," *El Universal Digital*, 3 February 1999.

David Pion-Berlin

6

Civil-Military Circumvention
How Argentine State Institutions Compensate
for a Weakened Chain of Command

It is paradoxical that the country that exemplifies military subordination to
civilian power has the defense system with the greatest vulnerability.
—Horacio Jaunarena, former Argentine minister of defense

Chains are only as strong as their weakest links, or so they say. If a key link in
the civil-military chain of command was weakened, perhaps critically so,
would that cause a democratic government to lose control of its armed forces?
One would think so given the vital importance that has been attributed to the
officials and institutions that make up a state's central defense organizations. In
his classic study *The Soldier and the State*, Samuel Huntington left little doubt
about the need for a strong civilian-led institution situated between the president and the military command, calling that ministerial control.[1] Generations
of scholars since have echoed his concerns. Martin Edmonds says, "Indeed,
within the central organizations of defense of all states is found the very
essence of civil-military relations within any society, and the core of the
relationship between armed forces and society."[2] Commenting on the Spanish
case, Felipe Agüero said that the empowerment of the defense minister and
ministry "was indispensable to unequivocally establishing the supremacy of
civilian authority."[3]

If the ministerial link in the chain of command is so critical, then the
Argentine case and undoubtedly others are puzzling. Argentina's defense ministries have never lived up to their responsibilities; they have not formulated
the defense policies or provided the institutionalized expertise needed to demonstrate civilian authority over military affairs. This is in part a product of
historical neglect. The ministry often existed in name only, with real power
residing in the military service chiefs. Argentine presidents were unwilling to
challenge their supremacy (Arturo Frondizi, 1958–62) or preferred direct,

personal links with their military commanders rather than bureaucratic ones (Juan Perón). Under the Juan Carlos Onganía government (1966–70) and during the Proceso dictatorship (1976–83), the ministry stood outside the chain of command entirely, supplanted either by a national security council or the junta itself. Thus it is not surprising that when the ministry was suddenly awakened from its dormant state at the start of the latest democratic period (1983–present) it was unprepared to assume the full burdens of defense management, as were those in charge of the agency.

Defense ministers and their staff come to the job ill-prepared to take on defense planning or strategizing. Instead, they attempt to hand off to the joint chiefs or the services these responsibilities or simply leave them unattended. In disavowing their duties, they create a policy vacuum that in theory should invite military encroachment and thus an erosion of the division of labor necessary to preserve civilian supremacy. Yet that does not appear to have occurred in contemporary Argentina, where the armed forces are arguably the most compliant in South America.[4] The military is respectful of the civilians who occupy positions above it. Thus we are faced with Jaunarena's paradox, namely that the military remains subordinate despite a ministry ill-suited to enforce that subordination. The rest of this chapter will be devoted to unraveling the paradox.

In brief, the argument to be advanced is as follows. There has been a compensation for ministerial frailty in the form of other civilianized centers of power in the executive and legislative branches of government. While lacking formal authority over the military, these centers have used their institutional strengths to chip away at the military's influence, leaving it in a weakened state and unable to exploit vulnerable defense organizations. Moreover, the public has distanced itself from political contacts with the military. Hence the armed forces can no longer rely on support from societal interest groups as a counterweight to "unfriendly" forces inside the state. As a result, there has been an undeniable shift in the overall balance of power in favor of governing officials. But this is *not* tantamount to full civilian control because policy makers have not used this advantage to demonstrate forceful leadership on defense issues in the state's defense organizations. And since the military has been unable to occupy those institutional spaces vacated by civilians, there exists an odd power vacuum at the core of the political military relationship.

What lies ahead is a state-centered, institutional explanation for these trends.[5] That means that the characteristics of governmental agencies that may have had an impact on the armed forces will be examined. The focus will be on the Economics and Foreign Relations Ministries along with the Congress.

First, I will identify the shortcomings of the Argentine Ministry of Defense (MOD) by comparing its levels of proficiency with those of the Ministries of Economics and Foreign Relations. I hope to demonstrate that these ministries (along with the Congress) do in fact represent alternative sources of institutional civilian power. The second objective will be to analyze what specific defense-related functions they have played and how those functions have both compensated for MOD frailties and led to an overall decline in military power.

The Ministries of Economics and Foreign Relations and the Congress have played key roles in diminishing three kinds of military influence. The first is material *resources* consisting of budget shares, salaries, force size, equipment, installations, and production centers. As Huntington has advised, "The larger the proportion of the national product devoted to military purposes, and the larger the number of individuals serving with the armed services . . . the greater will be the influence of the officer corps and its leaders."[6] The second is military *roles*, defined as the official missions the armed services are asked to undertake on behalf of the nation. Do they engage in missions that enhance their professionalism or diminish it? Are their actions restricted to national defense or more broadly gauged? To the extent that the armed forces' activities take them far afield from defense, the scope of their influence can widen appreciably as well.

Finally, there are *rationales*, namely the ability of the military to marshal knowledge to bolster its power. Because it has a near monopoly on defense expertise, the military can make claims about threats to national security that, however exaggerated, will seem compelling to unknowing politicians and thus be left unchallenged. The more persuasive the military is, the more resources it is likely to generate on its own behalf.

In Argentina, military resources have diminished, roles have narrowed, and rationales have been undercut. It remains to be seen just how civilian centers of institutionalized power have affected these changes.

An Institutional Approach

The point of focusing on state institutions is not to glorify government. One need not have any abiding faith in its agencies to be persuaded that institutions matter under certain restraining conditions. A critical condition arises when noninstitutional, society-centered channels of influence become unavailable to groups such as the armed forces. In the past, social connections would be forged and exploited by soldiers and civilians alike to impose harmful, sometimes fatal, pressures on democratic governments. If the military is now unable to amass influence outside of the state, then it is left with no choice but to maneuver inside the state.

A second constraint arises when, once inside, the military is limited in the means with which it tries to influence policy makers. If it finds itself unable to resort to intimidation or threats, then here too, the state's formal, institutional arrangements take on greater importance. The military may still exert considerable influence on policy makers, but it is influence that depends on built-in channels of access and will likely vary in strength from one institutional site to the next.

In short, the armed forces have to make their case within governing institutions or not at all and must do so in a way that observes those agencies' behavioral conventions.[7] Hence, the organizations that embody those conventions should become the subject of inquiry. These organizations are "collections of standard operating procedures and structures" that shape political behavior within their confines.[8] Rather than seeing the world as a collection of "freely-contracting individuals" who gain or lose depending on their own strategic acumen and interaction, most institutionalists insist it is organizations themselves that produce winners or losers.[9] Institutions exist in varied, structured contexts in which arrangements enable some and disable others and rules provide "procedural advantages and impediments for translating political power into concrete policies."[10] Commonly, those who can access, influence, or, better still, participate in key decision-making processes in institutions have the policy advantage; those who are left "out of the loop" do not.

It is the characteristics of the agency—not of the influence peddlers—that largely determine who is in and who is out. That perspective places institutionalists at odds with both liberal interest group theorists and Marxian structuralists who maintain that policy outcomes can be measured by the strength of initial demands that originate from society. State institutions are often portrayed as feeble, malleable entities that are easily manipulated by powerful social groups and political coalitions. Weak public officials would then design policies that respond directly to the will and preferences of the powers that be. Institutionalists, by contrast, would attribute greater powers to states and would argue that procedures within the state will shape the chances that demands from a given group will have an impact. The rules governing access are devised over time by relatively autonomous political actors who may be influenced by groups outside the state but who are not answerable to them and who are guided by their own interests.[11]

In this chapter, the focus will be on two institutional traits: autonomy and capacity. What about the organization allows its policy makers to keep military pressures at bay while crafting their own policies that affect military interests, often negatively so?[12] Autonomy, or the insularity and independence with which civilian actors can work, and the amount of expertise they bring to bear on their tasks are two sources of institutional strength. Agencies that are autonomous are free from military pressures. Organizational structures and procedures help sustain this sovereignty. Structures define barriers to entry for soldiers who would attempt to shape policy by placing greater bureaucratic distance between the military and centers of political power. Procedures alter the direction of influence. They determine who will actually deliberate over policy and ensure that the net flow of influence is from the center of the agency outward. Highly autonomous decision-making units then reduce the number of options the military has to amend, delay, or derail unwanted policy measures by placing the centers of decision-making power further out of its reach.

Agencies that can resist outside influences may very well fortify their own capacity. But autonomy alone cannot guarantee performance and may even serve the perverse function of shielding incompetence, which is why expertise is considered as well. Expertise is more elusive. While clearly it is individuals who bring their knowledge (or ignorance) to the job, there are also ways in which institutions produce and reproduce proficiency. They do so by building educational infrastructure (schools, institutes, research centers, libraries, extensions to universities, and the like) that allows expertise to become routinized. When state agencies are structured to cultivate the reproduction of knowledge, we can speak meaningfully of institutionalized expertise. Produced in this manner, knowledge can empower civilians to resist the temptation to defer to military views on defense-related policies.

Civil-Military Relations within and beyond Defense Organizations

Civil-military relations are complex, occurring at different levels and in different arenas. The defense organizations in the chain of command and the interactions that occur there constitute the micro foundations for most civil-military relations.[13] It is along this organizational ladder of influence that political overseers and soldiers interface on a daily basis, grappling with the organization, management, and deployment of the armed forces. Because central defense organizations along the chain of command constitute the key points of contact between political and military elites, their importance to the civil-military relationship cannot be easily disputed.

But beyond the confines of the micro world of defense organizations lie other sites where politicians and soldiers contest each other for influence. The military may command loftier heights outside of the defense organizations, enjoying privileged access in other state agencies or branches of government. It may use that access to its advantage by playing off one center of civilian power against another. Then there are less tangible sources of influence. The armed forces can control the terms of debate, suggesting when the nation's security is at risk and when it is not. In this manner they have at their disposal powerful rationales to demand more resources and influence.

Civilian leaders seemingly confront vulnerability at various points in the system. Perhaps that is why Claude Welch argues that "no military can be shorn of political influence, save through the rare step of total abolition."[14] All that civilians can do is set limits on that influence. But clearly the more options availed to the armed forces, the more formidable their task. Paradoxically, however, the multicentered civil-military relation affords civilians greater opportunity as well. They have several chances to curtail military influence precisely *because* there are other arenas. They may erode the military's formal authority within the state or, absent that, its informal influence outside of it. Should the military hold disproportionate sway over Defense Ministry officials, it may be barred from right of entry to officials in other key agencies. At a macro level, this suggests that the overall balance of power can be maintained in favor of civilians even in the face of micro-level deficiencies. Political leaders can, in other words, compensate for a weakened Defense Ministry by undercutting military influence at other sites, limiting the scope if not the degree of military power. Because the Argentine military has lost power in society, the key sites under consideration are those that reside within state institutions. It is, I submit, the power of state institutions outside the chain of command that permits this compensation.

This argument would seem to be plausible unless it could be shown that defense organization within the chain of command is the linchpin to civilian supremacy, that without demonstrable strength there, no effort outside of it would matter. It is doubtful that such an argument could be sustained. A quick review of institutional arrangements encountered in advanced, Western democracies uncovers serious if not striking deficiencies. In Israel, the military does not clearly submit to one political master by law or in practice and enjoys remarkably high levels of autonomy. In France, the president, prime minister, and defense minister all have their own direct lines of authority to the military chief of staff. In Britain, each service still reserves the right to appeal to the prime minister directly, bypassing the secretary of state for defense. And if we were to view matters in evolutionary terms, let us remind ourselves that by the end of World War II, and in its 162d year, the United States still had no secretary of defense, let alone any civilian institution to restrain the power of the Joint Chiefs of Staff. Adjustments to strengthen the U.S. chain of command were still being made well into the 1980s.[15]

The truth is that we really do not know just how indispensable defense organization is to the achievement of civilian control in developed or lesser developed countries. It is hard for us to imagine doing without it but equally hard to measure its relative weight. Scholars have suggested optimal designs for defense organizations along the chain of command.[16] But one would be hard-pressed to find examples of where a nation's failure to adhere to or approximate optimality has proved fatal. Indeed, there is so much variation in the patterns of authority governing contact between political and military elites that it is difficult to know what is essential and what is not. One would think that having a civilian-led Ministry of Defense would be a minimal requirement. Yet there has been a significant erosion of military influence in Brazil, which until 1999 had no Ministry of Defense.[17]

If defense organization is critical, then we are faced with the puzzle that so many leaders have endured for so long with seemingly flawed institutional ar- rangements. If it is not, then the question becomes, What else accounts for the stability of civil-military relations? Even though there are significant problems with defense organization within the chain of command, there are clear signs that civilian governments have made headway in their efforts to reduce mili- tary power and influence. Nowhere is this more apparent than in Argentina. A comparative discussion of state institutions will help us understand why.

The Ministry of Defense

There is no question that since the recovery of Argentina's democracy in 1983, the military's formal authority within the state has been reduced. Shortly after assuming office in 1983, President Raúl Alfonsín inserted the Defense Ministry into the chain of command between himself and the armed forces. The heads of each service were downgraded from commanders to chiefs of staff and had to answer directly to a civilian defense minister.[18] These organizational re- forms immediately reduced the decision-making autonomy enjoyed by each branch, while erecting a hierarchy from the president to his minister to his military subordinates.

The Defense Ministry, which had been in a moribund state of health for decades, was given a new lease on life with substantial powers to direct, regulate, and coordinate all spheres of defense activity not reserved for the president himself.[19] As the ministry assumed more and more tasks hitherto reserved for the armed services, the bureaucracy expanded as well, reflecting a need to delegate more duties to subordinates. These changes created additional layers of authority between the civilian officials and the military.

Of course, the ministry is just one, albeit central, component to the Argentine defense system. In addition, there is the military Joint Staff, or Estado Mayor Conjunto (EMC), which is a unit within the MOD but outside of the chain of command whose function it is to counsel the defense minister on joint military strategy, operations, and training.[20] Each of the three services is functionally—not operationally—accountable to the EMC when considering joint action and sends up mid-level officers to serve on the EMC staff. The 1988 Law of National Defense also created a National Defense Council (NDC) consisting of the vice president, cabinet ministers, and the head of intelligence, whose purpose it was to provide the president with advice on defense and security matters.

None of these organizational reforms should be underestimated. The fundamental problem, however, is that although the laws and structures are in place, they have not been effectively used. Civilian defense ministers and their staffs have not made policy.[21] For example, since the democratic transition, no general defense objectives have ever been proposed by the president, his minister, or his NDC. In fact, to my knowledge, the NDC has never been convened. With few exceptions, no specific defense plan or strategy has ever been hatched by the defense minister in consultation with his own staff.[22] The minister has repeatedly deferred to the EMC's military personnel to issue reports and recommendations that bear no stamp of civilian input. Besides, while many of the ideas contained in these reports regarding interservice collaboration were useful, they could not be easily enforced. The chief of the EMC lacks seniority over the chiefs of each service and hence could not invest the work of his agency with commanding authority.[23]

Students of the Argentine state may see nothing new in this portrayal of the Defense Ministry. The ministry's shortcomings, they may say, are symptomatic of more widespread and deeply rooted maladies of the state itself. These afflictions, the product of long-term neglect and abuse at the hands of political leaders, have reduced the state's performance by preventing it from producing and reproducing a cadre of technical support staff necessary to imbue its ministries with competency.[24]

By the same token, generalizations are risky. The state is not an undifferentiated political structure but an amalgam of unequally endowed institutions. One reason for this situation is that the desire for aptitude is problem-driven and therefore selective. For example, the need for a Third World country like

Argentina to solve its economic problems is imperative, often overshadowing other needs. This need may compel elected leaders whose political fortunes rise or fall with the economy to train the talent necessary to equip the Economics Ministry properly, while other ministries are left to languish. Similarly, a once isolated country like Argentina that now recognizes that its future is tied to that of other states, that it must forge stronger regional and international ties via diplomatic means, also has an incentive to invest scarce resources in its Foreign Relations Ministry.

Another reason for differences in ministerial proficiency has to do with the technical requirements of the tasks. It seems harder to settle for officials untrained in financial matters than it is, say, in the realms of defense, health, and labor. It is almost taken for granted in South America that a minister of economics, along with his principal underlings, will come to the job with a Ph.D. in economics from a reputable institution. Knowledge about taxes, budgets, inflation, interest rates, investment, and other specialties is not only essential but too complicated and specialized in nature to be left to officials who lack the relevant expertise. In sum, it would be ill-advised to discount ministerial analyses on the basis of overviews of state performance. It is worth examining the Argentine state in greater detail so that we may unveil important institutional differences, ones that will not only help place the Defense Ministry's problems in perspective but reveal how weaknesses in one corner of the state are compensated for by strengths in other corners.

Comparative Ministerial Competence: A Look from Above and Below

To the extent that civilians can deal knowledgeably and confidently with their subject matter, they can dispel notions that others like the armed forces can do the job better. Leadership at the top of the bureaucracy is always important insofar as a director can instill a sense of mission into an agency by tapping into and activating the motivational bases of its employees. It certainly helps if a minister comes to the job prepared in the specific subject matter at hand or remains there long enough to acquire it. A bureaucracy that is historically endowed with a well-trained civil service, however, is one that has institutionalized its own competence and is thus less dependent on top-rung political appointees to fill the void. For these reasons we need to examine the ministry from above and below, underscoring the capabilities of both its leaders and its employees. I have examined the longevity of those who have occupied the top posts in the Ministries of Defense, Economics, and Foreign Relations, along with their educational and career backgrounds. Additionally, I will look at the degree to which recruitment and training of personnel are institutionalized within the ministries.

How long do ministers serve in office? The answer tells us something about how well an agency's head can become acquainted with the complexities, peculiarities, and missions of the organization. If ministers are constantly shuffled in and out of office, the interruptions breed institutional memory failure. Those who leave do so hurriedly, emptying their offices of important documents, hardly giving a thought to the transition. New officials come and must frantically familiarize themselves with the issues and the agency without the help of adequate documentation. Without the benefit of accumulated record, wisdom, and experience, ministers have difficulty getting up to speed on issues.

The Defense Ministry has had a comparatively high turnover rate, as shown in Table 6.1. Under Alfonsín, discontinuity was unavoidable because of the sudden deaths of two ministers. Under Menem, it was intentional. Officials were posted there temporarily for expediency, only to be withdrawn when convenient. The Economics Ministry is traditionally the most precarious cabinet portfolio in Argentina. Ministers are quick to be fired whenever economic fatality strikes, a frequent occurrence in that country. Hence it would not be surprising to see substantial turnover there. Yet the Economics Ministry outperforms the Defense Ministry. Moreover, during the Alfonsín and Menem administrations, the two principal Economics Ministry czars survived for very long periods of time: Juan Sourrouille (forty-nine months) and Domingo Cavallo (sixty-five months). The Foreign Relations Ministry is substantially more stable than either the Defense or Economics Ministry. Through the end of the Menem presidency, only three individuals had served as foreign relations minister across three governments, and two of those had occupied the post for a combined span of almost 15 years.

Table 6.2 provides comparative information on the educational and career backgrounds of ministers who have occupied their posts during the democratic period in Argentina. For purposes of brevity, I have focused on those who have served at least one year in office. Thus not all cabinet appointees have been included.

It is evident that the Economics Ministry is in the best shape since its ministers have come to the job with good academic credentials and career-relevant, on-the-job training. Between 1985 and 1999, all ministers who served over a year had Ph.D.'s from top U.S. universities as well as experience in the Central Bank or in the ministry itself. This is to be contrasted with the defense ministers, none of whom had degrees or coursework in the realm of defense or security and only two of whom came to the ministry with relevant job experi-

TABLE 6.1 *Tenure of Argentine Ministers, 1983–1999*

MINISTRY	AVERAGE TENURE (MONTHS)	LONGEST TENURE (MONTHS)
Defense	19.5	39
Economics	25	65
Foreign Relations	59	93

Sources: 1983–87: *New York Times Index*; 1988–98: *Current World Leaders* 31, no. 1 (1988), to 41, no. 2 (1998).

ence.[25] The Foreign Relations Ministry occupies a middle position. One of the two longest serving ministers by far had the pertinent education (Dante Caputo) and the other had held a government position (Guido DiTella), but neither had both.

What most ministers bring to the defense job that is not captured in the table is a long, abiding friendship with the president and loyalty to his political party. That was not the case with the economics ministers, who were appointed mainly for their technical expertise. Ministers who are assigned to posts for political rather than professional reasons may be there because the president is worried that the ministry cannot respond effectively. The less faith he has in the agency, the more trust he must place in his political confidant to set things straight. But without a professional staff, an inexperienced director has his work cut out for him.

The Defense Ministry has no institute associated with it devoted to educating civilians in military affairs. In lieu of a ministerial institute, the National Defense School would seem to be a reasonable surrogate. Over the years the school has offered a series of interesting defense courses to military and civilians alike, but none are oriented toward ministerial service, nor is there any formal link between the school and the ministry. At the end of the 1997 academic year, Defense Minister Jorge Dominguez acknowledged the deficiency and anticipated that the new Law of Military Restructuring would authorize a linkage between the school's curricula and the work of the ministry. The law, passed in the spring of 1998, did not. What it did do was impose new responsibilities on the MOD, meaning that the agency had more obligations than in the past and fewer skilled civilians to carry them out.[26]

By contrast, the Foreign Relations Ministry is institutionally equipped to carry out its obligations. Since 1963, it has had an Institute for Foreign Service that recruits and trains future diplomats. Through countless administrations over more than thirty-five years, the institute has maintained a continuity that ensures that a coherent, consistent program is provided for future diplomats.

TABLE 6.2 *Argentine Ministers, 1983–1999: Education and Career Background*

MINISTER	RELEVANT EDUCATION?	EDUCATIONAL DETAILS	RELEVANT EXPERIENCE?	CAREER DETAILS
FOREIGN RELATIONS				
Dante Caputo, 1983–89	Yes	B.A., Ph.D. political science, Sorbonne; courses in international relations, Fletcher School	No	Professor of public administration; organized Alfonsín campaign
Domingo Cavallo, 1989–90	No	Ph.D. economics	No	President of Argentine Central Bank
Guido DiTella, 1991–99	No	Ph.D. economics	Yes	Ambassador to United States
ECONOMICS				
Juan Sourroille, 1985–89	Yes	Ph.D. economics, Harvard	Yes	Secretary of planning, Economics Ministry
Domingo Cavallo, 1991–96	Yes	Ph.D. economics, Harvard	Yes	President of Argentine Central Bank; undersecretary for development, Cordoba
Roque Fernandez, 1996–99	Yes	Ph.D. economics, University of Chicago	Yes	Director of Argentine Central Bank
DEFENSE				
Raúl Borrás, 1983–85	No	Economics degree	No	Minister of public works
Horacio Jaunarena, 1986–89	No	Law degree	Yes	Secretary of defense, Defense Ministry
Humberto Romero, 1990	No	Law degree	Yes	Secretary of defense, Defense Ministry
Antonio Erman González, 1991–93	No	Accounting degree	No	Minister of economics
Oscar Camilión, 1993–96	No	Law degree	No	Ambassador to Brazil; UN under-secretary general
Jorge Dominguez, 1996–99	No	Economics degree	No	Mayor, Buenos Aires

Sources: 1983–87: *New York Times Index*; 1988–98: *Current World Leaders* 31, no. 1 (1988), to 41, no. 2 (1998).

The institute has rigorous entrance requirements and a two-year curricula of courses on subjects oriented to conform with the needs of specific functions and departments in the ministry. The faculty, numbering over forty, draws from well-known authorities in academic and diplomatic circles. The institute also sponsors research in four centers of study where specialists prepare working papers and interact with officials from the ministry. With this institutionalization of competence, the ministry need not rely exclusively on the talents of its director.[27]

The Economics Ministry has evolved more slowly and unevenly. Decisions on privatization were, according to Osvaldo Iazzetta, improvisational, responding to the urgencies of the moment. That changed with the arrival in 1991 of Domingo Cavallo, who "produced a certain reconstruction of the state" that included a strengthening of technical expertise.[28] Iazzetta also admits, however, that the ministry demonstrated greater levels of proficiency earlier on in other areas such as taxation or budgets. This is important because the ministry's greatest impact on the armed forces concerns the defense budget. Indeed, Cavallo himself dismissed the notion that Argentina's previous failures to stabilize the economy had anything to do with technical incompetence but rather with a lack of political backing.[29]

Unevenness is now giving way to consistency with the creation in 1994 of the ministry's own Superior Institute of Governmental Economists. The institute's purpose is to promote a significant improvement in the quality of administrative and managerial personnel charged with the formulation and execution of economic policy. It too has tough entrance requirements (university degree, current public service, examination, and so on) and a four-semester-long graduate program in public economics with courses whose contents are tailored to the needs of the ministry.[30]

In sum, the Ministry of Defense is generally ill-prepared to assume the important tasks mandated to it. Its civilian ministers do not arrive on the job well versed in defense issues, nor do they stay on the job long enough to acquire the skills. And its staff has not reaped the benefits of professional training because there has been no institutionalization of expertise within the ministry. Comparatively speaking, the Ministries of Economics and Foreign Relations have done considerably better in all regards. The Defense Ministry's lack of ministerial competence and continuity translates into a deficiency of will. Being less confident in the area, its ministers are more reticent to demonstrate leadership, deferring instead to military judgment. I will now consider to what extent the institutional strengths of the Ministries of Economics and Foreign Relations and the Congress have been used to offset the weaknesses in the Ministry of Defense.

Reducing Military Power: The Role of Alternative Institutions

Economics

The Ministry of Economics, Works, and Public Services has been the principal instrument for reducing the military's resource base. Through its control of fiscal decisions and processes, it has effected enormous cuts in the military's budget shares, its personnel, and its facilities. The size of the armed services has declined by 52 percent between 1983 and 1997, by far the largest loss of personnel of any military force in the region. Its expenditures have decreased in real terms by more than a third in the same period, as shown in Table 6.3 and Figure 6.1. Installations have been closed, military-run factories have been privatized, pet missile projects have been suspended, and procurement has been curtailed—all at the insistence of the Economics Ministry. Decisions regarding the fate of the defense budget have been made deep within the chambers of the Ministry of Economics. It is here, not in the Defense Ministry or at army, navy, or air force headquarters, that ceilings for defense are established and officers are told what they can and cannot purchase.

The ministry has accomplished these tasks at the behest of two elected presidents and largely free from military pressures. Two elements define the ministry's autonomy. The first is procedural. On a decision as critical as a budgetary ceiling, one that will affect the nation's security, no one in the defense orbit is consulted, not the services, not the chiefs of staff, not the defense minister, not the National Defense Council. The preliminary decisions, which include the setting of tight spending limits for defense, are made to conform with general fiscal and monetary objectives, not with national security needs, and they are made by civilian technocrats thoroughly insulated from military pressures. Military officials do not wade into the decision-making waters until the end of the process, when they must decide how to prioritize the scarce resources delivered to them by the economists.

The second dimension to autonomy is structural. The technocrats are distant from military reach. The armed forces have no official presence in the Economics Ministry or its secretariat of finance. Bureaucratically speaking, the military is twice removed from the Economics Ministry, separated by the Defense Ministry and even further distanced from the budgeting office that resides within the finance secretariat. It must appeal through the MOD and hope that civilian functionaries there will adequately and fairly represent its interests. But defense officials are often poor advocates because unless there is a clear and present national security threat, they cannot overcome the rational

TABLE 6.3 *Military Expenditures in Argentina, 1983–1997*

YEAR	MILITARY EXPENDITURES (BILLIONS 1997 PESOS)	INDEX OF MILITARY EXPENDITURES (1997 = 100)	MILITARY EXPENDITURES AS % OF GDP
1983	6.167871393	154	3.5
1984	5.305161213	132	2.3
1985	4.914777951	122	2.3
1986	5.308153537	132	2.3
1987	5.386184154	134	2.3
1988	4.914777951	122	2.1
1989	4.085904056	102	1.9
1990	3.15091773	78	1.5
1991	3.562707621	89	1.5
1992	3.654088609	91	1.4
1993	3.588948006	89	1.3
1994	4.254625124	106	1.4
1995	4.116517838	102	1.4
1996	4.124343918	103	1.4
1997	4.016390056	100	1.2

Sources: Military expenditure and GDP figures provided by Thomas Scheetz. Index calculated by author. Raw data originally from the Ministry of Economics and the Central Bank.

objections of the Ministry of Economics to greater defense expenditures. For procedural and structural reasons, the military is largely left out of the loop.

The institutional arrangements governing budgeting decisions dealt a strong hand to Argentine presidents and their economics ministers. A ministry well insulated from pressures has an easier time staying the course even in the face of strenuous military objections to defense cutbacks. Chief executives are the beneficiaries of institutional strength as well. Not having to intervene personally to shepherd his budget through or bargain with his military commanders, the president can set his priorities and then distance himself from the policy fray while relying on agencies to faithfully execute his policies over and above military opposition.

It began with Alfonsín, who said he would trim the military's budget back to its historic level of 2 percent of GDP and did just that. Cuts hit the services hard, with reports of basic provisions in short supply, equipment lying in disrepair, units suspending activities and training exercises, and soldiers leaving the barracks at midday to find compensatory employment in the private sector. Sectors within the armed forces complained bitterly, to no avail, about how these losses had so damaged military operational capacity as to place the

FIGURE 6.1 *Military Expenditures in Argentina, 1983–1997*

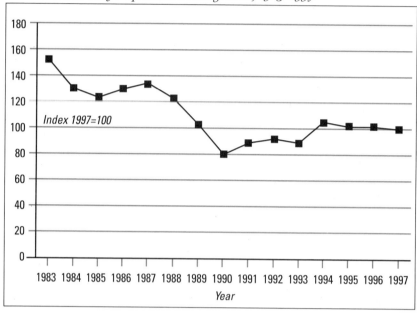

nation in a state of indefensiveness. The economics minister, Juan Sourrouille, along with his technocratic staff of financial experts and accountants, was invulnerable to military entreaties.

If the military thought it would get any fiscal relief with the coming to power of Peronist Carlos Menem, it was wrong. Personalities do not account for defense budget decisions in the democratic era; institutions and institutionalized interests do. The military's budgetary needs were no longer of transcending importance to Argentine governments; fiscal austerity and state shrinkage were. Shortly after Menem's adjustment plan was set in motion in 1991, the armed forces sounded the same alarms first heard under Alfonsín. Officers who took issue too strongly were scolded for complaining as if they were members of a union; others were summarily cashiered.[31] If the defense minister were to advocate on behalf of the military at cabinet meetings, the economics minister would usually have his way. Again, during the second wave of state restructuring that began in 1996, voices from the Defense Ministry and armed forces were cautioning that the country faced a "window of great [security] vulnerability" and that not one peso less could be spent on defense. In response, the military was chosen as a critical target for reform, and the Defense Ministry became the first state agency to be placed on the chopping block.[32]

Eventually, military complaints have given way to begrudging acceptance of its losses, yet another sign of its diminished power. A remarkable testimony to the military's compliance with civilian rule is its adjustment to the harsh realities of fiscal reform, a reflection of the power of institutions to shape strategies and preferences. Knowing that it lacks the power to alter budgeting rules and norms, it tries to stay one step ahead of these by proposing its own cost-saving measures rather than have the economics minister do it. Thus, in March 1996, a military study suggested that through liquidation of some of its properties and consolidation of others, it could save $300 million that could be reinvested in equipment.[33] While the military still pleads (as do all sectors fighting for budget shares), it also prioritizes. Which operations does it believe are most expendable? Which ones can it not do without? A hierarchy of needs is established so that anticipated cuts can be absorbed rationally while inflicting the least damage possible on force structure and personnel.

The military's attention to cost-benefit logic, not to mention its acceptance of more modest budgets, would have been unthinkable two decades before. Cognizant that a new culture of efficiency and fiscal prudence now pervades the corridors of power—corridors that it does not easily traverse—it adjusts its behavior accordingly. This is the modus operandi of a now vastly smaller, weaker organization compelled to operate according to new rules of the game. But if the Economics Ministry had a decisive hand in all this, it also received help from the Foreign Relations Ministry.

Foreign Relations

The Foreign Relations Ministry has played a key role in altering the military's threat environment. Its diplomatic offensives have locked erstwhile regional adversaries into a series of agreements that have arrested bilateral tensions, resolved border disputes, submitted future disputes to peaceful conflict resolution, and committed those same parties to strategies of economic integration. With the signing of historic nuclear treaties and protocols with Brazil, the nation's Foreign Relations Ministry capped a vigorous effort to break down the political, psychological, and military barriers that had separated these two South American giants for so long. The agreement paved the way for the talks that would result in the creation of the Southern Cone free trade bloc known as MERCOSUR.[34] President Raúl Alfonsín and his foreign relations minister, Dante Caputo, took the initiatives that led to the signing of the Treaty of Peace and Friendship with Chile, an accord that put an end to the age-old Beagle feud and obliged both countries to abstain from the threat or use of force.[35] His successor, Carlos Menem, and Foreign Relations Minister Guido DiTella and their counterparts in Chile followed up with resolutions to some two dozen other outstanding border disputes.

These diplomatic initiatives have greatly reduced the security risks to Argentina by lowering the political temperature between former enemies. In fact, Argentina is so safe from invasion that the nation no longer contemplates hypotheses of conflict with either of its neighbors.[36] Since defensive needs are assessed in proportion to risk, the armed forces have been stripped of persuasive rationales for rearmament. Even if it were true that budget cuts have left the nation ill-prepared to defend itself, vulnerability is less worrisome than it was before precisely because diplomacy has dramatically reduced the risk of confrontation with Chile or Brazil.

The military has had little choice but to go along with the regional peace offensives of the Foreign Relations Ministry. Even if it has lingering suspicions and fears about its neighbors—and in all likelihood it does—-its views do not penetrate the policy-making inner circles as they once did.[37] In fact, the armed forces can no longer use their institutional relation with the MOD to any appreciable advantage because the ministry itself has been supplanted by the Foreign Relations Ministry on external security and defense matters. True, the armed forces have set up liaison offices in the Chancellery so as to maintain access. But this is no substitute for the more extensive, regularized contact with the MOD. Additionally, ministerial procedures prohibit the military from weighing in on policy decisions.

Staffed by a highly autonomous, well-trained, politically savvy team of specialists, the ministry has won unprecedented influence over military affairs.[38] "Since 1990," comments Rut Diamint, "the definitional axis of security policy has been moved to the Ministry for Foreign Relations."[39] The Foreign Relations Ministry advises the president on how the nation's external defense objectives will be fulfilled, making key policy recommendations on regional security and international peacekeeping. In this respect, it has gone beyond its legal mandate, trespassing on ground that should normally have been reserved for the Defense Ministry. Nothing in the Constitution or Law of Ministries specifically allows it to "represent" the nation's interests in security or defense affairs, although it may do so in a host of other areas. Rather, it is limited to *participating in* two specific decisions: whether to allow foreign forces to traverse Argentine soil and whether to permit Argentine forces to depart. The ministry cannot recommend whether, when, or how the military forces shall be deployed once they have left Argentina.[40]

The Foreign Relations Ministry appears, however, to have done just that. It was Domingo Cavallo, then foreign relations minister, who helped Menem calculate that Argentina's best chance for development lay in a pragmatic reinsertion into the international community, within the parameters of the United States' "New World Order." To earn Washington's confidence, it was essential, thought Cavallo, that Argentina lend a military hand in internationalized conflicts. Aside from the president himself, it was the foreign relations minister who was the driving force behind Argentina's entry into the Gulf War against Iraq, not the minister of defense. It was the foreign relations chief who took the lead in defining the missions the military would have in the new world order. "From here on in," said Cavallo, "the armed forces are going to have very clear objectives. They are going to support international security at the same time they support national security."[41]

Cavallo's trespassing went beyond proclamations. In August 1990, Admiral Emilio Osses, then head of the EMC, said the military had reached a consensus about going to the Gulf. Cavallo, not the defense minister, swiftly rebuked Osses for remarks implying that the military had deliberated about its role. The political leadership decides, he said, while the military plays only a "technical, professional, and advisory role."[42] It is remarkable indeed that the head of foreign relations would discipline the military chief of staff instead of the civilian within the chain of command. In one of his last acts as minister, Cavallo traveled to Saudi Arabia in January 1991 to arrange for the financing and dispatch of Argentine navy vessels to the Gulf. At home stood an embarrassed, idle defense minister, Humberto Romero, who tried to cast the foreign relations minister's trip in a more general political light. But clearly Cavallo was up to his ears in military minutiae, as would be his successor, Guido DiTella. Why wasn't the defense minister or one of his secretaries in the Mideast handling these affairs?[43]

Whether it was the Gulf War, the termination of the air force missile project known as Condor II, or the involvement in UN peacekeeping forces in Yugoslavia and Cambodia, the Foreign Relations Ministry always seemed to be at center field while the Defense Ministry was relegated to the sidelines. This was true across administrations and regardless of which political appointee was at the helm of the ministry. The Chancellery's push to involve Argentine forces in peacekeeping has been particularly consequential because it has provided the military with a new, externally oriented, professionally enhancing mission. Although initially reticent, Argentine troops soon warmed to the idea of peacekeeping. They discovered the benefits of rubbing shoulders with the finest trained soldiers in the world, while the military organization discovered the advantages of having the United Nations pay for its services. Martín Balza, former chief of staff for the army, has said these ventures not only have helped restore the morale, confidence, and prestige of the military that were lost during its war with Great Britain but have literally transformed the internal culture of his service, helping to break down the walls that used to separate commissioned officers from noncommissioned officers.[44] He has the Foreign Relations Ministry, not the Defense Ministry, to thank for that. In short, the Foreign Relations Ministry has been instrumental in both stripping the military of rationales for resource expansion while shifting its preferences toward professionally rewarding, cost-saving, international security roles.

Congress

The primary missions of the Argentine armed forces have been fundamentally altered thanks in large part to the work of defense commissions in the Argentine Congress. Those commissions crafted the historic 1988 Law of National Defense (Ley 23554), which stipulated that military force be used to confront aggression of external origin only.[45] Previous laws had reserved for the military a significant and ongoing role in facing down domestic threats under the rubric of national security. Thus the new defense law represented a huge loss for the armed services and one they had lobbied vigorously to forestall.

While the impetus for new defense legislation derived from the Defense Ministry, the momentum quickly shifted to the Congress, where the law was written. It was largely in the defense commission of the House of Deputies in 1985 that the concept of defense was revisited, a defense system was proposed, distinctions between defense and security were elaborated, and the idea of confining military doctrine and deployment to external spheres was proposed. Though commission deputies drew ideas from diverse sources, they relied principally on their own civilian staffers for expertise. The commission and the full House did their work with dispatch, sending the bill on to the Senate, where some modifications were made by the defense commission to satisfy objections from Peronists who controlled the upper chamber. But upon its return to the lower chamber for final consideration, the bill stagnated under the weight of opposition from none other than the Defense Ministry itself. Horacio Jaunarena, then defense minister, had been under pressure to repair relations with the officer corps and hence tried to get Radical Party deputies to reconsider key provisions of the bill. It took the Semana Santa uprising of April 1987 to induce the government and the Peronists to reach consensus on a final bill that became law in April 1988.[46]

The congressional effort to refashion the Argentine defense system and the military's role in it was unprecedented. Never before had the legislative branch taken so active a role in defense matters with such an unexpected emphasis on long-term national interests rather than the sectarian politics of defense patronage or the urgencies of the moment. In commenting not only on the drafting of the defense law but on the informed floor debates leading up to it, José Manuel Ugarte, the principal author of the defense law, said, "In other words, it [the Congress] is a place where the short term can cede its place to the future, and where situational demands yield their place to structural reforms. For this reason it was in the parliament and not in the executive branch where the process of analysis and debate [of defense issues] took place."[47] Again the Defense Ministry failed to live up to its mandate. It is precisely within this central defense organization that the policies shaping the objectives, structure, capabilities, and limits of the national defense system should have been proposed. If there were to be constraints on military action, they should have been designed by Defense Ministry personnel. Instead, the Congress did so, joining the Ministries of Economics and Foreign Relations in compensating for fundamental weaknesses in the chain of command.

Conclusion

As indicated in the introductory chapter, powerful actors cannot automatically translate preferences into policy because their will is mediated by political institutions. An institutional approach has the advantage of explaining in what areas the military is and is not able to make its presence known. It does so by identifying those procedural or structural characteristics of governing agencies that either open up or restrict the military's access to centers of power. I have shown how higher levels of autonomy and expertise in the Ministries of Economics and Foreign Relations and the Congress have offset deficiencies in the Ministry of Defense, permitting civilians to make policy unimpeded by military pressures.

What do all of these ministerial and congressional initiatives add up to? Combined, they represent an impressive though indirect effort by political leaders to use institutions to place restraints on various forms of military power. Impressive, because these civilianized centers of power stripped the military of resources, roles, and rationales that in the past constituted vital sources of strength. That has permitted political leaders to sit atop the armed forces without fear of insubordination. Indirect because the efforts were undertaken outside of the chain of command, not within it. Operators without *formal* authority over the armed forces could nonetheless exert considerable influence over them because they made policy that directly and adversely affected their interests. They could do so because of the strengths of the institutions they inhabited.

Why would civilian leaders confronting military power do so by circumventing the core institutional sites? Defense institutions within the chain of command constitute the densest points of contact between military and civilian personnel. Nowhere else in or outside of the state do so many actors from the two sides meet and work together on a daily basis. That means the strengths and frailties of each are on full display for the other. Civilians who lack the requisite defense-related skills face careful scrutiny from military personnel close by—in fact, in the same building. Regardless of their legal authority, it is very hard for a defense minister and his undersecretaries to command respect from military subordinates when they are unfamiliar with the terrain. It is far easier for them to defer to the military, awaiting its recommendations, which then perhaps could be repackaged as their own.[48] No amount of repackaging, however, could conceal their dependence on the military, a dependence that deepens each time they relinquish responsibility.

Consequently, civilians stand a better chance of eroding military power where they can either demonstrate greater competence or operate at greater distance or both. The autonomy and capacity of institutions outside of the chain of command proved to be decisive. Budgets may have a defense component but demand the attention of trained economists and accountants, all of whom are civilians working in the inner chambers of the Economics Ministry. The Foreign Relations Ministry immerses officials in the world of diplomacy, where the artful skills of negotiation take precedence. It is a world where the armed forces are out of their element. And the Congress is a body of elected, nonuniformed representatives who haggle over legislative proposals. At each of these sites, civilians dominate, showing off skills, experiences, and styles of work that are often foreign to military personnel but relevant to their fates.

Where their work is military-unfriendly, they especially benefit from the autonomy they enjoy from the armed forces. They are not prey to direct military pressures, threats, or vetoes of any kind. The armed services have contacts with these centers, but they are less constant and intense than those found in the Defense Ministry. Moreover, they are official in nature, cordial, and limited in their impact, serving more to keep open communications than to provide avenues of penetration. Autonomy not only protects policy makers from unwanted influences but also prevents the military from playing off one center against another.

Does all of this add up to civilian control? That remains to be seen. What we can say with complete assurance is that the glass is at least half, probably three-quarters, full. The indirect application of civilian influence has weakened the military politically while focusing its attention on professionally enhancing missions. Ultimately, however, full subordination necessitates civilian leadership all along the chain of command. To date such leadership has not been sufficiently demonstrated.

The study of Argentina has implications for other countries of the region. The defense weaknesses mentioned here are not unique. They can easily be found throughout Latin America, where, if anything, they are compounded in magnitude. The civilian inferiority complex about defense is rampant in the region. It is a product of both the military's unwillingness to relax its tenacious grasp on a subject near and dear to it and politicians' disinterest in it. And it infects the defense organizations it comes into contact with. How lethal is the infection elsewhere? It is worthwhile exploring whether other countries have been able to compensate the way Argentina has. Such exploration would be especially warranted in countries where there is some evidence that military political influence has declined *despite* serious deficiencies in the chain of command. That would invite institutional approaches to the study of Uruguay, whose Defense Ministry has been dominated by military personnel, and Brazil, which until 1999 had no Defense Ministry.

By the same token, it would be interesting to take a look at nations where the military presence is stronger.[49] Have civilian leaders there missed opportunities to erode military power by not exploiting natural strengths found at other institutional sites in the state? Or are those states so weak that they afford no selective advantages? We need to know before rushing to judgment. The weakest link in the chain may be very weak indeed. But if Argentina is any clue, then civilians are resourceful enough to find other institutional means to ensure that the balance of power remains in their favor.

NOTES

I thank Deborah Norden and William C. Smith for their comments on an earlier version of this chapter.

1. Huntington preoccupied himself with the weaknesses of the U.S. secretary of defense, his office, and his staff. See Huntington, *Soldier and the State*, 87, 428–55.
2. Edmonds, *Central Organizations of Defense*, 2.
3. Agüero, *Soldiers, Civilians, and Democracy*, 197.
4. The strongest tests of subordination are those that evince military compliance with policies it opposes. Argentine examples of such subordination are more numerous than in any other state in South America. For instance, the military has complied with what is the most legally restrictive mission statement in the continent. It has lived within a defense budget that has been repeatedly cut more drastically than any other in the region. And it has gone along with the creation of an all-volunteer force it initially felt uncomfortable with.
5. On the theory of institutional analysis, see March and Olsen, "New Institutionalism," and Hall and Taylor, "Political Science and the Three New Institutionalisms." For an application of this approach, see Pion-Berlin, *Through Corridors of Power*, 19–41.

6. Huntington, *Soldier and the State*, 88.

7. This argument is made in Pion-Berlin, *Through Corridors of Power*.

8. March and Olsen, "New Institutionalism," 738.

9. Hall and Taylor, "Political Science and the Three New Institutionalisms," 941.

10. Immergut, "Rules of the Game," 59.

11. See Evans, Rueschmeyer, and Skocpol, *Bringing the State Back In*. Institutional approaches differ somewhat from earlier statist literature by their attention to substate variations in design, rules, and structures that influence policy outcomes.

12. By pushing through policies objectionable to the military, policymakers are likely to generate military opposition. So long as that opposition is confined to official corridors and its impact is minimized, it is not threatening to civilian control.

13. Feaver, "Crisis as Shirking."

14. Welch, *Civilian Control of the Military*, 2.

15. Also in Israel, the government deprives its defense minister of a civilian staff with which to evaluate military programs, defers to the military on the defense budget, and allows senior officers to appear at cabinet meetings to advocate policy preferences. See Etzioni-Halevy, "Civil-Military Relations and Democracy." See also Yariv, "Military Organizations and Policymaking in Israel." On France, see Marichy, "Central Organization of Defense in France." On Great Britain, see Edmonds, "Central Organizations of Defense in Great Britain." On the United States, see Huntington, *Soldier and the State*, 335–36, 374–99, 428–55.

16. Such a design would concentrate civilian power, deploy a single unambiguous chain of command, and furnish it with a well-trained and well-funded Defense Ministry that supervises an integrated military force. If authority is to be wielded effectively, it must maintain the delicate balance between political control and respect for military professional knowledge; hierarchical yet cordial and fluid contacts to maximize information flows; and sensible divisions of labor among policy, administrative, and professional functions.

17. Hunter, *Eroding Military Influence*.

18. On 7 December 1983 the military expressed to General Reynaldo Bignone, then head of the outgoing military government, its displeasure over the proposed law since it would relegate the chiefs of staff to administrative functions, stripping them of their autonomy (Foreign Broadcast Information Service–Latin America, 8 December 1983, B5).

19. *Legislación Argentina*.

20. República Argentina, *Ley de Defensa Nacional*.

21. In commenting on the desired traits of a defense secretary, Huntington said: "The secretary must be a man of policy. His greatest needs are breadth, wisdom, insight, and above all, judgment. He is neither operator, administrator, nor commander. But he is policymaker. He should have his own ideas on policy, and he needs initiative" (*Soldier and the State*, 455).

22. One exception is Decree 1116 drafted in 1996 and signed by President Menem and Defense Minister Jorge Dominguez. This Joint Military Plan suggests the principle of "strategic rationality," whereby military responses are designed in proportion to the aggressions encountered. See Decreto 1116/92, 2 October 1996, reprinted in Ser2000 Online Database of Security and Defense, http://www.ser2000.org.ar/protect/

archivo. Everything proposed here fits within the framework already devised by the Argentine Congress in its defense and internal security laws. Another is the ministry's release of the 1998 White Paper on National Defense, which is long on general objectives and activities—most of which were already known—but short on implementation details, which would have been valuable to know. See Ser2000 Online Database of Security and Defense.

23. This is one of the central weaknesses of the EMC, according to its former chief, Admiral Emilio Osses, in an interview with the author, 1 November 1994, in Buenos Aires. Osses wanted the EMC chief granted greater powers, but President Menem would not go along.

24. Sikkink, *Ideas and Institutions*, 188–95.

25. As can be seen in Table 6.2, although both Jaunarena and Romero had defense backgrounds, their combined services as defense ministers totaled only four of the sixteen years.

26. Ley de Reestructuración (24.948), in Diamint, *Argentina y la Seguridad Internacional*, 63–74.

27. República Argentina, Ministerio de Relaciones Exteriores, Instituto Del Servicio Exterior de la Nación, online http://isen.mrecic.gov.ar/.

28. Iazzetta, "Capacidades técnicas y de gobierno," 272.

29. Corrales, "Why Argentines Followed Cavallo."

30. República Argentina, Ministerio de Economía y Obras y Servicios Públicos, Instituto Superior de los Economistas de Gobierno, online www.mecon.ar/iseg.

31. Pion-Berlin, *Through Corridors of Power*, 125–26.

32. By November of that year, the ministry's physical plant had shrunk by 18 percent, including the loss of 2 secretariats, 2 undersecretaries, 10 departments, and 176 employees. The following April, the entire ministry was moved out of its premises and into army headquarters across the street to make way for the new headquarters for Buenos Aires's education department. See "La reforma del estado empezó por defensa," *La Nación*, 8 November 1996, and "Defensa vendió su sede a la ciudad," *La Prensa*, 24 January 1998, in Ser2000 Online Database of Security and Defense.

33. "Asegurán que el area militar podría ahorrar $300 million," *La Nación*, 11 March 1996, online Ser2000 Database of Security and Defense, http://www.ser2000.org.ar/archivo.

34. Sucesos, Agencia de Noticias online, "Mercosur," 1998, http://www.mercosur.com/htdocs/main.html.

35. Foreign Broadcast Information Service–Latin America, 23 October 1984, B3.

36. "Hipótesis de Integración y de Confianza," *La Nación*, 8 April 1998, Ser2000 Online Database of Security and Defense, 1–2.

37. The military was miffed about the government's decision to submit the Laguna del Desierto dispute to arbitration because in its view that area was unquestionably Argentine territory. But it played no role at all in the decision and complained to Guido DiTella for not having been even consulted in advance about the matter. See Foreign Broadcast Information Service–Latin America, 2 August 1991, 20–21.

38. Diamint, "Cambios en la política de seguridad"; Diamint, "Responsables ante la defensa," 13–14.

39. Diamint, "Responsables ante la defensa," 13.

40. See República Argentina, *Ley de Ministerios, Decreto 438/92.*

41. *La Nación,* 22 September 1990, 7. The pronounced role played by Cavallo was not a function of his personality or special influence with the president. When he left to become minister of economics and Guido DiTella took over as foreign relations head, the pattern continued. DiTella made the public statements about what military engagements would be taken in the Gulf, how long the armed forces would stay there, which ships would be used, and how they would be rotated in and out of action. His ministry also spearheaded Argentina's engagement in peacekeeping. See Foreign Broadcast Information Service–Latin America, 28 January 1991, 27.

42. Foreign Broadcast Information Service–Latin America, 24 August 1990, 23.

43. Ibid., 20 February 1990, 16.

44. Ibid., 29 July 1992, 17; 17 September 1992, 17–22.

45. República Argentina, *Ley de Defensa Nacional.*

46. The trials and tribulations of the Defense Law were conveyed to me by José Manuel Ugarte, its principal author, in an e-mail communication in October 1998.

47. Manuel Ugarte, "La Comisión de Defensa Nacional," 245.

48. These are principal agent problems characteristic of many large, hierarchical organizations. See Kiewiet and McCubbins, *Logic of Delegation.*

49. Even in Chile, where the military's overall influence is indisputably greater than in Argentina, the government is nonetheless able to demonstrate some autonomy regarding territorial security. When the Foreign Relations Ministry agreed to submit the disputed border area known as Laguna del Desierto to arbitration, the military was not pleased but did little to protest, even after the final ruling went against Chile. I am grateful to Scott Tollefson for pointing this out to me.

Harold A. Trinkunas

7

Crafting Civilian Control in Argentina and Venezuela

The global spread of democratization will not endure unless emerging democracies establish civilian control over their armed forces. Historically, democratization has been a cyclical process, with each wave producing only a few cases of consolidated democracies. The large majority of the regime failures in the most recent waves can be attributed to military intervention. In fact, between 1948 and 1977, there were 304 unsuccessful and 238 successful irregular transfers of power worldwide.[1] Harvey Kebschull cites 12 successful and 26 unsuccessful coups d'état worldwide from 1990 to 1992 alone.[2] Elected governments seem far more likely to collapse as a result of intervention by their own armed forces than revolution or war. Even though more than seventy countries have experienced transitions to civilian rule in the last two decades, many of these new regimes appear fragile at best, chronically unstable at worst.[3]

Military intervention is more than a danger to the survival of these regimes. The threat of this intervention provides outgoing authoritarian elites with the capacity to impose limits on the scope and quality of the institutions of a new democracy, preventing regime consolidation in countries such as Brazil, Chile, and Peru. Some countries with long histories of military intervention, however, such as Greece, Portugal, and Spain, have been able to reduce military jurisdiction over state activities in short periods of time and establish mechanisms of civilian authority over the armed forces. By excluding military interference in political processes, these regimes have been able to consolidate full democracy.

How is it that some civilian governments achieve and maintain the loyalty of their armed forces, even in the face of deep and troubling political, economic, and social problems? Why are some civilian governments able to exercise authority over the armed forces and exclude them from politics, while many are not? More important, how did these governments establish this degree of authority, and what are the circumstances under which other civilian rulers may be able to do the same? In other words, what is civilian control of the military and how do governments achieve it?

Emerging democracies often lack the leverage, legitimacy, and institutional capacity to compel the armed forces to accept civilian control. Nevertheless, transitions to democracy create an opportunity to craft this control, especially when they are characterized by high levels of civilian mobilization, disunity among authoritarian elites, and fragmentation within the armed forces. I argue that democratizers that act strategically to exploit the opportunity created by a transition can maximize their leverage over the armed forces.[4] The weakest strategies used by democratizers involve appeasing military commanders, trading off civilian control of the armed forces in favor of short-term regime survival. The most robust strategy combines high levels of civilian supervision of defense activities with sanctions against military rebellions and dissident officers. The combination of opportunity and successful civilian strategies creates regime leverage over the armed forces, leverage that can be used to eliminate military prerogatives and confine the armed forces to strictly professional tasks.

I also argue that civilian control is consolidated when elected officials transform strategies of control into institutions that permanently shift power away from the military and toward elected officials.[5] The regime's capacity to manage defense affairs is what allows democracies to create permanent institutions that sustain their leverage over the military. Democratizers that lack sufficient resources or civilian defense expertise will only be able to institutionalize relatively weak civilian control, regardless of the degree of leverage they have achieved over the armed forces. Only emerging democracies that benefit from strong opportunities, successful strategies, and a high degree of regime capacity will achieve strong institutionalized civilian control.

This chapter focuses on what civilian control of the armed forces is and how it may become consolidated in emerging democracies. After defining civilian control, I analyze the process by which civilian control develops and is institutionalized in emerging democracies. Here, I examine the opportunities available to democratizers to act strategically to generate leverage over the armed forces, as well as the obstacles they face to institutionalizing this leverage. In the third section, I will analyze four paths that emerging democracies may follow toward (and away from) civilian control. The next section examines the dependent variable, civilian control, and argues that by tracking shifts in civil-military jurisdictional boundaries, we can differentiate among different outcomes in emerging democracies. The final section illustrates the theoretical arguments made in this chapter with two cases: Argentina (1983–92) and Venezuela (1958–73). Both cases enjoyed broad opportunity structures following their transition from authoritarian rule, so this section will focus on the strategic interaction and institution building involved in crafting civilian control in each country.

Defining Civilian Control

Today, democratic civilian control of the armed forces is understood to mean military compliance with government authority rather than the absence of armed rebellion.[6] Civilian control exists when government officials have authority over decisions concerning the missions, organization, and employment of a state's military means. Civilian control also requires that officials have broad decision-making authority over state policy free from military interference.[7]

This definition differs from Samuel Huntington's traditional prescription for civilian control in both its subjective and objective forms. In Huntington's version of subjective control, political elites protect themselves from military intervention by ensuring that the armed forces share common values and objectives with them—often through a process of politicization of the officer corps. With respect to objective control, the military is independent from civilian interference. Instead, it is self-directed through strong norms of professionalism that include subordination toward duly constituted state authority and an apolitical attitude toward civilian government's policies and activities.[8] Here I argue that the essential component of strong democratic civilian control has two dimensions: institutionalized oversight of military activities by civilian government agencies in combination with the professionalization of military forces. In other words, civilian control exists when politicians and bureaucrats are able to determine defense policies and approve military activities through an institutionalized defense bureaucracy.

Maximizing civilian control in a democracy involves limiting the areas of state policy in which the armed forces hold ultimate jurisdiction. The ability of the armed forces to make decisions on state policy without civilian input or supervision is clearly incompatible with civilian control. The existence of enclaves of military autonomy within the state and institutional vetoes over civilian policy making threaten regime stability. Armed forces that have exclusive control over state revenues or industries outside the supervision of civilian authorities are more difficult to monitor and control. States in which the armed forces control internal security agencies have found it hard to prevent military intervention in politics.[9] In other words, broadly based and autonomous military participation in state activities not only prevents civilian control over the armed forces but also calls into question the very nature of a democratic regime. Furthermore, the military's participation in areas outside its primary mission has historically led to its politicization, friction between politicians and soldiers, and a significant reduction in military effectiveness.[10]

One way of assessing the degree of civilian control in a country is to examine a wide range of state activities and determine who governs military participation in each area. States have used their militaries to control riots, collect taxes, enforce unpopular domestic policies, and, most threatening to civil authority, protect or displace governments. But when the armed forces determine for themselves when and where they will engage in these activities, they evade civilian control. In other words, when the military has autonomous jurisdiction over important aspects of state activity—such as internal security, economic policy, and revenue collection—it prevents full democratization. To depict these jurisdictional boundaries, I have divided state activities into four concentric rings in Figure 7.1.

These concentric circles provide a visual representation of the possible areas of state activity wherein a civilian government and its military forces can participate. These areas are ordered in relation to their increasing functional distance from the war-fighting mission of the armed forces, as well as the increasing threat to civilian control posed by military involvement in them. External defense tasks involve preparing for and conducting war and related military missions, managing the military bureaucracy, training, and strategic planning. Internal security includes the maintenance of public order in emergency situations, preparation for counterinsurgency warfare, domestic intelligence gathering, and daily policing.[11] Public policy covers state budgets, the functioning of government agencies, and the crafting of public policy to achieve social welfare, development, and political objectives. State leadership selection involves decisions concerning the criteria and process by which government officials are recruited, legitimated, and empowered.[12]

But analyzing military participation in different areas of state activity is not sufficient to determine the presence or absence of civilian control in a country because it does not answer the question of who *governs* that activity. The armed forces can participate in leadership selection at many different levels, for example, ranging from vetoing presidential candidates, to running their own nominees, to simply assisting civilian election authorities by distributing materials and guarding polling stations. In the first two instances, the armed forces are acting independent of civilian guidance—suggesting a high degree of autonomy from government control. In the latter example, the military is presumably under the orders of civilian election officials in a democratic regime. In other words, who is in charge of making policy in a state activity determines whether civilian control exists.

FIGURE 7.1 *State Jurisdictional Boundaries: Where Is Military Participation Most Threatening to Democracy?*

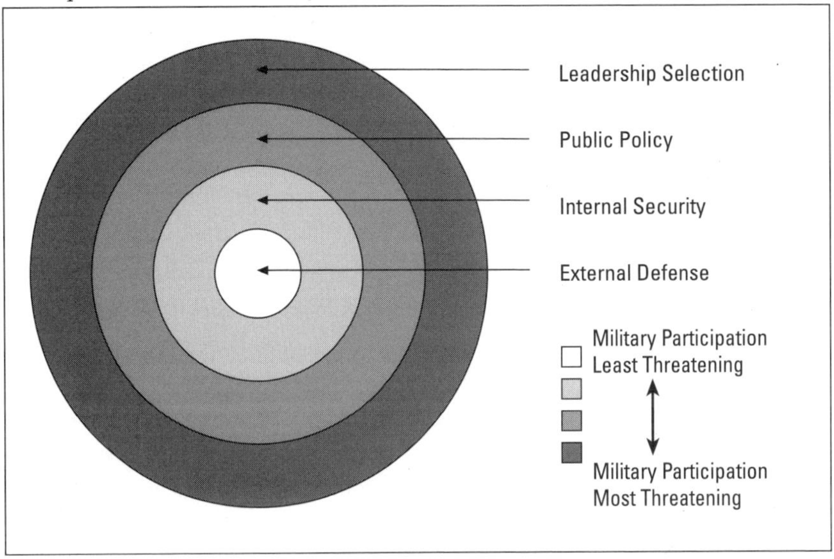

- Leadership Selection
- Public Policy
- Internal Security
- External Defense

□ Military Participation Least Threatening

■ Military Participation Most Threatening

Source: Trinkunas, "Crafting Civilian Control" (diss.), 11.

Military autonomy is defined by the degree to which the military is insulated from political and societal pressures and the process of boundary maintenance it carries out to exclude external civilian oversight of its internal operations. As David Pion-Berlin argues, a certain amount of autonomy is both necessary and functional to preserve the professionalism and efficacy of military forces. Nevertheless, a high degree of military autonomy can be used offensively by the officer corps to absorb new missions and prevent government oversight of their activities, thus rendering civilian control meaningless. Building on Pion-Berlin's work in this area, I focus on three degrees of military autonomy: civilian dominant, shared authority, and military dominant.[13] By tracing variation in both military autonomy and participation over time, I argue that it is possible to track shifts in civil-military jurisdictional boundaries over time.

Crafting Civilian Control

Two variables influence progress toward or away from civilian control: regime leverage over the armed forces and regime capacity to supervise national defense. Regime leverage is affected by the opportunity structure that accompanies a transition and the civilian strategy that allows democratizers to compel the armed forces to accept reduced jurisdictional boundaries following a dictatorship. Regime capacity, defined as a combination of government attention, resources, and trained personnel focused on defense issues, is what allows democratizers to institutionalize civilian control. Without regime capacity, governments in emerging democracies will be unable to supervise military activities effectively, preventing the consolidation of strong civilian control.

Broad versus Narrow Opportunity Structures

Theoretically, all transitions create an opportunity for civilian control, yet some provide greater opportunities than others. The scope of the opportunity structure created by a transition to democracy is determined by the degree of fragmentation of the armed forces, the degree to which civilians have mobilized and established a consensus on democratization, and the development of a civilian agenda to control the armed forces.

A broad opportunity structure is characterized by high fragmentation of the armed forces, a high degree of civilian popular mobilization, and an elite consensus on democratization. The nature of the crisis leading up to a transition to democracy determines the breadth of opportunity for democratizers to impose control on the armed forces.[14] Political and economic failures attributable to the policies of a dictatorship, particularly if they are compounded by defeat in war, are likely both to hasten the collapse of the regime and to increase recrimination and distrust among outgoing ruling elites.[15] The political, economic, and strategic failures of dictatorial rule also establish a basis for a broad civilian consensus opposing a return to authoritarianism.[16] A high degree of consensus on democratization will reduce the likelihood of significant elites "knocking on the barracks doors" and appealing for renewed military intervention.[17] The combination of mass mobilization and elite consensus can provide a powerful counterweight to military threats to the democratic process.

Narrow opportunity structures are found in transitions characterized by a high degree of military unity, a low degree of civilian consensus on democratization, and the absence of a democratic agenda to establish control of the armed forces. The positive performance of an outgoing dictatorship empowers authoritarian elites and the armed forces vis-à-vis democratizers. Furthermore, a legacy of positive government performance under authoritarian rule is likely to deepen divisions among civilians, as occurred in Chile following the 1989 transition. Under these conditions, democratizers face much greater constraints on their power and are unlikely to successfully shift jurisdictional boundaries in the direction of civilian control.[18]

In both broad and narrow opportunity structures, civilian control is not necessarily a top priority on the agenda of many new democratic regimes. A country's experience of authoritarianism can as easily teach accommodation to the demands of the armed forces as confrontation and vigilance over military activities. In addition, civilian politicians are likely to prefer gaining credit for improving economic conditions and the general welfare of the population than for military reform. Only in countries where civil society has mobilized around the issues of human rights abuses under a previous authoritarian regime is civilian control likely to be a major domestic political issue.

Selecting Strategies to Defend Democracy

Broad opportunity structures do not necessarily lead to a shift toward civilian control. For example, Colombia and Venezuela experienced pacted transitions to democracy almost simultaneously in the late 1950s, yet the Colombian armed forces retain a considerably higher degree of autonomy than those of their neighbor.[19] The difference between these cases lies not in the configuration of opportunities available to democratizers but rather in the strategies that early civilian leaders used to generate regime leverage.

The basis of regime leverage lies in modifying the fears, interests, and beliefs of military officers to induce compliance with government orders. Militaries comply with the directives of civilian leaders only when it is convenient for them to do so, when they fear the consequences of disobedience, or when their internal norms and beliefs lead them to accept civilian supremacy. Democratizers select strategies of civilian control to achieve one or more of these conditions, allowing government leaders both to protect their regime and to enforce their policies in the face of military opposition. I argue that civilian leaders have traditionally relied on four short-term strategies to reduce the threat of military intervention: appeasement, monitoring, divide and conquer, and sanctioning. These strategies rely on co-opting, recruiting, or intimidating a sufficiently large number of military officers into supporting the government's agenda so as to prevent the armed forces from acting cohesively to oppose civilian control. These strategies are not designed to benefit the armed forces but rather are intended to defend a democratic regime from military threats.[20]

Appeasement strategies rely on governments adopting policies and budgets that satisfy the institutional and particular interests of the officer corps in the hopes of discouraging military intervention in politics. These strategies are likely to lead to high levels of military autonomy and little or no reduction in the boundaries of military jurisdiction over the state. Nonetheless, governments engage in a wide array of patrimonial, remunerative, and clientilis-tic practices to maintain the loyalty of their armed forces.[21] These practices include granting officers high salaries and benefits, modern weaponry and equipment, and vetoes over state policy making. In spite of its pernicious effects, appeasement is often the only feasible strategy available to democratic governments with narrow opportunity structures.

A somewhat more robust strategy, monitoring, relies on external and inter-nal agents to maintain surveillance over the armed forces and inform rulers of potential threats. This forewarning may allow civilians to adopt policies and take actions to dissuade military intervention. For example, reliable informa-tion on coup plots may allow governments to intervene early, arresting re-bellious military officers long before they are prepared to mobilize their units against a democratic regime.[22] Monitoring strategies can be very effective in alerting civilian leaders to problems in the armed forces, but unless they are coupled with more robust strategies, such as divide and conquer or sanction-ing, governments may lack sufficient power to head off military threats.[23]

Divide and conquer strategies generate regime leverage by exploiting inter-nal cleavages and encouraging competition within and among state security forces, raising the costs of military intervention. Civilian leaders either create new counterbalancing security forces, such as gendarmeries or national police forces, or they induce existing military units to balance against each other, creating deterrence within the armed forces. Faced with the possibility that any coup d'état may lead to open conflict between different security organizations, military leaders are less likely to intervene in politics. Furthermore, by intro-ducing competition for power and resources, civilian governments can rely on their security forces to monitor each other to prevent any single organization from become threatening or dominant. Although divide and conquer is a difficult strategy to implement, civilians can often rely on the characteristic fragmentation of the armed forces in the wake of transitions to democracy, as well as on existing institutional rivalries among armies, navies, and air forces.

Sanctioning strategies are designed to use the fear of punishment to induce military cooperation with a democratic regime. Democratizers may be able to use civilian and military courts, loyalists in the military command structure, or internal security forces to suppress military uprisings and punish rebellious officers. A sanctioning strategy does not require repeated confrontations with the armed forces because, if successful, it has the effect of modifying the interests of the officer corps. Officers who cooperate with a new democratic regime will tend to go on to successful careers and rapid advancement. Those that oppose it will find themselves imprisoned or retired if they participate in failed rebellions. These new incentives and the fear of punishment lead the armed forces to accept the jurisdictional boundaries set by civilians and cooperate with the government.

Opportunity structures do not determine what strategies are available to democratizers, only which ones are most likely to succeed. Governments facing relatively fewer possibilities can partially overcome these circumstances by using strategies to maximize regime leverage over the armed forces. For example, civilian leaders could appease the navy in return for its support for a sanctioning strategy against the army. Civilian leaders who blend strategies of appeasement, monitoring, and divide and conquer can achieve particularly powerful combinations, granting governments both early warning of military threats and the leverage necessary to avert them.

Military Counterstrategies against Civilian Control

Strategies act to focus and maximize civilian leverage over the armed forces created by an initial opportunity structure. These strategies, however, will inevitably be resisted by the armed forces, which will correctly perceive them as a means to limit their power and prerogatives. Fortunately for democratizers, the armed forces' use of strategies is often impeded by the dynamics of a transition. This is especially true of broad opportunity structures that fragment the unity of the armed forces. This fragmentation can prevent military commanders from coherently applying counterstrategies to civilian control. Divided armed forces can effectively defend institutional prerogatives only if they are supported by the lowest common denominator of opinion in the officer corps. Following the collapse of a military authoritarian regime, many officers may prefer to focus on professional duties, undermining the ability of their commanders to apply counterstrategies to defend their prerogatives in internal security or public policy. The internal divisions in the officer corps following a transition will tend to inhibit the ability of military commanders to defend expanded jurisdictional boundaries, facilitating efforts by democratizers to establish leverage over the military, and ultimately, civilian control.

Institutionalizing Civilian Control of the Armed Forces

The combination of opportunity and strategy can facilitate only a temporary shift toward narrower military jurisdictional boundaries. Just as the crises leading up to the collapse of authoritarian rule help achieve civilian control, new crises, such as wars, economic failures, and social unrest, can undermine the legitimacy of a democratic regime. A permanent shift in the civil-military balance of power occurs only when elected officials create institutions of civilian control and compel or induce the armed forces to obey them.

Institutions of civilian control most often arise when democratizers transform successful strategies of control (such as monitoring or divide and conquer) into institutions. These institutions are essentially bundles of rules that redistribute power away from the armed forces and toward a civilian government on a permanent basis. For example, civilian rulers who pursue monitoring or sanctioning strategies create congressional oversight committees with permanent staffs, civilian defense secretariats, and independent intelligence agencies. Governments that rely on divide and conquer strategies strengthen police forces and create multiple intelligence and security agencies. When temporary strategies become institutionalized as rules governing civil-military relations, they are transformed into permanently operating factors that sustain regime leverage.

For these institutions to become a permanent feature of a regime's civil-military relations, the rules that govern them must first be written and then must acquire authority. Rules emerge from new constitutions, executive decrees, legislative actions, or court decisions that define new military jurisdictional boundaries. Some of these rules will acquire the weight of authority through habituation, either because they appeal to a preponderant number of military officers or because the armed forces are too weak to resist them. In many cases, the enactment and enforcement of new rules is an inherently conflictive process as both politicians and soldiers attempt to manipulate or tailor the new institutions to suit their needs and protect their prerogatives. The outcomes of conflicts over strategies and institutions of control generate precedents and norms for future civil-military interactions. By continually prevailing, politicians convince military officers to accept their orders, facilitating the process of writing and enforcing the rules of civilian control.

The Role of Regime Capacity

Institutionalizing civilian control can be a costly process, requiring a regime to commit specialized material and human resources to its success.[24] I define "regime capacity" as the combination of budgetary resources, expert civilian personnel, and government attention specifically and exclusively committed to matters of civilian control and national defense. These resources may be found in state ministries, legislatures, and courts, as well as in an independent press or nongovernmental organizations focused on military-related issues. The commitment of substantial government resources and expertise, when combined with external monitoring by civil society, allows democratizers to maximize civilian control in emerging democracies.

Institutionalizing intrusive monitoring and sanctioning strategies demands a high level of regime capacity. Civilian defense experts are required to manage military bureaucracies, develop and allocate budgets, and institutionalize government oversight mechanisms. Monitoring and sanctioning strategies are most effective when civil society contains groups and associations such as think tanks or human rights organizations that are committed to sustaining regime control of the armed forces and providing the government with external sources of defense expertise.[25]

However, institutionalizing appeasement or divide and conquer strategies is attractive to democratizers precisely because they consume little regime capacity. Divide and conquer strategies rely on mutual vigilance and counterbalancing by military (as opposed to civilian) forces to deter intervention in politics. Rather than allocating scarce civilian experts and resources to the task of controlling the military, rulers modify the structures and governance of the security forces so as to increase internal competition for power and resources.[26] Appeasement strategies require little more than the acquiescence of elected officials to military demands, and though they may lead to higher defense budgets, they consume little in the way of government management capacity. Successful institutionalization therefore requires not only regime leverage over the armed forces but appropriate levels of regime capacity to transform strategies into durable mechanisms of civilian control.

Paths and Outcomes in Civilian Control

Not all emerging democracies achieve civilian control of the armed forces. For many, the opportunity structures associated with their transition to democracy will not provide sufficient scope for democratizers to develop authority over the armed forces. Even when they benefit from broad opportunities, leaders in emerging democracies may fail to act strategically to generate leverage over the armed forces. Finally, even when regime leverage is available, many emerging democracies will lack the regime capacity necessary to institutionalize civilian control successfully. Each of these potential obstacles is a crossroads in an emerging democracy's progress toward civilian control.

The crafting of civilian control is a largely path-dependent process, in which the particular degrees of regime leverage and regime capacity available to an emerging democracy determine the degree to which government control will become institutionalized. Depending on what combination of opportunity, strategy, and institutions are available, an emerging democracy can follow a path toward one of four potential outcomes: regime collapse, regime persistence, weak institutionalized control, and strong institutionalized control, as shown in Figure 7.2.

Regime collapse: Governments with little leverage over their armed forces and lacking in expertise and resources to manage them are unlikely *successfully* to pursue any strategy other than appeasement. Military autonomy and jurisdictional boundaries will remain high, and democracy will never be fully consolidated. In the face of excessive military demands or a severe crisis in government legitimacy, democracy is likely to collapse in these cases.

Regime persistence: In this outcome, a government faces constraints on its power and leverage over the armed forces, but its high degree of capacity in defense matters allows it to pursue a combination of monitoring and appeasement strategies. Information derived from monitoring may provide enough forewarning of threats from the armed forces to prevent successful military intervention. A combination of monitoring and appeasement may also allow civilians to negotiate somewhat lower jurisdictional boundaries with the armed forces, but the boundaries between civilian and military authority will be weak. Democracy will not become consolidated, but it is more likely to persist because of its superior government management capacity vis-à-vis the armed forces. This outcome should be rare because it is difficult to conceive of cases where elected officials have access to a broad base of civilian expertise in defense affairs yet have not achieved control over the armed forces.

Weak institutionalized control: Governments with high leverage over the armed forces but low regime capacity will not be able to institutionalize the narrowest jurisdictional boundaries. While the armed forces will be largely excluded from politics, only weak control will be established because of weakness in regime capacity needed to establish supervisory agencies. Such institutions of civilian control as do exist will focus on divide and conquer and appeasement strategies. In these cases, civilians will not be able to create the institutional tools necessary to oversee military spending or define its roles and missions. But when the threat of military intervention is contained, democracy is more likely to become consolidated.

Strong institutionalized control: Democratizers enjoying both high leverage and high regime capacity can pursue any combination of strategies to create civilian control. Because appeasement is largely unnecessary, governments are likely to institutionalize robust strategies to ensure both the exclusion of the armed forces from political activities and active civilian supervision of military affairs. Both strong civilian control and democracy are very likely to become consolidated in this outcome.

FIGURE 7.2 *Possible Outcomes in Civil-Military Relations following a Transition to Democracy*

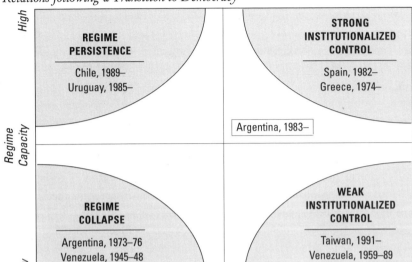

These outcomes are path dependent because the outcome of the strategic interaction among actors at each stage of the process of crafting civilian control determines what avenues are open to democratizers in the future. Initially, the mode of democratic transition conditions the potential leverage a new government will have vis-à-vis its armed forces. If a particular mode provides a narrow opportunity structure, civilian statecraft will be severely constrained and government control over the armed forces is unlikely to be established. Nevertheless, even strong opportunities can be squandered by poor civilian strategies, thereby dissipating government leverage, preventing the development of civilian control and impeding the consolidation of democracy. Given the obstacles, uncertainty, and risk associated with each step of this process, it is not surprising that few emerging democracies achieve strong institutionalized civilian control.

Examining the Dependent Variable: Civilian Control

How does a government know when it has achieved civilian control? How can an analyst differentiate between weak and strong institutionalized civilian control? More important, how do either of them know if a country is moving toward or away from these goals? Although a broad consensus has emerged as to what democratic civilian control is, there have been only a few efforts to measure the degree of civilian control in any given case.[27] I argue that the presence or absence of civilian control of the armed forces can be measured by the shape of the jurisdictional boundaries separating civilian and military authority within the state. I define these boundaries by the degree of military participation in state policy making and by the degree of autonomy enjoyed by the armed forces in their operations. In this section I examine the possible range of variation in military autonomy and participation, define a set of jurisdictional boundaries compatible with civilian control of the armed forces, and establish a means for identifying whether the boundaries in a given case are moving toward or away from civilian control of the armed forces.

I measure military participation by the presence of the armed forces in the process of making or implementing state policy in four separate categories: external defense, internal security, public policy, and state leadership selection. Arrayed in concentric circles, as in Figure 7.1, these policy areas permit coding of jurisdictional boundaries from the historical record of individual cases. Boundaries range from those of functionally specialized militaries, whose tasks are confined to war fighting and bureaucratic management (external defense), to highly interventionist militaries with multiple roles in economic policy, industrial affairs, and veto power over political candidacies and elections (public policy and state leadership selection).

Within this broad range, some forms of military participation are more threatening than others to civilian control. For example, army participation at the government's request in securing polling stations during an election is considerably less menacing to civilian control than a military veto of a presidential candidacy, even if both reflect military participation in the policy area of state leadership selection. Jurisdictional boundaries can be accurately represented only by capturing the degree of military autonomy in making and enforcing decisions in each of these areas of state activity.

The degree to which militaries act independently of government authority can be captured by assessing the relative roles of civilian and military actors in decision making and policy implementation on any given issue. Building on Pion-Berlin's work in this area, I focus on three degrees of military autonomy. The military-dominant category applies to those situations in which the armed forces have highly autonomous decision-making authority over policy. Shared authority applies to those situations in which both the armed forces and civilian rulers have relatively equal authority in devising and implementing a given policy. Civilian dominant refers to areas of state policy in which civilian rulers have exclusive decision-making authority yet the armed forces may have a role in implementing civilian decisions. This is the lowest level of military autonomy.[28] Returning to the previous example, army participation in providing security at polling stations would represent military participation in state leadership selection but would be unobjectionable given civilian dominance.

The concentric circles shown in Figure 7.1 can be used to derive maps for the jurisdictional boundaries of the four outcomes predicted in Figure 7.2: regime collapse, regime persistence, weak institutionalized control, and strong institutionalized control. For each map, the presence or absence of military participation and the armed forces' degree of autonomy can be coded by color, ranging from the dark gray of military dominant to the white of civilian dominant. Each map represents the outer limits of the jurisdictional boundaries for a predicted outcome (no map is presented for the first outcome, regime collapse, for the simple reason that the outer limits of jurisdictional boundaries in this case would be represented by military dominance of all areas of state activity). By comparing maps of the jurisdictional boundaries found in particular cases with the ones based on the theoretical outcomes predicted in this chapter, we can determine the presence or absence of civilian control in an emerging democracy.

Figure 7.3 compares the limits of jurisdictional boundaries for three possible civil-military outcomes following a transition from authoritarian rule. Regime persistence, shown in the uppermost set of concentric circles, is a case of a country that lacks civilian control of the armed forces but has managed to sustain civilian rule (low regime leverage/high regime capacity). In this case, even though civilians dominate the selection of state leaders (as shown by the light shading of the outermost ring), the armed forces continue to play a significant role in public policy (medium gray in the public policy ring represents shared authority). Furthermore, the armed forces continue to control internal security and external defense policy (shown by the dark gray, representing military dominance, of the two innermost rings). This pattern of jurisdictional boundaries closely approximates that of several South American countries, including Brazil and Chile.

Jurisdictional boundaries for weak institutionalized civilian control are shown in the central set of concentric circles. Here, civilians dominate all aspects of political life not directly related to security, and the armed forces are dominant in the area of external defense, exhibiting strong professional autonomy. Because civilian supervision is lax, the armed forces may also be able to maintain or absorb some internal security missions, often with the connivance of political leaders. This leads to "fuzzy" jurisdictional boundaries between civilian and military authority.

FIGURE 7.3 *Types of Jurisdictional Boundaries in Emerging Democracies*

Strong institutionalized civilian control is depicted in the lowermost set of concentric circles in Figure 7.3. It exists when civilians dominate most areas of state policy making but share authority with the military over some aspects of external defense policy in the interest of maximizing the effectiveness of armed forces' war-fighting capabilities. Under strong civilian control, government defense agencies can continuously monitor civil-military jurisdictional boundaries, supervising external defense performance and limiting armed forces' involvement in internal security and public policy to extraordinary situations.

A comparison of the jurisdictional boundaries in Figure 7.3 indicates that achieving civilian control of the armed forces involves both reducing their participation in state activities (shifting jurisdictional boundaries toward the innermost circle, external defense) and reducing the autonomy of the armed forces to such an extent that civilian dominance becomes the norm across most areas of state policy making. Simply put, as long as we observe that the areas of military jurisdiction in a given case shift toward the center of the concentric circles and become lighter gray (as military autonomy is reduced), civilian control over the armed forces is increasing.

Comparing Cases of Weak and Strong Institutionalized Control

This section compares the Argentine (1983–92) and Venezuelan (1958–73) experiences with crafting civilian control. In both cases broad opportunity structures existed, although the configuration of each differed to some extent. Figure 7.4 illustrates the baseline jurisdictional boundaries experienced in each case. In Argentina, the armed forces dominated all areas of public policy during the period of the Proceso dictatorship (1976–83), with military officers leading almost all government bureaucracies, state governments, and security services. Although they started from a disadvantageous position, Argentine democratizers benefited from the near collapse of armed forces' cohesion in the wake of the military, economic, and political failures associated with the authoritarian regime. In Venezuela, General Marcos Pérez Jiménez tightly restricted participation in the state to a circle of close allies during his dictatorship (1948–58), many of whom were civilian. Furthermore, democratizers benefited from the collapse of military cohesion during the final weeks of the Pérez Jiménez regime, as senior officers and civilians competed for power following the failed coup attempt of 1 January 1958. By contrast, civilian elite consensus was sustained at a high level throughout the transition by political pacting. When supported by mass mobilization, this process provided a useful counterweight to military hostility toward democratization. Interestingly, while both cases experienced broadly similar opportunity structures, political leaders in Argentina and Venezuela followed substantially different approaches to establishing civilian control.

Alfonsín's Strategy for Civilian Control in Argentina

Following his election, President Alfonsín was in a quandary: he had unexpectedly won, in large part by campaigning on a platform of justice and

FIGURE 7.4 *Baseline Jurisdictional Boundaries*

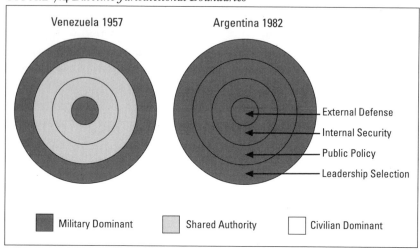

punishment for human rights abuses, yet achieving all of his publicly stated objectives would likely lead to a military reaction that would threaten the survival of the new democratic regime. Furthermore, the president and his advisers knew they faced a critical opportunity to establish civilian control and believed that prosecuting large numbers of military officers would undermine the reforms they planned to implement.

To achieve this, the Alfonsín administration planned to selectively combine strategies of sanctioning and appeasement. The sanctioning strategy would take advantage of the relative weakness of the military following the transition to empower the civilian Ministry of Defense and drastically reduce the defense budget. The appeasement strategy was designed to prevent a military rebellion by prosecuting only those officers who had given orders to commit human rights abuses and those who had exceeded their authority in carrying out orders. Alfonsín further eased the blow by directing the military judicial system to manage a self-purge of guilty officers.[29] Unaware of the sheer scope of both the number of officers who had participated and the crimes committed during the "Dirty War," the Alfonsín administration failed to understand that it would be impossible to limit the number of military trials through administrative measures, nor would the Argentine public accept this limitation.[30]

The government's strategies, sanctioning and appeasement, worked at cross-purposes. The officer corps interpreted the sanctioning strategy as revenge. The appeasement strategy, however, was interpreted as weakness, and post-Malvinas military reforms became blocked by interservice rivalries and bureaucratic inertia. Most critically, by directing the armed forces judicial system to conduct the initial trials of officers accused of torture and disappearances, the Alfonsín administration allowed the military to obstruct justice long enough for parts of the officer corps to reacquire sufficient cohesion to rebel. The delay in the trial process discouraged the administration's allies in the human rights community and undermined regime leverage.

Civilian and Military Counterstrategies in Argentina

The only objective on which the Argentine officer corps wholeheartedly agreed was the need to prevent a judicial revision of the repression it had conducted during the Dirty War. Other priorities, such as using the lessons of the Malvinas war to reorganize the armed forces, were rapidly abandoned because of the inability to reach a consensus among the services.[31] Although not all officers had participated in the Dirty War, a large enough percentage had been involved that many felt that either they or a colleague were at risk of standing trial. According to Norden, between nine hundred and thirteen hundred officers directly participated in repression, although the figure may have been much higher.[32] In the army, the officer corps was split generationally. Junior officers advocated a proactive defense of the institution and vindicated their role in the Dirty War, while the military high command favored a defensive "judicial battle" that would minimize convictions. Despite this divergence in their specific preferences, both junior and senior officers initially pursued a counterstrategy of delay in the face of human rights prosecutions.[33]

Human rights organizations also rejected President Alfonsín's strategy toward the armed forces, and they used the courts to pursue their own strategy of "unlimited" sanctions. Argentina's judicial system was open to citizen-initiated prosecutions, and the groups were highly successful in expanding the scope of human rights trials. Alfonsín lacked the control over civil society and the legal process that would have enabled him to enforce a compromise by executive fiat. The moral authority of the human rights organizations made them an effective pressure group, able to influence public opinion strongly against the president's strategies. Also, by assembling evidence and providing legal expertise in support of victims of the Dirty War, human rights organizations could force the pace of the government's military policy by filing new indictments against officers.[34]

Politically, Alfonsín often found himself outflanked on the left by human rights organizations and the progressive wing of the Peronist Party. Their public criticism cast his policies in a negative light, but he felt unable to match this leftward movement for fear of provoking a military backlash. As a result, Alfonsín postponed taking decisions he knew would be politically unpopular, and he timed major initiatives on military affairs to fall after national elections. Though it was a successful electoral strategy, Alfonsín's approach had the effect of delaying a resolution of the human rights trials until a time when the opportunity structure had narrowed. This situation in turn played into the hands of the military high command, fighting its judicial battle, and alienated the army's junior officers, setting up the conditions for the Holy Week rebellion of 1987.[35]

The Collapse of Regime Leverage under Alfonsín and Its Reconstruction under Menem

Between 1984 and 1987, regime leverage in Argentina appeared substantial but was based on weak foundations. The pace and timing of Alfonsín's sanctioning strategy slipped from his control, and his appeasement efforts proved to be a failure. Under these conditions, regime leverage could remain high only as long as the majority of the officer corps felt it was useless to resist government authority. Until this resistance began to emerge, Alfonsín was able to accomplish a substantial reduction in jurisdictional boundaries, confining the actual operations of the military to external defense.

Between 1984 and 1987, senior officers saw no point in open rebellion as a means to resist civilian efforts to sanction the armed forces.[36] By 1986, however, growing overt and covert resistance by junior and mid-ranking officers led Alfonsín to place greater emphasis on appeasing the officer corps through legal measures. Once the number of indictments for human rights abuses had reached into the hundreds, Alfonsín forced the Full Stop Law through the legislature, setting a two-month deadline for the filing of new charges against military officers. Both the human rights community and the Argentine judiciary were partially successful in resisting this law by accelerating the tempo of indictments before the deadline. Paradoxically, rather than appeasing the armed forces, the Full Stop Law reinforced the military's perception of a government focused solely on a sanctioning strategy.[37]

Military resistance culminated in the 1987 Holy Week rebellion by a small group of military officers.[38] The rebellion led to the collapse of the government's leverage over the armed forces. A pure sanctioning strategy could work only as long as the armed forces were prepared to accept civilian punishment. It is a measure of the degree of military fragmentation and demoralization that no rebellion occurred until three years into Alfonsín's regime. As the failure of the Full Stop Law demonstrated, Alfonsín's policy of appeasement had a negative impact on the officer corps, reinforcing the perception that civilians were duplicitous (since no improvement resulted from the law) and bent on punishing the armed forces.

The extent of the failure of Alfonsín's strategy was exposed by the inability of the government to secure any military support to repress the small numbers that actively participated in the Holy Week rebellion in 1987. Faced by a hostile and newly confident military, the president was forced to negotiate a humiliating end to the uprising. He ended prosecutions of most military officers for human rights abuses by asking the legislature to pass the unpopular Law of Due Obedience, which established strict limits on who could be prosecuted for the human rights abuses of the dictatorship.[39] Essentially, Alfonsín had to abandon sanctions and pursue a policy of heightened appeasement.

The rebellion of 1987 and the two that followed in 1988 provided the armed forces with enough leverage to broaden their jurisdictional boundaries into internal security and halt progress toward civilian control. As the Argentine economy began to collapse and social unrest grew after 1987, civilian politicians became increasingly unwilling to defend narrow jurisdictional boundaries, fearing that the military would be needed to contain public disorders. In the face of his declining ability to govern effectively, Alfonsín decided to step down six months early and transfer power to the newly elected Peronist president, Carlos Menem, in 1989.[40]

President Menem was able to resurrect regime leverage over the armed forces by repackaging the civilian strategies of sanctions and appeasement into a quid pro quo: blanket pardons for convicted officers in return for military obedience. Almost immediately after taking office, Menem issued two amnesties that covered all officers threatened with prosecutions for their actions during the Dirty War. By accepting the political cost of this action, President Menem gained the confidence of many military officers. This amnesty also removed the only common ground that provided some degree of military cohesion in the face of civilian strategies of control.

Following the amnesties, the post-1982 fragmentation of the military reemerged. When junior officers and sergeants under Colonel Seineldín rebelled for a fourth time in December 1990, President Menem had little trouble securing the support of the military high command for the use of force against them.[41] This action ended the cycle of insubordination and enabled the government to reassert civilian control. Menem was able to use this control to reshape the military, transforming it from an expensive source of instability into a cheaper instrument compatible with his neoliberal economic policies and useful in his realignment of Argentine foreign policy toward cooperation with the United States.[42]

Strategies and Counterstrategies for Civilian Control in Venezuela

Venezuelan democratizers entered the 1958 transition with a clear sense of the mode of civilian control they wished to achieve and the strategies they intended to use. During the decade of dictatorial rule (1948–58) by General Pérez Jiménez, civilian politicians, particularly those in the Acción Democrática (AD) Party, analyzed the problem of defending the regime after a transition to democracy. They concluded that successful democratization would require political consensus among major parties and fragmentation within the armed forces.

As early as 1949, the AD leadership began to discuss a combined strategy of divide and conquer and appeasement, designed to split the navy, air force, and junior officer corps away from the army-dominated high command. The goal of this package of strategies was to decentralize authority and access to resources in the armed forces, preventing any one military leader from assembling a coup coalition. Meanwhile, the officer corps were to be promised greater resources and professional opportunities, as well as an amnesty for political crimes to reconcile them to the new democracy. While this strategy was largely conceived by Acción Democrática, the pacting process of 1957–58 led other parties to accept it as well.[43]

When Pérez Jiménez fell in January 1958, factions in the military began to maneuver for advantage and autonomy. Within weeks, the armed forces had split into three competing groups, each with its own political agenda. Junior army and air force officers, led by Lieutenant Colonel Hugo Trejo, represented the populist wing of the armed forces that led the initial rebellion against the dictator. The navy faction backed its former commander, Admiral Wolfgang Larrazábal, who became head of the interim government and quickly allied itself with democratizers to defend the transition process. Conservative authoritarians in all services supported the new minister of defense, General Jesús María Castro León, in his efforts to place conditions on the transition. With the armed forces split into three hostile camps, efforts by any one faction to restrict the democratization process were met by determined resistance from the others. As a result of this competition, the military as a whole was unable to develop effective counterstrategies to oppose democratizers' plans for civilian control.[44]

The effectiveness of the divide and conquer strategy was reflected in the rapid elimination of two of the three factions during the transition to democratic rule. The leader of the populist faction, Lieutenant Colonel Trejo, was quickly shunted into a staff position and eventually appointed ambassador to Costa Rica through the connivance of the other faction leaders and civilian political leaders.[45] Only months later, the minister of defense, General Castro León, was forced into exile after leading a failed coup attempt that was defeated by the combined efforts of civilian political leaders and the navy.[46] By mid-1958, cohesive military opposition to democratization had been eliminated as a result of counterbalancing among various armed factions.

Venezuela faced further military insurrections during the transition and the first democratic administration of President Rómulo Betancourt, but none threatened the survival of the regime. Moreover, officers who participated in these failed insurrections were purged, while others of known loyalty to the regime were rewarded with promotions and more powerful positions. Quickly, the logic of rebellion was replaced by one of obedience to the new regime.

Even though the new government faced economic constraints as the result of an ongoing recession, the new logic of obedience was reinforced by measures of appeasement. These included an informal amnesty for military crimes committed during the dictatorship, increased autonomy for the air force and navy, and the easing of barriers to promotion for junior officers.[47] The final key to regime leverage over the armed forces was provided by the growth of Marxist guerrilla organizations in Venezuela after 1961. Combating these groups cemented officers' allegiance to the new democratic regime.[48]

Regime Leverage and Civil-Military Outcomes in Argentina and Venezuela

Venezuelan democratizers were more successful at generating regime leverage precisely because their strategy choices provided them with a measure of force with which to defend the new government. The combination of divide and conquer and appeasement allowed democratizers to rely on the armed support of a significant military faction, led by the navy. This backing was combined with a high degree of civilian mobilization under the control of political parties, providing democratizers with a substantial counterweight to military rebellions. This allowed them to achieve relatively rapid shift in jurisdictional boundaries toward civilian control, as Figure 7.5 shows.

Yet Argentine strategies under President Alfonsín were workable only as long as the armed forces felt it was hopeless to resist. Unlimited sanctions proved a rallying point for the otherwise fragmented armed forces. Simultaneously, because it failed to implement alternative strategies successfully, the democratic government had no reliable supporters in the armed forces. As a result, the *carapintadas* were able to rebel with relative impunity despite Alfonsín's initial success in reducing jurisdictional boundaries. Figure 7.5 shows the jurisdictional boundaries Argentina experienced during the period of mili-

FIGURE 7.5 *Transitional Jurisdictional Boundaries*

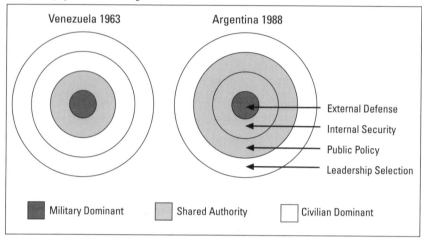

tary rebellion, when the armed forces were able to reassert a limited internal security role and force change in public policy (amnesty legislation).

Comparing the Institutionalization of Civilian Control in Argentina and Venezuela

The institutions of civilian control in both Argentina and Venezuela were flawed by the enduring shortage of regime capacity in each country. Venezuelan democratizers sought to establish strong boundaries between civilian and military authority but made little effort to supervise military activities. Early civilian leaders in Venezuela understood that they had little expertise in defense issues, nor were there any electoral incentives to sustain civilian interest in the military once the Marxist insurgency of the 1960s was defeated. The Argentineans, in contrast, deliberately set out to craft institutions of civilian control similar to those found in advanced industrialized democracies. They were successful at confining the armed forces to external defense duties in 1984, but they initially lacked the regime capacity to operationalize civilian oversight. In the long run, this meant that civilian control could not function effectively in preventing rebellions, let alone ameliorating military unrest caused by reduced budgets and low morale. Only under the Menem administration was civilian control institutionalized, albeit through peculiar channels that tended to undermine the role of the Ministry of Defense.

Institutionalizing Civilian Control in Argentina

Once it took office, the Alfonsín administration moved rapidly to expand civilian supervision over military affairs. It reinvigorated the Ministry of Defense by placing it in the chain of command and granting the civilian minister the power to supervise joint military activities and discipline high-ranking officers. New civilian secretariats were created to oversee military spending, planning, and operations. Military influence over public policy, once exercised through officers appointed to head state enterprises, was reduced by transferring control of these enterprises to the civilian-led ministry. Internal security forces previously controlled by the army and navy were also placed under civilian supervision. Military budgets, which had peaked during the dictatorship at 5.1 percent of GDP, were slashed within two years to their historic level of approximately 2.3 percent of GDP. The army was hit hardest, since its budget sank from 1.8 percent of GDP in 1983 to 0.6 percent in 1989, all in the context of a contracting economy.[49] Meanwhile, the members of the military juntas during the 1976–83 period were placed on trial and convicted of human rights abuses, an unprecedented achievement for a new democracy. This broad-based attack on military privileges rapidly confined the armed forces to narrow jurisdictional boundaries.

Argentine democratizers, however, lacked the defense expertise and resources to staff these new institutions of control effectively. This shortage of regime capacity operated against civilian authority in several instances, reflected in the inability of Defense Ministry officials to reform the military force structure in light of budget cuts, the failure to pass legislation redefining roles and missions until 1988, and the mismanagement of prosecutions of officers for human rights abuses. Congressional productivity in defense legislation was notably low until after the 1987 Holy Week rebellion. Throughout, the staff of institutions for controlling the security forces, the military, and the intelligence agencies continued to be recruited largely from active-duty or retired members of the same, which made elected officials suspicious of their advice.[50]

As a result, civilian oversight of the armed forces never became fully operational in Argentina. In its absence, the government was unable to monitor military activities for signs of rebellion or to address military discontent through effective reform measures. After the *carapintada* uprisings began in 1987, the institutions of civilian control largely ceased to function, and the minister of defense was reduced to the role of a mediator between the newly confident military high command and a demoralized President Alfonsín.[51]

President Menem succeeded in resurrecting regime leverage after 1990 but was less successful at consolidating civilian control because of his penchant for favoring personalistic or noninstitutional channels. Menem bypassed the authority of the minister of defense by establishing personal relationships with the commanders of the armed forces as a means of managing civil-military relations. The Ministry of Defense, theoretically the lead institution of civilian control, was further weakened by the rapid succession of ministers, six of whom were appointed between 1989 and 1995. Amid this turmoil in the leadership of the ministry, it was difficult to develop a stable cadre of experienced civilian defense experts. The authority of these ministers was called into question when some were accused of sympathizing with the *carapintada* rebels (until 1990) and another was convicted of corruption.[52] Taking advantage of the presidentialist nature of Argentine democracy, Menem often bypassed the congressional defense committees, even though these committees increasingly acquired the expertise necessary to pass effective defense legislation.[53] Thus the two principal channels associated with supervision of the armed forces in states with strong civilian control (the Ministry of Defense and the legislature) were shunted aside during the Menem administration.

In part, this state of affairs was a by-product of the economic catastrophe inherited by Menem in 1989 and his efforts to correct it. Menem prioritized economic recovery over all other aspects of state activity, adopting a neoliberal structural adjustment program to restructure the economy. As a result, the Ministry of the Economy and the Ministry of Foreign Affairs (which sought external support for economic reform through a substantially closer relationship with the United States) became the "power" ministries of the Menem administration, extending their authority even over military questions. During the hyperinflationary crisis of the early 1990s, the Ministry of the Economy achieved complete control over government budgeting and spending, including those of the armed forces. As part of a general trend to reduce unnecessary government spending, military budgets declined from 18.2 percent of government expenditures in 1989 to 10.6 percent in 1993, although they remained relatively stable in dollar terms. Simultaneously, defense industries were privatized, reducing government and military influence in the economy.[54]

Budgets are prepared with little consideration for defense needs. Rather, they conform to overall government targets for reduced public spending and balanced budgets. Indirectly, the Ministry of the Economy sets the limits for the overall size and structure of the military. Similarly, the Ministry of Foreign Affairs now plays an unprecedented role in determining the deployment of Argentine military forces through its focus on peacekeeping operations and regional collective security. Peacekeeping missions occupy the bulk of serious military effort, with 25 percent of all Argentine officers and noncommissioned officers having rotated through peacekeeping missions by 1995.[55] In other words, the president, the Ministry of the Economy, and the Ministry of Foreign Affairs play the central role in determining the size, readiness, and missions of the Argentine military. While this indicates that civilians have control over the armed forces in Argentina, the fact that this authority is exercised through peculiar institutional channels raises questions about its degree of consolidation.

Institutionalizing Weak Civilian Control: The Case of Venezuela

Unlike the Argentines, Venezuelan democratizers were well aware of the limitations of their regime capacity following the 1958 transition, and they developed their institutions of control accordingly. During 1958, the transitional government was able to embed its strategy of divide and conquer into concrete military institutions. By decree, they eliminated the Prussian-style General Staff, which maintained central control over the armed forces, and replaced it with a Joint Staff, which had no operational authority over the individual services. Decentralization was reinforced by devolving administrative and operational control from the Ministry of Defense to the army, navy, air force, and National Guard. This made the Ministry of Defense coequal in power and authority with each individual service. Joint military educational institutions were eliminated, allowing each service to train its officers independently, thus reducing the possibility of interservice collaboration among potential conspirators. Officers' careers were shortened to thirty years, which had the effect of increasing competition among younger officers, who now had many fewer years in which to accumulate the postings and promotions necessary to reach the highest ranks. Congressional and presidential approval for promotions to colonel and general became necessary, which led ambitious officers to support the new regime as a means of securing their advancement.[56] This set of institutions transformed the temporary loss of cohesion experienced by the Venezuelan military during the transition into an institutionalized fragmentation of its power and authority.[57]

Venezuela's first president of the democratic period, Rómulo Betancourt, deepened and defended these institutions adroitly. In effect, he became the mediator of intramilitary disputes, gaining a substantial measure of civilian control as a result. He also strengthened institutions of appeasement, providing better salaries and benefits, and improved professional opportunities. The effect was to deradicalize the officer corps and incorporate it into the prodemocratic middle class. Betancourt also exploited Venezuela's burgeoning guerrilla conflict to focus military energies away from attacking the democratic system and onto defending the new regime against a Cuban-sponsored adversary. Thus Betancourt increasingly divided military officers among themselves: colonels and generals, who needed civilian approval for promotion, versus the junior officers, who did not; the army, navy, and air force against each other in struggles over power and resources; officers satisfied with their new professional standing versus those who were discontented with the political system; officers who believed in democracy against those who feared civilian rule. In effect, Betancourt achieved multiple and crosscutting cleavages within the armed forces, which made it nearly impossible for them to resist his authority in any corporate manner.[58]

The peculiar genius of this set of institutional reforms was that they were broadly acceptable to military officers, who saw in them new opportunities for service autonomy, accelerated promotions, and professional development. Democratizers were thus able to secure civilian control and narrow jurisdictional boundaries while facing only localized military rebellions, which could be quickly suppressed by the growing number of pro-regime officers in the armed forces.

None of the reforms carried out by civilians during this period required a high degree of regime capacity. All of the new institutional arrangements were designed to function with little civilian supervision, relying only on the self-interest of military officers to sustain their effectiveness. This would be very important in the future because while politicians were highly focused and motivated to achieve civilian control in 1958, there was no guarantee that even this amateurish interest could be sustained. The low degree of regime capacity led presidents, beginning with Betancourt, to concentrate all authority over the military in their office. The many demands on a civilian president's time limited the amount of expertise and supervision the government could dedicate to military affairs on a permanent basis. As a result, Venezuelan institutions of civilian control were better at maintaining low military jurisdictional boundaries than at supervising the activities in them.

The cases of Argentina and Venezuela suggest that without civilian authority over the armed forces, democratic rule in both states would have collapsed in the face of military rebellion relatively early in the process of regime consolidation. As Figure 7.6 illustrates, both countries achieved a form of institutionalized civilian control of the armed forces: strong in the Argentine case, weak in the Venezuelan one. In Argentina, jurisdictional boundaries became quite low, particularly if the final configuration achieved under Menem is compared with the half-century of military intervention in politics that preceded it. Venezuelan jurisdictional boundaries were somewhat higher by 1973 because civilians never attempted to establish substantial oversight over

FIGURE 7.6 *Final Jurisdictional Boundaries*

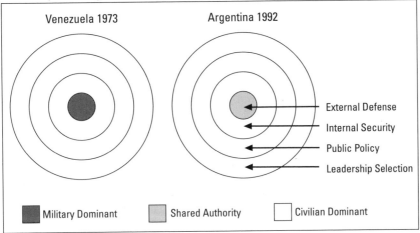

the armed forces and the borders between civilian and military authority remained porous. Venezuelan elected officials delegated considerable authority over some aspects of internal security to the military, even though this role was largely formal between 1973 and 1989. This suggests that while both countries achieved civilian control by the time period illustrated in Figure 7.6, the institutional underpinning for their authority was weaker than that found in advanced industrialized democracies.

Conclusion

The consolidation of civilian control is crucial not only to the survival of emerging democracies but also to the quality of their governing institutions. In one sense, civilian control is subject to the same opportunities, processes, and sequences that govern democratization. But civilian control is also the key tool in the struggle between democratizers and authoritarians over institutional arrangements. If an emerging democracy does not achieve it, supporters of the previous regime can credibly continue to threaten the new regime and place limits on it. Once civilian control is established, authoritarian forces are far less likely to affect the quality of democratic institutions.

Civilian control does not mean that elected officials are free to structure a regime's institutional arrangements as they please, yet it does mean that the limits on this process are imposed in the context of democratic rules of the game rather than by the use of force. Theoretically, elected officials should have the authority to make decisions in all areas of state policy, but in practice, authorities in all democracies face constraints on their power. For example, successful central banks today tend to enjoy a reserved domain over monetary policy, acting relatively free of political constraints in the interests of promoting economic stability. Like independent central banks, militaries hold substantial authority over a critical area of state policy. Even in highly democratic states, the power of civilian politicians constitutionally charged with military oversight is effectively constrained by the superior professional expertise of the officer corps, the defense constituency in the electorate, and the need for a credible defense. Any limits that the armed forces are able to place on political outcomes occur through lobbies, legislatures, and courts rather than through the use of force.

In this chapter, I have argued that the key to establishing civilian control in emerging democracies is the use of regime leverage to define narrow boundaries for military authority and institutionalize supervision of the armed forces. Regime leverage over the military allows civilians to resist conditions placed by outgoing authoritarian elites on democratic institutions. Without the support of the armed forces, authoritarian demands or conditions on emerging democracies are more difficult to sustain.

A second constraint on civilian control is the shortage of regime capacity in defense affairs that has prevented the deepening of the institutions of civilian control. Civil-military relations represent an area of state activity where there is a wide disparity in the technical expertise among the parties, which makes it difficult for civilians to assess the appropriateness of military plans and activities. The structuring of party systems, legislatures, and interest representation is often a familiar problem to democratic politicians, but national defense is not. Particularly in countries with negligible external threats and cyclical patterns of military intervention, politicians are unlikely to develop the expertise required to define low military jurisdictional boundaries and structure the institutions to monitor them, nor will militaries be eager to enlighten them.

I have also provided a measure for determining whether emerging democracies are moving toward or away from civilian control of the armed forces. By coding incidents of military participation in government activities onto jurisdictional boundary maps, we can generate snapshots of the shifting jurisdictional boundaries in emerging democracies. Taken as a time series, these maps allow us to detect trajectories in civilian control during a transition and consolidation to democracy. Furthermore, by comparing the final map of jurisdictional boundaries in a case (such as Argentina or Venezuela) with those of the predicted outcomes depicted in Figures 7.3, 7.4, and 7.5, we can determine whether a country has established civilian control and to what degree it has succeeded.

This chapter has focused on developing a theoretical model for how civilian control may become consolidated in emerging democracies following a transition from military authoritarian rule. The cases of Argentina and Venezuela illustrate the process by which weak and strong institutionalized civilian control is crafted. Further research needs to be performed before this model can be considered to have been adequately tested.[59] Cross-regional testing of this model should illuminate differences in the opportunities, processes, and sequences associated with crafting civilian control.

I have argued that there are four principal strategies used by civilians to render the armed forces more compliant and that the availability and successful application of any one of these hinges on the structure of opportunities that present themselves at the time of transition to democratic rule. Moreover, I have demonstrated that those strategies must be translated into institutional arrangements to sustain the gains achieved. Thus this study has confirmed that there is great utility in combining elements of strategic and institutional theories as outlined in the Introduction to this volume. In relating these approaches to the study of civil-military relations, Pion-Berlin suggests that politicians do have a portfolio of strategic options in dealing with the armed forces but that these depend on both the context they find themselves in and the power of the military they confront. Meanwhile, the military's abilities to exert its influence in a democratic order are, he says, "mediated by governing agencies via procedural and structural mechanisms which can either open or restrict the military's channels of influence." These points find corroboration in my study of crafting civilian control.

NOTES

1. Taylor and Jodice, *World Handbook*, 86–93.
2. Kebschull, "Operation 'Just Missed,' " 568.
3. Diamond, "Is the Third Wave Over?," 26.
4. Strategic interactions between democratizers and authoritarian elements dominate the period of regime transition, as O'Donnell and Schmitter suggest. The strategic interaction between democratic regimes, as they seek to assert civilian control, and the armed forces can be modeled as a deterrence game. See Schelling, *The Strategy of Conflict*, on strategic choice. For a formal model, see Hunter, "Negotiating Civil-Military Relations."
5. For the role of institutions and how they shape participants' decision making, see the

literature on historical institutionalism, particularly Steinmo, Thelen, and Longstreth, *Structuring Politics*.

6. Agüero, *Soldiers, Civilians, and Democracy*; Pion-Berlin, "Military Autonomy."

7. Agüero, *Soldiers, Civilians, and Democracy*, 19–21.

8. Huntington, *Soldier and the State*.

9. Stepan, *Rethinking Military Politics*, 93–127; Linz and Stepan, *Problems of Democratic Transition and Consolidation*, 209–11.

10. Pion-Berlin, "Military Autonomy"; Stepan, *Rethinking Military Politics*.

11. Stepan, "New Professionalism," 135–39.

12. Public policy and leadership selection are areas in which the armed forces in many countries attempt to lobby or exercise influence in support of military industrialization projects and budget allocations. But there is a clear distinction between influence, the threat of force, and direct military control of these processes. See Pion-Berlin, "Military Autonomy," 89, and Colton, *Commissars, Commanders, and Civilian Authority*, 231–45.

13. Pion-Berlin, "Military Autonomy," 84–86.

14. O'Donnell and Schmitter, *Transitions from Authoritarian Rule*.

15. Wars that incur heavy costs or end in defeat are likely to lead to violent regime change. See Bueno de Mesquita, Siverson, and Woller, "War and the Fate of Regimes."

16. Haggard and Kaufman, "Political Economy of Inflation."

17. Stepan, *Rethinking Military Politics*.

18. O'Donnell and Schmitter, *Transitions from Authoritarian Rule*, 20–21.

19. Hartlyn, "Military Governments and the Transition to Civilian Rule"; Karl, "Dilemmas of Democratization."

20. Indoctrination is excluded from this set of strategies because it operates on a different time scale. While monitoring and sanctioning strategies can be implemented in relatively short order, indoctrination strategies require military educational reform and a generational shift within the armed forces to fully implement.

21. Decalo, *Coups and Army Rule in Africa*, 25–47.

22. Countries practicing monitoring strategies can recruit officers on the basis of ethnic affiliations or introduce a political commissariat. In advanced industrialized democracies, monitoring strategies can depend on congressional committees, civilian-led defense ministries, and oversight by civil society and an independent press. See Farcau, *Transition to Democracy in Latin America*, and Feaver, "Delegation, Monitoring and Civilian Control of the Military."

23. Frazer, "Sustaining Civilian Control."

24. Fitch, *Armed Forces and Democracy*, 167–69.

25. McCubbins and Schwartz, in "Congressional Oversight Overlooked," argue that governments and legislatures rely on internal (police patrol) and external (fire alarms) oversight mechanisms to regulate bureaucracies.

26. Divide and conquer strategies may consume a great deal of military capacity in inefficient duplication of capabilities and unnecessary competitiveness, but they require relatively little in the way of civilian expertise and attention to regulate successfully.

27. Pion-Berlin and Arcenaux provide useful insights into this question in "Of Missions and Decisions."

28. Building on the low, mid, and high categories of autonomy used in Pion-Berlin's work, I argue that military autonomy is composed of two distinct roles: decision making and

policy implementation. Who decides what issue is the most salient aspect of military autonomy. Insofar as the armed forces retain a role in implementing civilian decisions on war, defense, internal security, and domestic policy, they retain an ability to influence the outcomes of state policy.

29. Pion-Berlin, *Through Corridors of Power*, 80–81.

30. Verbitsky, *Civiles y militares*, 43–47, 51–55.

31. Acuña and Smulovitz, "Militares en la transición Argentina," 162.

32. Norden, *Military Rebellion in Argentina*, 58–60.

33. Interview with Horacio Verbitsky, 27 June 1995, Buenos Aires; Norden, *Military Rebellion in Argentina*, 107–19, 127–30.

34. Pion-Berlin, *Through Corridors of Power*, 97–98.

35. López, *Ni la ceniza, ni la gloria*, 108–10.

36. Interview with Lieutenant Colonel Santiago Alonso, 12 July 1995, Buenos Aires.

37. Pion-Berlin, *Through Corridors of Power*, 97–99.

38. McSherry, *Incomplete Transition*, 213–16; Norden, *Military Rebellion in Argentina*, 128–30.

39. McSherry, *Incomplete Transition*, 213–16; Norden, *Military Rebellion in Argentina*, 128–30.

40. McSherry, *Incomplete Transition*, 194–97, 214–17.

41. Interview with Dr. Juán A. Ferreira Pinho, 17 May 1995, Buenos Aires.

42. Trinkunas, "Crafting Civilian Control" (diss.), 250–55.

43. Ibid., 95–99.

44. Ibid., 108, 114–16.

45. Burggraaff, *Venezuelan Armed Forces in Politics*, 176–77.

46. Interviews with President Rafael Caldera, 4 and 18 August 1992, Caracas; interview with General (AF) Antonio Briceño Linares, 26 October 1994, Caracas.

47. Interview with Ramón J. Velásquez, 3 April 1995, Caracas.

48. Müller Rojas, *Relaciones peligrosas*, 416–17.

49. López, *Ni la ceniza, ni la gloria*, 123.

50. Druetta, "Diputados y defensa," 232–43; Pion-Berlin, *Through Corridors of Power*, 164–66.

51. Interview with Deputy Horacio Jaunarena, 6 May 1995, Buenos Aires; Pion-Berlin, *Through Corridors of Power*, 158–59.

52. Pion-Berlin, *Through Corridors of Power*, 162–63.

53. Interview with Deputy Antonio Behrongaray, 20 June 1995, Buenos Aires; interview with Senator Eduardo Vaca, 7 October 1995, Buenos Aires.

54. Pion-Berlin, *Through Corridors of Power*, 122–36.

55. Child, "Guns and Roses."

56. Burggraaff, *Venezuelan Armed Forces in Politics*, 171–74.

57. Interview with Ramón J. Velásquez, 3 April 1995, Caracas; Schaposnik, *Democratización de las fuerzas armadas Venezolanas*.

58. Trinkunas, "Crafting Civilian Control" (diss.), 154–64.

59. Ibid.

Felipe Agüero

8

Institutions, Transitions, and Bargaining
Civilians and the Military in Shaping Postauthoritarian Regimes

Civil-Military Power Relations

Samuel P. Huntington's pathbreaking study of the military focused on civilian-military power relations and proposed conditions under which the political power of a professional military would be minimized.[1] Bengt Abrahamsson also focused on these kinds of relations, addressing military political power, its resources, and modes of mobilization the military could use to resist decisions concerning it.[2] Scholars working on Latin America borrowed from these orientations and looked at the empowering effects of military professionalization in the context of feeble social and political structures. Abraham Lowenthal, for instance, pointed to varying levels of military institutionalization—organizational resources, strength, and coherence—and their contrast with the institutionalization of civilian institutions,[3] a focus whose utility was reaffirmed by J. Samuel Fitch.[4] Guillermo O'Donnell, in turn, advanced several hypotheses on the military's empowerment that resulted from perceptions of change in its organizational capabilities relative to society,[5] and Alfred Stepan later reaffirmed a power perspective in his notions of military prerogatives and military contestation in the study of democratization.[6] It is thus clear, if hardly surprising, that dominant approaches in the study of military-state-society relations have pointed to crucial relations of power between civilian and military actors and institutions.

A power relations approach has served to analyze overt military intervention in politics, but it may also be used in the study of military accommodation in civilian-dominated regimes. Indeed, it has been applied to civil-military relations both in well-established democracies and civilian-controlled authoritarian regimes. In these cases, a focus on the scope and means of influence over decisions[7] and the agenda dominating civilian-military interactions has proved to be useful. The approach, therefore, does not assume that the normal and typical state of relations is one of conflict. Cooperation between military and civilian officials is observable even in newly democratized Latin American regimes whose polities have strong traditions of civilian-military conflict. In fact, such cooperation must take place for democratic politics to institutionalize into stable regimes. But the utility of a power relations approach is certainly enhanced in places like Latin America and southern Europe, where disputes over prerogatives, agenda-setting, and pending issues from an authoritarian past continued to mark the civilian-military rapport long after democratization.

A Focus on Founding Conditions

If the above is true, then it is critical to ascertain how civil-military power relations are shaped from their initial conditions. Initial conditions that form the basic parameters in the distribution of power between the military, on one hand, and the civilian elites and the rest of society, on the other, help delineate the contours of that relationship for long periods and, hence, the characteristics of the political regime and its dynamics of change.[8]

The study of civilian-military relations during a military regime, for instance, is facilitated by a clear view of the circumstances that launched that regime, the political alignments that made it possible, and the institutional arrangements that defined it in its early stages. Here, O'Donnell's analyses, such as those found in his *Modernization and Military Coups*, remain, in my view, paradigmatic. And just as a study of the conditions behind the founding coups of the military-authoritarian regimes of the 1960s and 1970s is essential to understanding civil-military relations in their midst, so is the identification of the founding conditions of other long-lasting periods of particular patterns of civil-military relations.

For instance, the contours of civilian-military relations in the period preceding the wave of militarism of the 1960s and 1970s were, in many cases, established by disruptions of the 1930s, which were, in turn, expressions of the profound political, social, and economic changes affecting the region. In Chile, the basic features of civilian-military relations that prevailed for most of the century were greatly influenced by the manner in which the dictatorship of Colonel Carlos Ibáñez came to an end and the *civilista* reaction that followed. In Argentina, the way in which the Yrigoyen civilian administration collapsed gave rise to a completely different pattern that opened the way to frequent military intervention. Later, the rise and demise of Peronist rule set into motion yet another dynamic based on the military-imposed, political exclusion of a large sector of Argentine society. In Peru, the mode in which the Alianza Popular Revolucionaria Americana (APRA) and the military violently collided early in the 1930s instituted a three-decade-long trend similar to the exclusionary pattern inaugurated with the fall of Perón in Argentina. In Venezuela, the manner in which the Pérez Jiménez regime witnessed its demise, and the way the opposition pacts were designed, strongly influenced the relations between soldiers and civilians that prevailed there until the early 1990s. Important junctures such as the ones just mentioned decisively helped to shape the balance and distribution of civil-military power relations for long stretches of the twentieth century.[9]

While initial conditions influence civilian-military interactions, how actors either reaffirm or change those conditions to their advantage is also of critical importance. The actual interchanges among players—replete with ideas, initiatives, mobilization, or incorporation of new resources—also influence changes in the pattern of their relations and the corresponding distribution of power. For instance, the decision to join the inter-American military system after World War II in most cases strengthened the military and affected its relations with civilians. The activation of the military's moderating role by political elites in Brazil and the formation of broad political coalitions such as that promoted by APRA and the Odriístas in Peru in the 1950s are examples of initiatives that affect the distribution of civil-military power. The formation of broad opposition coalitions and the mobilization of masses by civilian opponents to military-authoritarian regimes had similar impacts. A focus on founding conditions must, therefore, be balanced by a consideration of the actual ability and willingness of actors to pursue initiatives that strengthen their position within the existing parameters or to try to shake off the parameter's constraints.

Transitions and Institutional Outcomes

My interest here is civilian-military relations in the postauthoritarian regimes that emerged in southern Europe in the 1970s and in South America in the 1980s. In these cases, civilian-military relations evolved in diverse ways, exhibiting different distributions of power and modes of institutionalization. Spain and Greece, for instance, successfully attained civilian supremacy much earlier than Portugal and by different routes. In South America, Argentina has gone the farthest in removing the military from political center stage and advancing toward civilian control. These goals remain most elusive for Chile, and the other cases stand in intermediate positions. Overall, compared to southern Europe, South America has been much less successful in the pursuit of the democratic goal of civilian supremacy.

I argue here that many of the differences in civilian-military relations observed since the demise of authoritarian regimes may be accounted for by founding conditions of the successor democracies: the way the military exit took place, the main features of the transition, and the early institutional arrangements that gave shape to the new postauthoritarian order. I argue that the nature of the first postauthoritarian arrangement—the transition outcome— was strongly affected by the strength of the forces that helped produce it. For instance, a transition controlled by a unified military conducting its own withdrawal from office is likely to result in arrangements allowing for more military prerogatives than found in a full-fledged unrestrained democracy. In turn, a civilian-led transition in which the military has little agenda-setting or decision-making clout will likely lead to a new, postauthoritarian settlement that initially assigns fewer military entitlements. Thus the military's formal power, unity, and assertiveness at the outset are determinant in shaping the contours of the first postauthoritarian arrangement.

That arrangement then shapes the institutions that differentially empower the civilians and the military for the ensuing process and in which attempts to attain civilian supremacy and democratic consolidation take place. Since this arrangement is often the result of transactions and compromises reached after difficult negotiations and laborious efforts, it becomes very costly to change it. Unsatisfied actors will attempt to do so nonetheless, but they will have to bear the burdens of initiating action and rallying support. For instance, the inauguration of an unfettered democracy—although democracies, especially "transacted" postauthoritarian democracies, are seldom truly unfettered—would place heavier burdens on a military that, critical of the transition outcome, attempts to secure more privileges at the expense of an agreed-upon distribution of power. Conversely, in an incomplete democracy in which an entrenched military enjoys excessive prerogatives, the burdens of initial reformist action are placed on civilian democratizers. This reformist action is costly because, among other things, it calls into question more or less formalized guarantees previously given the military in the course of liberalization or during the transition.[10] Thus an important effect of initial conditions on the posttransition process is that they unevenly empower political actors in their attempts to change or maintain the contours of the first postauthoritarian arrangement.[11]

But however weighty the starting terms may be, strong actors may gradually be subdued, and initially weak actors may recover strength later in the process. In Spain, for instance, the military's subordinate position in the transition did not settle the military question once and for all. It did facilitate a clean democratic inauguration, placing the burden of subverting this order on the military, but ultimately it did not prevent the growth of military assertiveness, which severely tested the democracy and postponed the attainment of civilian supremacy and democratic consolidation. It took a failed coup attempt, civilian leadership, public support, and a set of specific policies to advance the movement firmly toward civilian supremacy. In Argentina, a transition initiated from the ashes of the armed forces' political and military defeat proved not to be an insurmountable impediment for the military's later reassertion. Here, too, a failed military uprising became the turning point that facilitated military subordination. In Uruguay, conversely, the military's control during the transition and its imposition of limits on the first democratic settlement did not in the end hinder the subsequent advancement of democracy. In Greece, where initial conditions were roughly similar to those of Argentina, democratization nonetheless proceeded much more smoothly, at a faster pace, and with greater success.

These cases suggest that even if initial conditions are critical in shaping the first transition outcome, which heavily influences subsequent events, the fortunes of this posttransition process are also affected by many other elements that come into play. It is up to the actors involved to mobilize, garner support, and prepare internally to exert the special effort to change the situation in pursuit of goals they value. They may decide they are not able to do this, that it is not worth the risks, or that the alternative does not appear to be so bad after all, or they may decide to jump in the dark, take the risks, and bear the consequences. Institutional settings and resources provide the constraints but also the opportunities, and it is up to the actors involved to use, exploit, or avoid them.

In the following sections I offer an approach for the study of civil-military relations in transitions from authoritarianism that highlights the role of bargaining resources for the empowerment of military and civilian actors in contexts of uncertainty, such as those of transitions.[12] Bargaining outcomes result in institutional arrangements—new political regimes—that distribute power unevenly among actors. These arrangements then heavily influence the bargaining process for the ensuing period, in which actors may try to redress that distribution. This section concludes with the application of this approach to the cases of southern Europe and South America. The final part of the chapter focuses more specifically on a within–South America comparison to probe the impact of initial conditions on the influence exerted by the military in the postauthoritarian regimes of those countries.

Interests, Uncertainty, and Guarantees during Transitions

The start of the transition finds the military and the civilians holding distinct, often conflicting, interests. The military, like any large complex organization, seeks to advance its institutional prerogatives. These are strongly defined by the military's previous partnership in the establishment and maintenance of the authoritarian regime that is initiating its retreat. This may mean in some cases that the military first tries to maintain some of the features of the old regime or to assist in shaping the contours of the new one. In most instances, however, it strives for internal control of the profession and for protection from external political control,[13] fearing and eventually resisting political change if it intrudes on the established allocation of prerogatives. Uncertainty over the nature and extent of the impact of regime change leads the military to attempt to maximize its autonomy.

Meanwhile, relevant civilian political groups seek the establishment of democracy. They may differ on the extent and specific nature of the democratic rules they would like to see enforced and the specific policies they would like to see implemented, but once the transition unfolds, they all share an interest in democratization. Even if some show less than enthusiastic support for democratization, no major political group actively and openly courts military intervention to advance its goals.

If they reside in the government, civilians will resist veiled or overt military pressures on policy in civilian areas and will attempt to move to impose greater control in military domains. This creates tensions with the military, which will worsen should there develop within society armed groups, widespread violence, uncontrolled social mobilization, or autonomous movements that, for instance, seek accountability for past abuses by military officers.

The military will make preemptive or reactive moves to maximize its autonomy and resist civilian "encroachments." The most extreme reaction is the attempt to block political change altogether, in the hope of an authoritarian reequilibration.[14] More often, however, the military tries to steer the course of change to its liking or attempts to obstruct change through the exertion of veto power or strong oversight capacity over government policies; threatens to use force to stop specific policies such as an expansion of political pluralism or the transfer of human rights violators to court; exerts control over intelligence agencies; rejects governmental or congressional "interference" with matters deemed internal; and takes other measures. In diverse combinations, such military maneuvers were observed in all the cases of concern here, and they were invariably aimed at gaining reassurances and decreasing uncertainty about its institutional future.

Guarantees, reassurances, and certainty form the crux of change in transitions involving the military and are critical to understanding military acquiescence to democracy. The military normally operationalizes its core interests in terms of "minimal conditions" that are made explicit in order to test the reaction of political actors, influence the policies they have outlined for the transition, and specify an eventual bargaining position. This will have the effect of moderating reformists' policies by imposing a "military ceiling" to reforms, even if this ceiling is eventually raised. The military attempts, in this way, to reduce the uncertainty that democratization brings about.

For the military, guarantees are those that secure its autonomy and protect it from external control. Furthermore, institutional guarantees are those that prevent outcomes in the political process that the military deems threatening to its institution and its views of national security. Obviously, not all these guarantees may be obtained, and their nature and extent will vary from case to case according to resources, perceived threat, and the institutional context itself.

In some cases, specific guarantees regarding immunity from prosecution for past abuses or the preservation of autonomy were demanded and offered, as were more general ones such as the formalization of a monitoring role. Guarantees may take the form of constitutional provisions that allow for direct representation of military interests, the preservation of institutions from the authoritarian past, or the continuity in power of formerly authoritarian elites who manage to mobilize enough popular support to play an important role under competitive conditions.

Assurances do not remain fixed, however, after the bargain that establishes the democracy is struck. Actors still try to redefine the boundaries of uncertainty or to change the content of guarantees. These areas may expand or shrink and will subsequently induce changes in the military's willingness to acquiesce or, at least, will affect the opportunity structure for alternative strategies. The point is that, to varying extents, the assertion of civilian supremacy demands that guarantees initially given the military be reduced, replaced, or reformulated.

Guarantees may be withdrawn or they may simply evaporate. For instance, political groups most congenial to military interests may fail to garner enough popular support in the competitive process, or they may grow increasingly distant from military interests. Whichever way guarantees disappear or weaken, they will be cause of substantial military frustration, such as experienced in Spain. The Franquist Right was not able to muster enough electoral support to present itself as a workable guarantee, and more moderate politicians whom the military initially saw as allies—the governments formed by the monarchy—pursued policies that challenged core military interests. They legalized the Communist Party and took positions during the drafting of the Constitution that destroyed a bond of trust that had originally served as an informal guarantee to the military.

In such situations, the military may attempt successfully or unsuccessfully to forcefully reinstate promises made. If it loses, it may be compelled to peacefully acquiesce to the new regime and hopefully to eventually redefine its goals so that they are commensurate with professional roles compatible with democratization. Accumulated frustration, however, may orient goal redefinition in the direction of greater contestation, reawakening a temporarily dormant assertive stance. In any case, changes in the structure of guarantees will renew and increase uncertainty, and civilians and the military will reassess the extent to which they regard each other as a continuing source of uncertainty. Ultimately, however, democratization entails a gradual and sensible elimination of this uncertainty on both sides.

Bargaining, Resources, and Empowerment

The offer and withdrawal of guarantees, reassurances, and threats during democratization are made when they may lead to desired and achievable outcomes in light of a given set of constraints. In gauging attainability, these actors assess the resources they can muster and develop expectations and calculations about the resources of others. Thus they relate to one another in a situation of interdependence within which they engage in communication and bargaining.

Bargaining does not necessarily entail a formal situation in which actors explicitly exchange agendas and mutual claims and demands, although it may. Rather, it is an ongoing process in which actors signal intentions and brandish resources with a view to producing reactions and responses that are in turn taken as signals for renewed interaction. The military, for instance, will resort to "voice" or veto, will manipulate fear induced by the powerful threat of a coup, or will spread the notion of a "military ceiling" to reforms.[15] Civilians may also use the military's coup threat to induce moderation and coalescence across the spectrum of political forces. They also may try to upgrade their bargaining capacities through the use of various resources such as mass mobilization, pacts, constitution making, issuance of policy packages, and legitimation via elections and referenda. Outcomes reached in a succession of bargaining exchanges institutionalize a new set of opportunities and constraints that unevenly empower the players, modifying strategic calculations for the subsequent series of exchanges.

Success throughout is a function of relative strengths. It is thus critical, for a proper understanding of different outcomes, to focus on the various resource settings, the resources available to different actors, and the ways they gain access to them, use them, and deny them to their opponents. The analytical starting point here is civilian and military actors developing resources to modify or strengthen institutional settings that bind them and differentially empower them.

Opportunities and Constraints

Resource strength at the dawn of a transition derives mainly from the way the military exit took place and the main features of the transition itself. During this period, the following factors (resources and institutions) are most likely to define the opportunities and constraints facing civilian and military actors, providing the context for their bargaining exchanges.

First, who is in control of the transition? If the elites who dominate are civilians, the military assumes a secondary role and finds it harder to influence the process in its favor. If, however, the elites in control are military, then the military is at the forefront of the negotiations leading to its retreat, holding the upper hand in the bargaining process that ensues, and imposing protective preconditions for itself.

Whether the military plays the dominant role is generally influenced by the formal position of power in the outgoing authoritarian regime. According to this idea, authoritarian regimes can be classified as civilianized or militarized. Militarized regimes are those in which the armed forces participate directly in the formulation of key policies and decide on the succession or rotation of those in executive office. Typically this is the case of governing "juntas" or other devices for direct institutional participation. The authoritarian regimes that existed in Greece, Argentina, Uruguay, Ecuador, Peru, Bolivia, Brazil, and Chile conform, in different ways, to this type. Civilianized regimes are those in which the civilians rather than the military make major policy decisions, although the latter may be given representation in the governing institutions. This distinction is commonly grounded in the duration of an authoritarian regime, with civilianization gradually taking over among regimes that lasted longer. The authoritarian regimes in Spain and Portugal are of this variety.[16] Based on this distinction, it may be argued that the military is in a better position to monitor change, set the agenda for the transition, and assure its interests in cases in which it occupied the core leadership positions in the exiting authoritarian regime.

Second, the transition path also affects the nature of the elites in control of the transition and the extent of their control. Transitions may be preceded by a gradual liberalization conducted by the authoritarian rulers and proceed more or less according to a schedule, and they may even follow, as in Spain, the long-anticipated death of an aging *caudillo*. In transitions that follow this pattern, the militarized or civilianized nature of the outgoing authoritarian regime is the critical factor in determining who will be in control of the transition. Transitions may also be launched unexpectedly, however, as a result of the sudden collapse of the authoritarian regime, and the elites formerly in command will be subsequently replaced with new ones.

Regimes may collapse because of a mass uprising, a coup, or a military defeat. If, for instance, a once civilianized authoritarian regime is overthrown by a military bent on liberalization and democratization, then it is the military that will guide the transition, regardless of the civilianized nature of the ousted dictatorship. This was clearly the case in Portugal.[17]

If military defeat or unbearable international humiliation causes the authoritarian regime to collapse (as in Greece and Argentina), the ruling elites will find their political strength swiftly eroded and will be pressured to transfer power. If the controlling elites are military and are replaced by civilians, then these cases should be considered civilian-controlled transitions. Such was the case in Greece, where civilian elites who started and guided the transition summarily replaced a militarized regime. In Argentina, however, military defeat led to regime collapse but not to the immediate transfer of power. The military held on for more than a year but, defeated and severely discredited, remained politically weakened. The transition path thus affects which elites control the transition and to what extent.

Third, the relative capacities of these actors greatly depend on a vital resource: the extent of their internal unity. The military's inherent might as a coercive force is vastly deflated politically unless it can display high levels of unity and institutional consensus. Because the officer corps is a hierarchical organization functioning by command and discipline, unity among its higher echelons becomes especially relevant when the military trespasses in areas outside its professional specialization, say from combat preparation to politics. Unity as a political resource is measured in the military by the extent to which definitions of institutional interests, mission, and role are shared, especially by senior officers.

Particular historical experiences, professional practices, international connections, and generational or "promotions" cliques all affect military unity during the transition. But especially important are the military's varying assessments about its own past governmental performance and about the performance of successor civilian governments. Unity is enhanced if the military's evaluation of its past performance is generally positive. Unity also is enhanced if the generalized perception develops that core institutional interests of the military are being harmed by the action of successor elites.

A certain level of consensus in the military may suffice to resist civilian attempts at military reform. But higher levels of consensus are necessary if the military wants to pursue a more assertive strategy. Consensus around a societal project, viewed as an alternative to civilian goals of regime transformation, is necessary if an assertive attempt to block civilian-led transformations is made.[18]

Fourth, unity is no less important for civilian forces. The ability of political parties and other organizations to coalesce around formal agreements on institutions and basic rules of governance is a factor of civilian strength. Pacts, accords, or informal but explicit understandings on mutual guarantees lend credibility to the forces that will staff democratic institutions. After the democratic election of leaders, the existence of such agreements will facilitate the emergence of a loyal opposition, that is, one that, even if substantively opposed to the party in power, will maintain its opposition within the boundaries permitted by democratic procedures.[19] Civilian coalescence on fundamentals will limit the range of resistance strategies available to the military.

Societal or ideological polarization may present obstacles to civilian unity, but it need not hinder coalescent possibilities. There are cases in which civilians have presented a united front despite ideological polarization, while in other cases, ideologically close actors have been unable to unite. In Uruguay, for instance, the ideologically close traditional parties could not coalesce in the Club Naval accords with the military. In Spain, in contrast, ideologically distant forces supported, overtly or tacitly, the reform proposals put forward by Adolfo Suárez and coalesced in the drafting of the new Constitution.[20]

Fifth, manifest citizen support for emergent civilian structures, leaders, and policies is a deterrent to antireformist military actions, as it signals increased costs to intervention and reduces the military's bargaining power. Successor governments depend on support especially when their views collide with the military's or when their reforms meet with strong military disapproval. Testimony to the possible risks of diminished support for governments facing aggrieved militaries were the coup attempts in postauthoritarian Spain and Argentina. The ability of civilian governments to garner electoral and mass backing is thus critical to preempting or deterring the military by signaling increased costs to insubordination. These measures include calls for elections or referenda and the timely publicizing of broad policy platforms that give the initiative to the government.[21]

The sixth factor is the existence of general orientations on national defense and military policy put forth by the civilian leadership, accompanied by appropriate civilian expertise. This entails a capacity for political leaders to understand the nation's security problems and threats and then define the nation's defense goals; to formulate a position on the armed forces' role and mission and specify views on military organization, professional norms, and education; and to construct policies on the allocation of resources for national defense and on the relationships that the military should establish with the rest of the state and society. These are the bases for adapting the military's mission and position in the state to the general goals of democratization.

The failure of civilians to conceive policy autonomously reinforces the military's claim to corporate autonomy and may facilitate the reconstruction of internal consensus in the military on terms contradictory to the goals of political democratization. Civilian efforts to promote military unity around professional views consistent with constitutional norms oblige the military to perceive the civilian leadership as competent. Therefore, the development of a conception and policy on national defense empowers the civilian leadership in the attempt to overcome corporate resistance and to advance democratic leadership in the defense area.

Civilian leaders generally have little, if any command of military and defense affairs when the transition to democracy starts. Delay in the formulation of policies, however, may not be harmful for civilians and may indeed be beneficial. Untimely civilian effort to initiate military reform may prove counterproductive. The need to reassure the military during the first years may, in fact, demand postponement of reform measures, particularly in areas deemed most sensitive. Civilian expertise is most effective if put into practice when at least some degree of confidence between the new authorities and the military has been cultivated.

Contextual and International Economic Factors

International factors played a role secondary to the dynamics of local processes, and they can be assessed more productively by focusing on the ways they filtered down to the views of domestic actors in strategic scenarios. External factors were indeed critical in several instances in triggering or encouraging the transition and in supporting processes of democratic consolidation later on. International armed conflict, for instance, played an important role in triggering the transitions in Greece and Argentina, as did the colonialist burdens in Portugal. Also, a strongly democratic regional environment attracted the participation of Portuguese, Greek, and Spanish elites in multifaceted European networks, greatly aiding the move toward democratization.

International factors also were influential as demonstration effects. The nearly simultaneous occurrence of regime changes in two or three countries influenced the perceptions of local actors. Revolutionary events in Portugal, for instance, were followed very closely by Spanish elites and certainly influenced their perceptions as they prepared for the imminent end of the Franquist era.

International pressures for democratization were more ambiguous in South America because of the role of changing foreign policy priorities of U.S. administrations and the stance of international financial agencies.[22] Specifically in regard to the question of civilian supremacy, regional military contexts of South America and southern Europe offered uneven opportunities for civilians. The North Atlantic Treaty Organization (NATO) provided special opportunities for the civilian leadership in Spain when that country finally decided to join the organization. Civilian governments could use this opportunity to empower themselves vis-à-vis the military in ways that simply were not available for civilian elites in South America.

Regarding the role of economic factors, more favorable conditions for democratization exist when successor governments are economically prepared to cope with the difficult legacies of authoritarianism and with the rising demands of a resurrected civil society.[23] Economic prosperity provides flexibility in governments' dealings with the military and assists in satisfying some of its material demands.

Economic difficulties, however, do not directly and inevitably stimulate the military's reentry into politics, especially in instances when its own governmental experience has shown the military how intractable problems in this area were and how risky it was to be placed in charge of solving them. Also, military evaluation of civilian competence is done on a broader basis than mere economic performance. For instance, when the military plotted against democracies in Spain and Argentina, neither the rebels' motives nor the governments' responses were directly related to economic issues.[24]

Nonetheless, the specific ways in which successor administrations handle economic problems and the effects their policies have on public support may affect the bargaining position from which governments face the military. Public support for democratic advancement has in most cases prevailed over frustration about economic difficulties.[25] Support for a democratic regime, however, is not the same as support for a specific government. And specific governments, especially in South America, had trouble maintaining enough popular backing to enable themselves to advance civilian supremacy.

Transition Conditions and Outcomes: A Summary Presentation

As outlined above, the opportunities and constraints presented to actors may be arranged in the following way in terms of their likely outcomes. Civilian reformers are ideally empowered to assert civilian supremacy if, either because the exiting regime was civilianized or because the military abruptly withdrew after collapse, they control the transition and set its agenda; they are able to coalesce around fundamental aspects of democratization and maintain substantial popular support that gives legitimacy to emerging structures; and they are able to develop, in due time, expertise on national defense from which they issue coherent military policies. If, at the same time, the military does not oppose them with an alternative project and its resistance to democratization is weakened by internal disunity, civilian reformers should be able to succeed, especially when, in addition, the international context is propitious.

Conversely, a decidedly less auspicious situation arises for civilian reformers when the military conducts its own extrication, controls the transition's agenda, and agrees on a coherent, alternative political project to that of civilian democratizers. If, in addition, civilian parties fail to align, to obtain popular support, and to devise mechanisms to expand what little support they may have, and they are unable to develop their own program on national defense and military policy, a much worse situation develops in which they confront military resistance or, barring that, fall short of advancing civilian supremacy.

More likely, however, are scenarios in which elements of civilian and military empowerment combine, as found in most of the cases considered here. These situations are roughly depicted in Table 8.1. The table highlights differences across cases with reference to factors that clearly precede the transition (such as the nature of the exiting authoritarian regime) jointly with factors that make their presence known during the transition itself or in the early stages of the posttransition period.[26] The table relates these factors to the level of success in attaining civilian supremacy.[27] After the end of transitions other elements emerge that either counter or reinforce the impact of the first transition outcome by affecting the disposition of those variables. A divided military, for instance, may unify in defense of hard-liners if it perceives threats to the military's core interests and mission. The intensification of terrorist threats against the military may ignite its contestational resolve, as it did in Spain, or

TABLE 8.1 *Opportunities/Constraints for Civilian Elites in Democratic Transitions*

	SPAIN	GREECE	PORTUGAL	ARGENTINA	BRAZIL	CHILE	PERU	URUGUAY
Authoritarian regime was civilianized	Yes	No	Yes	No	No	No	No	No
Transition substantially controlled by civilians	Yes	Yes	No	No	No	No	No	No
High civilian coalescence*	Yes	No	No	No	No	No	No	No
Manifest citizen support**	Yes-No-Yes	Yes	No-Yes	No-Yes	No	Yes	Yes-No	Yes
Civilian defense policies	No-Yes	Yes	No-Yes	No-Yes	No	No	No	No
Substantial divisions in the military	Yes	Yes	Yes	Yes	No	No	Yes	No
Military alternative project***	No	No	Yes	No	No	Yes	No	Yes
Favorable international opportunities	Yes	Yes	Yes	No	No	No	No	No
Success in civilian supremacy	High	High	High	Medium	Low	Low	Low	Medium

Source: Agüero, Soldiers, Civilians, and Democracy.

*High levels of civilian coalescence are found in different cases at various points in time. Only Spain is ranked Yes because of the high level of concentration in drafting the new constitution.

**Levels of popular support vary over time. The table focuses on level of support at critical junctures, such as referendums. No-Yes or Yes-No indicates change at different junctures.

***In cases ranked Yes, the military backed distinctly authoritarian constitutional designs.

invite political involvement that weakens progress in civilian control, as in Peru. A military at the helm of an authoritarian regime that then collapses following defeat in war may overcome its initial devastation (as in Argentina), turn highly assertive, and exact concessions, only to be partly subdued later on by newly strengthened civilians. Or a military that overthrows a civilianized authoritarian regime and commands the transition (as in Portugal) may ultimately weaken itself by inciting factionalism.

Civilian coalescence may be strengthened or weakened, as may the magnitude of public support for the successor government. International and economic factors, varying capabilities of civilian elites and successor governments for policy formulation, and the timing and pace[28] of policy proposal and implementation all influence the civil-military balance during the posttransition period in ways that cannot be predicted merely from knowledge of initial conditions. Also weighing in are unanticipated events that end up unexpectedly but decisively benefiting one or another set of actors. Coup attempts, especially failed coup attempts—such as those in Spain in February 1981, in Argentina in December 1990, and in Portugal in November 1975—are cases in point. In hindsight, these events proved to be decisive for the success of democratization.

The following section presents, in broad strokes, the results of efforts to attain civilian supremacy over the military in southern Europe and compares them with those obtained in South America. In the final section, a comparison within South America will help highlight factors critical to differences in outcomes in this region.

Southern Europe and South America: Compared Outcomes

Initial conditions in the civilianized transition common to Spain and Greece led to the two most successful cases of democratization. Civilian authorities there initiated the posttransition period with an advantage: they, rather than the military, controlled the transition. New constitutions and ordinances unequivocally established the primacy of elected officials in all policy spheres, including defense and the military, and these officials showed they could use the powers assigned to them in general policy decisions as well as in specific areas such as promotions and assignments.

Greece was the fastest in attaining success, marked by the 1977 reforms of the military command structure only three years after the changeover. This success was corroborated by the military's acceptance of the Socialist electoral victory in 1981. The quick pace of reforms was facilitated by the collapse of the colonels' regime in 1974, which allowed the next government to purge the military, albeit cautiously, and promote swift changes in it. The government could also benefit from the disrepute earned by the former ruling elites following the international circumstances surrounding their humiliating collapse. The exiting ruling elites had no support in the armed forces, whereas the civilian elites who controlled the interregnum mustered substantial backing in the election of a new parliament and the referendum against the reinstatement of the monarchy. The new parliament swiftly drafted a new constitution that further empowered civilian authority. Factions in the military contested decisions affecting it, but the government always prevailed. Former junta chiefs, whom the Karamanlis government had taken to court on charges of insurrection and treason, received life sentences. No major challenges from the military emerged after 1975.

In Spain, success came more slowly. Military challenges to democracy did not end until 1982, and the actual attainment of civilian supremacy became visible only in 1984—nine years after Franco's death—with the reform of the national defense organic law. In this case, with no collapse to speak of, a military led by generals who were hailed by the officer corps for their loyalty to the principles of Franquism remained intact throughout and well beyond the transition. The implication was that the military would resist democratic change for a longer period of time and that military reforms could be tackled only when that resistance was overcome.

Democratization in Spain commenced auspiciously and with much promise when, after Franco died, the king appointed a prime minister, Adolfo Suárez, who immediately called for elections for a constituent assembly. Early successes were soon eclipsed, however, by a mounting military threat, which nearly toppled the new regime. The posttransition route was, in fact, marked by bumps, ditches, and roadblocks that were not fully visible from the starting line at the transition's end. As in other cases, initial conditions here strongly influenced the power arrangements that ended the transition, but they could not fully confine subsequent developments.

The military, disappointed with the surprises of the transition and angered at the escalation of terrorism from Basque separatists, strengthened its contestational resolve, preventing civilian authorities from advancing their political supremacy. The times between the approval of the new democratic constitution in 1978 and the elections that brought the Socialists to power in 1982 were fraught with conspiracy and tension. It was not until the failed coup attempt of February 1981, which severely demoralized hard-liners and allowed for divisions to deepen, combined with the Socialist victory in the 1982 elections, that opportunities for the promotion of civilian supremacy opened up.

The Socialist government, elected in 1982 with an overwhelming mandate, which was willing to pursue military and defense reforms aimed at achieving civilian control, decisively exploited these opportunities. After 1982, the military no longer overtly challenged civilian authority. And with the major reforms of 1984–87, the extent of civilian preeminence reached in the defense hierarchy became comparable to that found in most of Western Europe.

Despite the relatively greater difficulties found in Spain, this country jointly with Greece came out of the transition with a cleanly inaugurated democracy. These were the only two cases in which the civilians controlled the transition. All the other democratic nations inherited legacies of military influence: tutelage, special prerogatives, a large number of posts reserved for uniformed men, or legal impediments to legitimate claims to retribution. The starting point after the transition ended was thus very different in these cases.

Portugal was the most troublesome of the southern European cases. The first to break away from authoritarian rule, it was also the last to attain civilian supremacy. Once the transition commenced, the military maintained a tutelary role for eight years until the constitutional revisions of 1982. It took several years following these revisions for civil-military roles to become defined. Aided by the election of a civilian president in 1986, further specification of civilian responsibilities in defense did not emerge until the late 1980s, and actual implementation of those roles did not begin until the 1990s. Beginning with a situation that came dangerously close to an all-out civil war, several factors, such as those listed in Table 8.1, operated to work gradually toward a successful outcome. Military divisions, the ascendancy of military moderates, the sharp reduction in military size, and the strength of the European pull all played significant roles in ways that cannot be fully specified here.

Compared to the southern European democracies, the new democracies of South America were less successful in their efforts to subordinate the armed forces. This difference is explained by the variables displayed in Table 8.1, with special emphasis on the civilian-dominated transitions in Greece and Spain. All the South American examples were, in turn, military-controlled transitions. Of course, many other factors, such as those operating in Portugal, others strictly related to bargaining situations, or international factors, were relevant as well and cannot be fully detailed for each case here.

Beyond the major differences between South America and southern Europe, much variation is found within the South American region. A more focused comparison of South American cases, which contrasts the institutionalized nature of authoritarian rule with the transition away from it, may allow us to revisit initial conditions—transition factors—and their impact on the military's clout in the postauthoritarian order. To what extent have predictions about democratic outcomes based on transitional modes held true? Does the present state of military influence in new democracies bear the imprint of the transitions or have those marks been wiped away? By contrasting the expectations borne out of regime change with the current state of military power and constraints on new democracies, we can gain insight into the impact of that change on the quality of democratic governance in the new regimes.[29]

Regime Institutionalization and Military Political Strength: Revisiting Initial Conditions in South America

All South American authoritarian regimes were military in nature. Thus transition from dictatorship meant military extrication from office and consequently foreshadowed a large military role in the transition. Particularly because they might be blamed for the regime's failures and crimes, these armed forces found added incentive to manipulate the transition in order to secure protection from retribution for themselves and their members before exiting.

Military regimes differed, however, in how institutionalized they were. A highly institutionalized, military-authoritarian regime sets down formal rules that regulate its power structure and assign government functions to nonrepresentative or semirepresentative bodies, including the armed forces. A good indication of the intent to institutionalize the regime was the adoption of a new constitution, such as in Brazil in 1967–69 and Chile in 1980.

One important consequence of institutionalization was stability in the military leadership. By having a minimum set of rules governing intramilitary and military-government relations, leadership succession—a critical problem for nondemocratic regimes[30]—acquired predictability. Usually this was accomplished by attaining some degree of separation between the military as institution and government. Stability in regime and military leadership—that is, the ability to maintain an unchallenged hierarchical structure and cohesion—strengthened the military's position during the transition.

In Uruguay, Peru, and especially Argentina, the absence of separation between the military as institution and government led to more internal bickering and, hence, instability at the top. Military and regime leadership was thus more uncertain than in Brazil and Chile, weakening the military's position during the transitions. Another, perhaps more important, consequence of institutionalization was that constitutions provided a framework from which to confront the opposition without improvised responses. While this was true in Brazil and Chile, it was not in the noninstitutionalized cases of Argentina,

Peru, and Uruguay, where the military was forced to devise a plan for extrication that reached out to the opposition.

An important distinction in transition modes is the degree of strength with which the ruling military entered the transition.[31] This factor determines whether the military may impose its own terms or must compromise with democratic forces in the execution of the transition. In Chile and Brazil, the military was comparatively stronger and could compel the opposition to submit to terms dictated by the outgoing authoritarian regime, terms whose entrenched regulations and mechanisms secured guarantees for the military's future interests.[32] These factors were not present in Uruguay, Peru, and Argentina, where the armed forces entered the period of regime change from a comparatively weaker position. They could not dictate their own terms and had to reach out to the democratic forces in an attempt to salvage some power after extrication from government. Uruguay and Peru are cases of compromise, while Argentina is a special case of attempted, but failed, compromise.[33]

Where the armed forces were weaker, the opposition extracted from them key concessions regarding the transition: free elections (except in Uruguay, where the military kept the most popular politician from running in the first election) and either a new democratically approved constitution or the resumption of the previous democratic constitution. In Brazil and Chile, by contrast, the military was not forced to compromise, and the opposition could not obtain the democratic process it desired and submitted itself to the authoritarian constitutions.

Expectations Raised from the Transitions

What expectations did these modes of transition create in terms of the military's capacity to constrain successor democracies? Clearly, it was anticipated that military restrictions on democracy would be greater in Brazil and Chile. In Brazil, this outlook was confirmed after the lamentable circumstances of Sarney's assumption of the presidency, which frustrated the opposition's hopes of a sharper break with military rule.[34] Democracy in these countries recommenced with ugly "birth defects,"[35] which were expected to limit the next regime severely.

The military would constitute an obstacle to a full resumption of democracy in the other countries as well, but it was thought that their mode of extrication would prevent them from imposing weighty restrictions on democratic governments. Still, the fact that in Uruguay a pact had been sealed in which the military had placed demands for specific action by the next government gave that democracy a constrained look as well. In Peru, the military exited with a few assurances of autonomy in specific circumstances and with the expectation that military matters would be dealt with carefully and in consensus with its leadership. As insurgency flourished during ensuing democratic administrations, the legislation that the military passed right before its exit proved to be significant in allowing it to operate independently in areas declared to be states of emergency. In Argentina, the military exited with no guarantees other than those it had bestowed on itself, which the successor government promised not to honor. Argentina was the only case in which the military left office with no laws or agreement with successor forces to protect it. In sum, transitions led to expectations of weighty restrictions on democracy in Chile and Brazil, moderate restrictions in Uruguay and Peru, and unfettered democracy in Argentina.

The issue of military human rights violations, however, caused extreme uncertainty in the transitions most affected by it: those of Argentina, Chile, and Uruguay. In the first two cases, the military had granted itself amnesty for crimes committed during the military-authoritarian period, and attempts to undo the amnesty would create unpredictable tensions. General Pinochet had at one point stated that he was staying on as army chief "so that my men are not touched." In Uruguay, the appointment of the last junta chief (General Hugo Medina) as defense minister in the newly installed democratic government posed a warning that his men were not to be touched either.

How do expectations raised from the transitions match present circumstances? Realities in Argentina, Chile, and Peru are as anticipated. Argentina and Chile stand at opposite ends of the spectrum, with many constraints in Chile and few in Argentina. Peru faces fewer limits than Chile, as predicted. Constraints are lower than expected in Uruguay and especially in Brazil.

Legacies of Transitions and Legal-Institutional Factors

The legacy of military rule is visible in all these countries. First, on the issue of human rights, even those nations that have enjoyed military restrictions on democracy have been unable to punish criminals and dispense justice. Second, the full assertion of civilian control is still a distant goal. Even in the most successful cases—Argentina and Uruguay—civilian officials have no influence over military education, and civilian court jurisdictions are narrowed while jurisdictions for military justice remain broad. Also, military reform and modernization programs have been mainly conceived and carried out by the armed forces themselves.[36] And where they are in control, civilians often have been guided by a desire to reassure the military that they would not conflict with its goals and interests.

Where military restrictions on democratic governance differ, however, the transition's impact appears most clearly and decisively where expectations and outcomes correspond most closely. Chile and Argentina reveal breaks with historic patterns of military involvement in politics. Argentina has departed from a century-long tradition of military political intervention, while Chile has broken with the pattern of *no* military intervention or participation in politics established in the democratic period between 1932 and 1973. In both cases, this departure is largely the result of the mode of transition.

I have noted that transitions produce outcomes that differentially empower the military and civilian officials for the postauthoritarian period. In Argentina, for instance, the transition allowed civilians to be assertive on human rights and to initiate military reforms. The armed forces were first placed on the defensive, but the attempts at retribution and reform ignited a military reaffirmation of its power, as the military rebelled repeatedly in pursuit of its goals. Finally, military contestation was eliminated when the Argentine government first appeased the military with amnesties and pardons and then crushed the last rebellious attempt, allowing the government to rid the army of mutinous leaders. The military's political clout was further weakened through economic and fiscal reform. In this sense, Argentina's has been a case of de facto demilitarization driven by budget reduction.[37] This, however, would have been impossible were it not for the transition, which returned unrestricted constitutional powers to civilian government facing a weakened military.

In Chile, in contrast, the transition produced a postauthoritarian arrangement based on the Pinochet Constitution, which assigned large prerogatives to the military. The burden of initiating constitutional reforms that would make possible the removal of the military from positions of influence fell on the successor government. Reforms were tried repeatedly but failed because of the rigidities imposed by the Constitution. Constitutional restrictions on the successor government inherited from the military regime found renewed sustenance from congressional parties of the right, which jointly with the nonelected senators denied the votes necessary for reforms. The power of the right has, in part, derived from the electoral system and the Constitution's clause on nonelected senators, both imposed by the military.

In Peru, the transition left the military with a significant level of autonomy, especially in its intervention against subversion. Trying not to antagonize the armed forces, the first successor government respected its autonomy and, by inaction, contributed to its expansion. After regime change, the military nurtured its independence and substantially expanded its capacity. This process was aided by the virtual freedom of action that civilian authorities gave the military to counteract the dramatic surge of subversive violence, notwithstanding the few attempts to the contrary during part of Alan García's failed administration. So much did this autonomy grow that, as Carlos Degregori and Carlos Rivera have convincingly argued,[38] Fujimori's decrees on expansion of the military role did no more than bring these in line with existing prerogatives. It is perfectly conceivable, however, that current military prerogatives could have been reduced had civilian administrations been assertive, thus lessening the impact of the transition. Their passivity, however, can be traced back to the transition itself, as it was based on the view that civilian rule could best be stabilized by leaving the military alone.

Turning to Uruguay, why couldn't the military sustain its privileges well into the future? The answer highlights the importance of legal-formal factors: unlike in Chile, the Uruguayan military failed to institutionalize its extrication from direct rule with an authoritarian constitution. In lieu of that, the military tried to hold on to its aspirations in a transition pact. Other than the restoration of elections and the previous constitution, this pact did not produce a binding agreement in part because there was no written document. Institutional Act 19, which followed the pact, allowed the National Security Council to continue for just a limited time. Only the Congress could have amended the constitution permanently to enshrine the military's interests. In addition to lacking a legal precedent or a binding agreement, the military also had to face up to the fact that during its rule it had antagonized all the major political parties. Therefore, on all issues other than the *ley de caducidad*, the Uruguayan military (unlike Chile's) had no party allies, nobody willing to defend and promote its legacy. Expectations arising from the transition could have been satisfied had military demands during the transition been made in formal-legal, binding terms. Then it would have been costlier for successor parties to have suppressed those demands because they would have had to risk altering a formalized agreement or law. Had the military's 1980 constitutional referendum passed, as it did in Chile, a transition would most likely have taken a very different course.

Along with Chile, Brazil's military entered the transition with strength and with an authoritarian constitution in hand, allowing it to reject the opposition's campaign for a new constitution or direct elections. Why, then, did military influence erode?[39] Why did expectations from the transition not materialize as they did in Chile? Again, the answer lies with legal-institutional factors, demanding a closer look at the authoritarian Constitution of 1967–69. Although the military had inserted into that Constitution several institutional acts highlighting its national security functions, the Constitution also established the primacy of the president over the armed forces and contained "liberal" elements such as the existence of a Congress, political parties, and opposition. Military rule thus relied on the primacy of the executive and its ability to secure a majority for its support party in Congress. For this, the president empowered himself with an additional resource—Institutional Act No. 5 (IA5)—which allowed him to dictate emergency measures at his discretion. When the military initiated the process of liberalization, it dropped IA5 and relied instead on specific decrees that could help it contain the rising electoral power of the opposition and its representation in Congress. The government ultimately failed in the attempt to control the forces unleashed by its own liberalization process that resulted in the 1985 election of a civilian president.

Without the control of the presidency, the military no longer could resort to emergency decrees to secure its interests. Now it could only rely on the Constitution, one that reserved national security roles for the armed forces but did not specify any special guarantees for a military out of government. In addition, no constitutional clause stood in the way of reform or the drafting of a new Constitution. Therefore, nothing impeded the new president from submitting in 1985 a constitutional amendment to enable the Congress elected in 1986 to produce a new charter. A constituent assembly thus offered an open-ended process that could substantially alter the legal-institutional basis of military power. This is a major difference with the case of Chile, where the Constitution assured the military that it could retain enhanced powers even after relinquishing control of the executive branch. The Chilean charter established high requirements for reform and specific military prerogatives in the National Security Council and was accompanied by organic laws of constitutional status that restricted presidential powers over the military.

The new centrality that the constituent process gave Congress in Brazil led the military to organize several ways of influencing its deliberations. While this influence obviously goes against the sovereignty of elected representation, it did at least signal the military's choice to accept the assembly as the locus of constitutional decision making and its willingness to abide by the assembly's decisions. The Constitution approved in 1988 reflected the military's influence on a number of issues, but it also denied some of the military's aspirations.

In sum, civilian elites in Brazil were freer to transform the military legacy than those in Chile. The military tried to maintain core elements of its power by influencing elected officials and negotiating with them instead of imposing a rigid legal-institutional legacy. This is why the Brazilian military's privileges are fewer than would have been predicted from the transition. Certainly peculiar features of Brazil's political system and parties facilitated the military's strategy of systematic lobbying on civilian officials: the weakness of political parties and the absence of party discipline.[40]

Conclusion

This brief comparative review of South American cases shows that differences in the manner in and extent to which military power constrains new democracies have been strongly influenced by the mode of transition from authoritarian rule. In none of the countries considered were the patterns of previous periods of democratic rule simply reproduced in the new democracies. Chile and Argentina represent a stark break with the past. In the other cases, the military's influence acquired new traits. This is also true for the southern European cases, although the significantly longer duration of authoritarian rule in Portugal and Spain had greater impact.

The expectations raised from the transition about the level of restriction the military would impose in new democracies were clearly matched in Argentina, Chile, and Peru. In Brazil and Uruguay, where military clout turned out to be less than expected, the major factors also were related to the transition. The comparative exercise undertaken here has highlighted the importance of formal legal-institutional elements in the transition and the type of institutionalization attained by military-authoritarian regimes. During the postauthoritarian era, the military will not be able to sustain the power and influence it had at the dawn of the transition if this power is not backed with formal-legal arrangements. These arrangements unevenly raise the cost of actions for contending actors in the process ensuing after the end of the transition. Clearly, for instance, it has been harder for Chilean authorities to curtail military power because such power is backed by an authoritarian Constitution than it has been for Uruguayan or Argentinean authorities not constrained by such realities.

These considerations are also valid for the southern European cases. The collapse of the colonels' regime in Greece allowed the new regime swiftly to create a new constitutional order. In Spain, the *reforma-ruptura* characterization of the transition pointed to the radical break with Franquism while proceeding from within its very institutions. Reformers were astute in using the regime's own legal mechanisms to promote blanket reforms: a referendum to end the old order and call for elections with constitution-making consequences. Reformers followed established legal routes to rid themselves of any legal-constitutional constraints. In Portugal, on the contrary, the collapse of authoritarian rule led to a new constitution conceived under heavy military tutelage. The establishment of full democracy had, therefore, to wait until those constraints were removed through constitutional reform, but a deadline for these reforms had originally been set already in the original Constitution. Constitutional constraints were thus strictly temporary, and their actual elimination depended on the actors' relative empowerment in the interim. These differences in southern Europe affected the nature and quality of early post-authoritarian arrangements.

It might seem somewhat of a paradox that formal-legal factors may play such a role, especially in South America, a region not known for exemplary rule of law. Although these elements may not pervade all spheres of politics and society, they certainly take added importance in the regulation of relations among state institutions. And though this role is not indicative of a special regard for the law on the part of actors that had not too long before toppled legally established regimes, it does support the notion that institutions and the legal-institutional arrangements that frame them do indeed have consequences.[41]

In the Introduction to this volume, it was noted how some institutionalists consider change to be possible but difficult because the "rules of the game" that constrain political action often constitute the embedded interests of key actors who first set up those rules. But strategic interactions with unanticipated consequences are still possible, and the way these interactions evolve depends not only on interests but on the comparative strength of the resources competitors for power can bring to the table. This chapter's analysis of civil-military relations during and after the transitions to democracy in Europe and Latin America makes similar observations. Because the stakes are high for those military and civilian actors involved in shaping the transition to democratic rule, what is done by them will not be easily undone by others. Thus the institutional arrangements they forge matter because whether they arise through bargaining, imposition, or law, they will set the confining context for new interactions. Where that context allows for maneuver, outcomes will depend on what resources each side commands and how it uses them.

Certainly the impact of the transition on the extent and manner of military influence in the new democracies ought not to obscure the role of other factors beyond the transition. The economy and its effect on budgets; political parties, their ties to the military, and the policies they put forth; subversion and political violence; international variables; bargaining processes animated by actors with changing relative empowerment; and other factors, joined with variables from an older past, have affected the transition legacy, strengthening or weakening it. This chapter has proposed an analytical focus that considers the actual ability and willingness of actors to pursue initiatives that strengthen their position within the existing pattern or to try and shake off its constraining impact on them. It has, at the same time, insisted that these actors' efforts must be viewed within the structuring impact of founding conditions. Just as the impact of civilian-military relations on the shape of political regimes during the military-authoritarian period or the preceding democratic periods could find their founding conditions in the background to the coups of the 1960s and 1970s and the social disruptions of the 1930s, so may the post-authoritarian period find defining characteristics in the founding conditions of the transitions.

NOTES

1. Huntington, *Soldier and the State.*
2. Abrahamsson, *Military Professionalization.*
3. Lowenthal, "Armies and Politics."
4. Fitch, "Armies and Politics."
5. O'Donnell, "Modernization and Military Coups."
6. Stepan, *Rethinking Military Politics.*
7. For this focus, see Colton, *Commissars, Commanders.*
8. For a more general statement of this approach, see Krasner, "Approaches to the State," and North, *Institutions, Institutional Change and Economic Performance.*
9. Collier and Collier's analysis of the political legacies of critical junctures in modes of labor incorporation could be applied to a study of the regime legacies of founding patterns of modes of civilian-military relations. See Collier and Collier, *Shaping the Political Arena.*
10. Inaction also may be costly in the long run if it leads to erosion of popular support for these civilian groups and to the institutionalized fixation of excessive prerogatives for the military.
11. For similar path-dependent approaches, see Stark, "Path Dependence," and Przeworski, *Democracy and the Market.* See also Cammack, "New Institutionalism."
12. These sections borrow heavily from my *Soldiers, Civilians, and Democracy.*
13. Perlmutter, *Military and Politics in Modern Times,* 2.
14. Linz, *Crisis, Breakdown and Reequilibration.*
15. Hirschman, *Exit, Voice and Loyalty.* O'Donnell and Schmitter pointed to the role of "playing coup poker [with] the coup that doesn't happen" (*Transitions from Authoritarian Rule*).
16. The importance of the extent of participation of the military in authoritarian regimes was highlighted in Linz, "Authoritarian Regime," and Linz, "Totalitarian and Authoritarian Regimes." The distinction between civilian and military influence in authoritarian regimes also was addressed in O'Donnell and Schmitter, *Transitions from Authoritarian Rule,* and O'Donnell, "Introduction to the Latin American Cases." Stepan argued that military-led transitions could be disaggregated into transitions led by the military as government or transitions led by the military as institution. Although these

distinctions are useful in highlighting different military dynamics in the transition, the basic contrast to be emphasized here is that between military-led and civilian-led transitions. See Stepan, "Paths toward Redemocratization."

17. This was also the case in Venezuela (1958–59), although civilian participation in the coup against dictator Pérez Jiménez was far greater than it was in the coup that ousted Marcello Caetano in Portugal.

18. In the period that preceded the 1966 coup in Argentina, the military succeeded in achieving cohesion and professionalization, which, according to O'Donnell, resulted in a feeling of organizational accomplishment that led the military to believe it "possessed a superior capacity to confront the social problems which the civil authorities evidently could not solve." The military empowered itself with a "political utopia" that guided the attempt to restructure the social (national) context (O'Donnell, "Modernization and Military Coups," 105, 120–21). From a different angle, Fitch maintains that these conceptions are influenced by the prior importance of particular doctrines or "role beliefs" ("Theoretical Model"). Depending on their pervasiveness and specific content, role beliefs operate as opportunities and as constraints for military action.

19. For a discussion of disloyal, semiloyal, and loyal opposition, see Linz, *Breakdown of Democratic Regimes*, 27–38.

20. Gillespie, "Uruguay's Transition." In Italy, much earlier, as in Spain, a broad spectrum of forces coalesced after the "svolta di Salerno," which led to the collaboration of all parties with the monarchy. See Di Palma, "Italy," and Pasquino, "Demise of the First Fascist Regime."

21. Good examples are Adolfo Suárez's early announcement of a timetable for the series of referenda and elections with which he garnered support for his plan of political reform in Spain; the skillful use of referenda by General Charles de Gaulle in France, which gave his government the upper hand in dealing with military opposition on the Algerian question; and President Alfonsín's submittal to referendum in Argentina of the sensitive Beagle territorial dispute with Chile, an action that helped remove a "national security" concern from exclusive military domains and helped settle a question otherwise prone to military utilization.

22. Lowenthal, *Exporting Democracy*.

23. For a discussion of this point, O'Donnell, "Transitions, Continuities, and Paradoxes."

24. Pion-Berlin, "Between Confrontation and Accommodation."

25. Linz and Stepan, "Political Crafting of Democratic Consolidation."

26. A basic time demarcation is that which separates the period before the end of the transition and the period that follows it. The demarcation line varies across cases; in Spain, for instance, the demarcation line is the approval of the 1978 Constitution and the following national elections; in Peru, the approval of the Constitution and the presidential elections of 1980; in Portugal, the Constitution of 1976 and the following elections; in Argentina, the assumption of power by President Alfonsín; and so on.

27. In the table Uruguay shows the same values as Chile, yet the outcome is different (low for Chile, medium for Uruguay). The reason for this difference lies in the success of the latter's enduring "constitutionalizing" authoritarian rule and is explained below, in the section on within–Latin America comparisons. Also, the table lists Peru's military as not having an alternative project of its own because this category considered only whether the military had backed a distinctly authoritarian constitutional design. This

was not the case in Peru; the military did entertain an alternative project, although this was one around which the military became divided over time.

28. For the importance of the time factor, see Linz, "Il Fattore tempo nei mutamenti di regime," and Linz and Stepan, "Political Identities and Electoral Sequences."

29. This section borrows heavily from my "Legacies of Transitions."

30. Linz, "Future of an Authoritarian Situation."

31. For other ways of classifying transitions in the literature, see Mainwaring, "Transitions to Democracy," and McGuire, "Interim Government."

32. The distinction of transition paths of *compromise* and *no compromise* is made in Bruszt and Stark, "Remaking the Political Field."

33. See McGuire, "Interim Government."

34. Sarney had been elected as vice president in the opposition ticket, but Tancredo Neves, the president-elect, suffered a stroke on the eve of the transfer of power and died a few weeks later. Until six months before the election, Sarney had headed the official party, which supported the military. He then led a splinter faction to join the opposition. The alliance of Sarney's group with the opposition allowed for their victory in the electoral college. Neves's death, however, lessened the successor government's break with the past. Sarney ruled with substantial military support, which helped him resist pressures to shorten his term. Also, the military intervened in a wide array of policy areas.

35. Karl, "Dilemmas of Democratization," 14; Hagopian, " 'Democracy by Undemocratic Means,' " 149.

36. Pion-Berlin, *Through Corridors of Power.*

37. Franko, "De Facto Demilitarization."

38. Degregori and Rivera, "Peru 1980–1993," 14.

39. Hunter, *Eroding Military Influence.*

40. Lamounier, "Brazil"; Mainwaring, *Rethinking Party Systems.*

41. Mussolini was, after all, demoted by the Fascist Council, opening the way for the king to force him out of office. See Pasquino, "Demise of the First Fascist Regime," and Barros, *Law and Dictatorship.*

David R. Mares

9

Latin American Economic Integration and Democratic Control of the Military

Is There a Symbiotic Relationship?

Latin American military autonomy from civilian control has traditionally been based on two sources of threat. Societies and governments in the region have historically identified internal opponents as "enemies," so it is no surprise that the military would also. Nationalists, including the military, have also historically identified neighboring countries as potential security threats. As a result, military leaders and their civilian allies[1] could argue powerfully that on matters concerning national security, the armed forces were entitled to an independent voice.[2] In this context, civilian control of the military was neither possible nor even desired by many sectors of society.

The current redemocratization of Latin American polities after unprecedented levels of repression presents serious challenges to military autonomy. Although most Latin American constitutions retain provisions that facilitate suspension of constitutional liberties in times of internal disorder,[3] the use of the military for domestic control has become unpopular, except in Colombia and Peru for idiosyncratic reasons.[4] Consequently, external defense missions of the militaries have become progressively more important in justifying military autonomy and prerogatives. Anything that diminishes those external threats makes it possible to demand further subordination of the military to government control and perhaps the military's elimination (for example, Costa Rica, Haiti, and Panama).

Many analysts and policy makers perceive the historically rapid rates of economic integration among various groups of Latin American nations as indicative of a decreased security threat environment.[5] New economic relationships are springing up even among states that in the past saw each other as rivals. The implications for civil-military relations of a possible link between economic integration and regional security could be profound if those links hold true.

At first glance, the empirical record suggests an intriguing but not conclusive association between economic integration and a decreased security threat in Latin America. Some of the oldest rivalries have resolved their security animosities at the same time they entered into economic integration projects (Argentina-Brazil and subsequently Argentina-Chile). Nevertheless, other rivalries have not stabilized even as economic integration has proceeded (Venezuela-Colombia and El Salvador–Honduras–Nicaragua). Some countries participating in economic integration schemes have dramatically restructured their defense sectors (for example, Argentina and Honduras) while others have not (for example, Venezuela and Brazil).

Such a seemingly mixed record may conceal a complex relationship between economic integration and democratic control of the military. This chapter uses a rational institutionalist approach to explore the potential impact of economic integration on civil-military relations. In this approach, social actors are assumed to be instrumentally rational. As such, social actors use their information (which may be incomplete and biased) to undertake and defend policies that they believe will further their material interests. As Douglass North states, "Institutions . . . are the humanly devised constraints that shape human interaction. In consequence, they structure incentives in human exchange." The institutional framework within which social groups interact influences the information they receive, as well as the behavior it engenders. Consequently, "institutional change shapes the way societies evolve through time and hence is the key to understanding historical change."[6]

Economic integration in Latin America occurs within an institutional framework. Economic integration might, therefore, affect the incentives that institutional framework provides for democratic control of the military. Four dimensions of the economic relationship are hypothesized to affect the impact of economic integration on the threat environment, which in turn structures the civil-military relationship. These are the international security risks of integration, the level of integration achieved, the rationales for which integration was pursued, and the existence of alternative sources of threat beyond the specific rivalry of the integrating partners. Depending on the specific manifestations of these four variables, economic integration can strengthen, weaken, or be irrelevant to democratic control of the military.

Preliminary evaluation of these arguments will be carried out by brief structured and focused comparisons between two Latin American economic integration schemes. El Salvador and Honduras pursued economic integration in the Central American Common Market of the 1960s despite an enduring rivalry. Argentina and Chile, longtime rivals, were on the verge of war in 1978 but subsequently chose to tie their economies more closely together.

The following questions guide the brief examination of the cases.

- What was the state of civil-military relations before economic integration began?
- Was an identifiable degree of democratic control of the military necessary for economic integration to develop?
- How extensive was (is) economic integration?
- Did (does) economic integration facilitate democratic control of the military?
- If so, how? If not, why not?

Conceptual and Theoretical Considerations

Democratic Control

The civil-military relationship can be structured in a variety of ways. At times the military as an institution governs itself and civil society, as in Argentina from 1976 to 1983 when the officer corps within each service branch debated the political and policy questions of the day.[7] If none of the other organs of the state (executive, legislative, or judicial) dominates the military, it may act as an equal partner in government, as in Indonesia under Soeharto and perhaps Alfredo Stroessner's Paraguay and Sandinista Nicaragua.[8] Or the civilian and military arenas might constitute entirely separate spheres of action requiring little substantive interaction. Chile between 1977 and 1981 came the closest to achieving this separation in Latin America.[9]

Military subordination to the leadership of the state can manifest itself in three ways. "Government control" indicates subordination to whoever is in the leadership position, including when the military as an organization is subordinate to a military junta. Chile under the regime of General Pinochet would provide a modal case.[10] Alternatively, the military might be under "civilian control," in which case the political regime could be totalitarian, authoritarian, or democratic. An example of a civilian totalitarian regime that controls the military would include most communist systems such as Cuba. Mexico is an example of a civilian authoritarian regime that controls the military.[11]

Following this line of reasoning, "democratic control" is a particular subset of "civilian control." It is clear from the Latin American experience that democracy per se does not guarantee civilian control of the military. Elsewhere I argue that democracy is compatible with various forms of civil-military relations. Only the liberal model of democracy requires civilian control of the military.[12]

Democratic control of the military is sustained by two bargains: one among civilian sectors and the other between civilians and the military.[13] In the first, civilians agree not to use the military for partisan advantages. The second bargain exchanges military subordination to civilian control for the degree of autonomy and resources necessary to carry out the military's functions. Democratic control is most likely to be sustained when the military's functions are oriented toward external defense because internal defense missions are likely to politicize the military as it questions why civilians have not been able to resolve the nation's problems without recourse to violence.[14]

We can usefully consider the domestic politics of the civil-military relationship as an institutional context within which three types of actors interact: those who favor military participation in politics, those who oppose it, and the military itself. The institutional context is defined by the nature of the democratic institutions and the specific roles that have been assigned to the military. Latin American democracies are presidentialist systems, with a chief executive and a legislature. In all countries with a military establishment, except Argentina, the military has a constitutionally provided role in maintaining internal order.

Economic Integration and the Threat Environment

For purposes of discussing civil-military relations, the threat environment is usefully distinguished by its external and internal dimensions. As hypothesized earlier, the international security risks of integration, the level of integration achieved, the rationales for which integration was pursued, and the existence of alternative sources of threat beyond the specific rivalry of the integrating partners constitute the key dimensions for understanding the relationship between economic integration and democratic control of the military.

The general theoretical logic about economic integration and international security risks builds on the work dealing specifically with trading relationships.[15] It begins with the idea that trade brings increased wealth to parties engaged in it. The security danger is that one, or both, of the parties may use that increased wealth to enhance its military capabilities to the detriment of the other partner. States therefore forgo strong trading relationships with states with which they are rivals.[16] The same logic, we can assume, applies to interdependence fostered by direct foreign investment, portfolio investments, and economic infrastructure projects.

Nevertheless, economic integration with a rival does not automatically produce negative security externalities. Such relationships freely entered into are expected to produce economic benefits to both sides, or they would not have developed. Whether such economic relationships generate an increased level of threat depends on three factors.[17] First, the nations involved must be able to cheat on the terms of the agreement, using barriers to shift the terms of exchange in their favor, thereby artificially gaining more than was expected by the other partner. Second, the cheater must be able to make use of those ill-gotten gains in a military fashion because if they accrue to economic actors (transnational corporations, internationalist oriented business, and so on) that will not allow those gains to be turned into military assets, no security externality will occur. Third, the advantaged actor must be able to turn its relative gain into a military advantage before the other side discovers this behavior and punishes it. The military advantage is not limited to victory in war but includes bullying tactics, coercive diplomacy, and so on. This is especially true in a region like Latin America, where war is rare but the use of force in foreign policy negotiations is ubiquitous.[18]

Integration can occur in a variety of ways, each with its peculiar characteristics. Eight levels of integration range from minimal to complete. Political forms without economic content are at the lowest levels: "instant friendship" in which integration is merely rhetoric. A "security community," in which the use of force is considered illegitimate regardless of the degree of economic interactions, forms the next level. Next comes "limited functional cooperation," in which coordination of policies proceeds in clearly delimited arenas for strictly technical reasons. Further up the scale of interdependence are five forms of integrating national economies. The least interdependent is "free trade," in which goods circulate among members free of tariffs. "Customs union" adds a common external tariff to free trade among members. When labor and capital, in addition to goods, are free to move among members, a "common market" has been established. Coordination of fiscal and monetary policies moves one farther up the interdependence scale, to "economic union." The highest level of integration is achieved with "total economic integration," in which economic policies are unified.[19]

Consideration of the potential impact of such integration on security and the strength of the military in domestic politics requires knowing how domestic interests are affected by integration. Higher levels of interdependence should affect more groups in society and affect them more intensely. Whether there will be more winners or losers in the process depends on the specifics of the integration. More winners should mean decreased influence of the military and greater democratic control, ceteris paribus. A large number of losers should produce the tensions discussed below in the section on alternative sources of threat and, consequently, a decrease in democratic control of the military.

The rationales for economic integration vary. Nationalist and geopolitical rationales can stimulate cooperation and even integration among rivals. The import-substitution industrialization model of development converges well with military geopolitical thinking in which developing countries band together to confront the biases in the international system that favor advanced nations.[20] The international economy is perceived to be a source of threat as long as the nation remains unindustrialized. Hence economic integration schemes are used to enlarge domestic markets by creating a protected regional market that provides captive consumers for infant industries.[21] This rationale for integration will, ceteris paribus, favor nationalist political forces, strengthen the military's prestige at home, and facilitate defending military autonomy, thereby undermining democratic control.

An alternative rationale for integration perceives opportunities in the international economy. National advantage is gained by making the most efficient use of one's resource endowment rather than implementing a costly industrialization. As this style of integration proceeds, the economies become structurally adjusted and efficient, more dependent on the flows of capital, and the influence of international financial actors increases. Domestic actors who favor liberalizing integration gain powerful international allies to use at home against the influence of the nationalist military and their civilian allies, whether or not the countries are democracies.[22] Military autonomy at home is undermined because the international context is perceived as conducive to national welfare rather than as a threat. Liberalizing integration, ceteris paribus, strengthens democratic control of the military.

Alternative sources of threat may be internal or external. The strength of the military's civilian allies in the political competition at home is directly affected by perceptions of internal threat as well. Economic integration contributes to these perceptions. When growth accelerates and is distributed broadly, social welfare improves and crime rates decline. Citizens feel more at ease and can address remaining security fears through private measures (for example, moving out of dangerous neighborhoods, hiring private security). If, however, economic integration produces high social costs, the losers in the process (for example, noncompetitive labor, business, agriculture, and the urban poor) may engage in increasingly disruptive protests. Examples abound in Latin America: the Caracazo riots in Venezuela in 1989; the Chiapas uprising in Mexico, which was inaugurated on the day the North American Free Trade Agreement (NAFTA) went into effect; and the massive street demonstrations in Ecuador against efforts by different presidents to implement structural adjustment. Crime will also rise. Under these conditions, the beneficiaries of the integration will demand greater governmental action against those threats. At the same time, the losers will look for allies in their struggles to interfere with market rationalization of the production process. In the Latin American context, the military will increasingly find itself courted as an ally by either or even both sides.[23] Military influence may once again rise, to the detriment of democratic control.[24]

An inverted U relationship may thus develop over time in the liberalizing cases. Early in the process greater economic integration may facilitate democratic control, as the external threat deriving from the old rival declines. But if the benefits of integration are not distributed widely, internal threats will rise to undermine democratic control.

While economic integration may produce decreased security anxieties toward an old rival, there may exist additional external threats that legitimate the military's continued claim on resources and political influence. For example, Brazil no longer fears Argentina but does worry about its ability to defend its Amazonian territory from Colombian narcotraffickers, rogue gold miners who create tensions on the Venezuelan border, and even developed nations that might decide that Brazil cannot defend the "world's lung" from environmental destruction.[25]

Although external sources of threat are most appropriate for democratic control of the military, when combined with internal threats, they increase the political weight of the military. If a society faces only internal threats, there will be pressure to eliminate or severely decrease the size of the military and strengthen civilian police forces. It is the combination of internal and external threats that poses the greatest challenge to democratic control of the military.

Latin American Cases

Historically, economic flows among Latin American countries have not been large. The underdeveloped nature of their economies as well as important geographic and climatic similarities meant that their production was not complementary and they tended to be short of capital. In addition, most Latin American neighbors experienced political tensions and mistrust over territorial, migratory, and natural resource issues well into the 1970s.

Economic integration in the region did not follow a single path. The Central American Common Market was launched in the 1950s as a hybrid of protectionist and liberal perspectives. A North versus South paradigmatic view of international politics began to dominate the region in the late 1960s and stimulated economic integration for protectionist and geopolitical rationales. The Andean Pact emphasized "southern" cooperation and helped the military governments of Ecuador and Peru lower the level of tension in their border dispute.[26] During the 1970s the Brazilian military government and Stroessner's authoritarian government in Paraguay embarked on the major hydroelectric projects that deepened their integration, and the military governments in Brazil and Argentina began the search for increased economic relations as a way of decreasing their rivalry.

After the debt crises of the 1980s delegitimated import-substitution industrialization, economic integration projects gained new life under more liberalizing rationales. NAFTA is the most liberalizing of the schemes, largely because its major partners (Canada and the United States) have liberal economies already. MERCOSUR falls between protectionist and liberalizing because its major partner (Brazil) seeks to use it to promote Brazilian industrialization.

Let us now turn to the two Latin American cases for some empirical evidence on the relationship between civil-military relations and regional-bilateral economic integration.

El Salvador and Honduras, 1960s

What was the state of civil-military relations before economic integration began?
El Salvador began a process of redemocratization in the 1960s, after years of dictatorial rule. The process was not without its problems, but by 1969 the country had progressed enough to merit a score of nine on the Polity scale of democracy.[27] The military had great influence because the traditional elite saw it as a guarantee against significant reforms if the center-left Christian Democratic Party gained office. In 1972 a military coup ushered in a new era of civil war, lasting almost two decades. Honduras had a brief flirtation with low levels of democracy in the early 1960s, but a military coup in 1963 terminated it.[28] The military would remain in power directly until the 1980s.

Was an identifiable degree of democratic control of the military necessary for economic integration to develop? How extensive was (is) economic integration?
The economic integration process began in 1951 with discussions among economists of the UN Economic Commission on Latin America and personnel of the Ministries of Economy of the various Central American countries. A series of bilateral free trade agreements led the way, yet the military remained a key and independent political force in all countries, usually governing itself, except in Costa Rica.

TABLE 9.1 *Central America's Institutional Context*

PUBLIC INSTITUTIONS

Permanent Secretariat of the General Treaty
Executive Council of the General Treaty
Central American Economic Council
Central American Bank for Economic Integration
Central American Institute of Research and Industrial Technology
Central American School of Public Administration
Central American Monetary Council
Central American Clearing-House
Superior Council for Central American Universities
Institute of Nutrition of Central America and Panama
Regional Plant and Animal Sanitation Organization
Council of Labor and Social Welfare
Central American Tourism Secretariat

PRIVATE INSTITUTIONS

Central American Air Navigation Service Corporation
Central American Institute of Business Management
Federation of Central American Associations and Chambers of Industries
Central American Institute of Labor Union Studies
Central American Federation of Chambers of Commerce

INTERNATIONAL INSTITUTIONS

UN Economic Commission on Latin America
U.S. Agency for International Development
Organization of American States
Inter-American Development Bank

Source: Central American Bank for Economic Integration, Investment Development Department, *Investment Opportunities in the Central American Common Market* (Tegucigalpa, Honduras, 1967), 62–63.

Table 9.1 lists the major organizations that structured the institutional context in which El Salvador and Honduras interacted. The number, character (public and private; global, hemispheric, and regional), and range of activities covered attest to the density and breadth of institutional ties. The achievements of the Central American Common Market (CACM) from 1960 to 1968 were substantial. The value of intraregional trade increased almost 800 percent while the value of exports to CACM partners increased from 7 to 25 percent of total. The composition of trade changed markedly: the value of industrial trade increased over 800 percent and three-fourths of intraregional trade was composed of manufactures and semimanufactures. Practically all intraregional transactions were carried out in domestic currencies through settlements in the

TABLE 9.2 *Trade Interdependence between El Salvador and Honduras, 1951–1970*

YEAR	EL SALVADOR				HONDURAS			
	TOTAL EXPORTS	TOTAL IMPORTS (CIF)*	% OF EXPORTS TO HONDURAS	% OF IMPORTS FROM HONDURAS	TOTAL EXPORTS	TOTAL IMPORTS (CIF)	% OF EXPORTS TO EL SALVADOR	% OF IMPORTS FROM EL SALVADOR
1951	85.5	65	1.99	4.77	66	62	5.45	3.37
1952	88.3	70.6	1.36	3.82	62.7	76	5.90	2.03
1953	89.6	73.4	1.34	5.45	67.5	71	5.78	2.17
1954	105	86.8	1.81	4.84	54.5	68	6.79	2.43
1955	106.9	91.9	1.78	4.35	47.2	72	8.47	2.75
1956	112.7	104.7	1.24	5.16	72.9	77	8.37	1.86
1957	138.5	115.1	1.73	4.34	64.9	91	7.86	2.78
1958	116	107.9	2.93	5.84	69.7	87	7.75	4.14
1959	113.3	99.6	3.62	6.43	68.6	71	9.18	5.35
1960	116.5	123	3.43	5.12	63	71.8	10.32	5.71
1961	119.2	108.7	3.86	6.07	72.9	72	8.92	6.53
1962	136.2	124.8	4.41	8.33	81.4	79.8	11.43	7.27
1963	153.8	151.8	5.53	7.11	83.3	95.2	11.04	8.30
1964	178.1	191.2	5.84	6.80	94.5	101.6	11.85	8.76
1965	188.7	200.6	7.47	7.83	127.2	121.9	10.38	10.09
1966	188.9	220.8	8.89	6.07	142.9	149	7.56	11.01
1967	207.2	223.9	9.65	5.54	155.2	164.5	7.09	11.73
1968	212.5	214	11.01	7.06	181.4	185.8	7.60	12.51
1969	201.8	208.5	6.35	3.51	168.3	184.3	4.23	6.74
1970	229.4	214.4	0.00	0.00	179.1	220.7	0.00	0.00

Source: International Monetary Fund, *Direction of Trade*, 1951–70.
*cif = cost, insurance, freight.

Central American Clearing-House. The Central American Economic Integration Bank disbursed $120 million in loans, divided equally between the private industrial sector and public infrastructure projects. Foreign capital inflows also increased by 300 percent.[29]

Table 9.2 presents the specific details of the Honduran-Salvadoran trade relationship. One can see that the levels of import and export interdependence between the two increased significantly over the 1960s. They fell to zero, however, after migratory and border tensions produced the 1969 One Hundred Hour War between them.

El Salvador, which along with Guatemala is one of the two largest and more developed economies in the region, benefited greatly from the integration scheme. Honduras, which had a large trade deficit with both El Salvador and Guatemala, demanded significant changes to increase the benefits to its smaller, less industrialized market. Economic analyses demonstrate that Honduran criticism of the Common Market was largely misplaced, but the elite as well as the general population perceived that the integration scheme was turning the country into a Salvadoran colony.[30]

Did (does) economic integration facilitate democratic control of the military?
If so, how? If not, why not?
Economic integration did not facilitate democratic control of the military in El Salvador, and Honduras's military dictatorship did not move toward democratization. Although the CACM increased economic relations between the two countries, it did not decrease each side's perception of the other as a rival. Examination of the security risks and rationales associated with economic integration in the CACM case helps us understand why the two remained rivals.

The security risks generated by the CACM for the two parties were not mitigated by any mechanisms in the process of integration. Arms purchases during the economic boom were not transparent, and military contact with the Consejo de Defensa Centro Americano (Central American Defense Council; CONDECA) was limited to fighting communism, not generating confidence between nations that had bilateral disputes. Civilian and military leaders in El Salvador believed they could win quickly if they attacked by surprise. As a result, they downplayed the possibility of a military invasion, and the Honduran government did not appreciate the seriousness with which the Salvadorans perceived the expulsions.

The rationale for integration under the CACM was protectionist, but the international political economy was identified as an ally in the industrialization process. The U.S. government, international financial organizations, and private foreign capital all played important roles in the CACM. At the time, "international communism" was a threat whose manifestation lay in domestic guerrilla movements, not invasion by foreign armies. Consequently, there was no alternative international threat against which all Central American countries needed to unite.

Xenophobic feelings were running high in both countries before the infamous soccer game riots that provide the war's better-known name, the Soccer War. Expulsion and mistreatment of Salvadorans in Honduras made the Salvadoran government appear impotent during a major crisis. The popular and elite consensus in the country was that Honduras had created this problem. The ruling Party of National Conciliation (PNC) had suffered large electoral losses to the opposition in the legislative and municipal elections of 1968, before the escalation of the crisis with Honduras. With more legislative and municipal elections scheduled in 1970, the government must have felt pressured to respond to the crisis.[31]

When the Salvadoran government announced a rupture of relations with Honduras on 26 June, crowds reacted to the news enthusiastically. Popular art denounced and ridiculed Honduran military abilities. The elite also united for war. Before June the opposition Christian Democratic Party (PDC) opposed military action, but thereafter it joined the Council of National Unity, pledged its support, and encouraged its student militants to volunteer. The PDC mayor of San Salvador, José Napoleon Duarte, even organized civilian patrols of the city to provide logistical support for the army during the war.[32]

The level of integration was high, but the skewed distribution of economic benefits created many perceived losers in both countries. The migratory flow to Honduras had served as an escape valve for the Salvadoran political economy. It would have been difficult to reincorporate the tens of thousands of migrants who were expelled or fled from Honduras into an economy already characterized by high rates of both unemployment and underemployment.[33]

In Honduras concentration of landholdings increased in the 1950s as the integration process helped produce a shift away from banana production to new commercial crops. Peasants had little land, and the level of industrialization in urban areas was not sufficient to provide an attractive alternative.[34] Honduran peasants were quite willing to blame Salvadoran migrants rather than Honduran landowners for their landless state. But the Honduran elite could not count on such diversions to safeguard its privileges and looked to the military to defend it against both external and internal threat.

The One Hundred Hour War between El Salvador and Honduras in 1969 resulted in between two thousand and five thousand deaths. War destroyed the Central American Common Market and increased the prestige of the militaries at home. Despite a military stalemate, Salvadoran troops were hailed as heroes because expulsions from Honduras ended. The pro-military governing party reversed its electoral fortunes in legislative elections in 1970, winning solid control. The Honduran military also gained prestige and civilian support for preventing a Salvadoran victory.[35]

Argentina-Chile, 1990–1999

What was the state of civil-military relations before economic integration began?
Argentina suffered through a disastrous military dictatorship, on both internal and external dimensions, from 1976 to 1983. Although disgraced by losing the Malvinas War and by the tactics it used during the internal Dirty War and with its top leaders in jail, some elements in the military nevertheless refused to accept the new state of civil-military relations. A series of isolated coup attempts challenged democratic control from 1987 to 1990. Under Carlos Raúl Menem (1990–99) the military was decimated and brought under a degree of democratic control heretofore unknown in Argentina.[36]

Chile underwent its redemocratization process only after General Augusto Pinochet lost a referendum in 1988. But Chile's military had not been defeated, and the right-wing political forces feared a return of the political challenges presented by Salvador Allende's regime in 1970–73. Consequently, an alliance of political and military forces was able to structure a transition to democracy that preserved for the military an important and independent voice. The new democratic institutions thus created weak democratic control of the military.

Was an identifiable degree of democratic control of the military necessary for economic integration to develop? How extensive was (is) economic integration?
Democratic control was not necessary for economic integration to begin. In the mid-1970s, Argentina's democratic government took advantage of the international repulsion of the Pinochet dictatorship to increase trade with Chile. Argentina accounted for two to three times more of Chile's total imports than Chile did for Argentina. On the export side the disparities were not as great, but Chile remained more sensitive to its trading relationship than did Argentina. The overall level of interdependence was low: for trade, on the order of 8–10 percent for Argentina and 13–22 percent for Chile, and most likely nil for finance.[37]

The war scare between the two countries in 1978 over the Beagle Channel decreased bilateral trade. The 1984 Treaty of Peace and Friendship that resolved the dispute contains a section titled "Economic Cooperation and Physical Integration." Article twelve created a permanent binational commission to

stimulate and oversee this process of economic integration.[38] Economic cooperation, however, did not progress quickly after the signing of the peace treaty.
The obstacles were primarily economic, although political-military factors
played a role as well.

Chile continued its neoliberal economic policies after the economic crisis of
1982 and would have been in a position to respond to opportunities in the
Argentine market. The military government in Chile would probably have
limited the extent of economic cooperation to ensure that "strategic areas" (for
example, key transportation links and sectors of the economy—see below)
remained under Chilean control. The Pinochet government did, however, sign
a bilateral agreement on nuclear cooperation in 1983 even before the final
resolution of the Beagle dispute.[39]

Chile's capital market expanded, deepened, and broadened dramatically in
the 1980s as a result of specific government policies and high rates of economic
growth. First, the reorganization and privatization of pension funds in 1980
created large institutional investors representing many sectors of Chilean society, including workers. The military government's revised privatization strategies after 1984 subsequently facilitated the growth of these and other investors.
The value of stocks transacted increased, in constant U.S. dollars, from 41.9
million in 1984 to 917.6 million in 1989.[40] Consequently, by the end of the
1980s a significant pool of Chilean capital was available for foreign investment.
Once the Argentine economy began to recover, Chilean investors would increase their presence in that market.

But the Argentine economy was in a constant state of crisis up to 1990 and
the market opportunities for closer economic ties were limited.[41] The Argentine economic situation was so bad that outgoing president Raúl Alfonsín
(1983–89) resigned early to allow his successor to begin implementing a
program for economic recovery. Menem took office with a great burst of
energy and the desire to extricate Argentina not only from its economic crisis
but also from its sense of political malaise. In the name of national reconcilia-
tion, he pardoned the junta members who had been sentenced for human
rights abuses during the military government. In addition, he dramatically
changed Argentine foreign policy, turning the country from a diplomatic
adversary of the United States into its closest ally in the Western Hemisphere.[42] As part of his new look for Argentina, Menem also sought closer
relations with the booming Chilean economy.

Political incentives complemented economic incentives after Chile democratized in 1990. The government of Patricio Aylwin (1990–94) was committed
to the military government's liberal economic development strategy. Economic reforms produced sustained high rates of economic growth, and the new

democracy's performance would be measured against those standards. In addition, the negotiated transition to democracy made it institutionally difficult to change policy dramatically. The government's own economic development strategy focused on spreading the wealth generated by the liberal development model (in 1990 38.6 percent of Chileans lived below the poverty line),[43] without redistributing wealth away from the current beneficiaries. Therefore, investments and markets had to grow in order to generate more wealth.

Under the military government Chile had simply opened its economy to anyone who was interested. The democratic governments of Aylwin and Eduardo Frei (1994–2000), actively sought to negotiate agreements that would accelerate Chile's integration into a world economy that was fast liberalizing and in which regional economic groups were playing a greater role.[44] The strategy paid dividends in 1998 when Chilean exports to countries with which it had trade agreements only fell 1 percent, as compared to an overall decline of 12 percent for all of Chile's exports.[45]

Chile's foreign economic strategy produced incentives for private and public investors that have increased economic cooperation with Argentina. The trade relationship itself is not very different from what it was in the 1970s: small and more important for Chile than for Argentina.[46] In addition, Chile has a large trade deficit with Argentina (and MERCOSUR). While there are sectoral benefits—manufactured goods accounted for 34 percent of Chile's exports to MERCOSUR from 1990 to 1995, while representing only 12 percent of Chile's total exports—the Chilean government worries more about its overall trade balance than it does about the specifics of a particular bilateral relationship.[47] Since the government is encouraging the import of natural gas from Argentina, it can expect the deficit to increase further.

It is in the area of financial and economic infrastructure integration that the relationship of the 1990s differs from that of the 1960s and 1970s. Table 9.3 shows the principal destinations of Chilean foreign investments; Chilean investments are principally in energy (55 percent) and industry (28.7 percent); only 2 percent in insurance and pension funds; 4.8 percent in banks; and 0.9 percent in communications.[48] As Table 9.4 illustrates, Argentine investment in Chile represents only a tiny fraction of total foreign investment in all sectors of the economy, except in transport.

Drawing implications from this relationship is difficult. Once again, this economic relationship is built largely on Chilean actions. But even this description may be misleading. A large proportion of what we identify as "Chilean" investment in Argentina may actually consist of European, U.S., and Japanese investment. For example, Enersis is a "Chilean" electricity-sector holding company that owns the Argentine power company that supplies Buenos Aires,

TABLE 9.3 *Principal Destinations of Chilean Foreign Investments, 1990–July 1997*

COUNTRY	CHILEAN FOREIGN INVESTMENTS (MILLIONS OF DOLLARS)	% OF TOTAL CHILEAN FOREIGN INVESTMENTS
Argentina	5,939.8	43.6
Peru	1,814.8	13.3
Brazil	1,471.0	10.8
Colombia	981.5	7.2
Mexico	499.8	3.7
Panama	387.5	2.8

Source: Comité de Inversiones Extranjeras, *El Mercurio*, 8 February 1998, cited in Fuentes and Martin, *La nueva agenda argentino-chilena*, 81.

Edesur. It is also one of the leading companies in the Chilean stock exchange, and energy stocks account for a large portion of the activity in that exchange. But the largest stockholder in Enersis is the Spanish company Endesa, with 32 percent of stock. The Spanish company was barely thwarted in its attempt to take over Enersis by purchasing 65 percent of its stock. Endesa also has stock in another "Chilean" energy company, Endesa-Chile. A U.S. company, Duke Energy, is currently attempting to take control of Endesa-Chile.[49] Any claims about the pacifying impact of "Chilean" investment in Argentina requires analysis of how third party investments affect the bilateral relationship.

Finally, there is the issue of physical infrastructure. The need to develop gas pipelines to bring the Argentine product (controlled by "Chilean" firms) to northern Chile and Santiago plays a fundamental role in this arena.[50] The infrastructure linking Chile with Argentina is also part of a broader vision of Chile as a "port country" (see section on regional factors below). Plans for the Mejillones port in northern Chile will make it the largest commercial port on South America's Pacific coast. Exporters from both Asia and South America are expected to use the port for exports of Chilean copper, its container facilities, and planned rail links into Argentina as well as the other MERCOSUR countries.[51] This physical integration of the two economies complements the trade and financial links to produce an economic integration far beyond that of the 1970s.

Economic integration between Argentina and Chile was facilitated by political rapprochement greater than that attempted in the 1960s. In early 1991 the Argentine-Chilean Mixed Commission on Borders (Comisión Mixta Chileno-Argentina de Límites) drew up a list of twenty-four territorial disputes to be negotiated. In August 1991 the two governments developed an agenda cover-

TABLE 9.4 *Argentine Foreign Investments in Chile by Sector, 1996*

SECTOR	TOTAL FOREIGN INVESTMENTS IN CHILE (MILLIONS OF DOLLARS)	ARGENTINE FOREIGN INVESTMENTS IN CHILE (MILLIONS OF DOLLARS)	ARGENTINE FOREIGN INVESTMENTS AS % OF TOTAL FOREIGN INVESTMENTS IN CHILE
Agriculture	16.8	0.0	0.0
Construction	27.6	2.3	8.3
Electricity, gas, and water	386.5	29.9	7.7
Industry	813.4	25.5	3.1
Mining	996.2	0.0	0.0
Fishing and aquaculture	41.4	0.0	0.0
Services	2,333.0	10.0	0.4
Forestry	19.9	0.0	0.0
Transport	55.9	35.3	63.1
Total	4,578.4	102.8	

Source: Government of Chile, Ministry of Foreign Affairs, Dirección de Promoción de Exportaciones, Pro-Chile 1997, cited in Fuentes and Martin, *La nueva agenda argentino-chilena*, 81.

ing forty issues in their bilateral relationship. Table 9.5 demonstrates the flurry of activity that occurred in this first year and a half characterized by democratic governments in both countries.[52]

Did (does) economic integration facilitate democratic control of the military? If so, how? If not, why not?

Economic integration with Argentina has not had much discernible effect on democratic control of the military in Chile. In the Argentine case, however, it may constitute a contributing factor to the consolidation of such democratic control. The four dimensions of the economic integration help us understand why its impact on democratic control has not been uniform.

The international security risks between Chile and Argentina declined even as integration proceeded rapidly. While Argentina benefits more than Chile through trade and perhaps investment (depending on the impact of third-party investors using "Chilean" firms), Chileans confront little military risk because the Argentine military has been decimated under Menem and cannot make use of the economic gains. Economic integration has also been accompanied by significant efforts to increase transparency in the military sphere and build confidence between the two militaries. Consequently, the threat of a sudden Chilean attack lacks credibility even on strictly military grounds.

TABLE 9.5 *Argentine-Chilean Economic Agreements, Acts, Protocols, and Studies, January 1991–June 1992*

MONTH / YEAR	SUBJECT	SECTOR
January 1991	Petroleum / gas	Government
February 1991	Telecommunications	Government
March 1991	Migration	Government
June 1991	Gas	Government
June 1991	Natural resources	Government
June 1991	Tariffs	Government
August 1991	Science and technology	Government
August 1991	Gas, environment, investment, customs	Government
September 1991	Trade	Private
October 1991	Customs	Government
November 1991	Visas	Government
March 1992	Merchant Marine	Government
April 1992	Stock market	Government
May 1992	Gas	Private
May 1992	Trade	Private
June 1992	Banking	Private

Source: Adapted from Fuentes and Mizala, "Chile-Argentina Después de Marzo de 1990," 6.

The level of integration between the two is still limited because neither external tariffs, nor labor markets, nor fiscal and monetary policies are coordinated. One of the reasons for this limitation is that Chile's economy not only liberalized before Argentina's but is more open to international trade. Were Chile to join MERCOSUR as a full member, integration with Argentina would most likely proceed faster and deeper because the common external tariff used by full members would make it more advantageous for Chile to buy and sell within MERCOSUR. Yet this state-managed integration would cost the Chilean economy because prices of affected goods and services would be raised by the common external tariff.[53] In addition, the architects and defenders of Chile's open economy fear the loss of international competitiveness that could very well result from close integration into a less open MERCOSUR. In contrast, Argentina wants Chile to tie its economic future to MERCOSUR.

The rationales for integration between the two countries are not identical. Argentina's foreign policy under Menem has become more liberal and internationalist than at any time since the Depression. Tying the value of its currency to the U.S. dollar and supporting MERCOSUR constitute the chief mechanisms through which the Menem government seeks to take advantage of the opportunities in the world market. Chile's opening of its economy is carried out in more nationalist terms. In this rationale, the international political economy contains threats. Unlike the period when countries sought to insulate their economies from international forces by protecting them, Chile's current strategy is to protect the national economy by diversifying its means of participating in the world market. Chile's rationale for integration with Argentina thus coexists well with nationalist perspectives on international politics and helps the military to retain its civilian allies. Argentina's liberal internationalist rationale for integration further diminishes civilian support for the military.

Argentina under Menem has not identified alternative sources of external threat. Even before integration with Chile progressed very far, Argentina had improved relations with its old rival Brazil. The perception after 1982 that British control over the Malvinas Islands cannot be effectively contested by military methods means that Britain does not constitute a relevant threat for the military. In short, Argentina does not confront external threats that can create a domestic constituency for military autonomy. This reality has facilitated Menem's ability to subordinate the military in Argentina.

Alternative internal sources of threat are also lacking in Argentina. The distribution of benefits from Argentina's integration schemes has favored the wealthy, and the country is confronting unemployment rates surpassing 15 percent. The fact that Menem has been the leader of the Peronist Party, however, has limited worker protest. In addition, Argentina's democratic Constitution separates internal from external security and does not provide the military with a role in the former. Consequently, the Argentine military cannot rely on internal sources of threat to develop important political allies.

Chile's military and civilian allies have been more successful in finding alternative sources of threat, both externally and internally. Given its liberal nationalist rationale, greater integration of the Chilean economy into the world market produces arguments for naval and air capabilities to defend sea and air lines of communication. The army and its civilian allies argue for an increased capacity to defend the overland routes between Chilean ports and the South American markets using them. These threats are not currently linked to any specific countries but are seen as potential security risks. Bolivia's continued claim on an outlet to the sea via territory Chile conquered in the War of the Pacific (1879–84), provides another potential external threat that can be addressed by military means. And the legacy of rivalry with Argentina is not yet forgotten. President Frei's chief adviser recently felt compelled to express a hope that the controversy over a Chilean company's responsibility for a major power outage in Buenos Aires would not deteriorate into a nationalist feud.[54]

The internal sources of threat continue to animate the Chilean military's allies. Although the democratic governments have distributed more of the benefits of economic integration to the poor, right-wing political forces in Chile still worry. The right fears that the losers in Chile's liberalization will elect a government with a sufficient majority in Congress to significantly alter the current rules governing the nation's political economy. The military's constitutionally sanctioned roles (in the National Security Council and in the Senate) make it a major ally in the right wing's ability to moderate the behavior of center-left governments. Consequently, strong democratic control of the military is opposed not only by the military but also by its civilian allies.

Conclusion

The relationship between economic integration and democratic control of the military appears to be complex. Latin America has made significant progress integrating its economies and subordinating the military to some degree of civilian control. But these economic and political processes are not yet reinforcing each other significantly. We should ask, "Why not?"

This chapter provides a speculative answer in the hopes of encouraging more research on the relationship between economic integration and democratic control of the military. There is much wishful thinking on the subject but little analysis. I have hypothesized that the best approach to studying the issue focuses on the impact of economic integration on the internal and external threat environment confronting the integrating countries. I also demonstrated that it would be misleading to think in terms of civilians versus the military; in these political struggles, civilians have military allies and military officers have civilian allies. I also proposed that using a rational institutionalist methodology facilitates systematic examination of purported causal links in the relationship.

In essence, this approach recommends an integration of the strategic and institutional perspectives identified in the Introduction to this volume. While political action between civilians and soldiers is driven by self-interest, the institutional environments in which these actors find themselves mold interests themselves. As those environments—both within and outside of the nation—change, individuals derive preferences for one behavior over another based on the "structure of incentives" established by the new order. Thus my approach affirms the value for civil-military studies of both identifying strategic self-interests and tracing the derivation of those interests to institutional sources.

The brief structured comparisons between two rivalries in which economic integration occurred suggests the plausibility of my approach. My analysis suggests that although the international security risks posed by the old rivalries have declined under the contemporary liberalizing integration, alternative sources of threat remain. The rationales for economic integration are not clearly supportive of greater democratic control of the military. And finally, the skewed internal distribution of the benefits of economic integration may constitute the greatest threat to both further economic integration and democratic control of the military.

As other scholars engage the topic we will learn more about the relationship between economic integration and democratic control of the military. My own initial thoughts will be further developed by the ensuing debates. And we will all contribute to the effort to make Latin America a more prosperous and peaceful region.

NOTES

An early version of this chapter was presented at the conference "Soldiers and Democracy in Latin America," 19–20 February 1999, in Riverside, California. I thank the Institute on Global Conflict and Cooperation of the University of California for supporting my efforts to study the relationship between democratic politics and regional conflict, David Pion-Berlin for helpful comments, and Daniel R. Lake for research assistance. The views presented here are my responsibility alone.

1. One should not conceptualize this relationship dichotomously as "civilians" and "the military" but rather as one in which some civilians oppose the military and its civilian allies. At times, the opposing groups may all be constituted by both civilians and military officers. For an elaboration, see Introduction to Mares, *Civil-Military Relations*.
2. The demands of civilians for military participation in "safeguarding" the state are made clear in Stepan, *Military in Politics*, and Loveman, *Constitution of Tyranny*.
3. Loveman, *Constitution of Tyranny*.
4. Colombia is still engaged in a civil war, and the military is a major ally in President Alberto Fujimori's still popular effort to rebuild the Peruvian political system. (His 1992 coup against Congress and the 1979 Constitution was very popular, and in March 1999 he still had approval ratings of over 60 percent in various polls.) See *El Comercio*, March 1999.
5. Compare with Escudé and Fontana, "Argentina's Security Policies."
6. North, *Institutions, Institutional Change and Economic Performance*, 3.
7. Russell, "El proceso de toma de decisiones."
8. Djiwandono, "Civil-Military Relations in Indonesia"; Lezcano, "El régimen militar"; Premio, "Redirection of the Armed Forces."
9. Compare with Silva, "Political Economy of Chile's Regime Transition."
10. Valenzuela, "Military in Power."
11. Dominguez, *Cuba*; Ronfeldt, *Modern Mexican Military*.

12. Mares, "Civil-Military Relations."

13. Huntington, *Soldier and the State*, 80–97. Huntington labels the type of control "objective control." "Subjective control" occurs when the military is subordinate to civilian forces, even democratic institutions, which require it to prepare for internal as well as external missions. By their very nature, internal missions draw the military into politics, thereby undermining the professionalism required to carry out their external mission.

14. Compare with Stepan, "New Professionalism."

15. Nye and Keohane, *Power and Interdependence*, began much of the discussion, but in their formulation economic interdependence characterized relationships in which the use of force as a policy instrument had already been rendered illegitimate.

16. Gowa, *Allies, Adversaries, and International Trade*.

17. Here I elaborate on Morrow, "When Does Trade Produce Security Externalities."

18. For an elaboration, see Mares, *Violent Peace*.

19. Nye, "Central American Regional Integration," 377–79.

20. On geopolitical thinking, see Kelly and Child, *Geopolitics of the Southern Cone*.

21. On import-substitution industrialization, see Little, Scitovsky, and Scott, *Industry and Trade in Some Developing Countries*.

22. Solingen, "Economic Liberalization, Political Coalitions."

23. "Knocking on the barracks door" is a time-honored strategy in much of Latin America. Compare with Stepan, *Military in Politics*.

24. Paraguay, a member of MERCOSUR and a country with a weakening economy, is a case in point. In June 1999 I was engaged in discussions concerning the new National Defense Law with active and retired military officers, as well as senators in Asunción. They articulated a need for the military to have an internal function for maintaining order in a variety of circumstances, including a strike that became a "threat" to public order. They also feared that General Lino Oviedo, implicated in both a coup attempt and the assassination of the vice president, was a populist demagogue.

25. Guedes da Costa, "Democratization and International Integration."

26. Mares, "Deterrence Bargaining in the Ecuador-Peru Enduring Rivalry."

27. Gurr et al., *Polity II*.

28. Durham, *Scarcity and Survival in Central America*, 162.

29. Grunwald, Wionczek, and Carnoy, *Latin American Economic Integration*, 42–47.

30. Anderson, *War of the Dispossessed*, 63–68; Grunwald, Wionczek, and Carnoy, *Latin American Economic Integration*, 48–49.

31. Armstrong and Shenk, *El Salvador*, 52–53.

32. Dunkerley, *Long War*, 82.

33. Anderson reports that in 1971 the unemployment rate was 20 percent while another 40 percent worked no more than 120 days a year (*War of the Dispossessed*, 141–42).

34. Durham, *Scarcity and Survival in Central America*.

35. Brzoska and Pearson, *Arms and Warfare*, 62–66, 70; Anderson, *War of the Dispossessed*, 173–74.

36. See David Pion-Berlin's chapter in this book.

37. International Monetary Fund, *Direction of Trade*; I could not locate financial data for this earlier period, presumably because it was unimportant.

38. The treaty and an analysis of its provisions can be found in Diaz Albonico, *El tratado de paz.*

39. Bernal Castro, "Argentine Nuclear Development," 98.

40. Hachette and Luders, *Privatization in Chile*, 59–61, 99–114.

41. For a discussion, see Gonzalez Fraga, "Argentine Privatization in Retrospect."

42. Pion-Berlin, "From Confrontation to Cooperation." The intellectual justification for this dramatic reorientation of foreign policy can be found in two books by one of Menem's advisers: Escudé, *Realismo Periférico* and *Foreign Policy Theory.*

43. Aninat, "Chile en las noventa."

44. Compare with Muñoz, *Las relaciones exteriores*; Muñoz, *Chile: Política Exterior*; and Varas, *Hacia el Siglo XXI.*

45. Chile Information Project (CHIP) News (http:www.chip.ci), "Trade Pacts Offset Export Slump," 16 February 1999.

46. International Monetary Fund, *Direction of Trade.*

47. Milet, Fuentes, and Rojas, "Introducción."

48. Government of Chile, Ministry of Foreign Affairs, Dirección de Promoción de Exportaciones, Pro Chile 1997, as cited in Fuentes and Martin, *La nueva agenda argentino-chilena*, 81.

49. CHIP News, "Enersis Shareholders Reject Endesa Spain Bid," 25 February 1999. The Spanish proposal received 73.96 percent of stockholder votes for the takeover but needed 75 percent. They are asking for a recount.

50. The energy sector is discussed in Fuentes and Martin, *La nueva agenda argentino-chilena*, 37–44, 58–61.

51. CHIP News, "COREMA Approves Mejillones Port Plans," 15 February 1999.

52. Caro, "Políticas de cooperación," 17, 28, 29; Fuentes and Mizala, "Chile-Argentina después de Marzo de 1990," 4.

53. Arteaga, "Los Empresarios y el MERCOSUR."

54. Enersis has had problems with blackouts in both its Chilean and Argentine (Edesur) facilities. There have been calls in Argentina to terminate its ninety-nine-year contract. See CHIP News, "Edesur Faces Possible Fines and Contract Loss," 22 February 1999; "Edesur Racks Up Fines of US$71 Million," 23 February 1999; and "Reaction to Power Situation Shows Chile Character," 25 February 1999.

Brian Loveman

10

Historical Foundations of Civil-Military Relations in Spanish America

Civil-military relations in Spanish America involve dynamic interactions among military institutions, government policy makers, other organized interests, and ordinary citizens.[1] They are conditioned by domestic and international variables, by short-term and long-term circumstances, and by particular features of each nation that constitute national social and political regimes. For almost every general observation on Latin American society and civil-military relations, nonconforming patterns in particular nations may be offered as inconvenient exceptions. Generalizations about politics in the region, including civil-military relations, must necessarily acknowledge this underlying diversity as a starting point.

Despite this "dilemma of diversity," this chapter identifies some more or less commonly shared historical patterns of civil-military relations in Spanish America bequeathed from colonial times and from the nineteenth century. These cultural, institutional, and historical patterns and efforts to sustain or alter them persist, with variation, as a frame for civil-military relations in the region at the end of the twentieth century.

The historical influence of customs, attitudes, values, institutional norms, professional standards, and political culture encumber and shape present civil-military relations in all modern polities—not just in Spanish America. In this sense, history is not "the past" or what has "passed" but rather a complex set of enduring (and sometimes antagonistic) collective expectations, beliefs, social memories, and institutionalized patterns of behavior that continue to operate as contingencies influencing the present—and the future. Such historical influences do not fully determine the present or the future, but they do form part of the complex, path-dependent course of social and political change in each nation and community. They operate more or less overtly, more or less consensually, more or less consciously, and more or less conflictively. They also operate to legitimate present actions whose ostensible purpose is to reaffirm historical commitments, values, and shared dreams or, alternatively, serve as obstacles, antiutopian politico-cultural barriers to the "revolution" or the "good society," however it is defined by social reformers and revolutionaries.

In Spanish America, both colonial and nineteenth-century patterns of civil-military relations have survived into the twentieth century, though they have not survived unchanged or uniformly within the region.[2] Nevertheless, certain aspects of civil-military relations and military institutions in Latin America and certain patterns of conflict over these patterns and institutions are recognizable common legacies of pre-twentieth-century developments. This chapter emphasizes some of the similarities across the region and notes the main variations up to World War I.[3] The chapter begins with colonial legacies and considers the impact of the wars of independence and early efforts at nation-building, the challenge of creating new constitutional regimes and the role of the armed forces in nineteenth-century constitutions, nineteenth-century national security laws and penal codes, and the impact of European military missions. Together these legacies form a "living past" that continues to influence civil-military relations. Examples of the influence of this living past are presented for illustrative purposes, but no effort is made to historicize or to compare systematically the diverse cases—a task for lengthier, more detailed historical research.

Iberian Colonial Legacies

The "Warrior-Priest Tradition" and Conquest of *Las Indias*

For over seven centuries before Columbus's voyage of "discovery" in 1492, the Iberian peninsula experienced intermittent dynastic warfare and war between factions of Christians and Moors, family feuds, territorial, economic, ethnic, religious, and cultural conflict. This on-again, off-again crusade (A.D. 711–1492), ostensibly to liberate Iberia from North African conquerors, engendered anomalous alliances, temporary truces, and illusory pacifications. Reconstructed historically as the *reconquista*, as if for seven centuries there existed a constant battle to recuperate Iberia for Christianity (and conveniently neglecting the seven centuries of miscegenation, cultural borrowing, and political pragmatism), this period gave birth to the foundational myths of Spanish nationalism and military lore. Américo Castro affirms that "the Reconquest was a loom on which the history of Spain was warped"; Claudio Sánchez Albornoz, asserts: "I consider the Reconquest the key to the history of Spain."[4]

Whatever the character of the "real" history of this period, as a foundational myth for Spain, the "unceasing monotone of the Reconquest was of Christian Spaniards against Moslem Spaniards, of Cross and Sword against Moorish Crescent."[5] Crown and church promised booty, privilege, and salvation to the Christian soldiers who fought and died for "King and God."[6] Gradually the various Iberian Christian kingdoms, *las españas* (Asturias, León, Castilla, Navarre, Aragón, Catalonia), consolidated their jurisdiction and pushed southward from Castile toward Andalucía. The dynastic union of Castilla-Aragón after the marriage of Ferdinand and Isabella in 1469, creation of the Inquisition in 1480, and the victory in Granada in 1492 melded military conquest with a religious crusade into a proto-Spanish nationalism. (The Inquisition was not abolished in Spain until 1820; religious toleration in Spain did not formally exist even in the early 1960s.) As it has been said, in Spain the Cross is on the Sword.

No other European nation-state has its origins in such a religious-military crusade or can date its consolidation so precisely in a fusion of historical myth and historical events. The historian John Crow's summary of the year 1492 is revealing: victory was gained in the *reconquista* against the Moors at Granada and the Cross planted on Alhambra Hill on 2 January 1492; the Inquisition expelled Jews from the country en masse; Rodrigo Borgia, a Spaniard, became pope; Columbus "discovered" America; and Antonio de Nebrija published the *Castilian Grammar*, the first grammar of any modern European language. According to Crow, when the queen asked the author, "What is it for?" Nebrija answered: "Language your majesty is the ideal weapon of empire."[7] Whether this account is accurate or apocryphal, the Spanish Crown ruled the first European nation with a *national* grammar.[8] It would export the warrior-priest tradition, the institutions and practices of the *reconquista*, the fusion of crusade, military conquest, and religious-cultural imposition to *las Indias*.[9] It may be that in some ways, as Benedict Anderson argues, nations are "imagined communities," but the Spanish monarchy and its overseas empire were a very real religious, cultural, political, and military presence in Europe and on the world scene from 1492.[10]

Iberian Catholicism, the Spanish language, Hispanic political institutions, and cultural patterns were implanted in *las Indias* by *conquistadores* accompanied by priests and sometimes by *conquistadores* who were priests. The union of the Holy Roman Empire under the Habsburgs on the accession of Charles V (Charles I of Spain, 1516–56), which made the Spanish Crown the point of the lance of the Counterreformation, added a global dimension to the extension of the Spanish crusade and reinforced the fusion of papal authority (the *donación* or "grant" that conferred *las Indias* on the Spanish Crown) and royal patrimonial authority. Charles V considered himself "as the personal champion of

Christendom"; in his view, the conquest of *las Indias* served the dual purposes of providing great wealth for his royal coffers and of extending the domain of the Universal Church, though he also "made war on the Pope and reduced the papacy to a role of subservience to the Spanish state" when his German troops sacked Rome in 1527. When his son Philip II inherited the throne (1556–98), he began his reign with an auto-da-fé at Valladolid; several heretics were burned at the stake. Philip II "would rather not rule at all if he had to rule over a nation of heretics."[11] This was the king who presided over the extended conquest and settlement of Spanish America and, briefly, of Brazil.

In practice, the exploration, conquest, and initial settlement of *las Indias* lasted almost a century, if permanent settlement at Buenos Aires (1580) is taken as a temporal-geographic benchmark — while periodic Indian rebellions into the eighteenth century made the "conquest" of bodies, souls, and territory an enduring mission.[12] Expansion and extension of the Spanish imperial administration and creation of new territorial divisions superficially replicated, albeit in a telescoped time period, the *reconquista* in Spain: a period of neofeudal conquest followed by creation of two viceroyalties (New Spain, Mexico, 1535, and New Castile, Peru, 1542), then gradual and recurrent imperial reorganization — culminating with the creation of the viceroyalty of New Granada (1739) and Río de la Plata (1776).

The founders and early governors of the new territories frequently bore the title of *adelantado*, an honor given to the *adelantados de frontera*, the military leaders of the *reconquista* on the Iberian peninsula.[13] And the motivations of these early *conquistadores* also mirrored the mixture of religious zeal and quest for instant riches depicted so well in the epic *Poem of the Cid*, describing the exploits of a heroic figure of the eleventh century who combined warring against the Moors with warring against Christian princes, collecting taxes on behalf of King Alfonso VI of Castile, and creating his own vast domain, all in the name of loyalty to Catholicism.[14] His appeals to recruit armies — "those who want to stop their toil and get rich, let them come with me to conquer and to populate this land," and the results, after a victory at Valencia — "those who came on foot are now mounted; gold and silver, it's more than one can count. All are now rich — every one of them who went," paralleled the dream and, sometimes, the luck of the *conquistadores* in the sixteenth century.[15]

The Spanish "warrior-priest" tradition came with Iberian *conquistadores* to the Western Hemisphere. The melding of conquest, governance, and religious-cultural intolerance persisted in colonial life to the end of the eighteenth century. This tradition permeated more deeply in major colonial centers than in frontier territories such as Costa Rica, parts of Venezuela, and Río de la Plata or Chile. But it was nowhere without some influence. Writing in 1967, Jacques

Lambert concluded, "Nowhere else have the initial forms of colonial domination left such a strong and lasting imprint on countries that have been independent so long."[16] Seemingly confirming Lambert's assertion, the military governments of Latin America from the 1950s into the late 1980s frequently
justified the movements that brought them to power and their subsequent
policies as efforts to defend "Western Christian Values" against "godless communism" and "subversion."[17]

Military Missions: External Security, Warfare, and Public Order

From the sixteenth century until the early eighteenth century Spanish rulers
were almost always at war, preparing for war, or recovering from war. Iberian
armies and mercenaries fought in Europe, North Africa, and Asia and against
Indian peoples from the southwestern United States to the southern tip of
South America. Spanish navies and their mercenary armadas fought in the
Mediterranean, the Atlantic, the Pacific, and the Caribbean. But in addition to
their external warfare roles, the officers and soldiers in Iberian military forces
were also responsible for law enforcement and maintenance of public order.
Neat distinctions between police and military functions did not exist. By the
early nineteenth century, the internal security missions of the armed forces had
increased greatly, both in Spain and in the colonies, as a result of the extended
Bourbon reforms that began after the War of the Spanish Succession that
ended in 1713–14 and intensified after the British occupation of Havana (1762–
63), riots in Madrid in 1766, and colonial rebellions from Mexico to the
Andean regions after 1765.

At the end of the War of the Spanish Succession (1714), the king redesigned
Spanish internal administration, replacing the old viceroyalties with provincial
captaincy-generals. First introduced in Aragón, Valencia, Mallorca, and Asturias from 1715 to 1717, this system finally prevailed throughout Spain, except
Navarre, by 1790. The captain-general, symbol of the transition from "kingdom" with local law and custom to province ruled by a centralizing Castilian
authority, became the most important administrative officer in Spain. Usually
he was president of the *audiencia*, the highest provincial civil and criminal
court, head of the provincial *consejo de guerra*, and commander of troops
stationed in the province. In his judicial functions he was advised by one of the
judges of the *audiencia*, called the *auditor de guerra* (a specialized civil-military
legal adviser—and a military designation still existent in some parts of Spanish
America at the end of the twentieth century).

This fusion of administrative, judicial, and military authority made military officers "the superior authorities of the entire administrative system and the ordinary justice system."[18] It responded to the king's belief that "in order to effectively legislate, enforce the laws, and implement judicial decisions, the existence of a permanent army was necessary, not only for external defense but within the kingdom. . . . This explains the position achieved by the military in Spanish territorial organization in the eighteenth century."[19]

Although the administrative reforms were resisted, applied unevenly, and even aborted in certain provinces, they gradually took hold from 1717 until Philip V's demise in 1746. He abolished the old provincial constitutions and conciliar government and made military officers the most important officials in public administration. Militarization of internal administration was an essential tool for forging an overarching Spanish *patria* from the collection of kingdoms and vicegeral jurisdictions inherited from medieval and Habsburg times.

These reforms from 1714 to the 1740s reflected the intensified Bourbon concern with consolidating centralized political control over the provinces— and the central role of the military in achieving this objective. In the words of Spanish historian José Ramón Alonso, "The army was converted into the foundation of Philip V's monarchy, a military monarchy from its origin, with an army almost always in action from the New World to Milan. Without the constant support of the army, Spain might have been dismembered, as England desired until 1715."[20] In addition to the militarization of public administration, in 1734 the king established a system of "disciplined militia" in Castile, a sort of home defense force to which was conceded many of the traditional military *fueros*. The Crown standardized militia organization, equipment, and uniforms. This militia further engaged numerous Castilians in military training and accustomed them to military discipline.

Militarization of internal administration and recruitment of civilians in militia was accompanied by militarization of politics. By the 1730s the army had grown tremendously, officers served in key government positions, as ambassadors, and as the king's principal advisers. Defense ministers directed Spain's foreign policy—indeed, managed much of Spanish public policy. In addition, all cases of treason, subversion, and sedition were transferred to the jurisdiction of military tribunals. Militarization of internal politics and public administration was part of the Bourbon effort to establish authority over Spain after ousting the Habsburg dynasty and to centralize authority over the various kingdoms, towns, ecclesiastical jurisdictions, and groups in society that enjoyed special privileges and immunities (*fueros*) in relation to royal authority. Military officers became "natural" participants in politics and government, from policy making to public works, from public order to collecting taxes.

Internal Security of the State and the Armed Forces

Riots in Madrid that spread throughout Spain in 1766 provoked military reforms that further militarized Spanish politics and administration. Urban riots protesting the liberal economic reforms (such as freeing the price of bread) and other policies of the Marquis de Quillache spread to Cuenca, Zaragoza, Salamanca, Extremadura, and Andalucía.[21] After containing the riots with promises of amnesties, rescinding unpopular decrees, and lowering bread prices, the king blamed the Jesuits for the disorders, expelled them from Spain and the colonies, and reorganized internal administration to prevent further such threats to internal order.

In July 1767 the province of Castile became the captaincy-general of New Castile, presided over by the captain-general and president of the Council of Castile, the Count of Aranda. Having fused civil and military authority, the king made Madrid a military department (*plaza de armas*) and stationed fifteen thousand troops in the capital and environs. Political opponents were subjected to the jurisdiction of ad hoc tribunals (*juzgados especiales*), and the government ordered secret executions and the "disappearance" of enemies. New militia were created in Castile, charged with fighting contraband and banditry and maintaining internal peace. In 1768 Carlos III decreed new military regulations (*reales ordenanzas*) that extended the jurisdiction of military tribunals over civilians for crimes committed during the riots (an ex post change of jurisdiction and of law that applied to the "crimes" against internal security). The king also gave military administrators authority to approve or prohibit public meetings and to take preventive measures, when the king requested. When disturbances occurred, regulations transferred territory for approximately five leagues from the garrison's base to military jurisdiction, essentially imposing martial law over the entire civilian population. Military forces were assigned many routine police functions and served as bailiffs in civil and military courts. All cases of treason (*infidencia*), subversion, and sedition were also transferred to military tribunals.

Further militarization of internal administration occurred in April 1774 with publication of a decree-law (*pragmática*) on popular tumult, essentially a public order or "internal security" law.[22] This *pragmática* outlawed display or dissemination of unapproved posters and placards. It also outlawed "subversive" writings (*papeles sediciosos*) and penalized those who, knowing of such materials, failed to report them to the local authorities. Further provisions regulated public meetings and authorized troops to use "whatever force necessary [*se usará contra ellos de la fuerza, hasta reducirlos a la debida obediencia*]."

From 1774 to 1779 the government created new militia units to repress high-waymen, bandits, and vagrants. In 1781 regular army troops were stationed in Andalucía and Extremadura to fight contraband and banditry, with orders to act "as if they were in a state of war [*como si lo executasen en guerra viva*]." In 1784 a Royal Instruction ordered the captains-general to compile lists and information concerning bandits in their jurisdictions and to share such information across jurisdictions, an internal intelligence function that, if taken literally, required a permanent political espionage system.[23]

Deliberate confusion between "bandits" and political adversaries became the rule in Spain (and, later, in Spanish America), since "bandits" were typically subject to military tribunals, immediate execution, and *ley fuga*.[24] It would be no accident that so many "bandits" were shot "attempting to escape" or that government authorities in twentieth-century Spanish America labeled rebel leaders such as Pancho Villa in Mexico and Augusto César Sandino in Nicaragua (1927–31) as "bandits"—a legal categorization that subjected the "bandits" to military jurisdiction, unprotected by civil liberties and rights (*garantías constitucionales*) or due process. Thus the Bourbon kings gradually militarized internal administration in Spain, established special courts for dealing with "subversives," "bandits," and many other categories of political opponents, and made civilians subject to military tribunals and military law. By 1805 army officers presided over every territorial tribunal in Spain. These patterns for dealing with internal security and political opposition, to greater or less extent, were extended to Spanish America and were retained after independence.

Due Obedience, Military Law, and Military Codes

Important sections and language of the military regulations of 1768 survived the independence struggles, nation-building, and constitution writing in the nineteenth and twentieth centuries to guide military behavior until almost the end of the twentieth. Assumptions about the duty of officers to obey orders without question and to innovate only in areas where regulations or orders left a vacuum shaped routine military operations and also operations in "internal war" and law enforcement in eighteenth- and nineteenth-century Spain and Spanish America. These same premises, couched in virtually identical language in military codes, would guide operations against guerrillas and leftist political movements in the region after 1959—operations that resulted in widespread human rights violations in much of Latin America.

What is striking is the resilience of these colonial regulations—the almost exact replication of the language and spirit of colonial military regulations in

nineteenth- and twentieth-century military codes. To illustrate, language from
the Spanish *ordenanças* of 1768 is reproduced below followed by language from
military codes in Colombia, Argentina, and Peru in the 1960s and 1970s. These
regulations are reproduced in Spanish in the text, with the relevant phrases
highlighted, to illustrate the longevity of both the spirit and the wording of
colonial military regulations and doctrine in Spanish America.

> *Spain, 1768, Article 9:*
>
> Todo oficial en su puesto será responsable de la vigilancia de su Tropa
> en él; *del exacto cumplimiento de las órdenes particulares que tuviere, y de
> las generales que explica la Ordenanța,* como de tomar, en todos los acci-
> dentes y ocurrencias que no le estén prevenidas, el partido correspon-
> diente a su situación, caso, y objeto, debiendo en los lances dudosos
> elegir el más digno de su espíritu y honor.
>
> *Chile, 1839, 1860, Ordenanța para el Regímen, Disciplina, Subordinación y
> Servicio de los Ejércitos de la República, Titulo XXXII (9):*
>
> Todo Oficial en su puesto será responsable de la vigilancia de su tropa
> en *el exacto cumplimiento de las órdenes particulares que tuviere, i de las
> jenerales que esplica la Ordenanța,* como de tomar en todos los accidentes
> y ocurrencias que no le estén prevenidas, el partido correspondiente a su
> situación, caso i objeto, debiendo en los lances dudosos elejir el más di-
> gno de su espíritu i honor.
>
> *Argentina, Reglamento de Servicio Interno, 1969:*
>
> El que comandare una tropa será responsable de la vigilancia de ella, *del
> exacto cumplimiento de las órdenes particulares que tuviere y de las dis-
> posiciones contenidas en las leyes y reglamentos,* como de tomar, en todos
> los accidentes y ocurrencias que no estén previstos, el partido corre-
> spondiente a su situación, caso y objeto, debiendo en los lances dudosos
> elegir él que considere más digno de su espíritu y honor.
>
> *Peru, Reglamento General del Servicio Interior, 1975:*
>
> Todo oficial es responsable de la vigilancia de su tropa, *del exacto
> cumplimiento de las órdenes particulares que tuviere y de las prescripciones
> reglamentarias,* así como de tomar en todos los accidentes y ocurrencias
> que no estén prevenidos, la actitud correspondiente a su situación, caso
> y objeto, debiendo en los trances dudosos elegir el más digno de su es-
> píritu y honor.[25]

The longevity of these provisions in military codes and the spirit that
pervaded them could not be foreseen in 1768. But the legacy of the 1766 riots
and the subsequent royal decrees profoundly, if not always consciously, influ-

enced civil-military relations in Spanish America. These military regulations and the internal security measures taken by the king and Aranda created the legal and policy foundations for managing political dissidence and protests in Spain and independent Spanish America. They also embedded in military regulations the concept of *obediencia debida* (due obedience) and its corollary, individual immunity for actions carried out under orders.

The consequences of disobedience could be drastic. Chile's first postindependence military code, adopted in 1839 and reformed in 1860, stipulated: "Any soldier, corporal or sergeant, on active service, who fails to obey all and any Officers of the Army, will be sentenced to death [*será castigado con pena de la vida*]."[26] Moreover, even when orders of superiors were possibly illegal, these codes required strict compliance (unlike the British and then United States tradition of "objecting" to illegal orders). Illustrative (and typical) language in this regard in the Guatemalan Código Militar (1878) stipulated: "Orders from superiors should be obeyed . . . without vacillation and without discussion, and without making observations of any sort, even when there is cause to do so, until after complying with the orders."[27] This clearly means that orders to interrogate, torture, or execute prisoners must be followed; any objections could be presented later.

And the consequences for disobedience? "Any soldier, corporal or sergeant who fails to obey every and any Army officer . . . will suffer the death penalty." The same penalty was prescribed for sergeants and corporals who did not obey their superiors, that is, higher-ranking noncommissioned officers.[28] Under these circumstances, it is easy to understand why "due obedience" would be a legal defense for soldiers and officers. The military codes did not recognize "illegal orders" as a proper rationale for failure to obey orders, and the penalties for disobedience could be drastic and immediate.

Almost everywhere in Latin America similar language was retained in military codes during the twentieth century.[29] Use of the concept of "due obedience" as a defense by military personnel in cases involving violation of human rights in the 1980s and 1990s is grounded in this pre-1948, pre-Nuremberg military doctrine.[30] The events of the 1980s and 1990s have, in some respects, reaffirmed this doctrine, whether by plebiscite in Uruguay or with the "due obedience law" in Argentina (1987).

Beyond the due obedience laws, many aspects of the colonial *ordenanzas* and the nineteenth-century military codes survived well into the twentieth century, including jurisdiction of military tribunals over civilians for many "political" crimes. This feature of Latin American legal culture invariably made the armed forces political actors.

The Military *Fuero* and Jurisdiction of Military Tribunals over Civilians

The military *fuero* in Spain and colonial Spanish America is a complex topic both legally and historically.[31] The concept of *fuero* refers to both "privileges and immunities" and "jurisdiction." Medieval towns obtained *fueros*, a royal charter of privileges from the king. Such *fueros* were the basis for local government, a sort of medieval "federalism" that was gradually eroded by the centralizing encroachments of the developing European nation-state to the time of the French Revolution (1789). *Fueros* also existed for special groups in society—nobles, religious orders, guilds, and the military. Priests and other religious figures pertaining to the ecclesiastical *fuero* enjoyed immunities from civil authority in certain stipulated cases and were subject to ecclesiastical courts. This might be "protection" against civil authority or it might mean lack of protection against ecclesiastical law by appeal to the "rights" of other subjects.

This was also true for the guilds (*gremios*) and for military personnel. Officers acting as military judges might protect their personnel against civilian claims, both in civil and criminal cases, but might also impose the extremely harsh penalties stipulated in the military codes for everything from bigamy to bestiality. Thus the military *fuero* could be a mixed blessing, despite its use as an enticement to military service in both the militia and regular army, especially when recruits were offered exemption from taxes and from ordinary jurisdiction in civil litigation and enhanced social position. In Spanish America these privileges were especially attractive to the "lower classes" and "people of color" (*pardos*, *mulatos*, and the various *castas*).

For purposes of understanding civil-military relations in Spain and Latin America, however, three main aspects of the *fuero* are essential.

1. Military personnel were subject preferentially to military jurisdiction and tribunals in cases of alleged criminal behavior, whether the alleged crimes were committed against civilians, against other military personnel, or against government authorities. Military officers acting as judges in *consejos de guerra* (courts-martial) heard such cases and had some incentive to find that military personnel had acted properly when accused of misdeeds—especially if they had acted under the orders of an officer. This aspect of the military *fuero* had variable impact from colony to colony and region to region within colonies. When the military *fuero* was extended to militia units and to black, mulatto, and *casta* troops in the eighteenth century, it also provided some social mobility and insulation from civil government authority. At the same time, it resulted in "a withering respect for justice, [an] undermining of the prestige and credibility of local government, and the establishment of

the military as a dominant force in the provinces [of Cartagena and Panama]."[32]

2. In many instances, civilians were subject to military jurisdiction, especially for crimes in which military personnel jointly participated with civilians, when the crime committed was rebellion, sedition, tumult, or other such crimes in which "internal security" was threatened (as already exemplified in the case of bandits, vagrants, and those who disseminated subversive writings).

3. Military jurisdiction generally meant that "normal" judicial protection and due process was not available to the accused. These patterns were maintained after independence in most of Spanish America, though the extent of military *fueros* and jurisdiction over civilians recurrently became a matter of political debate in the nineteenth century.[33]

The extent of military jurisdiction over civilians varied considerably in Spanish America after independence, as constitutional and legal changes reduced or eliminated both the military *fuero* and trial of civilians under military law. No systematic comparative historical investigation exists that documents the constitutional, legal, and political battles regarding military *fueros* and military jurisdiction over civilians. In some cases the military *fueros* were eliminated early: Costa Rica (1825), Venezuela (1830), Uruguay (1838), Bolivia (1839), and Mexico (1857). (In the Bolivian case, however, the 1839 Constitution was not implemented, and its successor in 1843 was labeled sarcastically by opponents the *ordenanza militar* because of its authorization of virtual martial law whenever the president judged that there existed "internal commotion" or "external danger.")

While systematic study of the politics associated with elimination of military *fueros* in the nineteenth century remains to be done, it is clear that persistence of military *fueros* and military jurisdiction over civilians for certain criminal proceedings on the model established in the colonial period and retained in the nineteenth century significantly influenced civilian-military relations in Spain and much of Spanish America until the late twentieth century.[34] Indeed, the jurisdiction of military tribunals over civilians and the application of military law "in time of war" to civilians, for "political crimes," was a crucial element in the human rights violations that characterized both military and civilian regimes in much of Spanish America from the 1960s until the 1990s.[35]

Such military jurisdiction over civilians was, for example, a permanent fact of life in Colombia from the late 1940s, with the country under states of siege governed by the language of the 1886 Constitution. Military jurisdiction over civilians in Colombia from 1948 to 1991 resembled that of late eighteenth-century Bourbon Spain.[36] In Chile, civilians continue to be prosecuted in military tribunals for a variety of "crimes," including "insulting military officers." And in Peru in the 1990s, President Alberto Fujimori greatly expanded military jurisdiction over civilians in certain types of cases involving "national security" and in parts of the country that the government declared "emergency zones." In contrast, in El Salvador and Guatemala, military jurisdiction over civilians ended as part of the reforms adopted after the "peace accords" that terminated the guerrilla wars in those two countries in the early 1990s.

Fusion of Military and Civilian Authority

Related to the internal security role for the armed forces and application of military law to civilians, both in Spain and the colonies in the eighteenth century, there existed, for some purposes, a routine overlap and fusion of civil and military authority. The Ordenanza de Intendentes del Río de la Plata (1782) and those of Nueva España (Mexico, 1786) gave viceroys, *intendentes*, and other *comandantes general* "total authority [*todo el lleno de la superior autoridad y omnímodas facultades*]." The Ordenanza de Intendentes reaffirmed this concentration of authority (except in Venezuela), recognizing the viceroys, captains-general, and *audiencia* presidents' "full and superior authority, consistent with their high rank [*superioridad y pleno ejercicio de todas las facultades propias de su elevada dignidad*]."[37] Almost all the viceroys in Mexico, Peru, Río de la Plata, and New Granada were military officers. The same was true in the captaincy-general of Chile and Guatemala and of the governors in Cuba and the Philippines. This trend was intensified in the 1760s and 1770s as a result of problems of internal order, the temporary loss of Havana and Manila to the British in the Seven Years' War (1762–63), and several serious rebellions from the mid-1760s in Quito (1765) to the 1770s and 1780s in Oaxaca, northwestern Venezuela, Arequipa, Cuzco, La Paz, Cochabamba, and Soccorro (in New Granada).

This wave of revolt, precipitated in great part as reactions to the Bourbon reforms that sought to enhance colonial revenues and reassert royal authority over local interests, culminated with the Túpac Amaru uprising (1780–81).[38] By the revolt's end, the Spanish army and militia numbered over seventeen thousand, a larger force than the regular garrison strength in Mexico, Peru, and New Granada combined. In the course of the fighting thousands died amid fear of a generalized race war. In 1784 Peru was divided into seven intendancies, with an additional two created in Chile under the command of Viceroy

Teodoro de Croix, former commandant general of the Frontier Provinces of New Spain. Thus as the Spanish colonies approached the nineteenth century, militarization of internal administration became ever more visible.

At the end of the eighteenth century the military establishment was an integral aspect of Spanish colonial administration. Civil and military authority often overlapped, military courts had jurisdiction over civilians for many crimes, especially those involving internal security and public order, and military officers and even enlisted personnel enjoyed certain privileges and immunities vis-à-vis civilian society, particularly the *fuero* militar. Tensions frequently existed between civil and military authorities, especially at the local level (*cabildo*), but the "special" status of the military was recognized in law and in practice. While the military was "subordinate" to government authority, it was also immune to oversight and subject to separate channels of authority that went directly to the king or, after independence, the president of the new Latin American countries.

The Armed Forces and Independence Movements

The wars of independence in Spanish America (1808–30+) were everywhere civil wars that divided all institutions and groups of the colonial order,[39] including military institutions, both the army and the militia, which saw officers and enlisted personnel fight to reaffirm the Spanish colonial regime and then to overturn it. Many of the leaders of the Spanish American independence movements defected from the Spanish army, and others were officers in the colonial militia.

The course of independence struggles varied greatly from Mexico to the southern tip of South America; in some cases independence cost thousands of lives and destruction of property and infrastructure (Venezuela, Río de la Plata, Chile), and in others independence came without significant warfare (most of Central America). Even when Spanish armies were finally defeated in Peru (1824) and southern Chile (1826), the region succumbed to territorial disputes, internal wars, foreign invasions, and naked struggles for power and control of government revenues. Efforts to create large confederal nations failed in Central America, northern South America, and the Río de la Plata region. Fragmentation led to creation of new nation-states that corresponded roughly to old colonial territorial jurisdictions (*audiencia*, captaincy-general, or lesser jurisdictions).

In these circumstances, military force, though usually not professional military organizations, became the arbiters of politics. This was the age of the *caudillos*, charismatic leaders, landowners, former military officers, and others who imposed their will or lost their lives at the head of armies composed of forcibly recruited peasants, former slaves, vagrants, ranch hands, urban "lower classes," and loyal henchmen.[40] The stakes for losers was high and the risks substantial enough to make control of violence literally worth *everything*. Every change in government potentially threatened catastrophe or proffered a windfall for the victors and their clientele.[41] With politics so crucial to their personal and professional fate and so volatile, "liberty, equality and fraternity gave way to infantry, cavalry, and artillery, as the republics bled themselves in constant warfare."[42] Such conditions reinforced the relative autonomy of armed forces in the region and eroded the limited credibility of enfeebled civil authority.

From the 1820s onward restoration of political order and effective law enforcement was at a premium. For many, the memory of relative calm under Spanish colonialism had great appeal. Though typically unsuccessful before 1880, with the arguable exception of Chile, political leaders sought to design institutions for "good government" that would somehow combine the spirit of Spanish, French, British, and North American liberalism with the more conservative social and legal regime of colonial Spanish America. Constitutional experimentation produced a vast array of failed regimes—including more than one hundred constitutions in Spanish America before 1900 (without counting the numerous short-lived "proto constitutions" and temporary constitution-like charters). Gradually, however, certain common institutions and practices prevailed in the region, including republican constitutions with relatively strong presidents, weak legislatures, and barely independent judiciaries. In the sphere of civil-military relations there also developed some common institutions and practices that, blended with the colonial legacies, continue to exercise influence in the twentieth century. Likewise, the definition and outcomes of conflicts in the area of civil-military relations—for example, efforts to eliminate or reduce the *fuero militar*—also continue to frame civil-military relations among the Spanish American republics.

Nation-Building and the Armed Forces

The Military and the Patria: Foundational Myths

The independence wars and the numerous regional and transnational wars that eventually established the boundaries of the new nation-states became the benchmarks for Latin American military institutions. The region's armies claimed a tutelary, guardianship role, what they called a "historical mission" to oversee the "transcendental destiny and values" of *la patria*. There arose an almost universal claim that national military institutions preceded the nation itself and that "the army is the soul of the present, because, assuring respect for the law, it prevents the nation from falling into barbarism; it is the soul of the future, because assuring order and security in the country, it favors its progress and helps it to achieve its destiny."[43] Put boldly, in the words of El Salvadoran lieutenant colonel Mariano Castro Morán: "In the process of creating nationality, in all epochs of the history of peoples, the ultimate and decisive stage is the formation of national armies, or, in modern times, the institutionalization of national armed forces. . . . Here in El Salvador, the National Army was created at the dawn of the Republic. . . . In effect, the history of our country in the nineteenth century is nothing more than the history of our men in uniform who created and reformed laws and institutions in the fields of culture and liberal, democratic humanism."[44]

Whatever the historical accuracy or credibility of such claims, they remain strong elements of military lore and military discourse in the late twentieth century. Indeed, they are disseminated on the ubiquitous Internet website maintained by the Latin American armed forces that proclaim boldly the prenational historical origins of national military institutions, the continuing relevance of the armed forces' historical mission of "overseeing" their nations' destiny, and the identity of military institutions with the core values of the nation-state. A Venezuelan website, for example, proclaims: "The Army is born with the Nation . . . its preamble in times of the conquest"; the Chilean army website declares that "the history of our nation has been the very history of its Army"; and an Uruguayan army website affirms, "The National Army is born with the Patria. It is a foundational army, principal actor in the Campaigns of Artigas [the "George Washington" of Uruguay], . . . reborn in the Liberating Crusade of 1825."[45] Similar language can be found on army, navy, and even air force websites across the region, in the military academy texts, and in official national histories. According to this version of Latin American history, the "national" armies predate the modern "*patrias*"; they created their nations and defended them against Spanish reconquest, foreign intervention, and internal strife that threatened dismemberment—they became their permanent guardians. These historical versions of the origins of military guardianship not only are validated in the "birth" of nations and their survival but are reinforced by the constitutional missions assigned to the armed forces in the nineteenth century.

Nineteenth-Century Constitutionalism and the Military

The desperate circumstances of the early nineteenth century in Latin America made reestablishing political stability and law enforcement a primordial task for nation-builders, whether they proclaimed themselves liberals or conservatives, republicans or monarchists, centralists or federalists. The traditional fusion of military and civil authority in territorial administration, the jurisdiction of military tribunals over "bandits" and others who threatened public tranquillity, and the dual mission of armed forces—internal order and external defense—were constitutionalized and codified in most of the region after independence. Of 103 constitutions adopted from independence until 1900, slightly over 80 percent defined the role of the armed forces in the constitution. Usually this definition included maintaining internal order, enforcing the law, and protecting the constitutional order against usurpation. In a few cases the military even had a mandate to supervise elections (a function adopted in the twentieth century in more Latin American countries), to ensure proper presidential succession, and to prevent *continuismo* (that is, "staying over" in office by presidents). These constitutions made the armed forces virtually a fourth branch of government, designated in constitutional language as permanent institutions of the various republics. Their constitutional authority and missions were stipulated with greater brevity than those of the legislature, judiciary, and executive branches of government, but nevertheless their elimination or the modification of their political authority and duties required constitutional reform. Moreover, these constitutions rarely specified who would decide when "disorder" warranted military intervention, when the actions of presidents, legislators, or local officials constituted threats to the "constitutional order" or to republican institutions, or when "internal commotion" (a common phrase in nineteenth-century constitutions) justified military action.

Arguably, this ambiguity gave the armed forces the authority or imposed on them the obligation to exercise the equivalent of "judicial review with bayonets." To illustrate, Peru's 1856 Constitution obligated the armed forces to disobey the government if it violated the Constitution or the laws. Víctor Villanueva, an expert on the Peruvian military and former officer, suggests: "This meant accepting, implicitly, that apart from the suffrage, sovereignty resided in the army rather than in the people. The latter had the right to elect governments and the army the duty of ousting them when it [the army] determined that they violated the constitution."[46] Even if Villanueva slightly overinterprets the constitutional phraseology, the basic point is valid: the Constitution appears to leave the armed forces as the arbiter of the constitutionality of government action, the "guardian" of constitutional rule. In the case of Guatemala, the treatise on "military duties" most widely read by the generations of officers from the 1950s to the 1980s instructed officers not to intervene in the activities of political parties "so long as their activities do not promote disorder nor threaten the integrity of national honor; if that occurs, then the armed forces, fulfilling their duty, must impose the law, subjecting [the parties] to the proper Authority [*deberá imponer los fueros de la legalidad, supeditando su obediencia, constante y absoluta, al Poder de que depende*]."[47] In short, if the situation "gets out of hand," it is the duty, that is, the constitutional duty, of the armed forces to protect national honor and "save" *la patria*.

While most nineteenth-century Latin American constitutions did not explicitly go this far, in defining the role of the armed forces, over 80 percent of the constitutions also recognized and reaffirmed the colonial military *fueros*. This constitutionalization of the armed forces' political functions, prerogatives, and privileges was reinforced further by incorporation of various constitutional regimes of exception into the political design of the Spanish American republics and the Brazilian monarchy. Importantly, however, in some cases (a bit less than 20 percent of the constitutions), the military *fueros* were explicitly abolished, and in slightly over 20 percent the constitutions prohibited jurisdiction by military courts and application of military law to civilians. This central issue in civil-military relations up to 1999 was engaged in some countries almost immediately after independence. Why certain countries went in this direction and the majority did not has not been investigated systematically, though it is clear that the struggle to eliminate or retain military *fueros* played an important part in politics in much of the region during the nineteenth century.[48]

Constitutional Regimes of Exception and the Military

Latin American constitutions, from the first wartime charters adopted during the independence struggles, included clauses that allow suspension of civil liberties and rights to meet all manner of emergencies: natural disasters, threats to constitutional order, insurgency, rebellion, "internal commotion," civil war, and many other contingencies. Illustratively, the charter of Gran Colombia (1821) authorized that "in times of internal commotion and armed conflict endangering the security of the Republic," the president "take whatever extraordinary measures, not within the normal sphere of his authority, that the case may require."

With variations, constitutional regimes of exception permit press censorship, restrictions on meetings and assembly, and suspension of habeas corpus and other procedural protections for those arrested or detained. Regimes of exception may also confer "extraordinary powers [*facultades extraordinarias*]" on the president and other government officials, including military officers. In some cases, regimes of exception are equivalent to imposing martial law, that is, assigning to military officers full government authority, suspending the operations of ordinary courts, and subjecting civilians to military law and tribunals.

Regimes of exception have different names and purposes from country to country and from time to time. Common regimes of exception are "state of siege," "internal war," martial law, and "state of emergency." But these names for regimes of exception do not imply similar political and legal meanings; thus "state of siege" in Chile before 1874 implied virtual constitutional dictatorship but after 1874, with constitutional reform, was much more limited regarding the "emergency powers" extended to the president. In all cases, however, regimes of exception are the result, in constitution making, of a priori philosophical, moral, and political decisions that, at times, civil liberties and rights, including basic "human rights," must be subordinated to "protecting *la patria*."[49] Argentina's 1853 Constitution's state of siege provisions, for example, amounted to virtual martial law, like Chile's up to 1874. This provision has been frequently used in Argentine history. More recently, well before the 1976 military coup, the elected government (1973–76) declared a state of war against terrorism. In the words of Argentine general Acdel Vilas, "The offensive against subversion presupposes in the first place freedom of action in all areas . . . a series of special procedures, an instantaneous response, a persecution to the death."[50] And in Chile in 1973, the military junta declared that the state of siege that it imposed, in accord with well-established Chilean practice since 1925, implied a "state of war" for legal and judicial purposes, as established in the Military Code of Justice.[51]

Constitutional regimes of exception extend, by definition, "exceptional" authority to government authorities and circumscribe civil liberties and rights. They are enforced by the armed forces and police, who exercise under such regimes expanded, if not unlimited, political and even judicial authority. Such regimes of exception since the independence movements of the nineteenth century have been, and remain, part of Latin American constitutionalism and political culture, though details vary from country to country. They are taken for granted throughout the region; they remain in place everywhere at the close of the twentieth century as essential elements of Latin America's "protected democracies" and a fundamental subtext of civil-military relations.

National Security and Military Law

From the late nineteenth century, most Latin American penal codes included special sections dealing with political crimes such as sedition, rebellion, and insurrection.[52] The penal code in effect in Argentina in 1888, for example, had a section titled "Crimes against Internal Security and Public Order." Crimes included under this section included "rising up in open hostility against the government of any Province, for any of the following purposes: to alter or destroy the Constitution; to depose the Governor or other authority or to impede transfer of power as specified in the Constitution; to extract any sort of decision from the authorities [*arrancar á los poderes constituidos alguna medida ó concesión*]; to impede the meetings of the legislatures, dissolve them, or interfere with their functioning; to reform the existing institutions by violent means; to promote disobedience by provincial or local authorities to the Government [*sustraer á la obediencia*]." Any of these actions constituted the crime of "rebellion," punishable by three and one-half years of exile. Other such crimes included sedition, "tumultuous assembly [*reunión tumultosa*]," *motín, asonada, atentado contra la autoridad,* and *desacato*—among many others.[53] The penalty for the crime of *desacato* ("those who resist or openly disobey the government [*la autoridad*]" or create a "grave disturbance," wherever "government officials are carrying out their functions") was from one to six months in jail. Chile's 1874 penal code had similar provisions regarding crimes and misdemeanors against the internal security of the state.[54] Laws regulating the press, censoring untoward comments on religion or offending the Catholic Church, and prohibiting offensive publications, posters, and speeches also sought to chill opposition to incumbent governments.[55]

In some instances these penal codes overlapped with the military codes; in others certain crimes were automatically assigned to military courts. In still other cases, crimes defined in penal codes or in special internal security laws, normally assigned to civilian courts (*fuero común*), were (and still are) assigned to military courts, if committed when the country, or a region of the country, is under a declared regime of exception such as "state of emergency," "state of siege," or "state of internal commotion." These overlapping and reinforcing constitutional, legal, and military code provisions establish a permanent regime of protected democracy, that is, an ostensibly constitutional regime whose architecture designs-in military guardianship, imposes restrictions on civil liberties and rights by civilian governments and, when necessary, by military institutions, and threatens civilians with military law and military tribunals if "*la patria* is threatened."

More important, this permanent regime of protected democracy came to be accepted as normal by many if not most civilians, indeed came to be viewed as an essential ingredient of constitutional "democracy" in the Latin American context. As long as there is no immediate crisis, no threat of disorder, no significant political polarization, such systems may operate as if they were "democratic." But the cumulative effect of these colonial and nineteenth-century patterns of civil-military relations was to fashion a political culture, or, more accurately, national political cultures, that have deeply embedded authoritarian and militarist political institutions and practices. Indeed, these institutions and practices are so deeply embedded in the "political mentality" of the region that well-known civilian politicians, regarded as "democrats," echo military lore and military political doctrine in times of crisis. Colombia's president Julio César Turbay, for example, addressing the thirteenth Conference of Commanders of Latin American Armies in Bogotá in 1979, commented: "Naturally, in extreme cases, confronted with an ostensible political vacuum that leads toward generalized anarchy, the Armed Forces must [*se ven precisadas*] exercise power to reestablish the rule of authority."[56] And Chilean ex-president Eduardo Frei Montalva, in an interview in Spain after the 1973 military coup in his country, declared: "The military have saved Chile. . . . They were called on by the nation and they fulfilled their legal duty. . . . If a people has been so weakened and harassed [*acosado*] that it cannot rebel, . . . then the Army substitutes its arms and does the work."[57]

These remarks by former presidents Turbay and Frei are not isolated viewpoints. The accretion of colonial legacies and nineteenth-century patterns of civil-military relations, converted into military lore, patriotic myth, national rituals, and military doctrine, pervade primary school textbooks, official histories, civic education, and daily political life. Their continuing influence at the end of the twentieth century varies from country to country, their persistence more or less subject to contestation and change. But nowhere in Latin America have these legacies been erased, nowhere have the cultural, institutional, and behavioral foundations of authoritarianism, militarism, and protected democracy been definitively eliminated.

European Missions and Professional Militarism: Patriotism and Antipolitics

In the late nineteenth century, another element was added to the accreted systems of civil-military relations in Latin America: the influence of European military missions contracted to "professionalize" and "modernize" the region's armed forces. The most important influences came from Spain, France, and Prussia / Germany and from diffusion of the technical, organizational, and doctrinal lessons of these missions through Latin American missions (especially the Chilean diffusion of Prussian influence) in northern South America and Central America. Frederick Nunn and other scholars have investigated the history of these missions and their influence.[58] For the purposes of the present chapter mention should be made of the most important legacies of the European missions, filtered by the local circumstances in each Latin American country: (1) the politicization of the region's armed forces; (2) the identification of the nation-state with the armed forces; (3) the dissemination of disdain for liberalism, for Marxism, for politicians, and for political parties; and (4) the nurture of a professional military "antipolitical" subculture.

Many Latin American countries contracted officers from Germany and France and sent their officers to academies in both these European nations. From Mexico to Chile military manuals, regulations, doctrine, and training regimen emulated French and German patterns, often merely translating European publications into Spanish. France and Germany had the most modern and admired military institutions in Europe. They were also the most politicized and antipolitical. The French and German concept of the "nation in arms," of making the barracks the "school of the people," was transferred to their Latin American pupils. Colmar von der Goltz's notion in *Das Volk in Waffen* (1883) that the army was the binding agent of citizenry and state was widely disseminated and popularized.[59] As Frederick Nunn notes in his investigation of "European military professionalism," Goltz believed that "the enigma to be solved . . . is how to produce a complete fusion of the military and the social and industrial life of the people, so that the former may impede the latter as little as possible, and so that, on the other hand, the full wealth of the resources of the latter may be evidenced by the healthy condition of the former."[60]

The European missions also taught, based on their own experience, that politics corrupted society, that politicians meddled in what should be "strictly professional" military affairs, and that "national development" depended on strong government supported by the armed forces. The French army, defeated by Prussia in 1870–71, repressed the Paris Commune in 1871 "in an appalling bloodbath"; by 1906 the General Labor Confederation declared that "in every strike the Army is for the employers" and denounced its recurrent use as strikebreakers.[61] In Prussia, Helmuth von Moltke despised politicians and believed that war had "become too serious a matter for soldiers to be able to tolerate the interference of civilians."[62] Like its French counterpart, the Prussian army maintained internal security and supervised surveillance of the Social Democratic Party and repression of political activism and labor movements. After 1896 no soldier was allowed to attend any meeting without an officer's permission, to sing any revolutionary or Social Democratic song, or to possess or distribute Social Democratic literature. German unification was a combined military-cultural mission that officers assigned to Chile, Argentina, and elsewhere in Latin America eventually shared with their students. The Prussians' star pupils in Chile and Argentina, Carlos Ibáñez and José Uriburu, would echo these antipolitical, antisocialist, antirevolutionary themes in their own brief dictatorships (Ibáñez, 1927–31, Uriburu, 1930–32), as would the most eminent pupil of the French mission in Peru, General Oscar Benavides, who arguably carried out the first coup of the Latin American "new military professionals" in 1914. Benavides graduated first in his class from the Escuela Superior de Guerra (Superior War College; ESG) in 1906, studied in France, and served on military commissions in Germany and Austria before becoming army chief of staff in 1913. He led troops against Peru's first "populist" president, Guillermo Billinghurst, after "the president dissolved congress, slashed the military budget, and threatened to arm his working-class supporters."[63]

Thus the "professionalization" of the Latin American armed forces through European missions, officer exchanges, and education in European academies inculcated a very particular version of military professionalism, a version inimical to liberal democratic politics, a version that reinforced the colonial and post-colonial elitism, social segregation, authoritarianism, and vanguardism of the Latin American officer corps. To the Iberian warrior-priest tradition, the legacies of Bourbon military institutions, and the multiple missions of nineteenth-century nation-building, the European tutors added romantic nineteenth-century European military nationalism, geopolitics, and a decided contempt for civilian politicians, legislatures, political parties, labor organizations, and "revolutionary" movements. Of course, this imported military "professionalism" and mysticism were superimposed on, and differentially filtered through, distinctive Latin American realities—from Chile's victory over Peru and Bolivia in 1884 to Brazilian, Argentine, Paraguayan, and Uruguayan reactions to the Paraguayan War (1865–70) and Porfirio Díaz's federal army in Mexico (1876–1910)—that translated German military regulations for the loading of the cavalry's horses, mules, and gear on the nation's new railroads in the 1890s.

Historical Legacies and the Challenge of Democratization

By World War I, most of the premises and practices that allowed the military to assume that it had the "acquired rights and privileges, formal or informal, to exercise effective control over its internal governance, to play a role within extramilitary areas within the state apparatus, or even to structure relationships between the state and political or civil society"—what Alfred Stepan refers to as "military prerogatives"—were solidly established.[64] In this sense, if "democratization" means, at least in part, reducing or eliminating these prerogatives, reference to "redemocratization" in Latin America in the 1980s or 1990s necessarily generates some confusion. Though the military governments from the 1960s to the 1990s may have visibly increased the direct role of the armed forces in governance, they did not *construct* the underlying "protected democracies" that existed in 1959 and reemerged in the 1980s and 1990s. The military governments selectively activated, for particular purposes, cultural, institutional, professional, and political elements of the Latin American civil-military schema that had evolved from the colonial era and the nineteenth century. Dormant in "normal times," these historically embedded options of Latin American politics become "operative" in times of "crisis." (Of course, the military governments violated the constitutions and the law when necessary to "save *la patria*," in accord with their understanding of the supra-constitutional "historical mission" assigned to them as "guardians." This is an essential part of the historical system of civil-military relations.)

Survival of these legacies remains, at the end of the twentieth century, a challenge for more than superficial democratization in the region in the twenty-first century. Part of that challenge consists of developing political leaders who do not share the basic premises of protected democracy, who do not believe that in times of "crisis" civil liberties and rights should be "suspended" and that the armed forces should exercise the guardianship mission stipulated in the Peruvian 1856 Constitution referred to earlier. Perhaps an ever more difficult part of the challenge consists of developing civilian institutions, both government and nongovernment, strong enough and resilient enough to nurture the long-term alteration of the authoritarian political culture and institutions bequeathed by Iberian imperialism, nineteenth-century *caudillismo* and militarism, and their reinforcement by the impact of the Cold War and the Cuban Revolution since 1959.[65]

Looking into the future, there can hardly be "redemocratization" where constitutional democracy with general respect for civil liberties and rights and the rule of law (not merely elections and civilian government) previously did not exist, or, at best, existed conditionally. The historical patterns of civil-military relations described in this chapter are living legacies of colonial and nineteenth-century development. Their modification or elimination requires changes in encoded cultural patterns, enduring institutional arrangements, and political practices of centuries—a task much more formidable than the restoration of an idealized "democratic" past.

Understanding Civil-Military Relations, Past and Future

This chapter surveyed the evolution of customs, attitudes, values, institutional norms, professional standards, political culture, and military and government institutions that shape present civil-military relations in Latin America. As a historical interpretation, it relied on diverse theoretical and empirical traditions, including the institutionalist, structural, cultural, and, to a lesser extent, strategic choice approaches outlined by David Pion-Berlin in the Introduction to this volume. My own approach to civil-military relations in Latin America has been eclectic; explaining the degree of "civilian control" over military actors at a particular moment in a particular country, for example, almost always requires analysis that melds idiographic and nomethetic approaches — and that relies on a combination of theoretical insights. Strategic choices always occur in institutional, cultural, and structural contexts and usually involve international, regional, and local influences. "Civilian control" (like most aspects of civil-military relations) is not simply a changing frame for strategic choices but rather a complex set of historically, culturally, and institutionally defined relationships that include ongoing choices by military and civilian actors. The past never fully determines the present or the future. Strategic choice never takes place in a vacuum. Neither history nor choice, neither institutions nor social structure, alone determines the changing configuration of civil-military relations. To be useful as history, as social science, and as input for policy makers, future research on civil-military relations must push forward eclectically on theoretical and empirical fronts, not allowing academic trends or disciplinary dogmatism to impede the accumulation and creation of knowledge.

NOTES

1. "Latin America" is a term without a clear geographical, cultural, or political referent. No nation in "Latin" America speaks Latin, and no territory was part of the Roman Empire. In the present essay I use the term "Spanish America" to refer to nation-states in the Western Hemisphere that were previously part of the Spanish Empire (thus excluding Puerto Rico and parts of the southwestern United States). I use the term "Latin America" to refer to Spanish America, Brazil, and Haiti. This definition is strictly for convenience and conforms to one common usage among competing definitions.
2. For example, Kuethe suggests that different patterns of adoption and implementation of the Bourbon military reforms in different regions of New Granada after 1765, including the resistance and adaptation to the racial implications of extending military *fueros* to *mulato*, *casta*, and black militiamen and soldiers, partially explain the relative strength

of civilian authority over the military in Colombia and the "elitist military tradition" in Ecuador, where civilian rule was much weaker (*Military Reform and Society*, 188–89).

3. Many other aspects of civil-military relations are not discussed in this chapter. A particularly intriguing example is the extent to which military budgets and expenditures overburdened Spain and the Spanish American republics, forcing serious compromises in foreign policies and inducing military rebellions from Habsburg times to the 1970s. See Porter, *War and the Rise of the State*, 85–86.

4. Cited in Crow, *Spain*, 78–79.

5. Ibid., 79.

6. Thus military-religious orders such as the Knights of Santiago, Calatrava, Alcantara, Templar and Hospitalers, the Hermandades de Castilla ("rural constabulary," called the "Holy Brotherhood" in the reign of Ferdinand and Isabella), and the Inquisition, established in 1480, were part of the process that made Spain a "church-state" in which political authority, military power, and control of religious doctrine and patronage were fused in the Crown.

7. Crow, *Spain*, 151.

8. A less theatrical interpretation of Nebrija's *Arte de la lengua castellana* (1492) relates that in dedicating the first grammar of a modern European language to the queen, the prologue noted the need for an official language as a "companion to empire" that would teach "the many barbarian peoples that will be conquered and governed by the laws of the conqueror" [*a los muchos pueblos bárbaros que serán vencidos y regidos por las leyes del vencedor*]" (quoted in Marín and del Río, *Breve historia*, 55–56).

9. Colin M. MacLachlan suggests that Pedro de Mendoza, the first *adelantado* of the Río de la Plata, more than likely carried with him to the "New World" a copy of the *Manual del soldado cristiano*, first published in Spain in 1526.

10. Anderson, *Imagined Communities*.

11. Quoted in Crow, *Spain*, 170.

12. Coincidentally, in 1580 King Philip II united the Iberian peninsula under one crown, temporarily combining the Spanish and Portuguese empires until 1640.

13. C. H. Haring estimates that of the seventy individuals who contracted with the Crown to subdue or colonize new areas in America in the sixteenth century, slightly less than half obtained the rank of *adelantado* (*Spanish Empire in America*, 22–23).

14. Standard texts on Spanish literature before the 1980s date the *Poem of El Cid* in 1140. Critical modern research suggests that a more likely date is approximately a century later and that the 1140 date is the result of revisionist history by partisans of Francisco Franco in Spain seeking to enhance and glorify "hispanicism."

15. Quoted in Crow, *Spain*, 90–91.

16. Lambert, *Latin America, Social Structures and Political Institutions*, 52.

17. There are so many examples of this sort of rhetoric that choosing any single example is a special challenge. A dramatic illustration in 1998 was an open letter from Chilean general Augusto Pinochet to his compatriots, after his arrest in London, on the request of a Spanish judge for his extradition in cases involving human rights abuses against Spanish citizens during his dictatorship. Pinochet wrote: "The dilemma was; or the Western Christian conception of existence would triumph, so that respect for human dignity and the survival of fundamental values would prevail [in the world] or the ma-

terialistic, atheistic vision of man and society, with its system that implacably oppresses liberties and rights [would prevail]. . . . Communism was this truly anti-religion . . . [that] sowed death and destruction . . . a universal evangelism of hatred and class conflict, . . . a gigantic genocide" ("Carta a los Chilenos," London, December 1998).

18. Hargreaves-Mawdsley, *Eighteenth Century Spain*, 10.

19. García Gallo, *Los orígenes españoles*.

20. Alonso, *Historia política*, 30.

21. For details on causes of the riots and the political opposition to King Carlos III, see Rodríguez, "Spanish Riots of 1766."

22. *Recopilación de leyes de los reynos de las Indias*, 5: 338–41.

23. A more detailed discussion of these provisions may be found in Loveman, *For la Patria*.

24. Article 288 of the "liberal" Constitution of 1812 declared that if "there is resistance [to arrest] or flight [*la fuga*] is feared, force may be used to secure [*asegurar*] the person." This language constitutionalized the practice of "shot while attempting to escape."

25. Quoted in Ministerio de Defensa Nacional, El Salvador, *Doctrina militar y relaciones*.

26. *Ordenanza para el rejimen, disciplina, subordinación*.

27. The translation does not entirely capture the sense of the Spanish: "Las órdenes del superior deben cumplirse, por sus subordinados, sin vacilación, sin murmurar y sin hacer observación ni reclamo alguno, aun cuando hubiere lugar á una ú otro, hasta después de haberlas cumplido" (Guatemala, *Código Militar de la República de Guatemala*, 1 August 1878, 2d ed. [Guatemala: Tipografía Nacional, 1898], 28).

28. Ibid., 28–29, Section 2a. Disobedience during active duty but not involving "in campaign or during war" brought lighter sentences: one to two years of prison and forced labor in public works projects (Article 71).

29. An important exception was the Ordenanza del Ejército de El Salvador (1934), which included almost the same language as the Guatemalan code referred to in the text but with an important addition, italicized here for emphasis: "Las órdenes *legales* del superior deben cumplirse por los subordinados sin hacer observación ni reclamación alguna, sin vacilación y sin murmurar; pero *podrán reclamar si hubiera lugar a ello, después de haberlas cumplido*" (Article 9). Thus, in this Salvadoran code, the possibility of "objecting" to "illegal orders" is recognized. Although the language that follows this section is ambiguous, it appears that if the superior provides *written orders*, the subordinate must nevertheless obey, having thereby eliminated his own responsibility, thus reaffirming the notion of "due obedience" as a proper defense. See Ministerio de la Defensa Nacional, *Doctrina militar y relaciones*, 58–62.

30. Thus Deborah Norden relates that in April 1986 the Argentine defense minister, Germán López, "directed an order to the Consejo Supremo to speed up the trials [of military personnel] and to expand the application of the due obedience clause in the Military Code of Justice." A public uproar caused the minister's resignation, but in December 1986, "the legislature passed the Punto Final [End Point] law, according to which any human rights cases not yet under consideration would have to be initiated within sixty days." When the courts accelerated their work and more military personnel were charged with human rights violations, a military uprising occurred in April 1987. Then, in early June, "the administration had succeeded in convincing Congress to pass an *Obediencia Debida* [Due Obedience] law, which effectively reiterated and ex-

panded the assumptions of the due obedience clause included in the reform of the Military Code of Justice [in 1987]" (*Military Rebellion in Argentina*, 103–4).

31. See McAlister, *"Fuero Militar."*

32. Kuethe, *Military Reform and Society*, 38.

33. This issue is discussed in more detail in Loveman, *Constitution of Tyranny*. An illustrative example is the Mexican case, where the liberal Constitution of 1857 prohibited military officers from exercising civil authority in times of peace (Article 122) and limited the jurisdiction of military courts to cases involving military discipline (Article 13). Military *fueros* were also eliminated in the Venezuelan Constitution of 1830, which prohibited trial of civilians by military tribunals (Article 219). In other cases, such as Chile, Peru, Colombia, and Guatemala, military jurisdiction over civilians remained extensive to the end of the twentieth century. In Guatemala, constitutional reforms in the 1990s finally emulated the Mexican example, severely restricting the jurisdiction of military tribunals over civilians.

34. Spain's *Código de Justicia Militar* assigned to military tribunals jurisdiction over cases in which military personnel or civilians "openly or covertly" defamed or offended the army or navy: "Los que de palabra ó escrito, por medio de la imprenta, grabado ú otro medio mecánico de publicación, en estampas, alegorías, caricaturas, emblemas, ó alusiones, injurien ú ofendan clara ó encubiertamente al Ejército ó á la Armada ó á instituciones, armas, clases ó cuerpos determinados del mismo, serán castigados con la pena de prisión correcional."

35. In many cases more specialized "antiterrorism laws," "arms control laws," and "national security laws" specifically established military jurisdiction over civilians for "political crimes." In other cases the Military Code of Justice has already established military jurisdiction in cases of rebellion, sedition, and related crimes. See, for extensive treatment of these issues, del Barrio Reyna and León Reyes, *Terrorismo, ley antiterrorista*.

36. See Leal Buitrago, *El oficio de la guerra*, 87–90.

37. García-Gallo, *Los orígenes de la administración territorial*, 982.

38. Scarlett O'Phelan Godoy lists more than eighty revolts from 1763 to 1783 in *Un siglo de rebeliones anticoloniales*.

39. For a detailed account of these movements, see Lynch, *Spanish American Revolutions*.

40. See Lynch, *Caudillos in Spanish America*.

41. For a more detailed discussion of this period, including the various international wars and the domestic conflicts, see Loveman, *For la Patria*, chap. 2.

42. Johnson, *Military and Society*, 37.

43. Solís, *Deontología militar*, 37.

44. Morán, *Función política del ejército*.

45. See http://www.ejército.mil.ve/ejehisto.htm; http://www.ejército.cl/bienvenda/bienvenda.html; and http://www.ejercito.gub.uy/muestra/cge/dptoeehh/reshst.htm. These sites were active on 31 December 1998. Similar sites and messages could be found for Brazil, Peru, Guatemala, Colombia, and Ecuador.

46. Villanueva, *Ejército peruano*, 66–67.

47. Solís, *Deontología militar*, 51.

48. In the Mexican case, for example, the independence movement took as one of its slogans *religión y fueros*, a response to the liberal government in Spain from 1820 to 1823. The struggle to abolish military and religious *fueros* was an important subtext to Mexican history from independence until the Ley Juárez and the 1857 Constitution. In Colombia, the Santander regime sought to dilute the military *fueros*, and in Venezuela, where the *fueros* were abolished, the "Revolution of the Reformists" (1837) sought to restore them.

49. The evolution and use of regimes of exception in Spanish American politics is the subject of Loveman, *Constitution of Tyranny*.

50. Quoted in Hodges, *Argentina's "Dirty War*," 125.

51. This interpretation was reaffirmed in the navy's response to the Rettig Commission in 1991: "Informe presentado ante el Consejo Nacional de Seguridad por el Comandante en Jefe de la Armada de Chile, Almirante Jorge Martínez Busch," 27 March 1991.

52. The Latin American penal codes relied on European models, particularly those of Spain, France, Belgium, and Germany. Laws to protect "internal security" were common in Europe and were emulated as the Latin American countries replaced or modified Spanish colonial criminal law.

53. "Código Penal de la República Argentina."

54. *Código Penal de la República de Chile*.

55. Interestingly, there were also provisions penalizing government officials who illegally banished, detained, or arrested citizens; held prisoners "incomunicado" or applied torture to prisoners; or "exercised judicial functions" and applied corporal or other punishment without proper judicial orders (*Código Penal de la República de Chile*, Articles 148–52).

56. Quoted in Leal Buitrago, *El oficio de la guerra*, 55.

57. Quoted in Johnson, *Algunas de las razones del quiebre*.

58. Nunn, *Yesterday's Soldiers*; Maldonado and Quiroga, *El prusianismo en las fuerzas armadas chilenas*; Masterson, *Militarism and Politics in Latin America*, chap. 1; Cobas, *Fuerza armada, misiones militares y dependencia*.

59. Nunn, *Yesterday's Soldiers*, has dealt with these issues in great detail; they are summarized here based largely on Nunn's research.

60. Cited in ibid., 83.

61. Horne, *French Army and Politics*, 27.

62. Kitchen, *German Officer Corps*, xx.

63. Masterson, *Militarism and Politics in Latin America*, 29.

64. Stepan, *Rethinking Military Politics*, 93.

65. This chapter does not address the period 1920–99. But obviously the state of civil-military relations in Latin America in 1999 is not simply the result of the colonial and nineteenth-century patterns discussed here. For an "update," see Loveman, *For la Patria*.

Bibliography

Abelson, Robert. "Beliefs Are Like Possessions." *Journal for the Theory of Social Behavior* 16 (1986): 233–50.

Abrahamsson, Bengt. *Military Professionalization and Political Power.* Beverly Hills: Sage Publications, 1972.

Acuña, Carlos, and Catalina Smúlovitz. "Militares en la transición Argentina: Del gobierno a la subordinación constitucional." In *La Nueva matriz política Argentina*, edited by Carlos Acuña, 153–202. Buenos Aires: Ediciones Nueva Visión, 1995.

Agüero, Felipe. "Debilitating Democracy: Political Elites and Military Rebels." In *Lessons of the Venezuelan Experience*, edited by Louis Goodman et al., 136–62. Washington, D.C.: Woodrow Wilson Center Press, 1995.

——. "Las fuerzas armadas y el debilitamiento de la democracia en Venezuela." In *Venezuela: La democracia bajo presión*, edited by Andrés Serbín et al., 187–203. Caracas: INVESP and North-South Center, 1993.

——. "Legacies of Transitions: Institutionalism, the Military, and Democracy in South America." *Mershon International Studies Review* 42 (November 1998): 383–404.

——. "The Military and Democracy in Venezuela." In *The Military and Democracy*, edited by Louis Goodman, Joanna Mendelson, and Juan Rial, 257–75. Lexington, Mass.: Lexington Books, 1990.

——. *Soldiers, Civilians, and Democracy: Post-Franco Spain in Comparative Perspective.* Baltimore: Johns Hopkins University Press, 1995.

Almeida Nieto, Galo. "La guerra revolucionaria." *Revista de las Fuerzas Armadas Ecuatorianas* (July 1985): 88–91.

Alonso, José Ramón. *Historia política del ejército español.* Madrid: Editora Nacional, 1974.

Alvarez Calderón, César. "El militar, educador y técnico al servicio de la Patria y la humanidad." *Revista de las Fuerzas Armadas Ecuatorianas* (February 1984): 20–22.

Anderson, Benedict. *Imagined Communities: Reflections on the Origin and Spread of Nationalism.* London: Verso, 1983.

Anderson, Thomas P. *War of the Dispossessed.* Lincoln: University of Nebraska Press, 1981.

Angell, Alan. "The Soldier as Politician: Military Authoritarianism in Latin America." In *Comparative Government and Politics: Essays in Honour of S. E. Finer*, edited by Dennis Kavanaugh and Gillian Peele, 116–43. Boulder: Westview Press, 1984.

Aninat, Eduardo. "Chile en las noventa: Las oportunidades del desarrollo." *Finanzas y Desarrollo* (March 2000): 19–21.

Armstrong, Robert, and Janet Shenk. *El Salvador: The Face of Revolution.* London: Pluto Press, 1982.

Arriagada, Genaro. *Pinochet: The Politics of Power.* Boulder: Westview Press, 1991.

——. *Por la razón o por la fuerza.* Santiago: Editorial Sudamericana Chilena, 1998.

Arrow, Kenneth J. *Social Choice and Individual Values.* New Haven: Yale University Press, 1951.

Arteaga, Domingo. "Los empresarios y el MERCOSUR." In *Chile-Mercosur: Una alianza estratégica*, edited by Paz Milet, Gabriel Gaspar, and Francisco A. Rojas, 165–71. Santiago: Editorial Los Andes, 1997.

Barros, Robert. *Law and Dictatorship: Military Constitutionalism and the Pinochet Regime in Chile, 1973–1989*. Cambridge: Cambridge University Press, forthcoming.

Bates, Robert H. "Area Studies and the Discipline: A Useful Controversy?" *PS: Political Science and Politics* 30 (June 1997): 167–69.

Bates, Robert H., Rui J. P. de Figueiredo Jr., and Barry R. Weingast. "The Politics of Interpretation: Rationality, Culture, and Transition." *Politics and Society* 26 (December 1998): 603–42.

Belkin, Aaron. "Domestic Survival and International Conflict: The Relationship between Coup d'Etat and War." Ph.D. diss., University of California, Berkeley, 1997.

Berman, Sheri. "Ideas, Norms, and Culture in Political Analysis." Unpublished ms., Princeton University, 1999.

Bernal Castro, José. "Argentine Nuclear Development." In *Averting a Latin American Nuclear Arms Race*, edited by Paul L. Leventhal and Sharon Tanzer, 96–110. New York: St. Martin's Press, 1992.

Bruszt, László, and David Stark. "Remaking the Political Field in Hungary: From the Politics of Confrontation to the Politics of Competition." In *Eastern Europe in Revolution*, edited by Ivo Banac, 13–55. Ithaca: Cornell University Press, 1992.

Brzezinski, Zbigniew, and Samuel Huntington. *Poder Político U.S.A.-U.R.S.S.* Vol. 2. Madrid: Ediciones Guadarrama, 1970.

Brzoska, Michael, and Frederic S. Pearson. *Arms and Warfare*. Columbia: University of South Carolina Press, 1994.

Bueno de Mesquita, Bruce, Randolph M. Siverson, and Gary Woller. "War and the Fate of Regimes: A Comparative Analysis." *American Political Science Review* 86 (September 1992): 638–46.

Burggraff, Winfield. *The Venezuelan Armed Forces in Politics, 1935–1959*. Columbia: University of Missouri Press, 1972.

Burggraff, Winfield, and Richard Millett. "More than Failed Coups: The Crisis in Venezuelan Civil-Military Relations." In *Lessons of the Venezuelan Experience*, edited by Louis Goodman et al., 54–78. Washington, D.C.: Woodrow Wilson Center Press, 1995.

Cammack, Paul. "The New Institutionalism: Predatory Rule, Institutional Persistence, and Macro-Social Change." *Economy and Society* 21 (November 1992): 397–429.

Camps, Ramón. "La subversión." *Revista de la Escuela Superior de Guerra* 443 (July–August 1979): 41–46.

Caro, Isaac. "Políticas de cooperación para la paz en Chile." Unpublished ms., Facultad Latinoamericana de Ciencias Sociales, 1992.

Carrillo, Cristóbal. "La guerrilla y los derechos humanos." *Revista de las Fuerzas Armadas Ecuatorianas* (October 1983): 41–47.

Catterberg, Edgardo. *Argentina Confronts Politics: Political Culture and Public Opinion in the Argentine Transition to Democracy*. Boulder: Lynne Rienner, 1991.

Child, Jack. "Guns and Roses." *Hemisphere* 6 (March 1995): 28–32.

Clausewitz, Carl von. *On War*. Edited and translated by Michael Howard and Peter Paret. Princeton: Princeton University Press, 1976.

Cobas, Efraín. *Fuerza armada, misiones militares y dependencia en el Peru*. Lima: Editorial Horizonte, 1982.

Código de Justicia Militar. Madrid: Talleres del Depósito de la Guerra, 1906.

"Código penal de la República Argentina." In *Códigos y leyes usuales de la República Argentina*, edited by Felix Lajouane, 184–93. Buenos Aires, 1988.

Collier, Ruth Berins, and David Collier. *Shaping the Political Arena*. Princeton: Princeton University Press, 1991.

Colton, Timothy J. *Commissars, Commanders, and Civilian Authority: The Structure of Soviet Military Politics*. Cambridge: Harvard University Press, 1979.

Congreso Nacional, República de Venezuela. *Constitución de la República de Venezuela*. Gaceta Oficial, no. 662. Extraordinario, January 1961.

———. *Ley Orgánica de las fuerzas armadas nacionales*. Gaceta Oficial, no. 3256. 26 September 1983.

Corrales, Javier. "Why Argentines Followed Cavallo: A Technopol between Democracy and Economic Reform." In *Technopols: Freeing Politics and Markets in Latin America in the 1990s*, edited by Jorge I. Dominguez, 49–93. University Park: Pennsylvania State University, 1997.

Crow, John A. *Spain: The Root and the Flower*. Berkeley: University of California Press, 1985.

Cruz, Consuelo, and Rut Diamint. "The New Military Autonomy in Latin America." *Journal of Democracy* 9 (October 1998): 115–27.

Danopoulos, Constantine P. *From Military to Civilian Rule*. New York: Routledge, 1992.

Decalo, Samuel. *Coups and Army Rule in Africa: Studies in Military Style*. New Haven: Yale University Press, 1976.

Degregori, Carlos Iván, and Carlos Rivera. *Perú 1980–1993: Fuerzas armadas, subversión y democracia*. Lima: Instituto de Estudios Peruanos, 1993.

del Barrio Reyna, Alvaro, and José Julio León Reyes. *Terrorismo, ley antiterrorista y derechos humanos*. Santiago: Universidad Académica de Humanismo Cristiano, 1991.

Desch, Michael. "Soldiers, States and Structure: The End of the Cold War and the Weakening of U.S. Civilian Control." Paper prepared for "A Crisis in Civilian Control? Contending Theories of Civil-Military Relations," Olin Institute Conference, 11–12 June 1996.

Diamint, Rut. "Cambios en la política de seguridad: Argentina en busca de un perfil no conflictivo." *Fuerzas Armadas y Sociedad* 7 (January–March 1992): 1–16.

———, ed. *Argentina y la seguridad internacional*. Santiago, Chile: FLASCO, 1998.

———. "Responsables ante la defensa." In *Argentina y la seguridad internacional*, edited by Rut Diamint, 13–14. Santiago, Chile: FLASCO, 1998.

Diamond, Larry. "Is the Third Wave Over?" *Journal of Democracy* 7 (July 1996): 26.

Diamond, Larry, and Marc F. Plattner. *Civil-Military Relations and Democracy*. Baltimore: Johns Hopkins University Press, 1996.

Díaz Albónico, Rodrigo, ed. *El tratado de paz y amistad entre Chile y Argentina*. Santiago: Editorial Universitaria, 1987.

Di Palma, Giuseppe. "Italy: Is There a Legacy and Is It Fascist?" In *From Dictatorship to Democracy*, edited by John H. Herz, 107–34. Westport: Greenwood Press, 1982.

Djiwandono, J. Soedjati. "Civil-Military Relations in Indonesia: The Case of ABRI's Dual Function." In *Civil-Military Relations: Building Regional Security and Democracy in Latin America, Southern Asia, and Central Europe*, edited by David R. Mares, 45–58. Boulder: Westview Press, 1988.

Dominguez, Jorge I. *Cuba: Order and Revolution*. Cambridge: Harvard University Press, 1978.

———. "Samuel Huntington's *Political Order* and the Latin American State." Paper presented to the Latin American Studies Association, Guadalajara, 17–19 April 1997.

Donoso, Juan Francisco. "A propósito de desarrollo, seguridad, y presupuestos." *Revista de las Fuerzas Armadas Ecuatorianas* (February 1991): 7–9.

Druetta, Gustavo. "Diputados y defensa: Radiografía de un poder tenue." In *Defensa y democracia: Un diálogo entre civiles y militares*, edited by Ernesto López et al., 196–239. Buenos Aires: Punto Sur, 1990.

Dunkerley, James. *The Long War*. London: Junction Books, 1982.

Durham, William H. *Scarcity and Survival in Central America: Ecological Origins of the Soccer War*. Stanford: Stanford University Press, 1979.

Eckstein, Harry. "A Culturalist Theory of Political Change." *American Political Science Review* 82 (September 1988): 789–804.

"Editorial." *Revista de las Fuerzas Armadas Ecuatorianas* (February 1984): 4–7.

"Editorial: Afirmación de la conciencia institucional." *Revista de las Fuerzas Armadas Ecuatorianas* (October 1979): 7–8.

Edmonds, Martin. *Central Organizations of Defense*. Boulder: Westview Press, 1985.

——. "Central Organizations of Defense in Great Britain." In *Central Organizations of Defense*, edited by Martin Edmonds, 85–107. Boulder: Westview Press, 1985.

Elster, Jon. *Ulysses and the Sirens: Studies in Rationality and Irrationality*. Cambridge: Cambridge University Press, 1979.

Escudé, Carlos. *Foreign Policy Theory in Menem's Argentina*. Gainesville: University Press of Florida, 1997.

——. *Realismo Periférico: Fundamentos para la nueva política exterior Argentina*. Buenos Aires: Planeta, 1992.

Escudé, Carlos, and Andrés Fontana. "Argentina's Security Policies: Their Rationale and Regional Context." In *International Security and Democracy*, edited by Jorge I. Dominguez, 51–79. Pittsburgh: University of Pittsburgh Press, 1998.

Etzioni-Halevy, Eva. "Civil-Military Relations and Democracy: The Case of the Military-Political Elite's Connection in Israel." *Armed Forces and Society* 22 (Spring 1996): 401–17.

Evans, Peter, Dietrich Rueschmeyer, and Theda Skocpol, eds. *Bringing the State Back In*. Cambridge: Cambridge University Press, 1985.

Farcau, Bruce. *The Transition to Democracy in Latin America*. Westport: Praeger, 1996.

Feaver, Peter. "Crisis as Shirking: An Agency Theory Explanation of the Souring of American Civil-Military Relations." *Armed Forces and Society* 24 (Spring 1998): 407–34.

——. "Delegation, Monitoring and Civilian Control of the Military: Agency Theory and American Civil-Military Relations." "U.S. Post Cold-War Civil Military Relations," working paper no. 4, John M. Olin Institute, 1996.

Fernandez, Pedro Javier. *Código penal de la República de Chile*. Santiago: Imprenta, Litografiai Encuadernación Barcelona, 1899.

Finer, S. E. *The Man on Horseback: The Role of the Military in Politics*. Boulder: Westview Press, 1988.

——. "The Retreat to the Barracks: Notes on the Practice and the Theory of Military Withdrawal from the Seats of Power." *Third World Quarterly* 7 (January 1981): 16–30.

Fitch, J. Samuel. *The Armed Forces and Democracy in Latin America*. Baltimore: Johns Hopkins University Press, 1998.

——. "The Armed Forces and the Politics of Democratic Consolidation in South America." In *Latin America and Caribbean Contemporary Record, 1986–87*, edited by Abraham Lowenthal, A17–A33. New York: Holmes and Meier, 1988.

——. "Armies and Politics in Latin America, 1975–1985." In *Armies and Politics in Latin America*, edited by Abraham F. Lowenthal and J. Samuel Fitch, 26–55. New York: Holmes and Meier, 1986.

——. *The Military Coup d'Etat as a Political Process: Ecuador, 1948–1966*. Baltimore: Johns Hopkins University Press, 1977.

——. "More on the Military in Politics." *Latin American Research Review* 12, no. 3 (1977): 203–7.

——. "The Theoretical Model Underlying the Analysis of Civil-Military Relations in

Contemporary Latin American Democracies: Core Assumptions." Interamerican Dialogue, 1987.

Fleischer, David. "The Cardoso Second Term Cabinet." *Brazil Focus* (January 1999), special report.

Flores, Leopoldo. "Intervención militar en política." *Revista de la Escuela Superior de Guerra* 469 (1983): 91–112.

Fontana, Andrés. "Percepciones militares acerca del rol de las Fuerzas Armadas en Argentina." Working paper, Fundación Simón Rodríguez, Buenos Aires, May 1993.

Franko, Patrice. "De Facto Demilitarization: Budget-Driven Downsizing in Latin America." *Journal of Interamerican Studies and World Affairs* 36 (Spring 1994): 37–73.

Frazer, Jendayi E. "Sustaining Civilian Control: Armed Counterweights in Regime Stability in Africa." Ph.D. diss., Stanford University, 1994.

Friedman, Jeffrey, ed. *The Rational Choice Controversy: Economic Models of Politics Reconsidered.* New Haven: Yale University Press, 1996.

Fuentes, Claudio, and Carlos Martin. *La nueva agenda argentino-chilena.* Santiago, Chile: FLASCO, 1998.

Fuentes, Claudio, and Gonzalo Mizala. "Chile-Argentina después de Marzo de 1990: Hacia la cooperación o el conflicto." *Fuerzas Armadas y Sociedad* 7 (July–September 1992): 3–17.

García Gallo, Alfonso. *Los origenes de la administración territorial de las Indias.* Madrid: Rivadeneyra, 1944.

———. *Los origenes españoles de las instituciones americanas.* Estudios de Derecho Indiano. Madrid: Rivadeneyra, 1966.

Geddes, Barbara. "Paradigms and Sand Castles in Comparative Politics of Developing Areas." In *Political Science: Looking to the Future*, vol. 2, edited by William Crotty, 45–75. Evanston: Northwestern University Press, 1991.

———. *Politician's Dilemma: Building State Capacity in Latin America.* Berkeley: University of California Press, 1994.

———. "Uses and Limitations of Rational Choice." In *Latin America in Comparative Perspective: New Approaches to Methods and Analysis*, edited by Peter H. Smith, 81–108. Boulder: Westview Press, 1995.

Geertz, Clifford. *The Interpretation of Cultures.* New York: Basic Books, 1973.

Gillespie, Charles. "Uruguay's Transition from Collegial Military-Technocratic Rule." In *Transitions from Authoritarian Rule: Latin America*, edited by Guillermo O'Donnell, Philippe C. Schmitter, and Laurence Whitehead, 173–95. Baltimore: Johns Hopkins University Press, 1986.

Gil Yepes, José Antonio. "Political Articulation of the Military Sector in Venezuelan Democracy." In *Venezuela: The Democratic Experience*, edited by John Martz and David Myers, 148–82. New York: Praeger, 1986.

Godoy, Scarlett O'Phelan. *Un siglo de rebeliones anticoloniales, Peru y Bolivia, 1700–1783.* Cusco: Centro de Estudios Rurales Andinos Bartólome de las Casas, 1988.

Gonzalez Fraga, Javier A. "Argentine Privatization in Retrospect." In *Privatization of Public Enterprises in Latin America*, edited by William Glade, 75–98. San Francisco: Institute for Contemporary Studies, 1991.

Goodman, Louis W., Johanna S. R. Mendelson, and Juan Rial, eds. *The Military and Democracy: The Future of Civil-Military Relations in Latin America.* Lexington, Mass.: Lexington Books, 1990.

Gordon, Dennis. "Withdrawal in Disgrace: The Decline of the Argentine Military, 1976–1983." In *The Decline of Military Regimes*, edited by Constantine Danopoulos, 199–224. Boulder: Westview Press, 1988.

Gowa, Joanne. *Allies, Adversaries, and International Trade.* Princeton: Princeton University Press, 1994.

Green, Donald P., and Ian Shapiro. *Pathologies of Rational Choice Theory: A Critique of Applications in Political Science.* New Haven: Yale University Press, 1994.

Grunwald, Joseph, Miguel S. Wionczek, and Martin Carnoy. *Latin American Economic Integration and U.S. Policy.* Washington, D.C.: Brookings, 1972.

Guedes da Costa, Thomaz. "Democratization and International Integration: The Role of the Armed Forces in Brazil's Grand Strategy." In *Civil-Military Relations: Building Regional Security and Democracy in Latin America, Southern Asia and Central Europe,* edited by David R. Mares, 223–37. Boulder: Westview Press, 1998.

"Guerrilla y delincuencia." *Revista de las Fuerzas Armadas Ecuatorianas* (February 1987): 56–61.

Gurr, Ted Robert, et al. *Polity II: Political Structures and Regime Change, 1800–1986.* Ann Arbor: Inter-University Consortium for Political and Social Research, University of Michigan, 1990.

Hachette, Dominique, and Rolf Luders. *Privatization in Chile: An Economic Appraisal.* San Francisco: Institute for Contemporary Studies, 1993.

Haggard, Stephan, and Robert Kaufman. *The Political Economy of Democratic Transitions.* Princeton: Princeton University Press, 1995.

——. "The Political Economy of Inflation and Stabilization in Middle Income Countries." In *Politics of Economic Adjustment,* edited by Stephen Haggard and Robert Kaufman, 270–313. Princeton: Princeton University Press, 1992.

Hagopian, Frances. " 'Democracy by Undemocratic Means'? Elites, Political Pacts, and Regime Transition in Brazil." *Comparative Political Studies* 23 (July 1990): 147–70.

——. Review of *Comparative Politics: Rationality, Culture, and Structure,* edited by Mark Irving Lichbach and Alan S. Zuckerman. *Comparative Political Studies* 31 (October 1998): 662–73.

Hall, Peter A., and Rosemary C. R. Taylor. "Political Science and the Three New Institutionalisms." *Political Studies* 44 (1996): 936–57.

Hamilton, Alexander, James Madison, and John Jay. *El Federalista.* Mexico City: Fondo de Cultura Económica, 1998.

Hargreaves-Mawdsley, W. N. *Eighteenth Century Spain, 1700–1788: A Political, Diplomatic and Institutional History.* London: Macmillan, 1979.

Haring, Clarence H. *The Spanish Empire in America.* New York: Oxford University Press, 1947.

Hartlyn, Jonathan. "Military Governments and the Transition to Civilian Rule: The Colombian Experience, 1957–1958." *Journal of Interamerican Studies and World Affairs* 26 (May 1984): 245–81.

Hernández Cajiao, Colonel Marco. "Disciplina y 'obediencia pasiva.' " *Revista de las Fuerzas Armadas Ecuatorianas* (October 1986): 27–32.

Hinostroza, Darío. "Subversión comunista: Sicopolita drogas terrorismo." *Revista de las Fuerzas Armadas Ecuatorianas* (February 1984): 86–96.

Hirschman, Albert. *Exit, Voice and Loyalty: Responses to Decline in Firms, Organizations and States.* Cambridge: Harvard University Press, 1970.

Hodges, Donald. *Argentina's "Dirty War": An Intellectual Biography.* Austin: University of Texas Press, 1991.

Horne, Alistar. *The French Army and Politics, 1870–1970.* London: Macmillan, 1984.

Hunter, Wendy. "Assessing Military Power and Privilege in Present-Day Latin America." Paper presented to the Latin American Studies Association, Chicago, 24–26 September 1998.

——. *Eroding Military Influence in Brazil: Politicians against Soldiers.* Chapel Hill: University of North Carolina Press, 1997.

——. "Negotiating Civil-Military Relations in Post-Authoritarian Argentina and Chile." *International Studies Quarterly* 42 (1998): 295–318.

——. "Reason, Culture, or Structure: Assessing Civil-Military Dynamics in Latin America." Paper presented to the conference "Soldiers and Democracy in Latin America," Riverside, California, 20 February 1999.

——. *State and Soldier in Latin America: Redefining the Military's Role in Argentina, Brazil, and Chile.* Washington, D.C.: United States Institute of Peace, 1996.

Huntington, Samuel P. *Political Order in Changing Societies.* New Haven: Yale University Press, 1968.

——. *El soldado y el estado.* Buenos Aires: Biblioteca del Oficial del Círculo Militar Argentino, 1964.

——. *The Soldier and the State: The Theory and Politics of Civil-Military Relations.* Cambridge: Harvard University Press, 1957.

Iazzetta, Osvaldo M. "Capacidades técnicas y de gobierno en las privatizaciones de Menem y Collor de Mello." *Desarrollo Económico* 37 (July–September 1997): 263–85.

Immergut, Ellen M. "The Rules of the Game: The Logic of Health Policy-Making in France, Switzerland, and Sweden." In *Structuring Politics: Institutionalism in Comparative Analysis,* edited by Sven Steinmo, Kathleen Thelen, and Frank Longstreth, 57–89. Cambridge: Cambridge University Press, 1992.

Inglehart, Ronald. *Modernization and Postmodernization: Cultural, Economic, and Political Change in 43 Societies.* Princeton: Princeton University Press, 1997.

International Monetary Fund. *Direction of Trade.* Washington, D.C.: International Monetary Fund, 1951–70.

Janowitz, Morris. *The Professional Soldier.* New York: Free Press, 1971.

Johnson, Carlos Molina. *Algunas de las razones del quiebre de la institucionalidad política.* Santiago: Estado Mayor del Ejército, 1987.

Johnson, Chalmers. "Preconception vs. Observation, or the Contributions of Rational Choice Theory and Area Studies to Contemporary Political Science." *PS: Political Science and Politics* 30 (June 1997): 170–74.

Johnson, John. *The Military and Society in Latin America.* Stanford: Stanford University Press, 1964.

Jowitt, Kenneth. "Moscow 'Center.'" *Eastern European Politics and Society* 1 (1987): 348–96.

Karl, Terry Lynn. "Dilemmas of Democratization in Latin America." *Comparative Politics* 23 (October 1990): 1–21.

——. "Petroleum and Political Pacts: The Transition to Democracy in Venezuela." In *Transitions from Authoritarian Rule: Latin America,* edited by Guillermo O'Donnell, Philippe Schmitter, and Lawrence Whitehead, 196–219. Baltimore: Johns Hopkins University Press, 1986.

Kebschull, Harvey G. "Operation 'Just Missed': Lessons from Failed Coup Attempts." *Armed Forces and Society* 20 (Summer 1994): 565–79.

Kelly, Philip, and Jack Child, eds. *Geopolitics of the Southern Cone and Antarctica.* Boulder: Lynne Rienner, 1988.

Kier, Elizabeth, and Jonathan Mercer. "Setting Precedents in Anarchy: Military Interventions and Weapons of Mass Destruction." *International Security* 20 (Spring 1996): 77–106.

Kiewiet, Roderick D., and Mathew D. McCubbins. *The Logic of Delegation: Congressional Parties and the Appropriations Process.* Chicago: University of Chicago Press, 1991.

Kitchen, Matin. *The German Officer Corps, 1890–1914.* Oxford: Clarendon Press, 1968.

Krasner, Stephen. "Approaches to the State: Alternative Conceptions and Historical Dynamics." *Comparative Politics* 16 (1984): 223–46.

——. "Sovereignty: An Institutional Perspective." In *The Elusive State: International and Comparative Perspectives*, edited by James A. Caporaso, 69–96. Newbury Park, Calif.: Sage Publications, 1989.

Krujit, Dirk. "Peru: The State under Siege." In *Beyond Praetorianism: The Latin American Military in Transition*, edited by Richard Millett and Michael Gold-Biss, 261–89. Miami: North-South Center Press, 1996.

Kuethe, Allan. *Military Reform and Society in New Granada, 1773–1808*. Gainesville: University Press of Florida, 1978.

Lambert, Jacques. *Latin America, Social Structures and Political Institutions*. Translated by Helen Katel. Berkeley: University of California Press, 1971.

Lamounier, Bolívar. "Brazil: The Hyperactive Paralysis Syndrome." In *Constructing Democratic Governance: Latin America and the Caribbean in the 1990s*, edited by Abraham F. Lowenthal and Jorge I. Domínguez, 166–87. Baltimore: Johns Hopkins University Press, 1996.

Lasswell, Harold. *Power and Society*. New Haven: Yale University Press, 1950.

Leal Buitrago, Francisco. *El oficio de la guerra, la seguridad nacional en Colombia*. Bogotá: Tercer Mundos Editores, 1994.

Legislación Argentina. Decree 15, 10 December 1983. Vol. B, Ediciones Jurisprudencia, 1926–27.

Levi, Margaret. "A Model, a Method, and a Map: Rational Choice in Comparative and Historical Analysis." In *Comparative Politics: Rationality, Culture, and Structure*, edited by Mark Irving Lichbach and Alan S. Zuckerman, 19–41. Cambridge: Cambridge University Press, 1997.

Lezcano, Carlos María. "El régimen militar de Alfredo Sroessner, fuerzas armadas y política en el Paraguay (1954–1989)." Working paper no. 1, Grupo de Ciencias Sociales, Asunción, Paraguay, 1989.

Lichbach, Mark Irving. "Social Theory and Comparative Politics." In *Comparative Politics: Rationality, Culture, and Structure*, edited by Mark Irving Lichbach and Alan S. Zuckerman, 239–76. Cambridge: Cambridge University Press, 1997.

Lichbach, Mark I., and Alan S. Zuckerman, eds. *Comparative Politics: Rationality, Culture, and Structure*. Cambridge: Cambridge University Press, 1997.

Linz, Juan J. "An Authoritarian Regime: Spain." In *Mass Politics*, edited by Erik Allardt and Stein Rokkan, 251–83. New York: Free Press, 1970.

——. *The Breakdown of Democratic Regimes: Crisis, Breakdown and Reequilibration*. Baltimore: Johns Hopkins University Press, 1978.

——. "Il Fattore tempo nei mutamenti di regime." *Teoría Política* 2 (1986).

——. "The Future of an Authoritarian Situation or the Institutionalization of an Authoritarian Regime." In *Authoritarian Brazil: Origins, Policies, and Future*, edited by Alfred Stepan, 233–54. New Haven: Yale University Press, 1973.

——. "Totalitarian and Authoritarian Regimes." In *Handbook of Political Science*, edited by Fred Greenstein and Nelson Polsby, 175–411. Reading, Mass.: Addison-Wesley, 1975.

Linz, Juan J., and Alfred Stepan. "Political Crafting of Democratic Consolidation or Destruction: European and South American Comparisons." In *Democracy in the Americas: Stopping the Pendulum*, edited by Robert A. Pastor, 42–48. New York: Holmes and Meier, 1989.

——. "Political Identities and Electoral Sequences: Spain, the Soviet Union and Yugoslavia." *Daedalus* 121 (Spring 1992): 123–39.

——. *Problems of Democratic Transition and Consolidation*. Baltimore: Johns Hopkins University Press, 1996.

Little, Ian, Tibor Scitovsky, and Maurice Scott. *Industry and Trade in Some Developing Countries*. London: Oxford University Press, 1970.

López, Ernesto. "Argentina 1991: Las nuevas oportunidades para el control civil." In *Democracia y cuestión militar*, edited by E. López and David-Pion Berlin, 147–202. Buenos Aires: Editorial de la Universidad Nacional de Quilmes, 1996.

——. *Ni la ceniza ni la gloria: Actores, sistema político y cuestión militar en los años de Alfonsín*. Buenos Aires: Editorial de la Universidad Nacional de Quilmes, 1994.

López, Ernesto, et al., eds. *Defensa y democracia: Un debate entre civiles y militares*. Buenos Aires: Pintosur, 1990.

Lopez, George. "National Security Ideology as an Impetus to State Violence and State Terror." In *Government Violence and Repression*, edited by Michael Stohl and George Lopez, 73–95. New York: Greenwood Press, 1986.

Loveman, Brian. *The Constitution of Tyranny*. Pittsburgh: University of Pittsburgh Press, 1993.

——. *For la Patria: Politics and the Armed Forces in Latin America*. Wilmington, Del.: Scholarly Resources, 1999.

——. "Latin American Civil Military Relations in the 1990s: The Armed Forces and the 'Democratization' Fad." Paper presented at the Latin American Studies Association, Chicago, 24–26 September 1998.

——. " 'Protected Democracies' and Military Guardianship: Political Transitions in Latin America, 1978–1993." *Journal of Interamerican Studies and World Affairs* 36 (1994): 105–89.

Loveman, Brian, and Thomas M. Davies Jr. *The Politics of Anti-Politics: The Military in Latin America*. Lincoln: University of Nebraska Press, 1989.

Lowenthal, Abraham F. "Armies and Politics in Latin America: Introduction to the First Edition." In *Armies and Politics in Latin America*, edited by Abraham F. Lowenthal and J. Samuel Fitch, 3–25. New York: Holmes and Meier, 1986.

——, ed. *Exporting Democracy: The United States and Latin America*. Baltimore: Johns Hopkins University Press, 1991.

Lowenthal, Abraham F., and J. Samuel Fitch. *Armies and Politics in Latin America*. Rev. 2d ed. New York: Holmes and Meier, 1986.

Lustick, Ian. "History, Historiograph, and Political Science: Multiple Historical Records and the Problem of Selection Bias." *American Political Science Review* 90 (1996): 605–18.

Luttwack, Edward. *Coup d'Etat: A Practical Handbook*. Cambridge: Harvard University Press, 1968.

Lynch, John. *Caudillos in Spanish America, 1800–1850*. New York: Oxford University Press, 1992.

——, ed. *The Spanish American Revolutions, 1808–1826*. New York: Norton, 1986.

Machillanda, José. *Cinismo político y golpe de estado*. Caracas: Italgráfica, 1993.

MacLachlan, Colin. *Spain's Empire in the New World: The Role of Ideas in Institutional and Social Change*. Berkeley: University of California Press, 1988.

Magallanes, Diego. "Estrategia psicosocial y opinión pública." *Revista de la Escuela Superior de Guerra* 472 (October–December 1984): 45–68.

Mainwaring, Scott. *Rethinking Party Systems in the Third Wave of Democratization: The Case of Brazil*. Stanford: Stanford University Press, 1999.

——. "Transitions to Democracy and Democratic Consolidation: Theoretical and Comparative Issues." In *Issues in Democratic Consolidation: The New South American Democracies in Comparative Perspective*, edited by Scott Mainwaring, Guillermo O'Donnell, and J. Samuel Valenzuela, 294–341. Notre Dame: University of Notre Dame Press, 1992.

Maldonado, Carlos, and Patricio Quiroga. *El prusianismo en las fuerzas armadas chilenas*. Santiago: Ediciones Documentas, 1988.

Manuel Ugarte, José. "La Comisión de Defensa Nacional: Un rol casi inédito." In *Defensa y democracia: Un debate entre civiles y militares*, edited by Ernesto López et al., 244–51. Buenos Aires: Puntosur, 1990.

March, James G., and Johan P. Olsen. "The New Institutionalism: Organizational Factors in Political Life." *American Political Science Review* 78 (September 1984): 734–49.

———. *Rediscovering Institutions: The Organizational Basis of Politics*. New York: Free Press, 1989.

March, James G., and Herbert A. Simon. *Organizations*. Cambridge, Mass.: Blackwell, 1993.

Mares, David R. "Civil-Military Relations, Democracy, and the Regional Neighborhood." In *Civil-Military Relations: Building Regional Security and Democracy in Latin America, Southern Asia and Central Europe*, edited by David R. Mares, 1–24. Boulder: Westview Press, 1998.

———. "Deterrence Bargaining in the Ecuador-Peru Enduring Rivalry: Designing Strategies around Military Weakness." *Security Studies* 6 (Winter 1996–97): 91–123.

———. *Violent Peace: Militarized Interstate Bargaining in Latin America*. New York: Columbia University Press, 2001.

———, ed. *Civil-Military Relations: Building Regional Security and Democracy in Latin America, Southern Asia and Central Europe*. Boulder: Westview Press, 1998.

Marichy, Jean-Pierre. "The Central Organization of Defense in France." In *Central Organizations of Defense*, edited by Martin Edmonds, 35–64. Boulder: Westview Press, 1985.

Marín, Diego, and Angel del Rio. *Breve historia de la literatura española*. New York: Holt, Rinehart, and Winston, 1966.

Masterson, Daniel. *Militarism and Politics in Latin America: Peru from Sánchez Cerro to Sendero Luminoso*. New York: Greenwood Press, 1991.

McAlister, L. N. *The "Fuero Militar" in New Spain, 1764–1800*. Gainesville: University Press of Florida, 1957.

———. "Recent Research and Writings on the Role of the Military in Latin America." *Latin American Research Review* 2 (Fall 1966): 5–36.

McCann, Frank. "Origins of the New Professionalism of the Brazilian Military." *Journal of Interamerican Studies and World Affairs* 21 (November 1979): 505–22.

McClintock, Cynthia. "The Breakdown of Constitutional Democracy in Peru." Paper presented at the 18th International Congress of the Latin American Studies Association, Atlanta, Georgia, 10–12 March 1994.

McCubbins, Matthew, and Thomas Schwartz. "Congressional Oversight Overlooked: Police Patrols versus Fire Alarms." *American Political Science Review* 28 (February 1984): 165–79.

McGuire, James W. "Interim Government and Democratic Consolidation: Argentina in Comparative Perspective." In *Between States: Interim Governments and Democratic Transitions*, edited by Yossi Shain and Juan J. Linz, 179–210. Cambridge: Cambridge University Press, 1995.

———. "Political Parties and Democracy in Argentina." In *Building Democratic Institutions: Party Systems in Latin America*, edited by Scott Mainwaring and Timothy Scully, 200–246. Stanford: Stanford University Press, 1995.

McGuire, William. "Attitudes and Attitude Change." In *Handbook of Social Psychology*, vol. 2., edited by Gardner Lindzey and Elliot Aronson, 233–346. New York: Random House, 1985.

McKinlay, Robert D. "Professionalization, Politicization and Civil-Military Relations." In *The Perceived Role of the Military*, edited by M. R. van Gils, 247–65. Rotterdam: Rotterdam University Press, 1971.

McSherry, J. Patrice. *Incomplete Transition: Military Power and Democracy in Argentina*. New York: St. Martin's Press, 1997.

———. "Military Power, Impunity, and State-Society Change in Latin America." *Canadian Journal of Political Science/Revue canadienne de science politique* 25 (1992): 463–88.

Milet, Paz, Claudio Fuentes, and Francisco A. Rojas. "Introducción: El Mercosur, nuevo actor internacional." In *Chile-Mercosur: Una alianza estratégica*, edited by Paz Milet, Gabriel Gaspar, and Francisco A. Rojas, 13–46. Santiago: Los Andes, 1997.

Ministerio de Defensa Nacional, El Salvador. *Doctrina militar y relaciones ejército/socieded*. El Salvador: ONUSAL, Talleres Gráficos CA, 1994.

Moncayo, Colonel Paco. "Introducción al Conocimiento de la Defensa Interna." *Revista de las Fuerzas Armadas Ecuatorianas* (July 1988): 49–63.

———. "Poder militar, partidos políticos, y grupos de presión." *Revista de las Fuerzas Armadas Ecuatorianas* (February 1991): 10–13.

Monroe, Kristen Renwick. *The Heart of Altruism: Perceptions of a Common Humanity*. Princeton: Princeton University Press, 1996.

———, ed. *The Economic Approach to Politics: A Critical Assessment of the Theory of Rational Action*. New York: Harper Collins, 1991.

Monteverde, Galo. "La Democracia." *Revista de las Fuerzas Armadas Ecuatorianas* (October 1987): 102–5.

Morán, Mariano Castro. *Función política del ejército salvadoreno en el presente siglo*. El Salvador: UCA Editores, 1984.

Morrow, James D. "When Does Trade Produce Security Externalities." Conference paper presented at the University of California, San Diego, 3–4 March 1995.

Müller Rojas, Alberto. *Relaciones peligrosas: Militares, política y estado*. Caracas: Fondo Editorial APU, 1992.

Munck, Gerardo L. *Authoritarianism and Democratization: Soldiers and Workers in Argentina, 1976–83*. University Park: Pennsylvania State University Press, 1988.

Muñoz, Heraldo. *Las relaciones exteriores del gobierno militar Chileno*. Santiago: PROSPEL-CERC, 1986.

———, ed. *Chile: Política exterior para la democracia*. Santiago: Pehuen, 1989.

Needler, Martin C. "Military Motivations in the Seizure of Power." *Latin American Research Review* 10 (Fall 1975): 63–79.

Norden, Deborah. "Democracy and Military Control in Venezuela: From Subordination to Insurrection." *Latin American Research Review* 33 (1998): 143–65.

———. *Military Rebellion in Argentina: Between Coups and Consolidation*. Lincoln: University of Nebraska Press, 1996.

Nordlinger, Eric. *Soldiers in Politics: Military Coups and Governments*. Englewood Cliffs, N.J.: Prentice-Hall, 1977.

North, Douglas C. *Institutions, Institutional Change and Economic Performance*. Cambridge: Cambridge University Press, 1990.

Nun, José. "The Middle Class Military Coup." In *Armies and Politics in Latin America*, edited by Abraham F. Lowenthal and J. Samuel Fitch, 59–95. New York: Holmes and Meier, 1986.

Nunn, Frederick. "The South American Military and (Re)Democratization: Professional Thought and Self-Perception." *Journal of Interamerican Studies and World Affairs* 37 (1995): 1–56.

———. *Yesterday's Soldiers: European Military Professionalism in South America, 1890–1940*. Lincoln: University of Nebraska Press, 1983.

Nye, Joseph S. "Central American Regional Integration." *International Conciliation*, no. 562 (March 1967). Reprinted in *International Regionalism: Readings*, edited by Joseph S. Nye Jr., 377–429. Boston: Little, Brown, 1968.

Nye, Joseph S., and Robert O. Keohane. *Power and Interdependence*. Boston: Little, Brown, 1977.

Obando, Enrique. "The Power of Peru's Armed Forces." In *Peru in Crisis: Dictatorship or Democracy?*, edited by Joseph Tulchin and Stephen Bland, 101–24. Boulder: Lynne Rienner, 1994.

O'Donnell, Guillermo. "¿Democracia delegativa?" *Cuadernos del Centro Latinoamericano de Económica Humana*, no. 61. Montevideo, Uruguay, 1991.

——. "Horizontal Accountability and New Polyarchies." Working paper no. 253, University of Notre Dame, Kellogg Institute, 1998.

——. "Introduction to the Latin American Cases." In *Transition from Authoritarian Rule: Latin America*, edited by Guillermo O'Donnell, Philippe C. Schmitter, and Laurence Whitehead, 3–18. Baltimore: Johns Hopkins University Press, 1986.

——. *Modernization and Bureaucratic-Authoritarianism: Studies in South American Politics*. Berkeley: Institute of International Studies, University of California, Berkeley, 1973.

——. "Modernization and Military Coups: Theory, Comparisons, and the Argentine Case." In *Armies and Politics in Latin America*, edited by Abraham Lowenthal and J. Samuel Fitch, 96–133. New York: Holmes and Meier, 1986.

——. "Transitions, Continuities, and Paradoxes." In *Issues in Democratic Consolidation: The New South American Democracies in Comparative Perspective*, edited by Scott Mainwaring, Guillermo O'Donnell, and J. Samuel Valenzuela, 17–56. Notre Dame: University of Notre Dame Press, 1992.

O'Donnell, Guillermo, and Philippe Schmitter. *Transitions from Authoritarian Rule: Tentative Conclusions about Uncertain Democracies*. Baltimore: Johns Hopkins University Press, 1986.

O'Donnell, Guillermo, Philippe Schmitter, and Laurence Whitehead, eds. *Transiciones desde un gobierno autoritario*. Vol. 4. Buenos Aires: Paidós, 1988.

Olson, Mancur, Jr. *The Logic of Collective Action: Public Goods and the Theory of Groups*. New York: Schocken Books, 1968.

Ordenanza para el rejimen, disciplina, subordinación i servicio de los ejércitos de la República. Santiago: Imprenta del Ferrocarril, 1860.

Pasquino, Gianfranco. "The Demise of the First Fascist Regime and Italy's Transition to Democracy, 1943–1948." In *Transitions from Authoritarian Rule: Southern Europe*, edited by Guillermo O'Donnell, Philippe C. Schmitter, and Laurence Whitehead, 45–70. Baltimore: Johns Hopkins University Press, 1986.

Pauker Gutiérrez, Francisco. "Movimiento revolucionario o fuerza revolucionario." *Revista de las Fuerzas Armadas Ecuatorianas* (July 1980): 107–19.

Pazmiño, Mario. "Las fuerzas armadas en la lucha contra la subversión." *Revista de las Fuerzas Armadas Ecuatorianas* (February 1985): 52–55.

Peña, Jorge. "The Military and Democracy in Ecuador: A Healthy Combination?" U.S. Army War College Strategy Research Project, Carlisle Barracks, Pa., 1996.

Perlmutter, Amos. *The Military and Politics in Modern Times*. New Haven: Yale University Press, 1977.

Perrow, Charles. *Complex Organizations: A Critical Essay*. 3d ed. New York: McGraw-Hill, 1986.

Philip, George. "Venezuelan Democracy and the Coup Attempt of February 1992." *Government and Opposition* 27 (Autumn 1992): 455–69.

Piccinali, Héctor. "Perspectiva estratégica de la integración latinoamericana." *Revista de la Escuela Superior de Guerra* 408 (1973): 65–76.

Picciuolo, José. "La cabellería del futuro." *Revista de la Escuela Superior de Guerra* 415 (1974): 77–130.

Pion-Berlin, David. "Between Confrontation and Accommodation: Military and Government

Policy in Democratic Argentina." *Journal of Latin American Studies* 23 (October 1991): 543–71.

——. "From Confrontation to Cooperation: Democratic Governance and Argentine Foreign Relations." In *Civil-Military Relations: Building Regional Security and Democracy in Latin America, Southern Asia and Central Europe*, edited by David R. Mares, 79–100. Boulder: Westview Press, 1998.

——. "Military Autonomy and Emerging Democracies in South America." *Comparative Politics* 25 (October 1992): 83–102.

——. "Strong Tests of Civilian and Military Power in South America." Paper presented to the Latin American Studies Association, Chicago, 24–26 September 1998.

——. *Through Corridors of Power: Institutions and Civil-Military Relations in Argentina.* College Park: Pennsylvania State University Press, 1997.

Pion-Berlin, David, and Craig Arcenaux. "Of Missions and Decisions: Military Roles and Civilian Controls in South America." Paper presented at the Western Political Science Association conference, Los Angeles, 19–21 March 1998.

——. "Tipping the Civil-Military Balance: Human Rights Policy and Institutions in Democratic Argentina and Chile." Paper presented to the Latin American Studies Association, 28–30 September 1995.

Porter, Bruce D. *War and the Rise of the State: The Military Foundations of Modern Politics.* New York: Free Press, 1994.

Power, Timothy. *The Political Right in Post-Authoritarian Brazil: Elites, Institutions, and Democratization.* College Park: Pennsylvania State University Press, 2000.

Premio, Daniel. "The Redirection of the Armed Forces." In *Nicaragua without Illusions*, edited by Thomas W. Walker, 65–80. Wilmington, Del.: Scholarly Resources, 1997.

Przeworski, Adam. *Democracy and the Market: Political and Economic Reforms in Eastern Europe and Latin America.* Cambridge: Cambridge University Press, 1991.

Quintana, Mayor Rodolfo. "Técnicas psicológicas en la guerra revolucionaria." *Revista de la Escuela Superior de Guerra* 418 (1975): 7–36.

Rapoport, David. "The Praetorian Army: Insecurity, Venality and Impotence." In *Soldiers, Peasants and Bureaucrats*, edited by Roman Kolkowicz and Andrzej Korbonski. London: George Allen & Unwin, 1982.

Recopilación de leyes de los reynos de las Indias. 5 vols. Madrid: Centro de Estudios Políticos y Constitutionales, Boletín Oficial del Estado, 1998.

Remmer, Karen. *Military Rule in Latin America.* Boston: Unwin Hyman, 1989.

——. "New Wine or Old Bottlenecks? The Study of Latin American Democracy." *Comparative Politics* 23 (October 1990): 479–95.

——. "The Process of Democratization in Latin America." *Studies in Comparative International Development* 27 (Winter 1992–93): 3–24.

República Argentina. *Ley de Defensa Nacional*, no. 23554. Boletín Oficial, 26 April 1988.

——. *Ley de Ministerios, Decreto 438–92.* Cámara de Diputados de la Nación Dirección de Información Parlamentaria, 1992.

Rial, Juan. "Armies and Civil Society in Latin America." In *Civil-Military Relations and Democracy*, edited by Larry Diamond and Marc Plattner, 47–65. Baltimore: Johns Hopkins University Press, 1996.

Ricci, María Susana, and J. Samuel Fitch. "Ending Military Regimes in Argentina, 1966–1973 and 1976–1983." In *The Military and Democracy: The Future of Civil-Military Relations in Latin America*, edited by Louis W. Goodman, Johanna S. R. Mendelson, and Juan Rial, 55–74. Lexington, Mass.: Lexington Books, 1990.

Rizzo de Oliveira, Eliézer. "A adaptaçao del militares a democracia no Brasil." Paper presented to the Inter-University Seminar on Armed Forces and Society, Baltimore, 20–22 October 1995.

Rodriguez, Laura. "The Spanish Riots of 1766." *Past and Present* 59 (1973): 117–46.

Rodríguez Solís, Manuel. *Deontología militar*. Guatemala: Ministerio de Defensa Nacional, 1964.

Ronfeldt, David. *The Modern Mexican Military*. Monograph Series 16. La Jolla: Center for U.S.-Mexican Relations, University of California, San Diego, 1984.

Ruiz Palacios, Colonel José. "El conflicto en la maniobra interior." *Revista de la Escuela Superior de Guerra* 473 (1984): 5–34.

Russell, Roberto. "El proceso de toma de decisiones en la política exterior argentina." In *Política exterior y el proceso de toma de decisiones en America Latina*, edited by Roberto Russell, 13–60. Buenos Aires: Grupo Editorial Latinoamericano, 1990.

Saín, Marcelo. *Los levantamientos carapintadas, 1987–1991*. Buenos Aires: Cedal, 1994.

Schaposnik, Eduardo. *Democratización de las Fuerzas Armadas Venezolanas*. Caracas: Editores ILDIS-Fundación Gonzalo Barrios Caracas, 1985.

Scheetz, Thomas. "The Evolution of Public Sector Expenditures: Changing Political Priorities in Argentina, Chile, Paraguay, and Peru." *Journal of Peace Research* 29 (1992): 175–90.

Schelling, Thomas C. *The Strategy of Conflict*. Cambridge: Harvard University Press, 1960.

Schmitter, Philippe. "The Consolidation of Political Democracies: Processes, Rhythms, Sequences, and Types." In *Transitions to Democracy*, edited by Geoffrey Pridham, 535–70. Aldershot: Dartmouth, 1995.

Schopenhauer, Arthur. *El mundo como voluntad y representación*. Mexico City: Editorial Porrua, 1997.

Scott, James C. *Weapons of the Weak: Everyday Forms of Peasant Resistance*. New Haven: Yale University Press, 1985.

Scott, W. Richard. *Organizations: Rational, Natural and Open Systems*. Englewood Cliffs, N.J.: Prentice-Hall, 1992.

Sikkink, Kathryn. *Ideas and Institutions: Developmentalism in Brazil and Argentina*. Ithaca: Cornell University Press, 1991.

Silva, Eduardo. "The Political Economy of Chile's Regime Transition: From Radical to 'Pragmatic' Neo-liberal Policies." In *The Struggle for Democracy in Chile*, edited by Paul Drake and Ivan Jaskic, 98–127. Lincoln: University of Nebraska Press, 1995.

Simon, Herbert A. *Administrative Behavior*. New York: Free Press, 1976.

——. "A Behavioral Model of Rational Choice." *Quarterly Journal of Economics* 69 (1955): 99–118.

Smith, Peter H. "The Changing Agenda for Social Science Research on Latin America." In *Latin America in Comparative Perspective: New Approaches to Methods and Analysis*, edited by Peter Smith, 1–29. Boulder: Westview Press, 1995.

Solingen, Etel. "Economic Liberalization, Political Coalitions, and Emerging Regional Orders." In *Regional Orders: Building Security in a New World*, edited by David A. Lake and Patrick M. Morgan, 68–100. University Park: Pennsylvania State University Press, 1997.

Stark, David. "Path Dependence and Privatization Strategies in East Central Europe." *East European Politics and Society* 6 (1992): 17–54.

Steinmo, Sven, Kathleen Thelen, and Frank Longstreth, eds. *Structuring Politics: Historical Institutionalism in Comparative Analysis*. Cambridge: Cambridge University Press, 1992.

Stepan, Alfred. *Brasil: Los militares y la política*. Buenos Aires: Editorial Amorrortu, 1974.

——. *The Military in Politics: Changing Patterns in Brazil*. Princeton: Princeton University Press, 1971.

——. "The New Professionalism of Internal Warfare and Military Role Expansion." In *Armies and Politics in Latin America*, edited by Abraham F. Lowenthal and J. Samuel Fitch, 134–50. New York: Holmes and Meier, 1986.

——. "Paths toward Redemocratization: Theoretical and Comparative Considerations." In *Transitions from Authoritarian Rule: Comparative Perspectives*, edited by Guillermo O'Donnell, Philippe Schmitter, and Laurence Whitehead, 64–84. Baltimore: Johns Hopkins University Press, 1986.

——. *Rethinking Military Politics: Brazil and the Southern Cone*. Princeton: Princeton University Press, 1988.

——. *The State and Society: Peru in Comparative Perspective*. Princeton: Princeton University Press, 1978.

Tarrow, Sidney. "Collective Action and Social Movements." In *Power in Movement: Social Movements, Collective Action and Politics*, edited by Sidney Tarrow, 9–27. Cambridge: Cambridge University Press, 1994.

Taylor, Charles Lewis, and David A. Jodice. *World Handbook of Political and Social Indicators*. 3d ed. New Haven: Yale University Press, 1983.

Trinkunas, Harold. "Crafting Civilian Control of the Armed Forces in Emerging Democracies." Ph.D. diss., Stanford University, 1999.

——. "Crafting Civilian Control of the Armed Forces in Emerging Democracies: The Cases of Argentina and Venezuela." Paper presented at the meeting of the Latin American Studies Association, Chicago, 24–26 September 1998.

Tsebelis, George. *Nested Games: Rational Choice in Comparative Politics*. Berkeley: University of California Press, 1990.

U.S. Arms Control and Disarmament Agency. *World Military Expenditures and Arms Transfers, 1996*. Washington, D.C.: ACDA Publications, 1997.

Valenzuela, Arturo. "The Military in Power: The Consolidation of One-Man Rule." In *The Struggle for Democracy in Chile*, edited by Paul Drake and Iván Jaskic, 21–72. Lincoln: University of Nebraska Press, 1991.

Valenzuela, J. Samuel. "La Constitución de 1980 y el inicio de la redemocratización en Chile." Working paper no. 242, University of Notre Dame, Kellogg Institute, 1997.

——. "Democratic Consolidation in Post-Transitional Settings: Notion, Process, and Facilitating Conditions." In *Issues in Democratic Consolidation: The New South American Democracy in Comparative Perspective*, edited by Scott Mainwaring, Guillermo O'Donnell, and J. Samuel Valenzuela, 57–104. Notre Dame: University of Notre Dame Press, 1992.

Van Doorn, Jacques. "The Officer Corps: A Fusion of Profession and Organization." *European Journal of Sociology* 6 (1965): 262–82.

Varas, Augusto. *Democracy under Siege: New Military Power in Latin America*. New York: Greenwood Press, 1989.

——, ed. *La autonomía militar en América Latina*. Caracas: Nueva Sociedad, 1988.

——. *Hacia el Siglo XXI: La proyección estratégica de Chile*. Santiago, Chile: FLASCO, 1989.

Vargas Meza, Ricardo. *Drogas, Máscaras y Juegos: Narcotráfico y conflicto armado en Colombia*. Bogotá: Tercer Mundo Editores, 1999.

Vasquez, John A. *The Power of Power Politics: From Classical Realism to Neotraditionalism*. Cambridge: Cambridge University Press, 1998.

Verbitsky, Horacio. *Civiles y militares: Memoria secreta de la transición*. Buenos Aires: Editorial Contrapunto SRL, 1987.

Vilas, Acdel Edgardo. "Reflexiones sobre la guerra subversiva." *Revista de la Escuela Superior de Guerra* 427 (1976): 7–16.

Villanueva, Victor. *Ejército peruano: Del caudillaje anárquico al militarismo reformista*. Lima: Editorial Juan Mejia Baca, 1973.

Weber, Max. *Economía y sociedad.* Vol. 1. Mexico City: Fondo de Cultura Económica, 1964.

——. *Economy and Society.* Vol. 2. Edited by Guenther Roth and Claus Wittich. Berkeley: University of California Press, 1978.

——. *The Methodology of the Social Sciences.* Translated and edited by Edward A. Shils and Henry A. Finch. Glencoe: Free Press, 1949.

——. *The Protestant Ethic and the Spirit of Capitalism.* Translated by Talcott Parsons. London: Unwin Paperbacks, 1985.

Weisberg, Herbert, Jon Krosnick, and Bruce Bowen. *An Introduction to Survey Research, Polling, and Data Analysis.* 3d ed. Thousand Oaks, Calif.: Sage Publications, 1996.

Welch, Claude E., Jr. *Civilian Control of the Military: Theories and Cases from Developing Countries.* Albany: State University of New York Press, 1976.

——. "Military Disengagement from Politics: Paradigms, Processes, or Random Events." *Armed Forces and Society* 18 (Spring 1992): 323–42.

Wiarda, Howard J. "Toward a Framework for the Study of Political Change in the Iberic-American Tradition: The Corporative Model." *World Politics* 25 (January 1973): 206–35.

Wiarda, Howard J., and Harvey F. Klein. "The Context of Latin American Politics." In *Latin American Politics and Development,* edited by Howard J. Wiarda and Harvey F. Kline, 3–14. Boulder: Westview Press, 1990.

Williams, J. Allen. "Interviewer Role Performance: A Further Note on Bias in the Information Interview." In *States of Social Research: Contemporary Perspectives,* edited by Dennis Forcese and Stephen Richer, 224–31. Englewood Cliffs, N.J.: Prentice-Hall, 1970.

Yariv, Aharon. "Military Organizations and Policymaking in Israel." In *Reorganizing America's Defense: Leadership in War and Peace,* edited by Robert J. Art et al., 108–29. Washington, D.C.: Pergamon-Brassey, 1985.

Zagorski, Paul. *Democracy vs. National Security: Civil-Military Relations in Latin America.* Boulder: Lynne Rienner, 1992.

Zald, Mayer, and Michael Berger. "Social Movements in Organizations: Coup d'Etat, Bureaucratic Insurgency, and Mass Movement." In *Social Movements in an Organizational Society,* edited by Mayer N. Zald and John D. McCarthy, 185–222. New Brunswick: Transaction Books, 1987.

Zald, Mayer, and Roberta Ash Garner. "Social Movement Organizations: Growth, Decay and Change." In *Social Movements in an Organizational Society,* edited by Mayer N. Zald and John D. McCarthy, 121–41. New Brunswick: Transaction Books, 1987.

Zaller, John R. *The Nature and Origins of Mass Opinion.* New York: Cambridge University Press, 1992.

Zaverucha, Jorge. "A Constituição Brasileira de 1988 e seu legado autoritário: Formalizando a democracia mas retirando sua essência." In *Democracia e instituiçoes Políticas Brasileiras no Final do Século XX,* edited by Jorge Zaverucha, 115–47. Recife, Brazil: Editora Bargaco, 1998.

——. "The Degree of Military Political Autonomy during the Spanish, Argentine, and Brazilian Transitions." *Journal of Latin American Studies* 25 (1993): 283–99.

——. *Rumor de Sabres: Tutela militar ou controle civil?* São Paulo: Editora Ática, 1994.

——. "Sarney, Collor, Itamar e as Prerogativas Militares (1985–1998)." Paper presented to the Latin American Studies Association, Chicago, 24–26 September 1998.

Contributors

FELIPE AGÜERO is Associate Professor in the School of International Studies of the University of Miami. He is the author of *Soldiers, Civilians, and Democracy: Post-Franco Spain in Comparative Perspective* (Johns Hopkins University Press, 1995) and coeditor, with Jeffrey Stark, of *Fault Lines of Democracy in Post-Transition Latin America* (North-South Center, 1998). His research interests are in the areas of democratization; the relations among state, military, and society; and party politics.

J. SAMUEL FITCH is Professor and Chair of Political Science at the University of Colorado in Boulder. His research focuses on civil-military relations in Latin America, particularly in posttransition regimes. He is the author of *The Armed Forces and Democracy in Latin America* (Johns Hopkins University Press, 1998); *Armies and Politics in Latin America*, with Abraham Lowenthal (Holmes and Meier, 1986); and *The Coup d'État as a Political Process: Ecuador, 1948-1966* (Johns Hopkins University Press, 1977).

WENDY HUNTER is Associate Professor of Political Science at the University of Texas at Austin. She is the author of *Eroding Military Influence in Brazil: Politicians against Soldiers* (University of North Carolina Press, 1997) and several articles on the military in Brazil and the Southern Cone. Her current research focuses on social policy issues in Latin America.

ERNESTO LÓPEZ is Professor and Researcher of the Universidad Nacional de Quilmes, Argentina, as well as Vice Rector of Institutional Relations and Director of the Armed Forces and Society Research Program. Since the early 1980s, he has been working in the fields of civil-military relations and regional security. He has written many articles and several books, including *Seguridad nacional y sedición militar* (Legasa, 1987), *Ni la ceniza ni la gloria: Actores, sistema político y cuestión militar en los años de Alfonsín* (Universidad Nacional de Quilmes, 1994), and, with David Pion-Berlin, *Democracia y cuestión militar* (Universidad Nacional de Quilmes, 1996).

BRIAN LOVEMAN is Professor of Political Science at San Diego State University. He has written extensively on civil-military relations in Latin America, Latin American politics, and inter-American relations. Among his books are *Chile: The Legacy of Hispanic Capitalism* (3d ed., Oxford University Press, 2001), *Constitution of Tyranny: Regimes of Exception in Spanish America* (University of Pittsburgh Press, 1993), and *For la Patria: Politics and the Armed Forces in Latin America* (Scholarly Resources, 1999). Two coedited volumes with Thomas M. Davies Jr. have been widely adopted as texts in universities in the United States: *The Military in Latin America: The Politics of Antipolitics* (3d ed., Scholarly Resources, 1997) and *Che Guevara on Guerrilla Warfare* (3d ed., Scholarly Resources, 1998).

DAVID R. MARES is Professor of Political Science and Adjunct Professor at the Graduate School of International Relations and Pacific Studies. His books include *Penetrating the International Market: Theoretical Considerations and a Mexican Case* (Columbia University Press, 1987), *Violent Peace: Militarized Interstate Bargaining in Latin America* (Columbia University Press, 2001), and *Coming in from the Cold: Chile–United States Relations at the Millennium*, with Francisco Rojas, and he edited *Civil-Military Relations: Building Democracy and Regional Security in Latin America, Southern Asia and Central Europe* (Westview Press, 1998).

DEBORAH L. NORDEN is Assistant Professor of Political Science at Whittier College. She has published widely on civil-military relations and democratization in Latin America, especially Argentina and Venezuela. Among her works are *Military Rebellion in Argentina: Between Coups and Consolidation* (University of Nebraska Press, 1996) and articles in *Comparative Politics, Latin American Research Review, Journal of Inter-American Studies and World Affairs, Armed Forces and Society, Party Politics*, and other periodicals. She is currently completing a book on U.S.-Argentine relations with Roberto Russell.

DAVID PION-BERLIN is Professor of Political Science at the University of California, Riverside. He is the author of *Through Corridors of Power: Institutions and Civil-Military Relations in Argentina* (Pennsylvania State University Press, 1997); *Democracia y cuestión militar*, with Ernesto López (Universidad Nacional de Quilmes, 1996); and *The Ideology of State Terror: Political Repression and Economic Doctrine in Argentina and Peru* (Rienner, 1989), along with numerous refereed articles and chapters. His current research centers on the military and economic adjustment programs and explaining institutional change in Latin America.

HAROLD A. TRINKUNAS is Assistant Professor in the Department of National Security Affairs at the Naval Postgraduate School in Monterey, California. His research and writing focus on Latin American politics, particularly democratization. Recent publications include "Crafting Civilian Control in Emerging Democracies" in the *Journal of Interamerican Studies and World Affairs* and "The Crisis in Venezuelan Civil-Military Relations: From Punto Fijo to the Fifth Republic" in *Latin American Research Review*. He is currently writing a book on civilian control of the armed forces in emerging democracies.

Index

Abrahamsson, Bengt, 7, 194
Acción Democrática (AD), 126, 182
Adelantado, 249
Agüero, Felipe, 9, 50, 124, 126, 135
"Alfaro Vive ¡Carajo!" guerrillas, 83
Alfonsín, Raúl, 45; human rights trials and, 60, 64,
    79, 80, 177–80; subjective civilian control and,
    103; Defense Ministry powers and, 141, 144; mili-
    tary budget and, 149–50; Chilean accord and,
    151; postauthoritarian transition and, 221 (n. 26);
    resignation in wake of economic crisis, 236
Alfonso VI, king of Castile, 249
Alhambra Hill, 248
Alianza Popular Revolucionaria Americana
    (APRA), 196
Allende, Salvador, 235
All-volunteer military (Argentina), 81
Alonso, José Ramón, 251
Amazon region, 37, 229
Andalucía, 248, 252, 253
Andean region, 10–11, 59–60, 250
Anderson, Benedict, 248
Andrés Pérez, Carlos, 123, 124, 128
Anthropology, 19–20
Antimilitary ideology, 94
Appeasement strategies, 167–68, 171, 172, 178, 182,
    183
APRA. *See* Alianza Popular Revolucionaria
    Americana
Aragón, 248, 250
Aranda, Count of, 252
Arequipa, 258
Argentina, 27, 95, 135–57; military attitudes, 7, 69–
    75, 86 (n. 24); military professionalism, 7, 137,
    221 (n. 18); European elitist military influences,
    7, 268; military budget, 11, 60, 80, 101, 149–50;
    military behavior, 26, 60, 78; military subordina-
    tion, 27–28, 63, 79–81, 84, 148–55, 156, 215;
    Chilean economic integration with, 29, 224, 235–
    42; military rebellions, 45, 52, 59, 88, 103, 120,
    180–81, 185; postauthoritarian regime transition,
    49, 52, 55, 60, 87 (n. 30), 198, 202–3, 204, 206,
    209, 214, 218, 221 (n. 26); Proceso de Reorga-
    nización Nacional and, 52, 136, 177; human

rights trials, 60, 64, 65, 79, 80, 81, 177–81, 185,
    214, 215, 236; *carapintadas*, 64, 65, 103, 183, 185,
    186; Dirty War, 65, 103, 178, 179, 181, 235; Law
    of Due Obedience (1987), 79, 181, 255, 272–73
    (n. 30); Malvinas / Falklands war, 81, 96, 103,
    116, 153, 178–79, 235; Condor missile program,
    81, 153; coups and coup attempts, 88, 195, 196,
    198, 204, 209, 221 (n. 18), 235; civil-military rela-
    tions, 89, 100, 104, 135–57, 162–63, 184–87,
    190–91, 195–196, 212–13, 214, 215, 225; military
    autonomy, 95, 138–39, 148, 155–56, 214; compe-
    tition among military branches, 116; Peronism,
    131, 179, 195–96, 241; military chain of com-
    mand, 135–57; diminished military resources of,
    137–38, 148, 185; Beagle Channel dispute, 151,
    221 (n. 21), 235, 236; Chilean accord with, 151–
    52, 235–36; peacekeeping operations and, 153,
    186–87; civilian control, 156–57, 177–81, 196,
    214, 215, 225; Laguna del Desierto dispute and,
    159 (n. 37), 160 (n. 49); White Paper on National
    Defense, 159–60 (n. 23); U.S. cooperation with,
    181, 236; military's historical control, 195–96;
    Honduran economic integration with, 224; Bra-
    zilian economic integration with, 224, 229, 230,
    241; military codes, 254; constitutional "state of
    siege" provision, 264; Constitution of 1853, 264;
    penal code (1888), 265; Punto Final (End Point)
    law, 272–73 (n. 30). *See also* Defense Ministry
    (Argentina); Economics Ministry (Argentina);
    Foreign Relations Ministry (Argentina)
Argentine-Chilean Mixed Commission on Borders
    (Comisión Mixta Chileno-Argentina de Límites),
    238–39
Arias Cárdenas, Francisco, 122–23, 127–28, 132,
    134 (n. 58)
Aristide, Jean-Bertrand, 81
Armies and Politics in Latin America (Lowenthal), xi
Arms and Politics in Latin America (Lieuwen), 4
Army. *See* Civil-military relations; *specific countries*
Arriagada Herrera, Genaro, 8
Artigas, José Gervasio, 261
Association of Retired Generals and Admirals, 83
Asturias, Miguel, 248, 250
Attitudes, military, 61, 67–76, 78; journals reflect